May It Please the Court

JUDICIAL PROCESSES AND POLITICS IN AMERICA

Brian L. Porto
College of St. Joseph

Longman

New York San Francisco Boston
London Toronto Sydney Tokyo Singapore Madrid
Mexico City Munich Paris Cape Town Hong Kong Montreal

Editor-in-Chief: Priscilla McGeehon
Senior Acquisitions Editor: Eric Stano
Marketing Manager: Megan Galvin-Fak
Production Manager: Ellen MacElree
Project Coordination, Text Design, and Electronic Page Makeup: Electronic Publishing
Services Inc., NYC
Cover Designer/Manager: Nancy Danahy
Senior Manufacturing Buyer: Dennis J. Para
Printer and Binder: Courier
Cover Printer: Coral Graphic Services, Inc.

For permission to use copyrighted material, grateful acknowledgment is made to the
copyright holders listed throughout this book, which are hereby made part of this copyright page.

Library of Congress Cataloging-in-Publication Data

Porto, Brian L.
    May it please the court : judicial processes and politics in America / by Brian L. Porto.
        p. cm.
    Includes bibliographical references and index.
    ISBN 0-321-03683-2 (pbk.)
        1. Political questions and judicial power--United States. 2. Justice, Administration
    of--Political aspects--United States. I. Title.

    KF8700 .P667 2001
    347.73--dc21
                                                                            00-035482

Please visit our website at http://www.awl.com

ISBN 0-321-03683-2

1 2 3 4 5 6 7 8 9 10—CRS—03 02 01 00

For my uncles,
John Parlapiano
and Anthony Porto,
mentors both

Contents

Figures

Preface

May It Please the Court is designed primarily for undergraduates in a liberal arts setting, but paralegal students and beginning law students can also benefit from reading it. The book stems from my conclusion that the judicial process texts currently available, despite their clarity and sophistication, have two significant limitations. First, they overstate the impact of political influences, especially judges' public policy preferences, on judicial decisions, and they understate the impact of legal influences (e.g., *stare decisis*, the justiciability doctrines, statutory and constitutional language) on those decisions. Second, they fail to convey the human drama of criminal and civil litigation. Thus, they portray an incomplete, inaccurate, and rather dull image of the judicial process.

This book, which reflects my experiences as a political scientist, law student, judicial clerk, and practicing lawyer, tries to redress that situation by giving well-deserved attention to legal influences on judicial decisions and to the trial process. That does not mean that political influences receive short shrift; instead, both legal and political influences receive considerable attention.

Indeed, each chapter reflects this book's premise that the judicial process operates at the intersection of law and politics. Chapter 1 explains how both law and politics affect judicial outcomes. It notes that a court decision that does not result from defensible legal rules, procedures, and arguments will draw substantial criticism, as will a court decision that conflicts with mainstream public opinion. Therefore, students must appreciate the power of both legal and political influences in order to understand the judicial process.

That theme runs throughout the remaining chapters. It informs the discussions of: (1) the structure of federal and state courts (Chapter 2); (2) the legal profession's history and culture, the challenges it faces, and the nature of modern legal training and practice (Chapter 3); (3) the selection and removal of federal and state judges (Chapter 4); (4) a hypothetical criminal prosecution for drug dealing (Chapter 5); (5) a hypothetical personal-injury suit that arises from a skiing accident (Chapter 6); and (6) the appellate proceedings in those two cases (Chapter 7).

Chapter 8 examines the legal and political influences on judicial decisions, and identifies the circumstances in which each category is most likely to affect case outcomes. Chapter 9 presents the debate about the legitimacy and the utility of judicial policy making. It then offers a centrist view of when and how courts should make public policy. Chapters 1 through 9 end with an illustrative case and questions designed to spark classroom discussion about the case and the chapter. Chapter 10 summarizes the previous chapters, then concludes that courts not only enforce norms and resolve disputes, but also, as a co-equal branch of government, shape the fundamental power relationships that drive American politics. Thus, the judicial process offers students a window on the entire American political system.

May It Please the Court aims to make the view from that window clear. It seeks to combine the lawyer's attention to detail with the political scientist's sensitivity to the extralegal forces that influence court decisions. It also strives to illuminate the strategy and the emotions that are part of criminal and civil litigation. I hope that it spurs students to ponder that strategy, to reflect on those emotions, and, most important, to appreciate the interaction between law and politics in modern America.

ACKNOWLEDGMENTS

A small group of talented and considerate people helped to make this book possible, and I owe them a great debt. Professor David Schultz, my friend and colleague, encouraged me to write the book, and his encouragement was a wonderful motivator.

Addison Wesley Longman Executive Editor Pam Gordon also offered encouragement, Acquisitions Editor Peter Glovin believed in the book, and Peter's successor, Eric Stano, skillfully guided it to completion. Kay Schlueter, Government Documents Librarian at the Kreitzberg Library of Norwich University, answered my many pleas for assistance with unfailing professionalism and good cheer. The circulation and reference staffs at the Cornell Library of Vermont Law School did the same.

I received valuable assistance from outside of academe too. JoAnn Welman McKee, Administrative Assistant to the Vermont Board of Bar Examiners, explained Vermont's program of law-office study, which enables one to gain admission to the Vermont Bar without having attended law school. John Quinn, Esq., Addison County (VT) State's Attorney, and Mark Zuckerman, Esq., Senior Assistant Attorney General and chief of the Criminal Bureau at the Office of the Attorney General of New Hampshire, furnished data and helpful hints about criminal litigation. Beth Robinson, Esq., of Langrock Sperry & Wool in Middlebury, Vermont, did the same with respect to ski-injury litigation.

I am also indebted to the following scholars whose critiques improved the manuscript considerably: Robert Carp, University of Houston; Cornell W. Clayton, Washington State University; Rebecca Davis, Georgia Southern University; Valerie Earle, Georgetown University; Marc Gertz, Florida State University; John Koslowics, University of Wisconsin–Whitewater; William P. McLauchlan, Purdue University; David R. Mugridge, Fresno Pacific University; Christopher Soper, Pepperdine University; and Thomas Walker, Emory University.

My wife, Sherrie Greeley, was immensely important to the completion of this book. Her knowledge of alpine skiing helped to inform Chapter 6, a photograph that she took appears on the front cover, and her continuing love and support kept me writing when it seemed that the project would take forever to complete. She makes my dreams come true.

Despite such expert assistance, errors may remain. If so, I alone am responsible for them.

BRIAN L. PORTO

Chapter 1

COURTS AND JUDGES IN THE POLITICAL PROCESS

LAW AND POLITICS: MYTH AND REALITY

In order to understand how courts work, it is necessary to understand the relationship between law and politics. That is no small task. Newspapers, periodicals,
and even some textbooks discuss both law and politics without defining either
term. Two enduring myths misconstrue the relationship between law and politics,
and cause much confusion about how courts work. The older myth is that law and
politics are unrelated; therefore, law is not political at all. The newer myth is that
law and politics are identical; therefore, legal reasoning is merely a justification
for judges' public policy preferences.

One famous example of the older myth is Alexander Hamilton's statement
in Federalist Paper Number 78 that courts "have neither force nor will, but merely
judgment."[1] Another famous example is the majority opinion that Justice Owen
Roberts wrote in *United States v. Butler*, in which the Supreme Court invalidated
the Agricultural Adjustment Act of 1933 on the ground that Congress lacked the
power under the Constitution to regulate agricultural production.[2] Justice Roberts
depicted judicial power in constitutional cases as minimal and as divorced from
politics. He wrote that when the Court considers a case in which there is a constitutional challenge to an act of Congress, "all [it] does, or can do, is to announce
its considered judgment upon the question."[3] He added that the Court "neither
approves nor condemns any legislative policy."[4] Instead, Justice Roberts observed,

> When an act of Congress is appropriately challenged in the courts as not conform-
> ing to the constitutional mandate the judicial branch of the Government has only
> one duty—to lay the article of the Constitution which is involved beside the statute
> which is challenged and to decide whether the latter squares with the former.[5]

1

The Hamilton and Roberts quotations ignore the political significance of court decisions. For example, there was considerable "will" involved in the Supreme Court's "judgment" that Congress lacked the power to regulate agricultural production, and that will reflected the Court majority's plainly "political" hostility to governmental regulation of business. There was also "force" in the Court's decision. It made President Franklin Roosevelt abandon, at least temporarily, his plans to boost farmers' incomes during the Great Depression by taxing the processors of crops, and then paying the proceeds to farmers who agreed to reduce their cultivated acreage.

An illustrative, but not so famous, example of the newer myth is a recent newspaper commentary about a decision that the Supreme Court reached during its 1996–97 term. That decision occurred in *Clinton v. Jones*, which arose from allegations by Paula Corbin Jones that President Bill Clinton sexually harassed her in 1991, when she was an employee of the State of Arkansas and he was the governor of that state.[6] The Supreme Court held in June 1997 that President Clinton was not immune from being sued during his presidency for actions unrelated to his official duties; therefore, Ms. Jones's lawsuit could proceed while Mr. Clinton was President of the United States.[7]

The newspaper commentary chastised the Court for its decision. The author stated that:

> By ruling, in effect, 9 to 0 that the sordid effort by Paula Jones to blackmail a sitting president can go forward, the tallest court in the land caved in to the band of Clinton-haters organized by political enemies in Arkansas to overturn the results of two national elections.[8]

That quotation is as misleading as the Hamilton and Roberts quotations. It assumes that law and politics are identical, and concludes that the Supreme Court permitted Ms. Jones's lawsuit to proceed during Mr. Clinton's presidency because the justices lacked the courage to thwart the efforts of Mr. Clinton's critics to discredit and to distract him. It fails to recognize that the legal question of whether the Constitution permits Ms. Jones's lawsuit to proceed during Mr. Clinton's presidency is separate from the political question of whether that lawsuit results from political hostility or from sexual harassment. The Supreme Court decided only the legal question because that was the only question it was authorized to decide.[9]

Both myths oversimplify the relationship between law and politics. This book rejects the myths, and begins from the premise that although law and politics are closely related and frequently intersect, they are not identical. It is necessary to define both terms before explaining the similarities and the differences between them.

Law is a system by which society makes choices that allocate its scarce resources and organize relations among individuals and institutions in order to achieve predictability in business and personal affairs.[10] Law includes the rules of conduct that govern human relations, such as the Vermont rule that a will is invalid unless three witnesses attest to it.[11] Law also includes the language that judges use to decide cases and to explain, in written opinions, the reasons for those decisions.[12] Finally, law includes public attitudes toward the rules of conduct and their enforcement.[13] For that reason, state laws against drunk driving became increasingly effective during the 1970s and 1980s, when an outraged public began to demand that those laws be strictly enforced. Law works best when those who are most likely to break it know that government will use its monopoly on the legitimate exercise of force to ensure compliance.

Politics is the acquisition, retention, and exercise of power for the purpose of collective action. That action allocates the benefits and the burdens of life in civil society. Simply put, politics determines "who gets what, when, how."[14] Politics and law are related because they both aim to organize human relations and allocate resources in a manner that promotes stability and predictability.[15] Nevertheless, they are different because law is about making choices, while politics is as much about obtaining and retaining influence as it is about exercising that influence. Law results from politics but it is not politics. There cannot be law without politics, but there often is politics without law, such as when legislators introduce bills that have little or no chance of enactment in order to curry favor with their constituents.

Thus, law is neither nonpolitical nor entirely political. Law and politics are distinct from one another, but they intersect because lawsuits frequently present courts with legal questions that arise from political controversies. Under such circumstances, judges' public policy preferences are likely to influence their legal conclusions. *United States v. Butler*, for example, presented the legal question whether Congress's constitutional authority to regulate "interstate" commerce enabled it to regulate the production of agricultural commodities. That question arose out of political opposition to President Roosevelt's "New Deal" plan for economic recovery from the Great Depression. The legal question and the political controversy that produced it were closely related; therefore, you should not be surprised that the majority's political philosophy influenced its decision in *Butler*.

That does not mean that judges have unfettered discretion to decide legal questions in a blatantly partisan fashion. We expect judges to resolve legal questions by means of legal reasoning. That is precisely what the Supreme Court did in *Clinton v. Jones*, when it concluded unanimously that the Constitution did not bar Ms. Jones from pursuing her lawsuit against President Clinton during his term of office. The justices were not free to resolve this dispute according to their political leanings; if they had been, Justices Ginsburg and Breyer, whom President Clinton appointed to the Court, might well have sided with the President.

THE POLITICAL CONTEXT OF JUDGING

Courts in the American Political System

United States v. Butler and *Clinton v. Jones* illustrate that courts operate in a political context. Cases regularly present legal questions that have either arisen from political controversy or that have generated political controversy while proceeding through the courts. The U.S. Supreme Court decides the most high-profile of those cases, but lower federal courts and state supreme courts also decide politically significant cases.

Courts operate in a political context because they exercise the coercive power of government. Their decisions allocate power among the branches of government, distribute wealth among individuals and corporations, and draw boundaries between personal freedom and governmental authority. Thus, courts are political institutions that make public policy decisions; politically important cases require courts to perform their **policy-making** function.The political significance of courts reflects America's **common-law tradition**. American law grew out of the **common law** of England, which the colonists brought to North America in the seventeenth and eighteenth centuries.[16] In America, as in England, the common law was judge-made law. It evolved through court decisions that created legal rules and principles that shaped the outcomes in later, similar cases. Gradually, those rules and principles became America's law of **contracts**, **property**, and **torts** (personal injuries).[17]

Judges are immensely important in the common-law tradition. The common law authorizes judges to review all acts of government agencies, and no person is beyond the jurisdiction of the courts.[18] The common law also gives to judges the primary responsibility for interpreting the law.[19] They interpret the law when they decide cases, and the power to interpret the law is the power to make the law, especially in cases in which there are few, if any, **precedents** (prior, similar cases) to guide them.[20] Such cases often become political disputes as well as legal disputes. A good example is the Vermont Supreme Court's 1999 decision that held that the Vermont Constitution entitles gay and lesbian couples to the same rights as heterosexual couples.[21] That decision spawned a lively debate in the Vermont Legislature about whether to: (1) permit gay and lesbian marriages in Vermont; (2) give gays and lesbians all the legal benefits of marriage without permitting them to marry; or (3) amend the Vermont Constitution so as to overturn the court's decision.[22]

Not all court decisions are politically significant, though, because not all cases have political implications; indeed, most cases that state courts and the lower federal courts decide lack political implications. In most cases, therefore, courts perform only the functions of **norm enforcement** and **dispute resolution**; those cases are undoubtedly important to the parties involved, but unlike policy making cases, they are important **only** to those parties, and not to society as a whole. For example, in State v. Coyman and McCormack, the New Hampshire Supreme Court held that the owner of a single-family home could consent to the warrantless entry and search by a police officer of the basement living room of the house that she shared with a tenant, who was the girlfriend of one of the defendants, even though the tenant was not present when the entry and the search occurred.[23] The search revealed stolen property and cocaine in plain view on a table in the basement. The court upheld the constitutionality of the search and affirmed the defendants' convictions because owner and tenant shared the basement living room, which authorized the owner to consent to the search. The court's decision enforced a legal norm in favor of "reasonable" searches and, of course, social norms against theft and the use of illegal drugs.[24] It also resolved a dispute between the State of New Hampshire and the defendants.

In *Alleyne v. Scandinavi Inn, Inc.*, the U.S. Court of Appeals for the First Circuit held that the Scandinavi Inn was not liable to Mr. Alleyne, an overnight guest, for the injuries that he suffered when he fell in his room.[25] Scandinavi had no vacancies when Mr. Alleyne stopped there during a snowstorm, but the innkeeper permitted him to sleep on a mattress for ten dollars. Unable to find the mattress or the innkeeper at bedtime, Mr. Alleyne located an unoccupied condominium with a loft bed in an unfinished section of the inn; he went to sleep, but later, on his way to the bathroom, he fell over a three-foot wall in the loft and landed on the first floor of the condominium, injuring his eye. The court rejected Mr. Alleyne's claims that the innkeeper was negligent for failing to show him the location of the mattress or of the bell that would summon the innkeeper, and for not preventing him from entering the condominium. In the court's view, Mr. Alleyne's injuries resulted from his own negligence, not from negligence by the innkeeper. That conclusion resolved a dispute between Mr. Alleyne and the inn, and it enforced the legal norm that I cannot hold you accountable for my injuries unless your action or inaction was responsible for my injuries.

United States v. Butler, on the other hand, was a policy-making decision because it temporarily stymied President Roosevelt's efforts to revive the American economy by means of federal regulation of production, thereby affecting the lives of millions of people.[26] *Clinton v. Jones* will not affect nearly as many lives as *Butler* did, but it is nonetheless a policy-making decision because it will prevent Bill Clinton's successors from postponing lawsuits in which they are defendants until they leave office.[27]

In his *Butler* opinion, Justice Roberts refused to acknowledge the policy-making function that courts perform. Today, though, most judges admit that courts make public policy. The main reason for this change is the influence of **legal realism** on the legal profession during the years since *Butler*. Ironically, legal realism gained prominence as an intellectual movement during the 1930s, when the Supreme Court decided *Butler*, but its greatest influence occurred decades later, when it became "gospel" among lawyers and judges. Legal realism maintained that when judges decided cases, they "made law" by choosing between conflicting values according to their individual public policy preferences.[28] It challenged and eventually supplanted the classical view of the judicial process, which Justice Roberts's opinion in *Butler* reflected.

The classical view held that a court decision was the predictable, almost mechanical, result of a judge's application of an unambiguous rule of law, contained in a statute, a constitution, or a prior court decision, to the facts of a particular case. Classical theorists argued, as Justice Roberts did in *Butler*, that a judge possessed little or no discretion to interpret such rules.[29] The Agricultural Adjustment Act (A.A.A.) at issue in *Butler* was unconstitutional because the Constitution expressly permitted Congress to regulate "commerce," but the A.A.A. sought to regulate "production," which was not "commerce"; therefore, Congress could not regulate production.

Legal realists responded that the Constitution mentioned commerce but not production, so it was not clear that commerce excluded the production of goods; if commerce included production, then Congress could regulate production pursuant to its power to regulate commerce. Therefore, the supposedly unambiguous distinction between commerce and production that the Court followed in *Butler* was actually quite ambiguous; it reflected the majority's distaste for federal regulation of the economy, not a hard-and-fast constitutional rule. Thus, legal realism's legacy is the recognition by today's lawyers and judges that "judgment" is not merely the application of a legal rule to the facts of a case, but instead, the choice of *which* rule to apply to that case and of *how* to apply it.[30]

There is virtually no disagreement today among political scientists and legal scholars that courts make public policy and that judges' policy preferences can influence case outcomes. There is disagreement, though, about the degree to which judges' policy preferences influence case outcomes. Some political scientists, known as **judicial behaviorists**, contend that political ideology is the most important factor that explains judges' decisions; some legal scholars, who belong to the **critical legal studies movement**, even argue that judges' decisions are merely political ideology expressed in, and obscured by, legal language.[31] For many judicial behaviorists and for critical legal studies scholars, the line between law and politics is indistinguishable.

This book perceives a much clearer distinction between law and politics than the critical legal studies scholars and many judicial behaviorists perceive. It proceeds from a **neo-institutionalist** perspective on the judicial process.[32] That perspective acknowledges that courts make public policy and that judges' policy preferences can and do affect case outcomes. On the other hand, it views court decisions as the products not only of judges' political philosophies, but also of case facts, legal principles, court rules, and of judges' views about how courts should function as institutions within the American system of government.[33] The remainder of this section will explain how both political factors and legal factors influence the judicial process.

Links Between Law and Politics

There are numerous links between law and politics in contemporary America. Perhaps the most obvious link is lawyers' participation in government at the local, state, and national levels. Locally, lawyers serve as city attorneys and as county prosecutors, offices to which they are either elected by the voters or appointed by elected officials. City attorneys represent their cities in non-criminal legal matters, which may be politically controversial, such as the distribution of condoms in city high schools to prevent teenage pregnancies.[34] County prosecutors, usually called county, district, or state's attorneys, prosecute violations of criminal law within their respective counties. The chief city attorney and the county prosecutor are often elected, which links them to politics.

At the state level, lawyers often serve as legislators or as governor. Other lawyers are employees of the state legislature, where they draft bills and furnish legal advice regarding proposed legislation. Lawyers also work in state agencies, including the office of the attorney general, which represents the state in lawsuits to which the state is a party. An assistant attorney general might, for example, defend a state department of education against a claim by the parents of a disabled child that the department failed to enforce the federal law that requires public schools to devise "Individual Education Programs" (IEPs) for disabled children.[35]

At the national level, lawyers are elected to Congress more often than are members of any other profession, and more lawyers than members of any other profession serve on the congressional staff. The staff lawyers draft bills and advise individual Senators and Representatives, as well as committees, about the legal implications of proposed and existing laws, which can be politically controversial. Lawyers also work for federal administrative agencies; they represent those agencies in disputes with individuals, and attempt to resolve disputes between individuals or institutions who come under their jurisdiction. They also draft regulations that, if adopted by the agency, will govern the behavior of individuals and institutions whom they are authorized to regulate. A Department of the Interior lawyer, for example, might mediate a dispute between an Indian tribe and non-Indian landowners concerning conflicting land claims that arise from a treaty that the tribe and the federal government signed more than a hundred years ago.[36] Such disputes occur often in the West; they arouse emotions, and they can thrust a lawyer into a political firestorm.

Another link between law and politics is the influence of politics on the selection and the work of judges. The political context of judging is clearest in the states because state judges enter the political arena when they run for election or reelection to the bench. State judges know that their decisions can become the subjects of nasty partisan attacks at election time. Even in states where judges are appointed, they may be subject to **retention elections**, in which voters answer a ballot question that asks whether one or more incumbent judges ought to remain in office.[37] Retention elections can be politically charged, as former Chief Justice Rose Bird and former associate justices Cruz Reynoso and Joseph Grodin of the California Supreme Court learned in 1986 when they lost their seats in a retention election because the electorate resented their votes to reverse death sentences.[38]

Former Justice Penny White of the Tennessee Supreme Court learned the same bitter lesson on August 1, 1996, when she lost her seat in a retention election less than two months after she voted in favor of a new death-sentence hearing for a convicted murderer. Justice White favored a new hearing because the prosecutors had failed to prove that the crime was "heinous, atrocious, or cruel," as Tennessee law required before a death sentence could be imposed.[39] The prosecutors could still try to prove, at the new hearing, that the death penalty was appropriate, but that subtlety was lost on the electorate in the midst of the Tennessee Republican Party's aggressive campaign to oust Justice White, a

Democrat.[40] Like her California counterparts ten years earlier, Justice White could not defend herself because ethical rules prohibit judges from commenting publicly about pending cases.

State judges may be more vulnerable to such attacks than federal judges are because state courts decide many more criminal cases than federal courts do, and criminal cases tend to inflame public passions. Nevertheless, federal judges are not immune from criticism by politicians or by the public. Harold Baer, Jr., a federal judge in New York City, came under heavy fire during the 1996 presidential campaign from both President Clinton and Mr. Clinton's opponent, Senator Robert Dole, for prohibiting prosecutors from introducing as evidence against a suspected drug trafficker eighty pounds of heroin and cocaine that police seized from her car. Judge Baer reversed himself after President Clinton's press secretary hinted during a press conference that Baer should resign from the bench.[41]

In 1987, federal judge Robert Bork, whom President Reagan nominated to the Supreme Court, was the subject of the most intense campaign in American history to convince the Senate to reject a Court nominee. The campaign was intense because the ideological balance on the Court was at stake. Bork would have replaced Justice Lewis Powell, a centrist who was the decisive fifth vote for the Court's liberal wing on abortion, separation of church and state, and affirmative action matters, but a reliable vote for its conservative wing in criminal and business cases. The Senate rejected the Bork nomination by a vote of 58–42.[42]

President Reagan nominated Judge Bork for his strident conservatism, and the Democratic majority in the Senate rejected him for the same reason. Four Democrats from Southern states voted no because blacks opposed the nomination, and black voters were responsible for the election of those four Democrats.[43] Other Senators voted no because politically moderate women's organizations opposed the nomination, a clear indication that it lacked the support of "mainstream" voters.[44] Thus, politics was responsible for Judge Bork's nomination to the Supreme Court, and politics was equally responsible for his defeat.

Supreme Court decisions are the most significant reflections of the connection between law and politics in contemporary America. Numerous cases illustrate that connection; the cases that probably illustrate it best are those in which the Court shapes the rules that govern American politics. Those cases address: (1) state regulation of political parties; (2) political patronage (public employment as a reward for political support); (3) ballot access for independent and third-party candidates; (4) the reapportionment and redistricting of legislatures; and (5) the financing of political campaigns.[45]

Baker v. Carr is the most important of those cases.[46] *Baker* held that courts could resolve lawsuits in which plaintiffs claimed that the methods by which their state legislators drew legislative district boundaries overrepresented rural residents and underrepresented urban residents, in violation of the Constitution. The justices reasoned that if courts relied on legislators to resolve such disputes, urban underrepresentation would persist because rural legislators would not voluntarily redraw district lines and relinquish power. *Baker* paved the way for later Supreme

Court decisions that revolutionized state politics by requiring legislatures to redraw district boundaries in order to represent urban and suburban residents fairly.[47]

Thus, law and politics are intertwined, and you might wonder why this book insists that they are not identical. The next section will explain how law and politics differ.

The Differences Between Law and Politics

One way to illustrate the difference between law and politics is to compare information gathering and decision making in a political and in a legal setting. A brief review of the 1991 Senate confirmation hearings of Supreme Court nominee Judge Clarence Thomas will make that comparison.

In the summer of 1991, President George Bush nominated Judge Thomas, a federal appellate judge, to the Supreme Court to succeed retiring Justice Thurgood Marshall. Judge Thomas's chances for confirmation by the Senate initially appeared to be excellent because of his compelling biography. He had overcome poverty and racial segregation in rural Georgia, had graduated from Yale Law School and served in the Reagan Administration, and had been appointed to the U.S. Court of Appeals while still in his early forties.[48] Judge Thomas's prospects for confirmation dimmed considerably, though, when Professor Anita Hill of the Oklahoma University Law School testified before the Senate Judiciary Committee that he had sexually harassed her a decade earlier, when she worked for him at two federal agencies.[49] The committee's hearings concerning Professor Hill's allegation against Judge Thomas demonstrated how law differs from politics.

The hearings were a "political free-for-all, with none of the safeguards and procedural rules used in court to ensure a fair trial."[50] Most of the committee members were lawyers, and they promised that they would "judge" the facts impartially, yet political, rather than legal, considerations dictated their behavior. For example, Republican members vigorously championed Judge Thomas's cause, and dismissed Professor Hill's testimony as unreliable. Their foremost goal was not truth or dispute resolution, but instead, the confirmation of a Republican president's Supreme Court nominee.

The rules that govern the introduction and presentation of evidence in a trial were not available at the hearings. Those rules require that only facts that tend to prove a matter that is in dispute at trial are admissible as evidence.[51] They prevent parties and witnesses from blurting out unreliable statements that are prejudicial to one side or the other.[52] Such statements, from Senators and witnesses, were standard fare at the "Hill–Thomas Hearings." For example, one witness speculated that Professor Hill was mentally unstable, and that she resented Judge Thomas because he rejected romantic advances that she had made to him in the past.[53] Several Republican Senators speculated that Professor Hill fabricated her allegation after reading a novel titled *The Exorcist* and a Kansas sexual harassment case that featured charges similar to those that she made against Judge Thomas.[54]

Unlike at trial, neither party at the Hill–Thomas hearings bore a clear burden of proof.[55] There was no standard by which the Senators could determine with reasonable certainty, even if they had all wanted to, whether Professor Hill's allegation was true. The Hill–Thomas hearings lacked the boundaries, the safeguards, and the finality of a judicial proceeding. The lack of boundaries or safeguards left Professor Hill and Judge Thomas at least as emotionally bruised as a trial would have, and the lack of finality left the American people bitterly divided about who had told the truth and who had lied. To make matters worse, neither the professor nor the judge could file an appeal to correct the deficiencies of the hearings; there is no right of appeal in the political process, as there is in the judicial process.

Thus, the Hill–Thomas hearings were a political exercise badly disguised as a legal proceeding. The disguise did not conceal the important ways in which law differs from politics.

Another way to illustrate how law differs from politics is to consider the distinction between a decision that is "good law" and a decision that is "good politics." A brief review of the work of Frank Johnson, who served as a federal district judge in Alabama from 1955 until 1979, will make that distinction clear.

During the 1960s, despite bitter opposition, Judge Johnson vigorously enforced the Supreme Court's 1954 decision, *Brown v. Board of Education,* [56] which held that the Constitution's **equal protection clause** prohibited racially segregated public schools.[57] In 1964, Judge Johnson ordered the Alabama State Board of Education and Governor George Wallace, a fiery segregationist, to refrain from further "interfering with court-ordered desegregation anywhere in the State of Alabama," and to cease financing private, segregated schools in order to evade court-ordered desegregation.[58] In 1967, after three years of resistance by the governor and by the state board of education, Judge Johnson imposed a statewide desegregation order that required each school district in Alabama to adopt a desegregation plan for all grades for the 1967–68 school year.[59] Thereafter, Judge Johnson and other federal judges in Alabama supervised the implementation of his order, and desegregation began to occur in earnest as the 1960s ended.

During the 1970s, Judge Johnson again aroused the wrath of many Alabama citizens when he concluded that conditions at the state's prisons violated the Constitution, and ordered state authorities to dramatically improve services and facilities for prison inmates. Judge Johnson found that unsanitary and dangerous conditions existed in Alabama's prisons; he characterized those conditions as "barbarous" and "shocking to the conscience."[60] Judge Johnson reasoned that prison policies were constitutional only when they furthered the legitimate correctional goals of deterrence, rehabilitation, and security. The filthy, unsafe conditions under which Alabama confined its prisoners negated those goals; therefore, they were "cruel and unusual punishment" in violation of the Eighth Amendment to the Constitution. Judge Johnson ordered prison authorities to implement a detailed list of "minimal constitutional standards."[61]

Judge Johnson's decisions concerning school desegregation and conditions for prisoners in Alabama were good law because they extended human rights contained in the Constitution to persons who were unable to protect their rights in the political process. Those decisions were bad politics, however, because they required Alabama to devote resources to persons whom the state's political leaders had long neglected and probably would have preferred to ignore. Therefore, state officials resisted implementing Judge Johnson's orders as long as they possibly could. The judge paid a price for his decisions; he endured social ostracism, no-holds-barred attacks by Governor Wallace, and hate mail from angry Alabamians. Alabama's Republican leaders convinced President Richard Nixon not to appoint him to the Supreme Court in 1969, 1970, or 1971 because they feared that his appointment would hurt their party's chances to attract the support of conservative white voters.[62]

The Hill–Thomas hearings and the career of Judge Johnson illustrate that law differs from politics and that politics without law threatens the rights of those whose views do not command the support of the majority. Nevertheless, law that disregards politics is also potentially dangerous. Court decisions must satisfy public opinion often enough that opponents of a particular decision will obey it because they acknowledge the legitimacy of the court that made it. Thus, courts must reconcile law and politics in order to ensure that citizens will obey the law and that courts will remain featured actors in the American political drama. The next section will explain how courts reconcile law and politics.

RECONCILING LAW AND POLITICS

Courts reconcile law and politics when they make decisions, especially in controversial cases, that reflect both defensible legal reasoning and sensitivity to political realities. The Supreme Court's 1992 decision in *Planned Parenthood of Southeastern Pennsylvania v. Casey* reflected such sensitivity.[63]

At issue in *Casey* was whether a state may, despite the constitutional guarantee of a right to abortion, restrict that right by requiring a woman to give informed consent to the procedure, wait twenty-four hours before having the abortion, inform her husband if she is married, and obtain the consent of one parent if she is a minor. The Court, in a plurality opinion that Justices Anthony Kennedy, Sandra Day O'Connor, and David Souter wrote jointly, reaffirmed its 1973 opinion in *Roe v. Wade* that "before [her fetus is viable, that is, able to survive outside the womb,] a woman has a right to terminate her pregnancy,"[64] but upheld all of the above restrictions except spousal notification because only spousal notification imposed an **undue burden** on a woman who sought a legal abortion.[65]

Even though Justices Kennedy, O'Connor, and Souter doubted the wisdom of *Roe*, they affirmed its core principle in *Casey* because American women have relied on that principle since 1973, and the three justices did not wish to destroy that reliance or public support for the Court by overruling *Roe*. They observed that:

> [F]or two decades of economic and social developments, people have organized intimate relationships and made choices that define their views of themselves and their places in society, in reliance on the availability of abortion if contraception should fail. The ability of women to participate equally in the economic

and social life of the Nation has been facilitated by their ability to control their reproductive lives. The Constitution serves human values, and while the effect of reliance on *Roe* cannot be exactly measured, neither can the certain cost of overruling *Roe* for people who have ordered their thinking and living around that case be dismissed.[66]

Justices Kennedy, O'Connor, and Souter also reminded their readers that:

[T]he [Supreme] Court cannot buy support for its decisions by spending money and, except to a minor degree, it cannot independently coerce obedience to its decrees. The Court's power lies, rather, in its legitimacy, a product of substance and perception that shows itself in the people's acceptance of the Judiciary as fit to determine what the Nation's law means and to declare what it demands.[67]

Thus, despite their qualms about *Roe*, the three justices voted to affirm it because "[a] decision to overrule *Roe's* essential holding under the existing circumstances would address error, if error there was, at the cost of both profound and unnecessary damage to the Court's legitimacy, and to the Nation's commitment to the rule of law."[68]

The *Casey* decision reconciled law and politics. On the one hand, it followed *stare decisis*; that is, it applied to a current case a rule of law announced in an earlier case, which in this instance was *Roe v. Wade*. On the other hand, it followed the rule of *Roe* out of concern for the degree to which American women rely on abortion rights and the Supreme Court relies on continued public support, respectively.

In reconciling law and politics, *Casey* showed that forces other than judges' public policy preferences can influence court decisions; among those forces are collegial interaction, a desire for continuity in the law, and a wish to preserve the institutional strength of one's court. In other words, judges sometimes make decisions that conflict with their **political philosophies**, or public policy preferences, because of their **judicial philosophies**, that is, their views about the way in which law should develop and about the role that courts should play in the American political system.[69] It is necessary to grasp the relationship between judges' political philosophies and their judicial philosophies in order to understand how courts work. This book will help you understand how courts work by painting a vivid picture of that relationship in the chapters that follow.

CONCLUSION: LAW, POLITICS, AND JUDICIAL DECISIONS

Contrary to myth, law and politics are neither unrelated nor identical. Politics influences court decisions because judges do not forget their public policy preferences when they go on the bench. *United States v. Butler* illustrates that point. Neither do judges forget their legal training when they go on the bench; therefore, legal factors influence court decisions too. *Clinton v. Jones* illustrates that point.

Law and politics, then, are not identical twins, but they are close relatives and they both influence courts, sometimes even in the same case, as *Planned Parenthood of Southeastern Pennsylvania v. Casey* illustrates. Therefore, you must appreciate the importance of both legal and political influences on judicial decisions in order to understand how American courts work. The reprinted Supreme Court opinion that appears in the next section will help in that regard. As you read it, try to identify the legal and the political influences in both the majority opinion and the dissent; when you finish reading, consider whether the majority opinion or the dissent makes a more convincing argument.

Epilogue: The Law and Politics of Flag Burning

United States v. Eichman
496 U.S. 310 (1990)

JUSTICE BRENNAN delivered the opinion of the Court.

In th[is] appeal, we consider whether [the] prosecution [of Eichman] for burning a United States flag in violation of the Flag Protection Act of 1989 is consistent with the First Amendment. Applying our recent decision in *Texas v. Johnson* (1989), the district court held that the Act cannot constitutionally be applied to [Eichman].

We affirm.

I

The United States prosecuted [Eichman] for ... knowingly setting fire to several United States flags on the steps of the ... Capitol while protesting various aspects of the Government's domestic and foreign policy. [Eichman] moved to dismiss the flag-burning charge on the ground that the Act ... violates the First Amendment. [**Editor's Note:** the federal district court that previously considered this case found the Act unconstitutional, and dismissed the charges against Eichman].

II

Last term in *Johnson*, we held that a Texas statute criminalizing the desecration of venerated objects, including the United States flag, was unconstitutional.... [Under] [t]he Texas statute,... "desecrate" meant to "deface, damage, or otherwise physically mistreat in a way that the actor knows will seriously offend one or more persons likely to observe or discover his action." We reasoned that the State's asserted interest "in preserving the flag as a symbol of nationhood and national unity," was an interest related to the suppression of free expression ... because [that interest] is implicated only when a person's treatment of the flag communicates some message. [W]e concluded that the State's interest could not justify [an] infringement on [Johnson's] First Amendment rights.

After our decision in *Johnson*, Congress passed the Flag Protection Act of 1989. The Act provides that:

> Whoever knowingly mutilates, defaces, physically defiles, burns, maintains on the floor or ground, or tramples upon any flag of the United States shall be fined … or imprisoned for not more than one year, or both.

The Government contends that the Flag Protection Act is constitutional because, unlike the statute addressed in *Johnson*, the Act does not target expressive conduct on the basis of the content of its message. The Act proscribes conduct (other than disposal) that damages or mistreats a flag, without regard to the actor's motive, his intended message, or the likely effects of his conduct on onlookers.

Although the Flag Protection Act contains no explicit content-based limitation on the scope of prohibited conduct, it is nevertheless clear that the Government's asserted *interest* is related to the suppression of free expression, and concerned with the content of such expression. The Government's interest in protecting the "physical integrity" of a privately-owned flag rests upon a perceived need to preserve the flag's status as a symbol of our Nation and certain national ideals. [T]he secret destruction of a flag in one's own basement would not threaten the flag's recognized meaning. Rather, the Government's desire to preserve the flag as a symbol for certain national ideals is implicated "only when a person's treatment of the flag communicates [a] message" to others that is inconsistent with those ideals.

The Act criminalizes the conduct of anyone who "knowingly mutilates, defaces, physically defiles, burns, maintains on the floor or ground, or tramples upon any flag." Each of the specified terms—with the possible exception of "burns"— unmistakably connotes disrespectful treatment of the flag.... And the explicit exemption in [the Act] for disposal of "worn or soiled" flags protects certain acts traditionally associated with patriotic respect for the flag.

Although Congress cast the Flag Protection Act in somewhat broader terms than the Texas statute at issue in *Johnson*, the Act still … suppresses expression out of concern for its likely communicative impact…. [T]he Government's interest [in preserving the flag as a national symbol therefore] cannot justify [the Act's] infringement on First Amendment rights. We decline the Government's invitation to reassess this conclusion in light of Congress'[s] recent recognition of a purported "national consensus" favoring a prohibition on flag-burning. Even assuming such a consensus exists, any suggestion that the Government's interest in suppressing speech becomes more weighty as popular opposition to that speech grows is foreign to the First Amendment.

III

… Government may create national symbols, promote them, and encourage their respectful treatment. But the Flag Protection Act goes well beyond this by criminally proscribing expressive conduct because of its likely communicative impact.

If there is a bedrock principle underlying the First Amendment, it is that the Government may not prohibit the expression of an idea simply because society finds the idea itself offensive or disagreeable. Punishing desecration of the flag dilutes the very freedom that makes this emblem so revered, and worth revering.

Affirmed.

JUSTICE STEVENS, with whom CHIEF JUSTICE REHNQUIST, JUSTICE WHITE, and JUSTICE O'CONNOR join, dissenting.

[T]he Federal Government has a legitimate interest in protecting the symbolic value of the American flag. [That value] has at least these two components: in times of national crisis, it inspires and motivates the average citizen to make personal sacrifices in order to achieve societal goals of overriding importance; at all times, it serves as a reminder of the paramount importance of pursuing the ideals that characterize our society.

[T]he Government may—indeed, it should—protect the symbolic value of the flag without regard to the specific content of the flag burner's speech. The prosecution in this case does not depend upon the object of [Eichman's] protest. It ... does not entail any interference with the speaker's freedom to express his or her ideas by other means. It may well be true that other means of expression may be less effective in drawing attention to those ideas....

This case therefore comes down to a question of judgment. Does the admittedly important interest in allowing every speaker to choose the method of expressing his or her ideas that he or she deems most effective or appropriate outweigh the societal interest in preserving the symbolic value of the flag?...

[T]he First Amendment embraces ... the right to communicate [ideas] effectively. That right, however, is not absolute—the communicative value of a well-placed bomb in the Capitol does not entitle it to the protection of the First Amendment.

Burning a flag is not, of course, equivalent to burning a public building. Assuming that the protester is burning his own flag, it causes no physical harm to other persons or to their property. The impact is purely symbolic, and ... some thoughtful persons believe that impact, far from depreciating the value of the [flag], will actually enhance its meaning. I most respectfully disagree. Indeed, what makes this case particularly difficult for me is ... the damage to the [flag] that has already occurred as a result of this Court's decision [in *Texas v. Johnson*].

The symbolic value of the American flag is not the same today as it was yesterday. [S]ome [Americans] now have difficulty understanding the message that the flag conveyed to their parents and grandparents....

Given all these considerations,... it might be appropriate to [join] the majority and merely apply the doctrine of *stare decisis* [and the rule of *Texas v. Johnson*] to the case at hand. That action, however, would not honestly reflect my considered judgment concerning the relative importance of the conflicting interests at stake.

Accordingly, I respectfully dissent.

QUESTIONS FOR DISCUSSION

1. What federal law did Eichman violate when he burned American flags on the steps of the United States Capitol? What conduct did that law prohibit?
2. On what basis did Eichman move to dismiss the charge against him?
3. How did the Supreme Court's decision in *Texas v. Johnson* affect its decision in *Eichman*?
4. What was Congress's response to the Court's decision in *Texas v. Johnson*? How does that response illustrate the political context in which courts operate?
5. On what basis did the federal government argue that the federal law at issue in *Eichman* was sufficiently different from the Texas law at issue in *Johnson* that the federal law was constitutional even though the Texas law was unconstitutional?
6. On what basis did the Court majority reject the federal government's argument that the federal law was constitutional even though the Texas law was unconstitutional?
7. Why did the exemption contained in the federal law for the destruction of "worn or soiled" flags reinforce the majority's conclusion that the federal law was unconstitutional?
8. Why did public support for a prohibition on flag-burning not convince the Court majority to decide *Eichman* in favor of the federal government?
9. Should public support for a prohibition on flag-burning have convinced the Court majority to decide *Eichman* in favor of the federal government? Why or why not?
10. What value did the majority protect by its decision in *Eichman*? How does that value choice illustrate judicial policy making?
11. What value did the dissenters wish to protect instead? How does that value choice illustrate judicial policy making?
12. Who do you think reached the correct result in this case, the majority or the dissenters? Why?

NOTES

1. The Federalist Papers are a series of essays that Alexander Hamilton, James Madison, and John Jay published in 1788 in an effort to convince delegates to state ratifying conventions to ratify the Constitution that the delegates to the Constitutional Convention in Philadelphia had adopted in 1787. See Roy P. Fairfield, ed., *The Federalist Papers*, Second Edition (Baltimore: Johns Hopkins University Press, 1981).
2. 297 U.S. 1 (1936).
3. *Id.*, pp. 62–63.
4. *Id.*, p. 63.
5. *Id.*
6. 117 S. Ct. 1636 (1997). The Supreme Court decision to which President Clinton and Ms. Jones were parties was *Clinton v. Jones* because President Clinton was the

plaintiff in that case; that is, he brought the lawsuit, and asked the Court to postpone Ms. Jones's sexual harassment suit against him until after he left office. The sexual harassment suit was *Jones v. Clinton* because Ms. Jones was the plaintiff and President Clinton was the defendant in that suit. The plaintiff's name always appears first in the case name.

7. The Supreme Court **remanded** (i.e. returned) the Jones case to the federal district court in Little Rock, Arkansas, where it began, so that it could proceed to a resolution. On April 1, 1998, Judge Susan Webber Wright dismissed the case because Paula Jones had failed to prove that President Clinton had subjected her to sexual harassment. Ms. Jones appealed Judge Wright's decision to the U.S. Court of Appeals for the Eighth Circuit, but before that court could hear oral arguments, the parties agreed to settle the matter. On November 13, 1998, President Clinton offered to pay Ms. Jones $850,000, which she accepted in return for ending her lawsuit against him. President Clinton admitted no wrongdoing and offered Ms. Jones no apology under the terms of their settlement agreement. See: "The President's Women," *The Economist*, November 21, 1998, p. 29, col. 1.

8. David Nyhan, "The Trials Inflicted by the Supreme Court 9," *Boston Sunday Globe*, July 6, 1997, p. C 4.

9. Several commentators have argued that the Supreme Court decided *Clinton v. Jones* incorrectly. The commentators have charged that the Court wrongly predicted that a civil suit during a president's term of office would impose no serious burden on the president. The *Jones* case, however, occupied much of President Clinton's time and attention for more than a year following the Supreme Court's ruling, and it diverted the attention of the press and the public from his job performance to his legal predicament. See, e.g. Suzanna Sherry, "What the Jones Case Meant, After All: The Judicial System Worked, Despite an Iffy High Court Decision," *The Washington Post National Weekly Edition*, April 13, 1998, p. 21. Thus, the Supreme Court may have read the law correctly in *Clinton v. Jones*, while, arguably, it misread the political reality that a sexual harassment suit against a sitting president would divert the president, the press, and even the people, from the conduct of the people's business for an extended period. Under these circumstances, a plaintiff's gain might be democracy's loss.

10. Kermit L. Hall, *The Magic Mirror: Law in American History* (New York: Oxford University Press, 1989), p.3; Roscoe Pound, *The Spirit of the Common Law* (Boston: Beacon Press, 1963), p. 140.

11. The three-witness requirement is contained in Title 14 of the *Vermont Statutes Annotated* at section 5.

12. Lief H. Carter, *Reason in Law*, Fifth Edition (New York: Addison Wesley Longman, 1998), p. 5.

13. Lawrence M. Friedman, *American Law* (New York: W. W. Norton, 1984), p. 22.

14. Harold D. Lasswell, *Who Gets What, When, How* (New York: Meridian Books, 1958).

15. Herbert Jacob, *Law and Politics in the United States*, Second Edition (Boston: Little, Brown and Company, 1986), p. 26.

16. Theodore F.T. Plucknett, *A Concise History of the Common Law*, Fifth Edition (Boston, MA.: Little, Brown, 1956), p. 13.

17. Brian L. Porto, *The Craft Of Legal Reasoning* (Fort Worth, TX.: Harcourt Brace College Publishers, 1998), pp. 99–101.

18. Arthur R. Hogue, *Origins of the Common Law* (Hamden, CT.: Archon Books, 1974), p. 179.

19. *Id.*, p. 190.

20. Porto, *The Craft Of Legal Reasoning*, pp. 100–101.

21. *Baker v. State*, No. 98–32 (December 20, 1999). You can locate this decision on the Internet at www.dol.state.vt.us. by using links to the judiciary and to recent Vermont Supreme Court decisions.

22. That debate ended on April 26, 2000, when Govenor Howard Dean signed legislation that conferred on same-sex couples all of the benefits of marriage, in "civil unions", but did not permit same-sex marriages. "Civil unions" were a legislative compromise.

23. 130 N.H. 815 (1988). This case is now more than ten years old, but it remains fresh in my mind because I researched and helped to write the New Hampshire Supreme Court's opinion that resolved it during the enlightening year that I worked as a law clerk to Associate Justice William Johnson. Law clerks are recent law school graduates whom state and federal court judges and justices hire to assist them with their work, usually for one or two years.

24. The fourth amendment to the U.S. Constitution and part I, article 19, of the New Hampshire Constitution both prohibit *unreasonable* searches and seizures. The U.S. Supreme Court has held that warrantless entries are generally unreasonable, but that they are permissible when they occur subject to the consent of a person who is authorized to consent. Similarly, warrantless seizures of property are generally unreasonable, but when the officer is entitled to be on the search premises and when, as in this case, the items seized are in *plain view*, a search warrant is unnecessary. The New Hampshire Supreme Court has interpreted the New Hampshire Constitution in the same way.

25. 955 F. 2d 132 (2d Cir. 1992). This case, in which I assisted Mr. Alleyne's lawyer, illustrates the "stranger-than-fiction" fact patterns that occur surprisingly often in personal injury litigation. It also illustrates the emotional roller coaster that lawyers and clients can experience during lengthy litigation. The jury returned a verdict in Mr. Alleyne's favor at trial, but the innkeeper appealed, and the appellate court overturned the jury's verdict.

26. *Butler* was only a temporary bar to President Roosevelt's economic recovery program because, beginning in 1937, Justice Roberts and Chief Justice Charles Evans Hughes switched their votes and created a 5–4 Court majority that upheld the constitutionality of the Roosevelt program on the ground that Congress's power to regulate interstate commerce encompassed the power to regulate the production of goods. Hughes and Roberts switched their votes after President Roosevelt proposed legislation to add several new justices to the Court who would support his economic program. The Senate defeated this "Court-packing plan," but President Roosevelt accomplished his goal when Hughes and Roberts changed their votes in the "switch in time that saved nine."

27. That is unfortunate for future presidents, because the Court's decision in *Clinton v. Jones* appears to have underestimated the extent to which permitting the Jones lawsuit to go forward would divert the attention of both President Clinton and the media from the important issues that Mr. Clinton was elected to address. See Suzanna Sherry, "The Judicial System Worked Despite an Iffy High Court Decision," *The Washington Post National Weekly Edition*, April 13, 1998, p. 21. Professor Sherry's article recalls that there was tremendous media attention to the lawsuit early in 1998, before the trial judge dismissed it for lack of sufficient evidence to support Ms. Jones's claims, including sexual harassment.

28. Wilfrid E. Rumble, Jr., *American Legal Realism: Skepticism, Reform, and the Judicial Process* (Ithaca, N.Y.: Cornell University Press, 1968), p. 22.

29. Rumble, *American Legal Realism*, p. 49.

30. *Id.*, pp. 97–98.

31. The critical legal studies scholars argue further that legal reasoning is designed not only to camouflage the political choices that judges make when they decide cases, but also to "protect and preserve the propertied interest of vested white and male power." Allan C. Hutchinson, *Critical Legal Studies* (Totowa, N.J.: Rowman and Littlefield, 1989), p. 4. Thus, the critical legal studies movement openly advocates a particular political viewpoint, that of the radical left. Judicial behaviorists agree that judges act on the basis of their political ideologies, but judicial behaviorists do not advocate a particular political viewpoint. Instead, they advocate the rigorous application of scientific methods to the study of judicial policy making. Chapter 8 discusses the work of the judicial behaviorists in detail.

32. For more complete explanations of the neo-institutional perspective in political science, see Rogers M. Smith, "The 'New Institutionalism,' and the Future of Public Law," *The American Political Science Review* 82, no. 1 (March 1988); and James G. March and Johan P. Olsen, "The New Institutionalism: Organizational Factors in Political Life," *The American Political Science Review* 78, no. 3 (September 1984): 734–749.

33. Ronald H. Kahn, *The Supreme Court and Constitutional Theory, 1953–1993* (Lawrence, KS.: University Press of Kansas, 1994), p. 3; Howard Gillman, *The Constitution Besieged: The Rise and Demise of Lochner Era Police Powers Jurisprudence* (Durham, N.C.: Duke University Press, 1993), p. 17; Rogers M. Smith, "Political Jurisprudence, The 'New Institutionalism,' and the Future of Public Law," *The American Political Science Review* 82, no. 1 (March 1988): 89–107.

34. Brian L. Porto, "Law, Courts, and the Political Process," in David A. Schultz, ed., *Law and Politics: Unanswered Questions* (New York: Peter Lang Publishing, 1994), p. 108.

35. *Id.*, p. 109.

36. *Id.*

37. Twenty-one states initially select judges by election. Thirty-eight states require judges to keep their seats by means of some sort of retention election, either by the voters or by the state legislature. Only three states do not subject their judges to a retention election or reappointment. See John Gibeault, "Taking Aim," *American Bar Association Journal* (November 1996): 50–55.

38. Porto, "Law, Courts, and the Political Process," p. 110.

39. Gibeault, "Taking Aim," p. 53.

40. *Id.*, p. 54.

41. *Id.*, p. 51.

42. Ethan Bronner, *Battle for Justice: How the Bork Nomination Shook America* (New York: W. W. Norton, 1989), p. 327.

43. *Id.*, p. 286.

44. *Id.*, p. 185.

45. For a discussion of Supreme Court decisions concerning these issues, see Brian L. Porto, "Law, Courts, and the Political Process."

46. 369 U.S. 186 (1962).

47. For a discussion of those later cases, see Porto, "Law, Courts, and the Political Process," pp. 126–130.

48. Jane Mayer and Jill Abrahamson, *Strange Justice: The Selling of Clarence Thomas* (New York: Plume/Penguin, 1995), p. 16.

49. *Id.*, p. 291.
50. *Id.*, p. 274.
51. Shirley A. Wiegand, "Analyzing the Testimony from a Legal Evidentiary Perspective: Using Judicial Language Injudiciously," in Sandra L. Ragan, ed., *The Lynching of Language: Gender, Politics, and Power in the Hill-Thomas Hearings* (Urbana, IL.: University of Illinois Press, 1996), p. 6.
52. *Id.*
53. Mayer and Abrahamson, *Strange Justice*, p. 296.
54. *Id.*, p. 302.
55. Wiegand, "Analyzing the Testimony from a Legal Evidentiary Perspective," p. 9.
56. 347 U.S. 483 (1954).
57. The equal-protection clause, which is contained in the Fourteenth Amendment to the Constitution, provides that "[n]o State shall deny to any person within its jurisdiction the equal protection of the laws."
58. *Lee v. Macon County*, 231 F. Supp. 743, 755 (M.D. Ala. 1964).
59. Tinsley E. Yarbrough, *Judge Frank Johnson and Human Rights in Alabama* (Tuscaloosa, AL.: University of Alabama Press, 1981), pp. 139–140.
60. *Newman v. Alabama*, 349 F. Supp. 278, 281 (M.D. Ala. 1972).
61. *Pugh v.Locke*, 406 F. Supp. 318, 332–335 (M.D. Ala. 1976).
62. Yarbrough, *Judge Frank Johnson and Human Rights in Alabama*, pp. 146–150.
63. 505 U.S. 833.
64. *Id.*, p. 870.
65. *Id.*, pp. 893–894.
66. *Id.*, p. 856.
67. *Id.*, p. 865.
68. *Id.*, p. 869.
69. For interesting discussions about the influence of factors other than political philosophy on court decisions, see Ronald H. Kahn, *The Supreme Court and Constitutional Theory, 1953–1993*; and Howard Gillman, *The Constitution Besieged: The Rise and Demise of Lochner*, Era Police Powers Jurisprudence.

Chapter 2

American Courts— Structures and Procedures

Federalism and the Judiciary

The United States is the only country in the world that contains two parallel court systems, one for the nation and one for each state, including separate national and state trial courts.[1] America's dual court system is a result of federalism, one of the core principles that underlies the U.S. Constitution. Federalism divides power between the national, or federal, government and fifty state governments.[2]

American federalism is the product of a compromise that occurred among the delegates to the Constitutional Convention in 1787. Staunch supporters of a strong national government wanted the states to be administrative units that would merely execute the policies of the national government. Staunch supporters of state power wanted states to retain the supremacy that they enjoyed under the **Articles of Confederation**, which governed America in 1787. The two sides reached a compromise, namely, federalism, which substantially increased the power of the national government, but retained the states as **sovereign** (possessed of authority over their territory), but inferior, political entities.[3] For example, under the Constitution, the national government can regulate interstate and foreign commerce, which it could not do under the Articles of Confederation.[4] State governments can regulate commerce within their borders, provided their regulations do not burden interstate commerce, such as by banning from their interstate highways trucks that federal regulations permit.

Federalism aims to achieve national unity, but also to preserve the diversity of traditions and values that exists within the states. It preserves diversity by giving states power to make important value choices about issues that affect them.[5] Capital punishment highlights that diversity. Texas executed thirty-seven people in 1997 alone, while Vermont refuses to enact a capital punishment statute.[6] Thus, a dual court system and variations in state law are two noteworthy consequences of federalism. Both consequences were evident in the much-publicized case of Karla Faye Tucker, whom Texas executed on February 3, 1998.[7] The dual court system enabled Ms. Tucker's lawyer to seek a stay of execution for her from the U.S. Supreme Court, even though a state court had convicted her of murder pursuant to the criminal law of Texas. After the Supreme Court rejected Ms. Tucker's petition, Texas carried out her death sentence. Had she committed the same crimes in Vermont, her sentence would have been life imprisonment instead of death.

The remainder of this chapter will explain in detail the consequences of federalism for the judicial process. The next section will discuss state courts, and subsequent sections will examine, in turn, federal courts, federal court administration, and the relationship between state and federal courts.

STATE COURT SYSTEMS

Introduction

Each state is responsible for creating its own court system; therefore, there is considerable variation between states in the structures and procedures of their respective courts. Despite such variation, it is possible, for discussion purposes, to place state courts into four categories. Those categories are (1) **trial courts of limited jurisdiction**, (2) **trial courts of general jurisdiction**, (3) **intermediate appellate courts**, and (4) **courts of last resort**. Trial courts of limited jurisdiction and trial courts of general jurisdiction are the first courts to hear cases. They resolve cases by determining the facts, and then applying the relevant law to those facts. In contrast, intermediate appellate courts and courts of last resort hear **appeals** by parties who lost in the trial courts. They do not reconsider the facts; instead, they review trial court procedures and rulings (e.g. on the admissibility of evidence) for conformity to statutory and constitutional requirements. In short, **appellate** courts determine whether trial court proceedings were fair. Figure 2.1 depicts the four categories of courts discussed, and it shows the paths that appeals can take in states that lack intermediate appellate courts and in states that have them.

Trial Courts of Limited Jurisdiction

Trial courts of limited jurisdiction consider civil (e.g., personal injury, contract, and property) claims up to a specified dollar amount, crimes punishable by less than one year in jail and a $1,000 fine, traffic, family, estate, juvenile, and small claims cases. The number of trial courts of limited jurisdiction varies from one state to the next; New York State has eight, whereas Kansas has one.[8] Court reformers have long advocated that states consolidate these courts, as Kansas has done, in order to save money and to increase efficiency. Consolidation is often politically unpopular, though, because it reduces the opportunities for political parties to reward their supporters with jobs in the local courthouse.

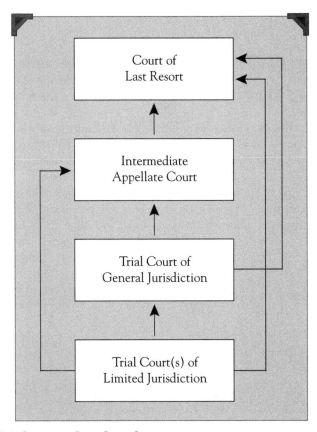

FIGURE 2.1 Composite State Court System
Source: Court Statistics Project, *State Court Caseload Statistics*, 1996, p. 7. (Williamsburg, VA: National Center for State Courts, 1997). Reprinted with permission.

Some states that have more than one trial court of limited jurisdiction refer to them, respectively, as **traffic court, probate court** (resolves estate matters), **family court, juvenile court,** and **small claims court**; other states assign them more general names, such as **magistrate's court, justice court,** or **municipal court.**

Nowadays, the presiding officer in nearly all trial courts of limited jurisdiction is a judge who is a licensed lawyer in the state in which the court is located. Nevertheless, Arkansas, Delaware, Louisiana, Montana, Ohio, and South Dakota still have courts in which nonlawyers preside, most often in traffic and in small claims matters, but also in minor civil and criminal cases.[9] Court reformers have long urged state legislators to abolish such courts, known as **justice of the peace, mayor's,** or **aldermen's courts,** because the presiding officers are often ignorant of legal rules and of the rights of parties. Traditionally, those presiding officers also earned their incomes from the fees that they assessed, primarily traffic fines, which gave them a financial stake in the results of cases, and invited biased judging. Consequently, most states have abolished such courts. In the states where they survive, they operate almost exclusively in rural areas.

The business of trial courts of limited jurisdiction is not confined to small-scale matters, nor is it less significant than the business of trial courts of general jurisdiction. Admittedly, the civil and the criminal jurisdiction of these courts is "limited" to the dollar amount and to the degree of seriousness, respectively, at which the authority of trial courts of general jurisdiction begins. However, the jurisdiction of family courts and probate courts is "limited" only by subject matter, not by dollar amount or by degree of significance. There is nothing "small scale" about a family court's revocation of parental rights, or about a probate court's resolution of a will contest over a multimillion dollar estate.

Trial courts of limited jurisdiction hear different types of cases in different states. In many states, they hear civil cases; indeed, they heard 57 percent of the civil cases that state courts resolved nationwide in 1996.[10] States limit the dollar amount that can be in controversy in such cases; for example, California caps it at $25,000,[11] and Kentucky caps it at $4000.[12] A trial court of limited jurisdiction might hear a suit by a homeowner who alleges that the defendant, a roofing company, failed to complete the work it agreed to do on her house, or a suit by a furniture store that seeks to collect the balance due on the living room furniture that the defendant purchased.

Some states permit trial courts of limited jurisdiction to hear criminal cases. Those cases almost always involve **misdemeanors**, which are minor offenses for which the penalty is a jail term of less than one year and a fine of less than $1,000 ($5,000 in some states). Minor assaults, drunk and disorderly conduct, and possession of a small amount of marijuana suitable only for personal use are examples of misdemeanors.

Civil and criminal caseloads in trial courts of limited jurisdiction are enormous. Those courts resolved almost 3,100,000 civil cases and more than 2,500,000 criminal cases in 1996.[13] Therefore, time is of the essence, and judges in limited jurisdiction courts dispose of cases as quickly as they can, often in a matter of minutes. Trials, either by the judge or by a jury, are rare; in civil cases the parties usually agree to settle the dispute for a certain sum, and in criminal cases the defendant typically **plea bargains**—that is, pleads guilty, usually to a lesser charge than he originally faced, and pays a fine and/or accepts some form of punishment (i.e., jail, probation, home confinement, suspension of driver's license).

Much of the business of trial courts of limited jurisdiction consists of small claims and of traffic cases. Traffic cases are the largest category; they comprise nearly 50 percent of the caseload.[14] **Commissioners, hearing officers,** or **judges pro tempore,** who are lawyers hired by the court to hear cases part-time, often decide traffic matters, especially in large cities.[15] They usually take only about ninety seconds to either resolve a case or to set a trial date for it, because they often must address 250 cases in an afternoon.[16]

Small claims are also numerous; in 1990, they were approximately 40 percent of all the non-criminal cases filed in trial courts of limited jurisdiction nationwide.[17] Small claims cases typically concern efforts by businesses to collect debts, and attempts by individuals to obtain compensation for a bodily injury, property damage, or defective goods or services. The amount in controversy must not exceed the court's jurisdictional limit, which ranges from $1,000 to $5,000 in most states.[18] Speed is essential, and judges try to avoid trials by encouraging the parties to resolve their differences without a trial. When trials occur, they usually last from a half-hour to forty-five minutes, and the presiding officer, who might be a regular judge or a part-time judge pro tempore, is likely to decide the matter immediately thereafter.[19]

States have experimented in recent years with a variety of mechanisms designed to reduce their small claims and traffic caseloads. Connecticut, the District of Columbia, and Vermont have transferred the collection of fines for minor traffic offenses to a nonjudicial office or agency in order to reduce caseloads and paperwork, and to give courts more time to consider major traffic cases.[20] Small claims courts in many states now refer cases to **mediation**, in which the parties attempt to resolve their dispute with the aid of a neutral third party, who is known as a **mediator**. The mediator advises the parties, and may offer suggestions, but the parties must resolve the dispute themselves. Mediation can save many hours of judge time, and the cost of a **mediation coordinator** is much less than the cost of an additional judge.

Such experiments will probably continue, even increase, in the future. It is important that they succeed because Americans most often participate in the judicial process in traffic and small claims courts, and their experiences in those courts shape their views about the entire legal system.

Trial Courts of General Jurisdiction

You are probably familiar, at least indirectly, with trial courts of general jurisdiction. Films and television programs regularly depict fictional and actual murder trials; actual murder trials occur in state courts of general jurisdiction. For example, the criminal trial in which a jury acquitted former football star O. J. Simpson of the 1994 murders of his ex-wife and her friend occurred in a state trial court of general jurisdiction in California. So did the subsequent civil trial in which the victims' families recovered financial compensation from Mr. Simpson.

Most states call their trial courts of general jurisdiction **superior court, district court**, or **county court**. As the Simpson cases illustrate, these courts often hear both criminal cases and civil cases. Criminal cases present disputes between a person or persons and the state that arise from alleged violations of the criminal law. Civil cases present disputes between individuals (e.g., you and another motorist), between institutions (e.g., your college and the food service that operates its cafeterias), and between individuals and institutions (e.g., you and an insurance company) that commonly arise from personal injuries, broken business agreements, and/or damage to property.

Every state has at least one trial court of general jurisdiction. Its criminal jurisdiction includes **felonies**, which are major crimes (murder, rape, arson, armed robbery, etc.) that are punishable either by death or by a prison term of more than one year. The same court's civil jurisdiction encompasses cases in which the amount of compensation that the plaintiff seeks exceeds the cap that exists in the trial court of limited jurisdiction. For example, in North Carolina, the limited jurisdiction court can hear civil cases in which the amount in controversy is $10,000 or less, and the general jurisdiction court hears all civil cases that involve more than $10,000.[21]

Civil cases are more numerous than criminal cases, and trials are rare in both types of case. Trial courts of general jurisdiction resolved approximately 4 percent of criminal cases at trial in 1996;[22] similarly, in 1992, they resolved just 3.3 percent of civil cases at trial.[23] They resolve approximately two-thirds of their criminal cases by means of plea bargains and another 20 percent by means of a prosecutor's decision not to prosecute (**nolle prosequi**) or a judge's decision to dismiss all charges.[24] Despite its prevalence, plea bargaining is controversial. Supporters argue that without it, several times as many judges, prosecutors, and defense attorneys as presently exist would be necessary in order to manage the criminal caseload. Opponents counter that it can induce an innocent defendant to plead guilty rather than to risk a more severe sentence if convicted at trial, or enable a serious offender to receive less punishment than his crime warrants. This debate is likely to continue, but so will plea bargaining in most courts.

Plea bargaining will continue partly because the U.S. Supreme Court supports it. Nearly thirty years ago, the Court stated that:

> If every criminal charge were subjected to a full-scale trial, the States and the Federal Government would need to multiply by many times the number of judges and court facilities.[25]

In the same case, the Court described plea bargaining as an "essential element of the administration of justice."[26]

The Supreme Court has rejected the argument that plea bargaining induces innocent defendants to plead guilty. It has held that defendants who receive advice from competent lawyers prior to entering their pleas are "presumptively capable of intelligent choice in response to prosecutorial persuasion," and are unlikely to be induced to plead guilty despite their innocence.[27] Thus, although the Court recognizes that the prospect of a reduced sentence may put pressure on defendants to plea bargain, it has long held that plea bargaining is not so coercive as to deprive defendants of their constitutional rights.[28]

Still, a plea bargain is constitutional only when a defendant enters into it "voluntarily and intelligently."[29] In order to satisfy that requirement, a judge must address a defendant in person in **open court** (ie. a courtroom that is open to the public), and, before approving the plea bargain, must indicate the maximum sentence that applies under the plea agreement. A judge must also inform a defendant that, by pleading guilty, the defendant will give up the privilege against compulsory self-incrimination, the right to a jury trial, and the right to confront accusers in court.[30] Furthermore, a judge must ask a defendant whether the defendant: (1) entered into the plea agreement voluntarily, and (2) understands its consequences. Finally, a judge must advise a defendant that the defendant can plead "not guilty" and go to trial.[31] Regardless of a defendant's answers, a judge can reject a plea bargain, in which case a defendant usually can withdraw a guilty plea if she wishes.[32]

Plea bargaining is prevalent primarily because it is efficient, but even if the courts were able to try every case, there would still be cases in which plea bargaining would be appropriate. An example is a case that appears, at the time of indictment, to warrant a charge of **first-degree murder** (a planned homicide), but that, after an investigation, seems instead to warrant a charge of **manslaughter** (an unintentional homicide). In that case, a plea bargain in which the defendant pleads guilty to manslaughter ensures a conviction for the prosecutor and a just punishment for the defendant.[33] Thus, plea bargaining is not a "necessary evil;" it is often necessary, but it can be an instrument of justice too.

Trial courts of general jurisdiction resolve more than 60 percent of their civil cases by means of a **settlement** by the parties or by a decision by the plaintiff to withdraw the case.[34] Settlements, in which the parties typically agree that the defendant will pay the plaintiff a sum of money in return for the plaintiff's promise to end the lawsuit, are popular with parties and with judges because they avoid the expense and the unpredictability of a jury trial. They frequently occur on the eve of trial, when the parties become eager to avoid the costs and the uncertainties of the fast-approaching trial. Another 25 percent of civil cases end in a **default judgment**, wherein the plaintiff wins because the defendant has failed to defend herself, or in a dismissal of the case by the court because the plaintiff has not pursued her claim against the defendant.[35]

When a trial occurs, it is either a **jury trial** or a **bench trial**. In a jury trial, a jury of ordinary citizens determines whether, in a criminal case, the defendant is **guilty** or **not guilty**, and whether, in a civil case, the defendant is **liable** for the plaintiff's injury. The judge informs the jury about the legal principles (unconstitutional searches, negligence, etc.) that govern the case, but the jury applies those principles to the facts of the case in order to reach a **verdict**. In a bench trial, a single judge applies law to facts and reaches a verdict. Judges who preside in trial courts of general jurisdiction use several devices to help them manage cases efficiently. One is **alternative dispute resolution (ADR)**, which employs means other than lawsuits to resolve disputes. Besides mediation, those means include **arbitration** and **minitrials**. Arbitration features a neutral decision maker, known as an **arbitrator**, who renders a decision after hearing presentations by both parties. It is faster than a lawsuit because it dispenses with the rules for introducing evidence that apply in a trial. Minitrials, in which retired judges hear cases, also shed traditional courtroom procedures for presenting evidence. Mediation, arbitration, and minitrials save the parties and the judiciary time and money. However, the decisions reached are not binding precedents on which other parties can rely in future disputes.[36]

Thirty-nine states and the District of Columbia permit juries of less than the traditional twelve members in civil trials, although some of them require agreement of both parties in order to reduce the size of a jury.[37] Proponents argue that smaller juries are more efficient, less expensive, and require less time to select than twelve-member juries.[38] Similarly, thirty-four states permit nonunanimous juries in civil cases, although two of them do so only when both parties agree to it.[39]

Judges must depend on legislators for the authority and the funds necessary to implement the reforms just discussed. Unfortunately, legislators are often slow to furnish those tools to judges because legislators rarely derive the political benefits from court reform that they derive from anticrime or antidrug initiatives.[40] Thus, politics influences reform efforts in state trial courts as much as heavy caseloads do.

Intermediate Appellate Courts

In thirty-nine states, at least one **intermediate appellate court** is located just above the trial court of general jurisdiction in the hierarchy of state courts.[41] Most of those states refer to this court as the **court of appeals**, and this book will do the same. Fourteen states divide their courts of appeals into geographic districts; the judges assigned to each district hear appeals from decisions of the trial courts of the counties located in that district. All courts of appeals are divided into three-judge panels to hear cases; in other words, the court might include fifteen judges, but only three judges will hear any particular case.

Courts of appeals are **appellate** courts, which means that they consider only **appeals** filed by parties who have been unsuccessful in a lower court, usually a trial court of general jurisdiction. They exist to correct **errors of law**, which occur, for example, when the trial judge gives improper instructions to the jury about what the law requires. Courts of appeals are different from trial courts in two ways. First, they decide only **questions of law**, whereas trial courts decide both questions of law and **questions of fact**. At trial, for example, a jury will decide whether the defendant meets the physical description of the person whom a witness saw leaving the scene of the crime, a question of fact. The trial judge will decide whether to exclude certain evidence against the defendant that the police obtained by means of a constitutionally dubious search, a question of law. The constitutionality of the search is a suitable basis for an appeal, whereas the accuracy of the witness's testimony is not.

Second, courts of appeals do not conduct trials; they conduct **oral arguments** in some of their cases, but only the judges and the lawyer for each party participate. There are no witnesses, and there is no testimony. Each lawyer typically is allotted fifteen minutes to present arguments to the judges, some of whom repeatedly interrupt the lawyer by asking questions designed to probe the weaknesses and the ramifications of her arguments.

Courts of appeals hear mostly **mandatory appeals**, which **appellants** have a constitutional right to file. That enables **courts of last resort** (i.e., **state supreme courts**) to hear **discretionary appeals**, which are not mandatory, but which demand a hearing because they raise important legal and public policy issues. Nevertheless, courts of appeals are important because state supreme courts review only a few appellate decisions each year. In 1996, state supreme courts reviewed an average of 11 percent of the discretionary appeals they received from parties who had lost in courts of appeals.[42] Thus, courts of appeals often have the final say on questions of state law.

Court of appeals judges seek to manage heavy caseloads. They have become more efficient by deviating, at least in some cases, from the traditional model of appellate court procedure. That model includes a review of the parties' written briefs, an oral argument followed by a conference during which the judges discuss the case and reach a tentative decision, and the writing of an opinion by one judge that explains the reason(s) for the court's decision. Large caseloads prevent appellate judges today from following the traditional model in every case.

Therefore, many courts of appeals use "shortcuts" that attempt to resolve cases expeditiously, while still giving them the attention that they deserve. For example, in the Arizona Court of Appeals, oral argument is available in criminal and in civil cases only when the attorney for one of the parties requests it,[43] and the court grants few requests for oral argument; those conditions also apply in the Florida District Courts of Appeal.[44] Lawyers customarily submit cases to courts of appeals **on the briefs**—that is, without requesting an oral argument. Courts of appeals usually decide routine cases by means of **unpublished opinions**, which circulate among the judges and the lawyers in the case but do not appear in the bound volumes that contain the court's published opinions. Unpublished opinions require less time to prepare than published opinions do.

Law clerks research and write drafts of court opinions, which judges then edit. That enables each judge to produce many more opinions annually than would otherwise be possible. Law clerks, who usually serve for a year or two, are recent law school graduates who compiled excellent academic records. Each judge typically employs one or two clerks every year. Heavy caseloads have made courts of appeals judges editors instead of authors of most of the opinions that bear their names. They nevertheless retain the power to decide cases, and there is power in the editor's pencil too.

New Jersey's intermediate appellate court uses two-judge panels instead of the traditional three-judge panels to hear most appeals.[45] That reduces the time that lapses between the submission of briefs and oral argument. In order to protect the quality of their decisions, the New Jersey judges write an opinion in every case heard by a two-judge panel.[46] That delicate balance between efficiency and quality will continue to challenge state appellate judges in the future, because caseload growth is the most pressing problem for courts of appeals.[47] Deviations from the traditional appellate model are here to stay.

Courts of Last Resort

Every state has at least one **court of last resort**, and Oklahoma and Texas have two—one that hears criminal appeals only and one that hears civil appeals only.[48] Forty-two states call this court the **supreme court**, as this book will do.[49] In the states that have a court of appeals, most of the caseload of the supreme court is discretionary; the court will hear an appeal only if a majority of its members wishes to do so. The court's mandatory jurisdiction might be limited to **capital cases**, wherein a trial court has sentenced a criminal defendant to death, or cases in which two separate panels of the court of appeals have interpreted a state law or a provision of the state constitution differently.

State supreme courts consist of between five and nine **justices**. They typically hear cases **en banc**, which means that all members of the court hear oral arguments together, rather than in panels of two or three. Oral arguments follow the pattern described above; the lawyer for each side usually receives fifteen minutes to argue her case, but often spends the bulk of that time responding to questions from the bench. State supreme courts hear only appeals, and they decide only questions of law. They hear mostly appeals from decisions reached in the courts of appeals, but they also hear appeals from decisions by trial courts of general jurisdiction when state law authorizes a direct appeal to the supreme court. In the eleven states that lack a court of appeals, the supreme court hears appeals mostly from decisions of the trial court of general jurisdiction, and in nine of those states the supreme court *must* hear those appeals, regardless of their legal significance.[50]

Even supreme courts that have discretionary jurisdiction have adopted "shortcuts" designed to resolve cases more quickly. Some decide their less significant cases by means of **orders**, which are one or two lines long, and which indicate whether the court has **affirmed** or **reversed** the lower court's decision in that case. Others make oral argument optional, and some hear routine cases in panels of three justices. Law clerks research and write draft opinions, which justices edit.

Discretionary jurisdiction liberates state supreme courts from merely correcting errors, and enables them to be important policy makers. They decide cases that affect the lives of all the residents of their respective states, not just the parties. Those cases often involve interpretations of state constitutions that give greater protection to individual rights than does the federal Constitution. Federalism permits state courts to grant their residents more rights than the federal constitution does if those rights rest exclusively on state law. Thus, even though the federal Constitution does not include a right to an education,[51] numerous state supreme courts have held that their state constitutions guarantee the right to an education, and that reliance on local property tax receipts to fund public schools deprives children who live in poor communities of that constitutional right.[52] Sometimes the cutting edge of judicial policy making is not in Washington, D.C., but is instead in Montpelier, Madison, and Frankfort.

THE FEDERAL COURT SYSTEM

Introduction

A federal court system functions alongside the fifty state court systems in the United States. The federal court system includes: (1) **specialized federal courts**; (2) the **U.S. district courts**; (3) the **U.S. courts of appeals**; and (4) the **U.S. Supreme Court**. The remainder of this section will discuss each of those components in turn. Figure 2.2 depicts the federal court system.

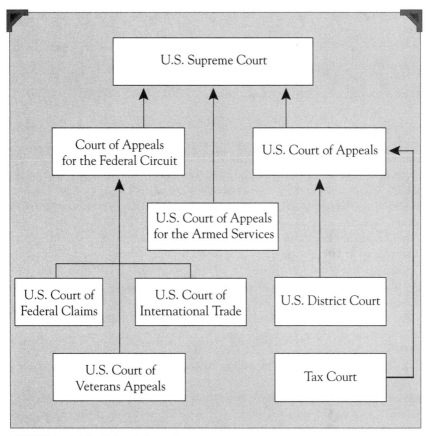

FIGURE 2.2 The Federal Court System
Source: Material extracted from Robert S. Want, ed., *Want's Federal-State Court Directory, 1998 Edition* (New York: Want Publishing Company, 1997). Reprinted with permission.

The Constitution did not require Congress to establish any federal court other than the Supreme Court. That is because Article III states: "The Judicial power of the United States, shall be vested in one supreme court, and such inferior Courts as the Congress may from time to time ordain and establish." That language reflects a political compromise between delegates to the Constitutional Convention who favored a strong national government that would include lower federal courts and delegates who favored states' rights and opposed the creation of lower federal courts. The latter delegates argued that state courts could hear all cases initially, and that a right of appeal to the Supreme Court would protect the interests of the national government and ensure a uniform interpretation of federal law nationwide.[53]

The Constitutional Convention could not resolve this debate, so the delegates agreed to let Congress decide in the future whether or not to establish lower federal courts. In the Judiciary Act of 1789, Congress established thirteen federal district courts and three regional **circuit courts** (southern, middle, and eastern); the circuit courts, in which two Supreme Court justices and a district judge heard cases, including some appeals, were the predecessors of the U.S. Courts of Appeals.[54] More recently, Congress has established the specialized federal courts that are the subject of the following section.

Specialized Federal Courts

The five specialized federal courts include: (1) the **Court of Federal Claims**; (2) the **Court of International Trade**; (3) the **Court of Appeals for the Armed Forces**; (4) the **Tax Court**; and (5) the **Court of Veterans' Appeals**.[55] Except for the Court of International Trade, these courts are known as **legislative courts** or as **Article I courts,** because Congress created them pursuant to its power under Article I, Section 8, clause 9 of the Constitution to "constitute tribunals inferior to the Supreme Court." They often have administrative as well as judicial duties, and they are sometimes created for the express purpose of helping to administer a particular federal law.

Those characteristics distinguish Article I courts from **Article III courts**, or **constitutional courts**, of which the district courts, courts of appeals, and Supreme Court are the most familiar. Article III courts exist pursuant to Congress's power under Article III, Section 1, to "from time to time ordain and establish" courts inferior to the Supreme Court. The Court of International Trade is the only specialized federal court that is an Article III court. Judges who serve on Article I courts do not enjoy the lifetime tenure or the protection against salary reductions while they are in office that judges who serve on Article III courts enjoy.[56] Thus, Article I courts are less independent of the elected branches of the federal government than Article III courts are.

All of the specialized federal courts have their headquarters in Washington, D.C. The Court of Federal Claims is a trial court that hears primarily breach-of-contract claims that individuals and corporations bring against the federal government. The Court of International Trade is a trial court that hears disputes that arise from product classification and valuation decisions made by the U.S. Customs Service, plus appeals of unfair trade practices decisions made by the federal Department of Commerce and by the International Trade Commission. The Court of Appeals for the Armed Forces is an appellate court, comprised of civilian judges, which hears appeals from court-martial convictions in military courts. The Tax Court is a trial court that resolves disputes about underpayments or overpayments of federal taxes. The Court of Veterans Appeals reviews decisions of the Board of Veterans Appeals about claims for veterans' benefits.

U.S. District Courts

The district courts are the federal system's trial courts of general jurisdiction. Section 2 of the Judiciary Act of 1789 established one district court, with one district judge, in each state; in other words, each state was a federal judicial district.[57]

Today, there are ninety-four federal district courts in the United States, ninety of which are located within the fifty states; the remaining four are located in Puerto Rico, the Virgin Islands, Guam, and the Northern Mariana Islands, respectively. Each state, as in 1789, contains at least one district court, now served by at least two judges, but the larger states are subdivided into districts, each of which might have several judges, depending on its caseload. For example, Wyoming has one district court served by two judges, whereas New York State has four districts; the **U.S. District Court for the Southern District of New York**, which includes the New York City boroughs of Manhattan and the Bronx, has twenty-eight judges.[58] There are 649 district court judges.[59]

District courts have **original jurisdiction**, which means that they hear cases in the first instance, not on appeal, in both civil and criminal matters. They conduct jury trials and bench trials in both civil and criminal cases, although trials are as rare in federal court as they are in state courts. For example, in 1995, only 3.4 percent of the civil cases in district courts nationwide went to trial.[60] A single judge presides over most cases in district court. However, in cases that concern the **reapportionment** (redistribution of seats based on census figures) of state legislatures, congressional **redistricting** (the redrawing of boundary lines between districts), and certain civil rights matters, three judges preside, including two district court judges and one appellate judge. The criminal jurisdiction of district courts pertains to offenses that violate federal criminal law. Examples include the interstate theft of an automobile, the importation of illegal drugs, and the murder of a hiker in Yellowstone National Park; the murder would be a federal offense not because of the act itself, which is ordinarily a state crime, but because it occurred on federal property.

The civil jurisdiction of district courts pertains to disputes that derive from conflicting interpretations of a federal law or treaty, or of a provision of the federal constitution. These disputes raise **federal questions** that Congress has authorized district courts to resolve. In 1996, a district court in Louisiana resolved a federal question when it held in *Pederson v. Louisiana State University* (L.S.U.) that L.S.U. had violated a federal law that prohibits sex discrimination in education by failing to provide intercollegiate athletic opportunities for its female students that were equivalent to those it provided for its male students.[61]

District courts also hear civil cases pursuant to their **diversity-of-citizenship jurisdiction**. **Diversity cases** are disputes between residents of different states in which the plaintiff's claim amounts to $50,000 or more. For example, if a Maine resident injured a New Jersey resident in a skiing accident in Maine, the New Jersey resident could sue the Maine resident either in state or in federal court, and either in New Jersey or in Maine, if his claim exceeded $50,000. Federal district judges have long argued that Congress ought to abolish diversity jurisdiction because (1) diversity cases clutter federal courts with matters that belong in state court, and (2) state courts are no longer biased against nonresidents, so there is no reason to preserve diversity jurisdiction.[62] It survives because a transfer of diversity cases to state courts would add to their caseloads at a time when they, like federal district courts, are already overloaded with cases.[63]

Finally, district courts hear civil cases in which prisoners bring petitions pursuant to the **writ of habeas corpus,** which ask district judges to order prison authorities to either show cause why they are holding a prisoner or to release him.[64] These petitions are civil matters, even though they arise out of criminal cases, because they are private disputes between prisoners and prison wardens. A state or federal prisoner can file a petition for habeas corpus review of the reasons for his incarceration, which a district court can consider if the petitioner makes a credible argument that law enforcement authorities violated one or more of his *federal* rights, such as the **right to a fair trial** guaranteed by the Sixth Amendment to the federal Constitution.[65]

District courts face large caseloads. In 1996, plaintiffs filed 272,700 civil cases in district courts nationwide; since 1991, when plaintiffs filed 207,700 civil cases, the number of civil filings has increased each year.[66] Prosecutors brought 47,100 criminal cases in the district courts in 1996, an increase of nearly 3,000 cases over 1995 and of almost 9,000 cases since 1985.[67] That is a far cry from the late eighteenth and early nineteenth centuries, when district courts heard mostly *admiralty* cases, which concern navigation and commerce on lakes, rivers, and oceans, and endured second-class status relative to state courts.[68]

Another change, though, is that district court judges now have tools with which to manage their caseloads. They have authority to appoint **magistrate judges** to assist them with their work; there are now 478 magistrate judges working in the federal court system, of whom 381 work full-time.[69] Magistrate judges serve eight-year terms, and conduct preliminary proceedings in both civil and criminal cases. If the parties consent, a magistrate judge may conduct all proceedings in a jury or a nonjury civil matter, and may decide the case; a magistrate judge may also conduct a trial in a misdemeanor criminal case if the defendant consents.[70]

Bankruptcy judges also assist district judges by hearing and resolving petitions for personal and corporate bankruptcy. In 1984, Congress made the bankruptcy courts units of the district courts; there is a bankruptcy court for each district. Bankruptcy court judges are appointed by the judges of the U.S. Courts of Appeals, and they serve fourteen-year terms.

District judges also use law clerks, technology, alternative dispute resolution, and court rules to manage their caseloads. District court law clerks perform a greater variety of tasks than appellate court law clerks do. They not only research and write opinions, they also draft jury instructions, communicate with the lawyers in each case, and evaluate the parties' pretrial requests to each other for information.[71] That enables judges to preside at trials, which are time-consuming despite their infrequency. Personal computers, computerized legal research, and teleconferences between judges and lawyers involved in a case speed the resolution of cases and the production of court opinions. Unpublished opinions help too. So does **court-annexed arbitration**, which is compulsory but nonbinding. The court informs the parties that before they can have a trial, they must submit their dispute to a panel of arbitrators who are practicing attorneys. The parties do not have to accept the arbitrators' decision, but that decision might tell them enough about the likely outcome of a trial to induce a settlement.[72]

In 1990, Congress enacted the **Civil Justice Reform Act**, which required district courts to devise and implement plans for reducing costs and delays in civil litigation. Pursuant to the Act, district courts have experimented with mediation and with minitrials in an effort to make civil justice faster and cheaper.[73] They have also tried **summary jury trials**, **early neutral evaluation**, and more active judicial management of cases. Summary jury trials allow parties to present their case in summary form to an **advisory jury**, which then renders a nonbinding decision; the parties can proceed to trial if they wish, but the advisory jury's decision can encourage them to settle. Early neutral evaluation features a nonbinding conference, which the parties and their lawyers attend early in the pretrial period; an experienced lawyer evaluates the parties' prospects at trial, which can also encourage a settlement.[74] Judicial management of cases includes setting early, firm trial dates, requiring the parties to appear in person at settlement conferences or to be available by telephone, reducing the time allowed for discovery, and beginning judicial participation in a case soon after it is filed.[75] Finally, district judges can impose **sanctions**, usually payment of the opponent's attorney's fees and court costs, on parties who file frivolous claims, defenses, and/or appeals.[76] No one has conducted a scientific study to determine the effects of technology, unpublished opinions, arbitration, or sanctions, so it is not clear whether they have increased the productivity of district courts. Most district judges, though, believe that sanctions have reduced caseloads slightly.[77] The quest for suitable means of caseload reduction is likely to continue.

U.S. Courts of Appeals

The U.S. Courts of Appeals are the intermediate appellate courts of the federal system. They are the final authority on most questions of federal law, because the Supreme Court decides fewer than 5 percent of the cases that parties file there annually.

The courts of appeals are a comparatively "modern" addition to the federal court system. Congress established them in 1891 as the "Circuit Courts of Appeals."[78] Before that, the old circuit courts that the Judiciary Act of 1789 established, in which Supreme Court justices and district judges sat together, heard appeals during two court sessions per year. That arrangement imposed a strenuous travel burden on the Supreme Court justices. Still, states' rights forces in Congress, who disliked federal courts, opposed the creation of a new appellate court until 1891. In 1911, the Circuit Courts of Appeals became the U.S. Courts of Appeals, the name they retain today.[79]

Like the district courts, the courts of appeals no longer operate in the shadows of state courts; the breadth of federal law today and the Supreme Court's reduction of its docket in recent years have made the courts of appeals more powerful and more visible now than ever before.

The courts of appeals are organized into twelve regional circuits and one national circuit. The twelve regional circuits hear criminal and civil appeals from the district courts located within their respective circuits. For example, the U.S. Court of Appeals for the First Circuit hears appeals from district courts located in Maine, Massachusetts, New Hampshire, Rhode Island, and Puerto Rico. Eleven of the circuits bear their respective numbers in their names; the twelfth regional circuit is the District of Columbia Circuit, which hears appeals from the district court in Washington, D.C., and from federal government agencies. The one national circuit is the Federal Circuit, also located in Washington, D.C., which hears appeals from district court decisions nationwide in patent, copyright, and trademark cases, and all appeals from the Court of Federal Claims and the Court of International Trade.[80] The First Circuit, which sits in Boston, is the smallest of the courts of appeals, with six judges, and the Ninth Circuit, which sits in San Francisco, is the largest, with twenty-eight judges. There are 179 judges on the courts of appeals.[81] Figure 2.3 lists the federal appellate circuits and the district courts from which they hear appeals.

Federal appellate courts hear only appeals; therefore, they do not conduct trials, and they consider only questions of law, not questions of fact. They usually hear cases in panels of three, but they occasionally hear or rehear a case **en banc**. Thus, federal appellate proceedings are similar in many ways to the proceedings of state appellate courts. However, federal appellate courts are organized regionally. Consequently, the judges live and do most of their work in separate locations. They ordinarily meet for three to five days each month in order to hear oral arguments, then they return home for three or four weeks to research and write six to ten opinions.[82] During a typical year, each judge, who is usually assisted by three law clerks, will produce approximately fifty published opinions and an equal number of unpublished opinions.[83]

The judges have become more productive in recent years in response to their caseloads. In 1996, the courts of appeals resolved 26,988 cases, as compared to 21,006 cases in 1990 and 10,607 cases in 1980.[84] Nevertheless, the median number of months between the commencement and the resolution of a case increased only slightly between 1980 and 1996, from 8.9 to 10.3.[85] Several factors account for this improved productivity. One factor is law clerks. Another is technology. Personal computers, computerized legal research, and the circulation of draft opinions between judges via electronic mail have increased the speed with which judges can produce opinions. A third factor is an intensified effort to settle appeals; **settlement officers**, who are full-time court employees, meet with lawyers and attempt to mediate settlements before the lawyers file briefs.[86]

Other factors that account for improved productivity are decreases in the frequency and the length of oral arguments, in the numbers of published opinions, and changes in the **standards of review** that govern appeals. Today, the courts of appeals hear oral arguments in only about 40 percent of appeals, and they typically allot only fifteen minutes per side, a 50 percent reduction since the 1960s.[87] Along with the decrease in orally argued cases has come an increase in unpublished opinions, which now resolve cases that have not been argued orally, and

First Circuit (Boston)

Maine
Massachusetts
New Hampshire
Puerto Rico
Rhode Island

Second Circuit (New York City)

Connecticut
Eastern New York
Northern New York
Southern New York
Western New York
Vermont

Third Circuit (Philadelphia)

Delaware
New Jersey
Eastern Pennsylvania
Middle Pennsylvania
Western Pennsylvania
Virgin Islands

Fourth Circuit (Richmond)

Maryland
Eastern North Carolina
Middle North Carolina
Western North Carolina
South Carolina
Eastern Virginia
Western Virginia
Northern West Virginia
Southern West Virginia

Fifth Circuit (New Orleans)

Eastern Louisiana
Middle Louisiana
Western Louisiana
Northern Mississippi
Southern Mississippi
Eastern Texas
Northern Texas
Southern Texas
Western Texas

Sixth Circuit (Cincinnati)

Eastern Kentucky
Western Kentucky
Eastern Michigan
Western Michigan
Northern Ohio
Southern Ohio
Eastern Tennessee
Middle Tennessee
Western Tennessee

Seventh Circuit (Chicago)

Central Illinois
Northern Illinois
Southern Illinois
Northern Indiana
Southern Indiana
Eastern Wisconsin
Western Wisconsin

Eighth Circuit (St. Louis)

Eastern Arkansas
Western Arkansas
Northern Iowa
Southern Iowa
Minnesota
Eastern Missouri
Western Missouri
Nebraska
North Dakota
South Dakota

Ninth Circuit (San Francisco)

Alaska
Arizona
Central California
Eastern California
Southern California
Western California
Guam
Hawaii
Idaho
Montana
Nevada
Northern Mariana Islands
Oregon
Eastern Washington
Western Washington

Tenth Circuit (Denver)

Colorado
Kansas
New Mexico
Eastern Oklahoma
Northern Oklahoma
Western Oklahoma
Utah
Wyoming

Eleventh Circuit (Atlanta)

Middle Alabama
Northern Alabama
Southern Alabama
Central Florida
Northern Florida
Southern Florida
Middle Georgia
Northern Georgia
Southern Georgia

FIGURE 2.3 Federal Appellate Circuits and Component Districts*
*Excludes District of Columbia Circuit and Federal Circuit.

Source: Marie T. Finn et. al., eds., *The American Bench: Judges of the Nation,* Ninth edition (Sacramento, CA: Forster-Long, 1997/98). Reprinted with permission.

some cases that have been argued orally. The courts of appeals have also adopted standards of review that defer to the district court or the federal agency whose decision they are reviewing; district court decisions must be **clearly erroneous** and agency rulings must be **arbitrary or capricious** or **unsupported by substantial evidence** before courts of appeals will reverse them. Such standards hasten the resolution of appeals because an appellate court can decide more quickly whether a lower court's decision was reasonable than whether it was correct.[88]

Finally, the increased use of sanctions to punish and to deter the filing of frivolous appeals has improved productivity. A court rule empowers the judges to require a party who files a frivolous appeal to pay the attorney's fees and the court costs of the opposing party.[89] They are quicker to invoke that rule today than they were in years past; they will undoubtedly continue to do so, and will further modify the traditional appellate process, if caseloads continue to grow.

U.S. Supreme Court

The Supreme Court is the most powerful court in America, and the only court that the Constitution mentions by name. It is comprised of nine **justices** who hear all cases *en banc*, and it has both original and appellate jurisdiction. That means that the Court hears some cases in the first instance and other cases on appeal. Its original jurisdiction includes cases that involve ambassadors from other countries and cases in which a state is a party. The plaintiffs in those cases can bring their claims directly to the Supreme Court. However, the Court is only *required* to hear original jurisdiction cases that present disputes between two states, such as *New Jersey v. New York* (1998); that case involved a dispute about which state owned Ellis Island in New York Harbor, which was the point of entry into the United States for 12 million immigrants from 1892 to 1954.[90] In such cases, the Court's jurisdiction is **original and exclusive**; those are the only cases that the Court actually hears in the first instance. In other original jurisdiction cases, such as when a state is *one* of the parties, the Supreme Court's jurisdiction is **original and concurrent**, which enables the Court to transfer the case to a district court. Thus, the Supreme Court rarely hears an original jurisdiction case; it has done so approximately 160 times since 1789.[91]

Appellate matters dominate the Supreme Court's **docket** (calendar); more than 95 percent of the cases that are filed in the Court each year are appeals from decisions of lower courts.[92] The justices have almost complete discretion whether to hear those cases, and they choose to hear less than 5 percent of them. In 1996–1997, **petitioners** (appellants) filed 7,602 cases at the Court, of which the justices agreed to hear only 140.[93] Appellate cases arrive by three alternate routes: namely, the **writ of certification**, the **writ of appeal**, and the **writ of certiorari.**

The *writ of certification* is the least likely route; it is a request by a lower federal court, usually a court of appeals, for a final answer to questions of law in a particular case. The Supreme Court, after considering the **certificate**, may decide to hear the case itself. These cases are infrequent; they do not occur even every year.

The *writ of appeal* is a more common route to the High Court, primarily because federal law requires the Court to accept and decide cases that arrive by this method. However, the Court need not hear oral arguments or write opinions in these cases; consequently, they often merit only a one- or a two-line **order** that indicates whether the justices have affirmed or reversed the decision of the court of appeals. Few cases reach the Court by writ of appeal today because in 1988, Congress reduced the Court's mandatory appellate jurisdiction to reapportionment cases, some **antitrust** (anticompetive business practices) matters, certain civil rights cases, and cases that involve the public financing system for presidential elections.[94]

The *writ of certiorari* is the most common route to the Supreme Court. The Judiciary Act of 1925 gave the Court discretion to grant or deny a petition for certiorari.[95] If four justices decide to **grant cert**, the Court requests a certified copy of the case's written record from the lower court, and places the case on its docket. Petitioners whose cases the Court accepts, except the federal government and those who filed **in forma pauperis** (in the form of a pauper), must pay a filing fee of $300; they must pay another $100 if the Court grants their requests for oral argument.[96] Petitions for certiorari range from elegantly printed, bound documents to single hand-written sheets of prison stationery. They constitute more than 375,000 pages annually, which the justices review with the help of a **cert pool** comprised of their law clerks. The cert pool began in 1972 in response to an increased volume of petitions: it had become impossible for each justice to review each petition.[97] The clerks review petitions and write memoranda to the justices that evaluate the "certworthiness" of each petition. The justices then decide whether to grant or deny cert, or to investigate further before they reach a decision.[98]

The review of cert petitions constitutes a "boot camp" of sorts for law clerks. They begin their year of service at the Court in July, when the Court is out of session and the justices are enjoying the pleasures of their respective retreats. Supreme Court law clerks are the creme of the crop of recent law school graduates. Some of them clerk for a federal court of appeals judge before coming to the Supreme Court. Their first assignment is to review and to write memoranda about the certworthiness of the petitions that arrive during the summer. In late September, several days before the Court's **preterm conference**, the **chief justice** will prepare a list of the petitions that warrant discussion and a vote at the conference; a petition that fails to make this **discuss list** is automatically denied cert unless another justice asks that it be added to the list. Approximately three-quarters of the petitions that the Court receives fail to make the discuss list, and most of those that make it are rejected too. Thus, even before its annual term begins on the first Monday in October, the Court has disposed of about 1,000 petitions, and it has rejected about 800 of them without discussion.[99] That pattern continues throughout the term, which ends in late June or in early July. The Court considers new cert petitions each week, and it rejects all but a few of them, usually without a discussion.

During the term, the justices hear oral arguments, decide cases, and write opinions besides considering new cert petitions. Their clerks research and write first drafts of opinions besides considering new cert petitions. The term is divided into **sittings** and **recesses**; the Court hears oral arguments from 10 A.M. until noon and from 1 P.M. until 3 P.M. on Mondays, Tuesdays, and Wednesdays during seven two-week sittings that begin on the first Monday in October and end in mid-April. Each case receives one hour of oral argument (thirty minutes per side), so the Court can hear up to twelve cases per week. Two-week recesses occur between sittings; during the recesses, the justices decide cases, write opinions, and manage other Court business.[100] Between late April and the end of the term, they concentrate on writing opinions.

It is both demanding and exhilarating for a lawyer to argue a case before the Supreme Court. The justices study the parties' briefs and review their clerks' **bench memoranda** about each case beforehand, and they arrive at oral argument armed for intellectual combat. They show no mercy to the lawyer who begins her argument by saying: "I plan to make three main points...."[101] According to journalist David Savage:

> A knowing glance goes between Justices John Paul Stevens, Antonin Scalia and David H. Souter. 'Before you go to that first point,' Stevens interrupts in the politest of tones, 'would you explain for me....'[102]

That gentle request commences a flood of pointed questions and probing hypotheticals from various justices that expose the heart of the case and the weaknesses of the lawyer's argument. According to Savage:

> After 25 minutes or so of rapid-fire questions, the justices sometimes pause, as if the matter is now clear to them. At this point, the lawyer, pummeled but still standing, sometimes looks down at the notes spread on the lectern. 'As I was about to say ...,' the lawyer begins, as time runs out.[103]

Oral argument can be exasperating for a lawyer, but it can be immensely useful for the justices. They sometimes learn more about the case from their colleagues' questions than they learn from the lawyers' arguments or from briefs; therefore, a justice can leave an oral argument with a different view of a case than he had when the argument began.[104] Oral argument is also valuable for lawyers and their clients because it is the only time when their particular case commands the undivided attention of the Court.

The justices decide cases during **conferences** that occur each week of the term. Conferences occur on the Friday prior to the beginning of the next two-week sitting, and on Wednesdays and Fridays during sittings. At the Wednesday afternoon conference, the justices discuss and decide the cases that they heard the previous Monday. At the Friday conference, which lasts all day, they discuss and decide the cases that they heard the previous Tuesday and Wednesday, and they consider new cert petitions too.[105] The conference proceedings are secret, and only the justices attend. The most junior justice serves as doorkeeper and messenger, sending for reference materials and receiving messages during the conference. Each conference begins with handshakes between the justices, who then consider new cert petitions and decide cases. The **chief justice** speaks first about each case to be decided, briefly outlining its facts, and indicating how he will vote. Then, each **associate justice**, in order of seniority, comments on the case, and indicates how he or she will vote. A majority is necessary to decide a case, which usually means five votes.

Conference discussions have changed in recent years because the Court now receives many more petitions than it did in the past. The increased workload has reduced the amount of time that the justices can devote to each case in conference. "In fact," says Justice Antonin Scalia, "to call our discussion of a case a conference is really something of a misnomer. It's much more a statement of the views of each of the nine justices."[106] Thus, justices do not try to persuade their colleagues of the correctness of their views in conference; they do that in their written opinion drafts instead.

After the justices vote on a case, the chief justice, if he is in the majority, assigns a member of that majority to write the opinion of the Court. When the chief justice is in the minority, the most senior justice in the majority assigns a member of the majority to write the opinion. The designated author then begins work on the **majority opinion**; often, a law clerk prepares an initial draft, and the justice revises it.[107] When a satisfactory draft opinion is complete, the author circulates it among the other justices. Members of the majority suggest changes, and the author then makes the changes necessary to preserve a majority. Sometimes, the author must revise the opinion several times in order to satisfy her colleagues. Occasionally, it is impossible to satisfy one's colleagues, and the original majority collapses. For example, in *Bowers v. Hardwick* (1986), then-Justice Lewis Powell voted at conference to overturn a Georgia antisodomy law, but he changed his mind after conference, and a 5–4 vote to overturn the law became a 5–4 vote to uphold it.[108]

The final majority opinion is therefore the product of negotiations, albeit quiet, dignified, negotiations that are usually conducted in writing. The Court's heavy workload forces the justices to communicate with one another primarily by letters and memoranda. Each **chambers** (justice's office), which is comprised of a justice, three or four law clerks, one or two secretaries, and a messenger, operates largely independently of the others. Former Justice Powell once observed: "As much as 90 percent of our total time, we function as nine small, independent law firms."[109] That makes for quiet surroundings, which contrast with the passions that the Court's cases can arouse in the hearts and minds of the public and of the justices. The cases often present in lawsuit form the most divisive public policy disputes that this country faces, from abortion to affirmative action to physician-assisted suicide. Former Justice Oliver Wendell Holmes, Jr., captured that contrast when he observed that the Court was quiet in the same way that a "storm center" was quiet.[110]

The justices vote as independently as they work. One or more justices will often write a **concurring opinion** or a **dissenting opinion** in a case. A concurring opinion agrees with the majority's conclusion, but for reasons other than those that persuaded the majority. A dissenting opinion disagrees with the majority's reasoning and with its conclusion. Dissenting opinions are common nowadays;

during the 1996–1997 term, for example, the Court was unanimous in only 45 percent of its signed opinions; the comparable figure for 1995–1996 was 41 percent.[111] The justices do not strive for institutional consensus today as much as they did in the past.[112]

A Supreme Court decision in a **full opinion case**, which features a signed written opinion, is not final until a justice announces it orally in open court. The Court announces decisions on Tuesdays and Wednesdays during weeks when it hears oral arguments, and on Mondays during the other weeks. The justice who wrote the majority opinion announces the Court's decision and occasionally reads portions of the opinion aloud. Justices who wrote concurring or dissenting opinions sometimes state their views too. The Court's announcements can command the attention of the entire nation, especially in cases like *Clinton v. Jones* and *Texas v. Johnson.*

FEDERAL COURT ADMINISTRATION

Several institutions oversee or assist the federal courts. The **Judicial Conference of the United States** is the governing body for all federal courts except the Supreme Court. It is comprised of the Chief Justice of the United States, the chief judges of the courts of appeals, the chief judge of the Court of International Trade, and a district judge from each circuit. The entire membership meets twice a year, and committees meet more often.[113] The Judicial Conference determines both the needs of the federal judiciary, such as additional judges, higher judicial salaries, or improved courtroom security, and the size of the budget necessary to meet those needs. It also initiates changes in the **Federal Rules of Criminal Procedure** and in the **Federal Rules of Civil Procedure,** which govern the consideration and the resolution of cases in the federal courts. The Supreme Court and Congress must approve such changes before they can become permanent. A **circuit judicial council**, comprised of appellate and district judges, and chaired by the chief appellate judge, acts as a counterpart to the Judicial Conference in each region of the country.

The **Administrative Office of the U.S. Courts** is the federal courts' housekeeping agency. It distributes office supplies to the courts, arranges for them to have sufficient courtroom and office space in federal buildings throughout the country, maintains the personnel records of their employees, and collects data about their caseloads. It also furnishes statistical information to the Judicial Conference, and is the clearinghouse for information and proposals directed to the Judicial Conference. Finally, the Administrative Office is the federal courts' advocate before Congress; it presents to Congress budget proposals, requests for additional judgeships, suggested changes in procedural rules, and other recommendations of the Judicial Conference.[114] **Circuit executives** perform comparable functions regionally.

The **Federal Judicial Center** also supports the federal courts. It conducts research about and recommends changes in the management of the federal courts, and it develops educational and training programs for court personnel.

RELATIONS BETWEEN STATE AND FEDERAL COURTS

State courts and federal courts often interact with each other; a diversity of citizenship case is one example of that interaction. Recall that a New Jersey plaintiff can sue a Maine defendant in state court or in federal court. If the plaintiff sues in a state court in New Jersey, the defendant can **remove** the case to a federal court in New Jersey. The federal court would then decide the case according to the state law of New Jersey because federal courts must follow state law in diversity cases.[115] If the district judge were unclear about a point of New Jersey law necessary to decide the case, she would **certify** her question to the New Jersey Supreme Court, and would await that court's answer before proceeding with the case.

Criminal cases also spur interaction between state courts and federal courts. Defendants who are convicted of crimes in state courts frequently appeal their convictions on the grounds that they were deprived, before or during trial, of rights guaranteed by the U.S. Constitution. For example, a defendant might argue before a state supreme court that the trial judge erred in allowing the introduction at trial of evidence that resulted from a coerced "confession" that violated the Fifth Amendment's prohibition against **compulsory self-incrimination**. If the state supreme court rejected the defendant's claim, the defendant could appeal that decision to the U.S. Supreme Court because his claim would raise an issue of federal law. The U.S. Supreme Court, of course, would be free to reject the case.

The jailed defendant could instead challenge his conviction by petitioning a federal district court to grant *habeas corpus* review of his case. The prisoner would sue the prison warden; the suit would ask the district court to review the state court's decision to use the "confession" at trial, and to determine whether that decision violated the Fifth Amendment. If the federal court agreed with the prisoner, it could issue an order that (1) released him from custody, (2) reduced his sentence, or (3) sent the case back to state court for a new trial or for resentencing.[116]

There are limits to the interaction between state courts and federal courts. The doctrine of **preemption** prohibits state courts from hearing cases about subjects that Congress has assigned exclusively to federal courts, such as bankruptcy, antitrust, and Indian treaty matters. Federal law preempts state law in those cases, so only federal courts can hear them.[117] The doctrine of **abstention** prohibits federal courts from deciding cases in which questions of state law remain to be answered, and the answers could resolve the cases. Recall, for example, the criminal defendant who lost in a state supreme court, and filed a *habeas corpus* petition on Fifth Amendment grounds. The federal district court that received the petition would not review it if state courts had not yet resolved the defendant's companion claim, namely, that his actions did not meet the state's legal definition of the crime for which he was convicted. If the defendant later lost on that claim, he could again seek *habeas corpus* review on Fifth Amendment grounds in the federal district court. Thus, abstention sometimes postpones, rather than prevents, consideration of a case by a federal court.[118]

There is no limit on informal interaction between state judges and federal judges. Indeed, thirty-four states have **judicial councils**, which enable state judges and federal judges to discuss issues of common concern to both groups, such as alternative dispute resolution and the tracking of *habeas corpus* petitions. The West Virginia council has been especially active; it coordinates alternative dispute resolution in state and federal courts there, and it tracks *habeas corpus* petitions filed by West Virginia's state and federal prisoners.[119] Federal–state cooperation could be the wave of the future in judicial administration

CONCLUSION

Federalism divides judicial power in America between a federal court system and fifty state court systems. The federal system and the state systems contain trial courts and appellate courts, and each system has a court of last resort that is the final arbiter of disputes within its jurisdiction. Federal courts and state courts have different jurisdictions; that means that state courts cannot decide exclusively federal matters, such as bankruptcy cases, and that federal courts cannot decide issues of state law. Nevertheless, diversity cases, *habeas corpus* petitions, and federal constitutional claims in state criminal cases cause state and federal courts to interact. State and federal judges also interact off the bench, in judicial councils, because they face common administrative problems to which state—federal judicial cooperation could be an answer.

The relationship between state courts and federal courts is much clearer today than it was early in the nineteenth century, when the Supreme Court decided the case reprinted below. After you read the case, consider how the relationship between state courts and federal courts, and the relationship between the states and the federal government, would be different today if the Court had reached a different conclusion.

Epilogue: The Roots of Judicial Federalism

Martin v. Hunter's Lessee
14 U.S. (1 Wheat.) 304 (1816)

[Editor's Note: This case arose when a federal district court upheld Martin's land claim, which was based on a treaty between the United States and Great Britain. Hunter claimed the same land pursuant to a grant from the State of Virginia. The Virginia Court of Appeals, the highest court in that state, reversed the federal district court. In 1813, the Supreme Court set aside the state court's decision, but the state court refused to obey the Supreme Court. The Virginia Court of Appeals contended that the Supreme Court lacked the authority to reverse the decision of a state court because Section 25 of the Judiciary Act of 1789, which conferred that authority, was unconstitutional. The constitutionality of Section 25 was the issue in this case.]

JUSTICE STORY delivered the opinion of the Court.

The constitution of the United States was ordained and established, not by the states in their sovereign capacities, but emphatically, as the preamble of the constitution declares, by "the People of the United States." There can be no doubt, that it was competent to the people to invest the general government with all the powers that they might deem proper and necessary; to extend or restrain these powers according to their own good pleasure, and to give them a paramount and supreme authority. As little doubt can there be, that the people had a right to prohibit to the states the exercise of any powers which were, in their judgment, incompatible with the objects of the [constitution]; to make the powers of the state governments, in given cases, subordinate to those of the nation, or to reserve to themselves those sovereign authorities which they might not choose to delegate to either.

The constitution was for a new government, organized with new substantive powers, and not a mere supplementary charter to a government already existing. The constitution was an act of the people of the United States to supersede the [articles of] confederation, and not to be engrafted on it....

This leads us to the consideration of the great question, as to the nature and extent of the appellate jurisdiction of the United States. [**Editor's Note:** Justice Story then observed that Article III of the Constitution extended the appellate jurisdiction of the federal courts "to *all* cases arising under the constitution, laws and treaties of the United States....]

If the constitution meant to limit the appellate jurisdiction [of federal courts] to cases pending in the [federal] courts, it would necessarily follow, that the jurisdiction of these courts would, in all the cases enumerated in the constitution, be exclusive of state tribunals. How, otherwise, could the jurisdiction extend to *all* cases arising under the constitution, laws and treaties of the United States ...? If some of these cases might be entertained by state tribunals, and no appellate jurisdiction as to them should exist, then the appellate power would not extend to *all*, but to *some*, cases.

But it is plain, that the framers of the constitution did contemplate that cases within the judicial cognisance of the United States, not only might, but would, arise in the state courts, in the exercise of their ordinary jurisdiction. With this view, the sixth article declares, that "this constitution and the laws of the United States which shall be made in pursuance thereof, and all treaties made, or which shall be made, under the authority of the United States, shall be the supreme law of the land, and the judges in every state shall be bound thereby, anything in the constitution or laws of any state to the contrary notwithstanding."

It must, therefore, be conceded, that the constitution not only contemplated, but meant to provide for cases within the scope of the judicial power of the United States, which might yet depend before state tribunals. It was foreseen, that in the exercise of their ordinary jurisdiction, state courts would incidentally take cognisance of cases arising under the constitution, the laws and treaties of the United States. Yet, to all these cases, the judicial power, by the very terms of the constitution, is to extend. It cannot extend, by original jurisdiction, if that was already rightfully and exclusively attached in the state courts, which (as has already been shown) may occur; it must, therefore, extend by appellate jurisdiction, or not at all. It would seem to follow, that the appellate power of the United

States must, in such cases, extend to state tribunals; and if, in such cases, there is no reason why it should not equally attach upon all others, within the purview of the constitution.

[**Editor's Note:** Justice Story then rebuts the argument that it violates "the spirit of the constitution" for a federal court to exercise appellate jurisdiction over a state court decision.]

The courts of the United States can, without question, revise the proceedings of the executive and legislative authorities of the states, and if they are found to be contrary to the constitution, may declare them to be of no legal validity. Surely, the exercise of the same right over judicial tribunals is not a higher or more dangerous act of sovereign power.

Nor can such a right be deemed to impair the independence of state judges. It is assuming the very ground in controversy, to assert that they possess an absolute independence of the United States. In respect to the powers granted to the United States, they are not independent; they are expressly bound to obedience, by the letter of the constitution; and if they should unintentionally transcend their authority, or misconstrue the constitution, there is no more reason for giving their judgments an absolute and irresistible force, than for giving it to the acts of the other co-ordinate departments of state sovereignty....

... The constitution has presumed (whether rightly or wrongly, we do not inquire), that state attachments, state prejudices, state jealousies, and state interests, might sometimes obstruct, or control, or be supposed to obstruct or control, the regular administration of justice. Hence, in controversies between states; between citizens of different states; between citizens claiming grants under different states; between a state and its citizens, or foreigners, and between citizens and foreigners, it enables the parties, under the authority of congress, to have the controversies heard, tried and determined before the national tribunals. No other reason than that which has been stated can be assigned, why some, at least, of those cases should not have been left to the cognisance of the state courts.

This is not all. A motive of another kind, perfectly compatible with the most sincere respect for state tribunals, might induce the grant of appellate power over their decisions. That motive is the importance, and even necessity of uniformity of decisions throughout the whole United States, upon all subjects within the purview of the constitution. Judges of equal learning and integrity, in different states, might differently interpret the statute, or a treaty of the United States, or even the constitution itself: if there were no revising authority to control these jarring and discordant judgments, and harmonize them into uniformity, the laws, the treaties and the constitution of the United States would be different, in different states, and might, perhaps, never have precisely the same construction, obligation or efficiency, in any two states. The public mischiefs that would attend such a state of things would be truly deplorable; and it cannot be believed, that they could have escaped the enlightened convention which formed the constitution. What, indeed, might then have been only prophecy, has now become fact; and the appellate jurisdiction must continue to be the only adequate remedy for such evils....

On the whole, the court are of opinion, that the appellate power of the United States does extend to cases pending in the state courts; and that the 25th section of the judiciary act, which authorizes the exercise of this jurisdiction in the specified cases, by a writ of error, is supported by the letter and spirit of the constitution. We find no clause in that instrument which limits this power; and we dare not interpose a limitation, where the people have not been disposed to create one.

Strong as this conclusion stands, upon the general language of the constitution, it may still derive support from other sources. It is an historical fact, that this exposition of the constitution, extending its appellate power to state courts, was, previous to its adoption, uniformly and publicly avowed by its friends, and admitted by its enemies, as the basis of their respective reasonings, both in and out of the state conventions [that ratified the Constitution]. It is an historical fact, that at the time when the judiciary act was submitted to the deliberations of the first congress, composed, as it was, not only of men of great learning and ability, but of men who had acted a principal part in framing, supporting or opposing that constitution, the same exposition was explicitly declared and admitted by the friends and by the opponents of that system. It is an historical fact, that the supreme court of the United States have, from time to time, sustained this appellate jurisdiction, in a great variety of cases, brought from the tribunals of many of the most important states in the Union, and that no state tribunal has ever breathed a judicial doubt on the subject, or declined to obey the mandate of the supreme court, until the present occasion. This weight of contemporaneous exposition by all parties, this acquiescence of enlightened state courts, and these judicial decisions of the supreme court, through so long a period, do, as we think, place the doctrine upon a foundation of authority which cannot be shaken, without delivering over the subject to perpetual and irremediable doubts....

It is the opinion of the whole court, that the judgment of the court of appeals of Virginia [in Hunter's favor], rendered on the mandate ... [that the Supreme Court had issued to the Virginia Court of Appeals in 1813 to decide the case in Martin's favor], be reversed, and that the judgment of the district court, held at Winchester, be, and the same is hereby affirmed.

Reversed.

QUESTIONS FOR DISCUSSION

1. What statute was at issue in this case, and why?
2. Who, in Justice Story's view, established the Constitution, and why?
3. What relationship did Justice Story say that the Constitution created between the federal government and the state governments?
4. What was the "great question" that the Supreme Court considered in this case?
5. Why did Justice Story conclude that Article III of the Constitution did not limit the appellate jurisdiction of the federal courts to cases that began in federal court?

6. What constitutional language suggests that the Founding Fathers believed that a federal court could review the decision of a state court on federal constitutional grounds, and that the state court would be bound by the federal court's decision?

7. What inference did Justice Story draw from his observation that federal courts could review the actions of state legislatures and of governors on federal constitutional grounds?

8. Why does federal court review of state court decisions on federal constitutional grounds not impair the independence of state judges?

9. What policy reasons exist for federal court review of state court decisions on federal constitutional grounds?

10. Did the Supreme Court find that Section 25 of the Judiciary Act of 1789 was constitutional? Which court did it affirm, and which court did it reverse?

11. What "historical facts," in Justice Story's view, supported that conclusion?

12. How would the United States be different today if the Court had found Section 25 unconstitutional, and the Supreme Court could not review the final decision of a state supreme court? Would any benefits result from that arrangement? Would any costs result?

NOTES

1. Sandra D. O'Connor, "Trends in the Relationship Between the Federal and State Courts," in Mark W. Cannon and David M. O'Brien, *Views from the Bench: The Judiciary and Constitutional Politics* (Chatham, N.J.: Chatham House Publishers, 1985), p. 244. Federalism also exists in Australia, Canada, Germany, India, and Mexico, but only in the United States are there separate federal and state trial courts. In the other **federal systems**, state or provincial courts conduct trials and federal courts hear appeals. *See* Daniel John Meador, *American Courts* (St. Paul, Minn.: West Publishing Company, 1991), p. 44.

2. J. W. Peltason, *Understanding the Constitution*, Thirteenth Edition (Fort Worth, Tex.: Harcourt Brace College Publishers, 1994), p. 18.

3. Merrill Jensen, *The Making of the American Constitution* (Melbourne, Fl.: Krieger Publishing Company, 1979), p. 8.

4. J. W. Peltason, *Understanding the Constitution*, Thirteenth Edition, p. II.

5. A. E. Dick Howard, "Federalism: The Historical Context," in *Politics and the Constitution: The Nature and Extent of Interpretation* (Washington, D.C.: National Legal Center for the Public Interest and the American Studies Center, 1990), pp. 94–96.

6. Sam Howe Verhovek, "Divisive Case of a Killer of Two Ends as Texas Executes Tucker," *The New York Times*, February 4, 1998, p. A1.

7. *Id.*

8. *See generally* Robert S. Want, ed., *Want's Federal-State Court Directory, 1998 Edition* (New York: Want Publishing Company, 1997).

9. *Id.*

10. Brian J. Ostrom and Neal B. Kauder, *Examining the Work of State Courts, 1996: A National Perspective from the Court Statistics Project* (Williamsburg, Va.: National Center for State Courts, 1997), p. 18.

11. *Id.*, p. 155.

12. *Id.*, p. 169.

13. Court Statistics Project, *State Court Caseload Statistics, 1996* (Williamsburg, Va.: National Center for State Courts, 1997), p. 137.

14. John A. Gaerdt, *Small Claims and Traffic Courts: Case Management Procedures, Case Characteristics, and Outcomes in 12 Urban Jurisdictions* (Williamsburg, Va.: National Center for State Courts, 1992), p. 111.

15. *Id.*, p. 114.

16. *Id.*, p. 155.

17. Id., p. 3.

18. *Id.*, p. 6.

19. *Id.*, p. 155.

20. *Id.*, p. 130. *See also* Court Statistics Project, *State Court Caseload Statistics, 1996*, p. 54, which identifies Vermont's Traffic and Municipal Ordinance Bureau.

21. Court Statistics Project, *State Court Caseload Statistics, 1996*, p. 41.

22. Ostrom and Kauder, *Examining the Work of State Courts, 1996*, p. 57.

23. *Id.*, p. 24.

24. *Id.*, p. 57.

25. *Santobello v. New York*, 404 U.S. 257 (1971).

26. *Id.*

27. *Bordenkircher v. Hayes*, 434 U.S. 357 (1978).

28. American Bar Association Criminal Justice Standards Committee, *ABA Standards for Criminal Justice: Pleas of Guilty*, Third Edition (Washington, D.C.: American Bar Association, 1999), pp. xiii–xiv.

29. *Boykin v. Alabama*, 395 U.S. 238 (1969).

30. American Bar Association Criminal Justice Standards Committee, *ABA Standards for Criminal Justice: Pleas of Guilty*, pp. 41–45.

31. *Id.*, p. xiv.

32. *Id.*, pp. 82–83.

33. Id, p. xv.

34. Ostrom and Kander, *Examining the Work of State Courts, 1996*, p. 24.

35. *Id.*

36. Harry P. Stumpf and John H. Culver, *The Politics of State Courts* (New York, N.Y.: Longman, 1992), p. 167.

37. Henry J. Reske, "Downward Trends," *American Bar Association Journal* (December 1996): 24.

38. *Id.*

39. *Id.*

40. Stumpf and Culver, *The Politics of State Courts*, p. 164. Nevertheless, lawyers and judges are at least partly responsible for the sluggish resolution of cases in some trial courts. In Massachusetts, despite a constitutional guarantee of speedy trials, one-third of the 6,000 criminal cases pending in superior court are more than a year old, and almost 15 percent are more than two years old. One Boston-area district attorney blamed this backlog on the legal "culture" in Massachusetts. He observed that: "The culture has been, you have to let a case cook for a year before you do anything about it. So if it's a little over a year old, the attitude is, 'No big deal.'" William F. Doherty, "Superior Courts Trying to Cut Backlogs," *Boston Globe*, November 27, 1997, p. D16.

41. Alabama, Tennessee, Indiana, New York, and Pennsylvania have two intermediate appellate courts each. Alabama and Tennessee have one intermediate appellate court for civil cases and another for criminal cases.

42. Ostrom and Kauder, *Examining the Work of State Courts, 1996*, p. 79.

43. Joy A. Chapper and Roger A. Hanson, *Intermediate Appellate Courts: Improving Case Processing* (Williamsburg, Va.: National Center for State Courts, 1990): p. 18.

44. *Id.*

45. *Id.*, pp. 21–22. New Jersey's intermediate court of appeals is known as the Appellate Division of Superior Court. Court Statistics Project, *State Court Caseload Statistics, 1996*, p. 38.

46. Chapper and Hanson, *Intermediate Appellate Courts*, p. 22.

47. Stumpf and Culver, *The Politics of State Courts*, pp. 138–139.

48. *Id.*, p. 14.

49. *See generally* Court Statistics Project, *State Court Caseload Statistics, 1996*; and Want, ed., *Want's Federal-State Court Directory, 1998 Edition*.

50. Those states are Delaware, Maine, Montana, New Hampshire, Nevada, North Dakota, Rhode Island, South Dakota, Vermont, West Virginia, and Wyoming. The New Hampshire Supreme Court has mandatory jurisdiction only in a capital case in which the trial court has imposed the death penalty. The West Virginia Supreme Court has no mandatory jurisdiction. *See generally* Court Statistics Project, *State Court Caseload Statistics, 1996*.

51. *San Antonio Independent School District v. Rodriguez*, 411 U.S. 1 (1972).

52. See, for example, *Claremont School District v. Governor*, 142 N.H. 462 (1997); *Brigham v. State*, 166 Vt. 246, 692 A.2d 384 (1997); *Roosevelt Elementary School District No. 66 v. Bishop*, 877 P.2d 806 (Ariz. 1994); *Tennessee Small School Systems v. McWherter*, 851 S.W. 2d 139 (Tenn. 1993); *Rose v. Council for Better Education, Inc.*, 790 S.W. 2d 186 (Ky. 1989); and *Edgewood Independent School District v. Kirby*, 777 S.W. 2d 391 (Tex. 1989).

53. Robert A. Carp and Ronald Stidham, *The Federal Courts*, Third Edition (Washington, D.C.: CQ Press, 1998), p. 2.

54. Id., p. 3.

55. *See generally* Want, ed., *Want's Federal-State Court Directory, 1998 Edition*, pp. 3–5.

56. Carp and Stidham, *The Federal Courts*, pp. 28–29.

57. *Id.*, p. 23.

58. *Id.*, p. 25.

59. *Id.*

60. U.S. Bureau of the Census, *Statistical Abstract of the United States: 1996* (Washington, D.C.: U.S. Government Printing Office), p. 215.

61. 912 F. Supp. 892 (M.D. La. 1996). The federal law at issue in *Pederson* was **Title IX** of the **Education Amendments Act of 1972**, which appears in the **United States Code** at 20 U.S.C. § 1681.

62. Diversity cases account for 17.5 percent of the current caseload in federal district courts. See Richard A. Posner, *the Federal Courts: Challenge and Reform* (Cambridge, Mass.: Harvard University Press, 1996), p. 210.

63. *Id.*, p. 219.

64. Article I, Section 9, clause 2 of the U.S. Constitution provides that the *writ of habeas corpus*, which American law inherited from English law, "shall not be suspended, unless when in cases of rebellion or invasion the public safety may require it."

65. Carp and Stidham, *The Federal Courts*, p. 43.

66. U.S. Bureau of the Census, *Statistical Abstract of the United States: 1997* (Washington, D.C.: U.S. Government Printing Office, 1997), p. 216.

67. *Id.*

68. Lawrence M. Friedman, *A History of American Law*, Second Edition (New York, N.Y.: Simon & Schuster, 1985), pp. 139–142.

69. Posner, *The Federal Courts*, pp. 130–131.
70. Carp and Stidham, *The Federal Courts*, pp. 30–31. In 1994, magistrate judges presided in 17 percent of the civil jury trials that occurred in federal district courts. Posner, *The Federal Courts*, p. 65.
71. For that reason, district court clerkships usually last two years instead of one year, and district court judges are increasingly hiring career law clerks. Posner, *The Federal Courts*, p. 158. It is difficult to learn the many tasks of a district court law clerk quickly, and it is frustrating for a judge to lose a clerk shortly after she has begun to perform those tasks well.
72. Posner, *The Federal Courts*, p. 238.
73. The Act appears in Title 28 of the *United States Code* at sections 471–482.
74. *United States Code Congressional and Administrative News* 8 (1990): 6832–6833.
75. Stephanie B. Goldberg, "Rand-ly Criticized," *A.B.A. Journal*, April 1997, pp. 14–16.
76. *Id.*, p. 183.
77. *Id.*, p. 184.
78. Friedman, *A History of American Law*, p. 387.
79. *Id.*
80. Marie T. Finn, Jeanie E. Clapp, Janet E. Breza, and Ruth A. Kennedy, eds., *The American Bench: Judges of the Nation*, Ninth Edition (Sacramento, Calif.: Forster-Long, Inc. 1997-98), p. 1.
81. Carp and Stidham, *The Federal Courts*, p. 17.
82. Frank M. Coffin, *On Appeal: Courts, Lawyering, and Judging* (New York: W. W. Norton, 1994), p. 73.
83. *Id.*
84. U.S. Bureau of the Census, *Statistical Abstract of the United States: 1997* (Washington, D.C.: U.S. Government Printing Office, 1997), p. 216.
85. *Id.*
86. Posner, *The Federal Courts*, p. 239.
87. *Id.*, p. 160; Coffin, *On Appeal*, p. 129.
88. Posner, *The Federal Courts*, p. 176.
89. That rule is Federal Rule of Appellate Procedure (F.R.A.P.) 38. *See* Coffin, *On Appeal*, p. 100.
90. 118 S. Ct. 1726.
91. Lawrence Baum, *The Supreme Court*, Fourth Edition (Washington, D.C.: CQ Press, 1992), p. 11.
92. David M. O'Brien, *Storm Center: The Supreme Court in American Politics*, Third Edition (New York: W. W. Norton, 1993), p. 197.
93. Kenneth Jost, *The Supreme Court Yearbook 1996–1997* (Washington, D.C.: CQ Press, 1998), p. 75. The Court heard oral arguments and produced signed written opinions in eighty of those cases, a typical number for recent years, but a considerable decline from the 1970s and early 1980s, when the Court decided 130–150 full opinion cases per term. It is not clear why the Court decides fewer full opinion cases today than in the past, but there are several theories that try to explain the decline. They posit, respectively, that: (1) the current conservative Court is satisfied with the generally conservative decisions of the federal appellate courts, and sees little need to review them; (2) seekers of social change distrust the current Court, so they are bringing their concerns to Congress, state legislatures, or state courts instead; (3) the justices, as conservatives, wish to reduce the role of the federal courts in political life; and (4) it is

more difficult to get four votes to grant cert today than it used to be because the justices no longer follow the traditional courtesy of furnishing the fourth vote when three judges wish to grant cert. *Id.*, p. 77; David O. Stewart, "Quiet Times," *American Bar Association Journal* (October 1994): 40–44.

94. See the **Improvement of the Administration of Justice Act,** P.L. 100–352, 102 Stat. 662 (6/27/88).

95. Jost, *The Supreme Court Yearbook 1996–1997*, p. 293.

96. O'Brien, *Storm Center*, p. 208.

97. *Id.*, p. 236.

98. Eight of the nine justices participate in the cert pool. Justice John Paul Stevens does not. Justice Stevens assigns his clerks to review cert petitions, and to prepare memoranda for him about those petitions that *the clerks* think deserve a hearing by the Court. Justice Stevens does not review the petitions that his clerks conclude are not worthy of the Court's attention. That is a significant grant of discretion to clerks, who are extremely bright, but who are also inexperienced lawyers.

99. O'Brien, *Storm Center*, p. 237.

100. Jost, *Supreme Court Yearbook*, p. 291.

101. David G. Savage, "Say the Right Thing," *American Bar Association Journal* (September 1997): 55.

102. *Id.*

103. *Id.*

104. The same phenomenon occurs in the U.S. Courts of Appeals and in state appellate courts. For a good discussion of the value of oral arguments, see Coffin, *On Appeal*, pp. 130–134.

105. Jost, *The Supreme Court Yearbook*, p. 299.

106. Quoted in O'Brien, *Storm Center*, p. 244.

107. It is debatable whether law clerks exercise excessive influence over the content of Supreme Court opinions because they write first drafts of those opinions. Some justices rely on clerks more than others do, but it is difficult to generalize about the clerks' substantive influence because the Court does most of its work out of the sight of journalists and scholars. Clerks have apparently influenced the style of Supreme Court opinions, though. Opinions are longer and more heavily footnoted today than they used to be. They reflect the style used in the **law reviews** (or **law journals**) that Supreme Court clerks edited when they were law students.

108. O'Brien, *Storm Center*, p. 273.

109. *Id.*, p. 164.

110. O'Brien, *Storm Center*, p. 13.

111. Jost, *The Supreme Court Yearbook*, p. 78.

112. O'Brien, *Storm Center*, p. 284.

113. Posner, *The Federal Courts*, p. 12.

114. Carp and Stidham, *The Federal Courts*, pp. 33–34.

115. That requirement is known as the "*Erie* doctrine" because the Supreme Court articulated it in *Erie Railway Co. v. Tompkins*, 304 U.S. 64 (1938). The doctrine holds that in a diversity case, a federal court must apply state **substantive law,** but federal **procedural law.** That means that in our hypothetical suit that arose from a skiing accident, the federal court would use the **Federal Rules of Evidence** to govern the admission of evidence, but it would apply New Jersey **tort law** to decide whether the defendant was legally responsible for the plaintiff's injury.

116. James G. Apple, Paula L. Hannaford, and G. Thomas Munsterman, *Manual for Cooperation Between State and Federal Courts* (Washington, D.C.: Federal Judicial Center, 1997), p. 44.

117. Other matters that are subject to exclusive federal jurisdiction are copyright, trademark, securities (e.g., stocks and bonds), and admiralty (sea-going commerce) law, suits against foreign diplomats, and, of course, federal crimes. Apple et al., *Manual for Cooperation Between State and Federal Courts*, p. 170.

118. *Id.*, p. 168.

119. *Id.*, p. 97

Chapter 3

Lawyers and Lawyering

Introduction

Law touches every aspect of contemporary American life. It accompanies us from the cradle to the grave. Statutes, administrative regulations, and/or court decisions govern the hospitals in which we are born, the schools we attend, the personal and professional relationships we enter into as adults, the security of our retirement funds, the medical technology that can prolong our lives, and the funeral services we cannot avoid. We want protection from bodily harm, financial ruin, emotional pain, injustice, and environmental hazards, but we do not trust government to protect us. Law enables us to protect ourselves by hailing into court the individual, school district, corporation, or government agency that has injured us or that has failed to prevent our injuries. Despite our skepticism about government, we seem to trust courts enough to sacrifice time and money there in pursuit of protection, restitution, or retribution.[1]

The daily newspapers contain ample evidence of this. In late 1997, they reported the following stories. A former cheerleader sued Marquette University for having required him to lift heavy female partners during stunts, which he alleged caused him to suffer a serious back injury.[2] A feud between two fifth-grade girls from a Detroit suburb ended up in court, where the judge issued a mutual-protection order that prohibited the girls from harassing each other, under penalty of incarceration in the local youth lockup.[3] The New Hampshire Supreme Court ruled that the local property tax-based system of financing public schools was unconstitutional, which meant that the legislature and the governor would have to devise an alternative.[4]

Americans routinely seek resolution of their disputes by courts, and lawyers run the courts; therefore, the legal profession exercises great influence over the relations between individuals and institutions in the U.S.. Indeed, you cannot understand how the judicial process works without first understanding how the legal profession works. This chapter will show you how the legal profession works.

A BRIEF HISTORY OF THE LEGAL PROFESSION

Lawyers have been influential in the U.S. throughout the country's history. Twenty-five of the fifty-six men who signed the Declaration of Independence in 1776 were lawyers, as were thirty-one of the fifty-five delegates to the Constitutional Convention in 1787.[5]

Lawyers were not as influential early in the colonial period as they became during and after the Revolutionary War. There was great hostility toward lawyers early in the colonial period, which was reflected in the laws of the colonies. Colonies such as Massachusetts Bay and Pennsylvania, which had been founded by religious sects and were governed by religious principles, were especially hostile to lawyers. The Puritans of Massachusetts Bay believed that the colony's leaders should govern strictly and firmly without interference from lawyers and lawsuits, which disrupted the natural, hierarchical order of social life. The Quakers of Pennsylvania, who sought government by consensus, resented the adversary system of English common law, which they believed sowed the seeds of disharmony in colonial society. An early eighteenth-century observer of life in Pennsylvania wrote to relatives in England about the Pennsylvanians that "[t]hey have no lawyers. Everyone is to tell his own case, or some friend for him…. 'Tis a happy country."[6]

Later in the eighteenth century, though, the colonists concluded that lawyers were a necessary evil because they proved to be useful for organizing life as populations and economic activity grew, and as religious constraints on behavior weakened. Lawyers began to thrive, as customers sued merchants and parties to land sales sought competently drafted purchase-and-sale documents. By 1750, despite lingering bias against lawyers, there was a competent, professional bar in all major population centers.[7] Lawyers' importance caused their ranks to grow dramatically in the late eighteenth and early nineteenth centuries. In Massachusetts, for example, there were approximately fifteen lawyers in a population of 150,000 in 1740, but by 1840 there were 640 lawyers, a tenfold increase relative to the state's total population.[8]

The westward expansion of the U.S. that began after the Revolutionary War was a great benefit to lawyers. Legal historian Lawrence Friedman has written that:

> No frontier town was too raw and muddy for lawyers. They were out to seek their fortunes in land and litigation, sometimes even in genteel larceny.[9]

Western lawyers bought and sold land for absentee owners, searched land titles, drafted deeds, collected debts, and loaned money at interest. Besides buying and selling land, they sometimes received payment for their services in land.

Early in the nineteenth century, most American lawyers lacked offices and steady clients. Practice consisted largely of **litigation** (trials), so lawyers traveled together from town to town within a judicial circuit, either by stagecoach or on horseback, accompanied by a judge. A lawyer would barely be off the horse or out of the stagecoach when several prospective clients would approach him, seeking his services. This arrangement made it difficult for lawyers to establish settled practices, so it gave way in most places, even before the Civil War, to the establishment of law offices. Those law offices were small, usually consisting of one or two lawyers.

In those days, lawyers became rich and famous by courtroom advocacy, in part because trials were public entertainment that eased the monotony of daily life, especially in rural areas, where entertainment options were limited. After the Civil War, big-city lawyers began to become rich, if not famous, by advising large corporations instead of by trying cases in court. The oratorical wizard gave way to the "Wall Street lawyer" at the top ranks of the legal profession.

At about the same time, the increasing sophistication of the economy spurred a movement for a more "professional" bar, which led to the establishment of the **American Bar Association (A.B.A.)** in 1878 and to calls for more stringent standards for admission to the practice of law. For more than a hundred years, those standards had generally been lax. Some states required more preparation than others, but the final hurdle was usually a rather casual oral examination by a judge that lasted approximately a half-hour. A candidate often passed because of a recommendation from a well-known lawyer, not because of the quality of his answers. At the urging of the A.B.A., states began, late in the nineteenth century, to require candidates for admission to the bar to pass a written **bar exam** that was more rigorous than the oral exam of yesteryear. The A.B.A. saw written exams as a means of improving the competence of lawyers, and of keeping out of the profession "price cutters and undesirables," which, unfortunately, usually meant the children of Irish, Italian, Polish, and Jewish immigrants.

The method of training future lawyers also changed in the late nineteenth century. For more than 100 years, most American lawyers had learned their craft by serving an apprenticeship with an established practitioner. The apprentice paid the practitioner a fee in return for the opportunity to read classics of English common law, copy legal documents, run errands, and generally observe the master at work. The quality of the apprenticeship depended largely on the teaching skills of the master; some masters relegated their apprentices almost exclusively to mind-numbing copy work, but a few were so good at teaching that they shifted from practicing law to teaching it.[10] The first law schools grew out of those specialized law offices; during the late nineteenth century, law schools replaced apprenticeships as the principal method of training lawyers in the U.S..

Law schools also changed from independent, for-profit businesses to university-based undergraduate departments. They would not become graduate programs within those universities until approximately 1920. The leader among law schools during these years was Harvard, where Christopher Columbus Langdell revolutionized legal education while serving as dean from 1870 until 1895.[11] Langdell made it harder to enter Harvard's law department by requiring passage of an entrance examination for applicants who lacked a college degree. He made it harder to graduate, too, by lengthening the program from one year to two years in 1871, and to three years in 1876. He divided the curriculum into "courses," each worth a fixed number of hours or units, and required first-year students to pass final examinations in their courses in order to proceed to the second year.[12] Thus, Langdell substituted a modern law school for the haphazard series of lectures that existed at Harvard (and in most other university law departments) when he became dean.

Langdell's most important innovation was the **Socratic method** of teaching law, which is still the standard method of teaching law. The Socratic method replaced lectures with classroom discussions of appellate court decisions that illustrated principles of law that the professor wished to convey. The professor asked the students questions about the decisions, and each answer generated another question from the professor, until the class had dissected a particular decision and had extracted from it the principle(s) of law for which it stood. Initially, the Socratic method caused a revolt among Harvard students, who cut Langdell's classes en masse, and a dramatic decline in enrollment because it required students to read assigned cases carefully and to answer questions about them in class.[13] To add insult to injury, the Socratic method enabled professors to ask endless questions of the students, while refusing to answer the students' questions, and to respond with biting sarcasm to answers that they thought were ill-considered, soft-hearted, or naive. It also taught law exclusively by examining the logic of court opinions, ignoring legislation, administrative regulations, and social and political influences on the law.[14] Despite those complaints, which students still voice today, the Socratic method became the dominant method of teaching law at Harvard and at every other American law school early in the twentieth century.

Perhaps the most significant development in the legal profession during the late nineteenth century was the creation of large, urban law firms, the principal clients of which were major corporations. These firms were a response to the industrialization and urbanization of post-Civil War America, and to the needs of business corporations, which were steadily increasing in numbers, size, and complexity. Large corporations needed a wide range of legal services, including the drafting of contracts and other business documents, advice about the legal implications of proposed business transactions, the collection of debts, and defense against personal-injury lawsuits. Corporate needs caused law firms to grow too, because law firms required specialists in numerous legal fields in order to represent corporate clients adequately.[15] In this new environment, law offices depended heavily on the technology of the day, including telephones and typewriters, employed support staffs of stenographer-typists, and divided legal work among **office lawyers**, who advised clients and drafted documents, and **litigators**, who tried cases in court.

Not everything about the legal profession changed rapidly in the years after the Civil War, though. White, Anglo-Saxon Protestant males controlled the bar throughout the nineteenth century and well into the twentieth century. The growth of night law schools near the turn of the century enabled the sons of Irish, Italian, Polish, and Jewish immigrants to become lawyers, but before World War II the prestigious law firms would not hire them. Therefore, most ethnic lawyers practiced among their relatives and neighbors in urban, ethnic enclaves.[16]

If ethnic lawyers were able to sneak in the back door of the legal profession, women and blacks found all entrances bolted shut. Women were excluded from the bar in every state before the 1870s, and they entered the profession at a glacial pace for many years thereafter. As late as 1960, only 3 percent of the lawyers in America were women.[17] In the early 1870s, when Myra Bradwell sought admission to the Bar of the State of Illinois, the law barred women from practicing in that state. Mrs. Bradwell challenged the Illinois law in litigation that ended in the U.S. Supreme Court in 1873.[18] Her lawyer argued that the Illinois law abridged the privileges and immunities that the Fourteenth Amendment guaranteed to Mrs. Bradwell and all American citizens, but the Supreme Court disagreed. A concurring opinion by Justice Joseph P. Bradley revealed the paternalism that underlay prohibitions against women practicing law. Justice Bradley wrote that:

> The paramount destiny and mission of women are to fill the noble and benign offices of wife and mother. This is the law of the Creator.[19]

The *Bradwell* decision forced women to seek admission to the bar on a state-by-state basis, which was a long, slow struggle. Still, by 1923, women had been admitted in every state.[20]

That did not mean that male lawyers welcomed women into the profession. Columbia University did not admit women to its law school until 1927; once women were admitted, the male students stomped their feet on the floor in unison whenever a woman spoke in class, so that nobody could hear her.[21] Harvard barred women from its law school until 1950.[22] The few women who enrolled in law school before the 1970s often found that their male professors and classmates either ignored them or treated them with contempt. The early women law students encountered similar hostility when they sought employment after graduation. When Sandra Day O'Connor, now an associate justice of the U.S. Supreme Court, graduated from Stanford Law School in 1952, she had difficulty finding work despite her high grades. One California law firm offered her a job as a secretary.[23] Justice O'Connor's colleague, Justice Ruth Bader Ginsburg, was tied for first place in her class at Columbia Law School when she graduated in 1959, but none of the major New York City law firms offered her a job.[24]

Circumstances changed during the 1970s and the 1980s, as women entered law school in large numbers. Women were 4 percent of law students in 1964, but nearly 40 percent by 1984.[25] During the 1970s and 1980s, the battleground in women's struggle for acceptance in the legal profession shifted from the law schools to the law firms, where male partners routinely denied partnerships to their female colleagues. By the 1980s, it was common for women to be 30 percent of the **associates** in a large law firm, that is, junior, salaried lawyers who do not share in the firm's governance or its profits, but less than 5 percent of its **partners**. The battle continues in the year 2000; women find that it is much easier to enter a major law firm as an associate than it is to "make partner." Once barred from the legal profession altogether, women are still grossly underrepresented in its top ranks.

Blacks were no more welcome in the legal profession than women were during the nineteenth century and most of the twentieth century. Aspiring black lawyers faced enormous barriers to obtaining training and employment, so their number remained small well into the twentieth century. Black lawyers, like the white ethnic lawyers of the urban Northeast, had to have broad practices that included both criminal and civil work, litigation and office work, in order to earn a living, because they did not receive the lucrative business of banks, large corporations, or wealthy individuals. Black lawyers represented primarily low- and moderate-income black clients. After the Civil War, many black lawyers received their legal educations at the Howard University Law School in Washington, D.C., which opened in 1869. At Howard, Dean John Mercer Langston trained a small group of black lawyers, many of whom were pioneers in the legal battle for black civil rights during the first thirty years of the twentieth century.[26]

Black women faced the longest odds of any group when they tried to become lawyers because they were burdened by the double whammy of being black and female. Despite such treatment, there were trailblazers who established a foothold in the legal profession for black women. For example, Ruth Harvey Charity practiced law in Danville, Virginia, during the 1940s, after her graduation from Howard Law School, and filed lawsuits that resulted in the desegregation of Danville's park and library.[27] Constance Baker Motley became the first black woman to serve as a judge of the U.S. District Court for the Southern District of New York when President Lyndon Johnson appointed her to that post in 1966.[28] During the 1970s and the 1980s, black women were among the growing numbers of women who entered law school and the legal profession. Black women law graduates became much sought after by legal employers during those years, as the federal government began to enforce aggressively the laws against employment discrimination. Ironically, the double whammy became a double benefit, at least in obtaining employment, if not in earning a partnership.

Perhaps the most dramatic recent change in the legal profession has been growth. In 1960, there were about 286,000 lawyers in the U. S.; by 1987, there were about 690,000, and by 1996, about 911,000 (including judges), which gave the United States more lawyers per person than any other country in the world.[29] The principal reason for this increase has been the entrance of women into the legal profession that began in the 1970s. In 1950, just 2.5 percent of America's lawyers were women; by 1987, that number had increased to 14 percent, and by 1996, it was up to 29 percent.[30] The percentage of women lawyers is likely to increase further in the future because women were 45.2 percent of America's law students in 1997.[31] Law firms grew rapidly during the late twentieth century too. In 1996 approximately 300 law firms each employed more than 100 lawyers, whereas in 1978 only forty-seven law firms were that large.[32]

Another major change has been the diversification of law practice. One example of that diversification was the development of **public-interest law firms** during the late 1960s and the 1970s. These are nonprofit law offices. Some of them, such as the **Legal Services Corporation**, which Congress established in

1966, exist to provide low-cost legal services to people who cannot afford to hire a private lawyer to represent them. Others, such as the **Conservation Law Foundation** or the **Institute for Justice**, bring lawsuits for the purpose of achieving specific public policy goals; they represent clients in order to further ideological aims, not to make a living. The Conservation Law Foundation and similar groups use the law to pursue "liberal" policy goals, such as preserving the habitat of the spotted owl by restricting logging in old-growth forests in the Northwest. The Institute for Justice and organizations like it use the law for "conservative" goals, such as ending race-based **affirmative action** programs in higher education.

By the 1980s, the practice of law had become so diversified that there were, in effect, many "legal professions" in which lawyers could choose to practice. Some lawyers worked for "megafirms" comprised of several hundred lawyers, with offices in several different American cities and in exotic locales overseas. Other lawyers worked alone or in small firms, in office towers in midtown Manhattan and on Main Street in Manhattan, Kansas. Some worked in government, as banking regulators, as counsel to state legislatures, and as legislative assistants to members of Congress. Others worked as **in-house counsel** to corporations, where they were both advisors to and employees of their respective clients, or as **public defenders** or **legal-aid lawyers**, providing free legal representation to impoverished clients in criminal and civil cases, respectively. The following section will examine this diverse legal profession as it exists at the beginning of the twenty-first century.

THE LEGAL PROFESSION TODAY

Entry

States determine the requirements for admission to the practice of law. In forty-three states and the District of Columbia, one must complete a three-year course of study in law school, preferably a law school approved by the American Bar Association, in order to be eligible to take the bar exam.[33] Seven states, including Alaska, California, Maine, New York, Vermont, Virginia, and Washington, permit the substitution of several years of law office study for law school.[34] In Vermont, for example, one can substitute for law school four years (at least twenty-five hours per week for at least forty-four weeks per year) of **reading law** in a law office; after completing that program, one can take the bar exam. Nevertheless, most of the people who take bar exams in this country nowadays have earned both a baccalaureate degree (B.A. or B.S.) from a four-year college and a **juris doctor** (J.D.) degree from an A.B.A.-approved law school.

The law school experience calls to mind the old adage that "the more things change, the more they stay the same." Much about legal education has changed during the past generation, but its core remains remarkably unchanged. Most professors still analyze appellate court opinions, using the Socratic method, which still strikes fear in the hearts of law students, who dread being "called on" in class.

Journalist Chris Goodrich, who attended Yale Law School, described that fear at work in his civil procedure class. He recalled that:

> [Professor Geoffrey] Hazard turned to the class list on the podium, and at that point no minds drifted. You could almost hear the adrenaline rush through the student body as Hazard chose his first victim. After some noisy fidgeting the class became deadly silent.[35]

The most significant change in legal education in the past generation has been the growth of **clinical studies**, elective courses in which students earn academic credit by representing, under faculty supervision, low-income clients in civil matters, prisoners, or persons accused of crimes who cannot afford a private attorney. They were a response to student demands during the late 1960s and early 1970s for more engaging and socially conscious courses during the second and third years of law school. Clinical studies have become a fixture at American law schools, and many second-year and third-year students now take such courses.

Another important change has been the creation of courses that relate law to subjects or to academic disciplines that law school curricula traditionally ignored. For example, when I was in law school, during the mid–1980s, I took courses titled "Law and the Social Sciences" and "Law and Sports," respectively; many of my classmates took "Law and Economics." This trend continues. The 1997–1998 Vermont Law School catalog includes courses titled "Moral Philosophy Seminar," "Environmental Justice," and "Native Americans and the Law Seminar." The addition of such courses was a less dramatic change than the creation of clinical programs, because professors usually teach the "law and" courses in the same way that they teach contracts or property, by discussing appellate court decisions, using the Socratic method. The "law and" courses nonetheless add vitality to the law school curriculum.

Despite these changes, the required first-year courses and other traditional courses such as corporations and income taxation remain preeminent. The reason for that is their presence on bar exams. Therein lies one important critique of legal education: it is part "trade school" and part graduate program in liberal arts. That hybrid status often confuses law students and makes them wish that faculty and administrators would choose between the two. It can frustrate both practice-oriented and academically oriented students; the former sometimes conclude that law school is inadequate preparation for law practice, while the latter often see it as a boring vocational school. So long as students enroll in law school for many different reasons, legal education will remain a hybrid, and the gulf between the study and practice of law will continue.

A related critique of legal education is that it trains students generally for a specialized profession. Few law graduates will find work in large corporate law firms, where their inexperience will not hurt the firm because there are plenty of seasoned lawyers available to do the most important work. Most graduates will find work in small firms, where they will probably be expected to counsel clients and to argue cases in court right away; their inexperience could have disastrous consequences. Similar problems can exist in state and local government agencies, where supervision of new lawyers is often minimal because of heavy caseloads and insufficient staff. Therefore, several critics recommend that law schools develop separate academic "tracks" from which students could choose, depending on their career aspirations.[36] They contend that it is nonsensical to train the student who will write simple wills and oversee residential real estate sales in Taos, New Mexico, in the same way as the student who will arrange major stock offerings on Wall Street or the student who will write automobile emissions rules at the Environmental Protection Agency. The future small-town lawyer will not need the extensive training in legal reasoning that law school provides, while the aspiring Wall Street lawyer will need more advanced training in business law than law school usually offers, and the E.P.A. lawyer-to-be will require more exposure to legislation and to administrative law than is common in law school.

It is unclear whether law schools will adopt these changes. On the one hand, they would probably help law schools to place a higher percentage of their graduates in jobs after graduation, which improves the schools' ability to attract future students. On the other hand, they would necessitate smaller classes and more professors, which could significantly increase the cost of law school.

Another critique of legal education is that it is too narrow; that is, it restricts every subject to a discussion of appellate court opinions. "Law and Sports," for example, is nothing more than what appellate judges have said in a series of contracts, torts, and constitutional cases that happened to arise in a sports context. That course will not examine the origins of professional sports in America, the educational implications of commercialized college sports, or the place of sports in the American psyche. Neither will a course in labor law review the historical context in which labor unions developed in the U.S. That is why critics have long charged that legal education tries to sharpen the human mind by narrowing it.

One critic recommends that law schools divide their curricula into three roughly equal components, including (1) doctrinal analysis (i.e., the existing case analysis); (2) field-based clinical education (which also exists, but to a lesser extent); and (3) advanced training in political economy, anthropology, philosophy, and related subjects. He argues that the third component would cure students of their mistaken belief that logic alone resolves legal disputes, rather than logic mixed with values, biases, and cultural conventions.[37]

A final critique charges that legal education indoctrinates students in a hyperrational and contentious method of problem solving that regards emotions as irrelevant to "thinking like a lawyer," and that values winning more than effective dispute resolution. Law school, like Marine boot camp, strips one of customary patterns of thought and behavior, and replaces them with new ones.[38] The student who adopts the new patterns graduates from law school "thinking like a lawyer," just as the recruit graduates from boot camp a "Marine."

Chris Goodrich, who wrote a book about his student days at Yale Law School, voiced this critique when he wrote that "in emphatically fostering students' intellectual selves, law school gives them—me, in this instance—license to ignore the more problematic, uncontrollable, emotional aspects of life."[39] It enables some students in property class, for example, to point out the economic reasons not to require landlords to maintain their low-income housing adequately, and to ignore the human tragedy of children living with rats, roaches, and leaky plumbing.[40] Other students, especially those who enter law school with strong ideological, religious, or professional perspectives, struggle to make accommodations between thinking like a lawyer and being an environmentalist, a Muslim, or a clinical psychologist.

Many students do not resolve such tensions until their second year in school, when another source of tension enters their lives: the job search. The job search typically begins during the second year of law school because that is when law firms, especially large law firms, hire law students to work in their offices during the following summer. If the **summer associate** experience is satisfactory for both parties, the firm will probably offer the student a position as a full-time **associate** when she graduates. Some government employers and small law firms also follow this pattern, but it is more common among large firms because, unlike other legal employers, they usually hire new attorneys every year,

The job search can be tense. Students whose grades put them in the top 10 percent or 15 percent of their class at a prestigious law school can agonize about whether to accept a job offer from a large firm in New York City, with a starting salary of more than $100,000 a year, or to follow their hearts and take a job for less than half that salary with the **Natural Resources Defense Council** or the **National Women's Law Center**.[41] Many students enter law school eager to do public-interest work after graduation, but the prospect of trying to pay off a student-loan debt of $100,000 or more and live in modest comfort, all on a salary of $40,000 or less, convinces them to join large law firms if they can. The salaries that large law firms offer, frequently to twenty-four- and twenty-five-year-olds, are seductive, especially to graduates of private law schools, who paid an average annual tuition in 1997 of $19,000.[42] Therefore, it is not surprising that only 15 percent of the class of 1997 entered government service or public-interest practice after law school.[43]

Recently, faculty and administrators, especially at the elite law schools, have concluded that their graduates are following too narrow a career path; therefore, they have offered loan forgiveness programs to students who accept low-paying public-interest jobs after graduation.[44] That is commendable, and more schools should do it. Law schools must also promote government service and public-interest work as career choices, just as they have long promoted corporate practice, and they must invite more government and public-interest employers to interview their students on campus. It should be just as easy for students to interview with those employers as it is for them to interview with large law firms.

Most students lack the academic credentials for employment with a large law firm, and some experience considerable tension when they seek employment. These students must identify potential employers by their own effort, because employers will not come to campus to interview them. They must also pay the costs of their transportation to and from interviews. Some of these students find employment via a personal friendship or a family relationship. Others volunteer, work part-time, or work for low wages during the summer, or even after graduation, in hopes of receiving an offer of full-time work. Most law graduates eventually receive that offer, usually from a small law firm comprised of between two and ten lawyers. Six months after graduation, 89.2 percent of the 1997 law graduates nationwide were employed, and 73.6 percent were employed full-time as lawyers.[45] Figure 3.1 shows the types of employment they obtained. Nevertheless, considering the effort that most law students expend to find employment, it is easy to understand why those who can join a large law firm that recruits them usually do so.

All aspiring lawyers, regardless of their class rank, must pass a bar exam in the state(s) where they plan to practice. Most students know before graduation where they wish to practice, and they enroll in a **bar review course** for that state's bar exam. Unlike law school courses, bar review courses use lectures that present a large quantity of information in a short time. Students must memorize that information, such as the requirements for a valid will or the elements of negligence, in order to be able to recall it quickly and use it to answer exam questions. The bar exam is usually a two-day affair. Forty-seven states and the District of Columbia

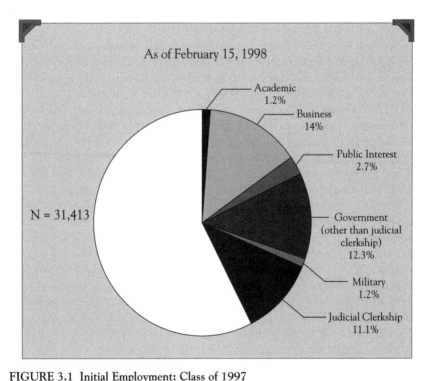

FIGURE 3.1 Initial Employment: Class of 1997
Note: Figures in this chart reflect legal and non-legal jobs. The category of "unknown employer type," which included 1.8 percent of the class of 1997, is not shown.
Source: National Association for Law Placement, *Selected Class of 1997 Employment Report and Salary Survey Findings* (NALP, 1998), p. 1. Reprinted with permission.

administer a **Multistate Bar Examination** on the first day; it consists of two-hundred multiple-choice questions on contracts, torts, property, civil procedure, criminal law, and constitutional law.[46] The second day of the exam consists of essay questions, written by the examining state's **board of bar examiners**, that test one's knowledge of the law in that particular state.

Bar exams are graded on a pass/fail basis, but they are by no means easy. Nevertheless, in most states, most examinees pass the bar exam the first time they take it. Bar exams are more difficult in some states than in others, as data from the July 1996 test date indicate. In Nebraska, 97 percent of the first-time examinees and 94 percent of all the examinees who took the July 1996 exam passed it. In contrast, 69 percent of the examinees who took the California bar exam for the first time in July 1996 (and 56 percent overall) passed. These variations reflect the different passing scores that states require on the multistate portion of the exam and differences in the difficulty of the essay questions from state to state.

Successful examinees will be formally sworn in to the bars of their respective states, and can begin their legal careers. They will have traveled a long, sometimes arduous road from law student to lawyer, and will perhaps have questioned the wisdom of their career choice along the way. Yet they can be proud of having successfully completed professional training that taught them a disciplined, careful way of thinking, and that gave them powerful tools with which to play a leadership role in American society.

Culture

Lawyers who are newly admitted to practice soon discover that, if they are not always admired or even respected, they are nonetheless prominent actors in American life. Their prominence results from several traditions in American political and legal thought that combine to make litigation a more common means of resolving disputes and of creating public policy here than it is in other countries. One such tradition is the **common-law tradition**, which developed from the English king's enforcement of his royal rights.[47] Its most fundamental principle is the **supremacy of law**, which states that all acts of government are subject to review in the courts, and that no person is beyond the courts' jurisdiction.[48] A related principle is that judges bear the major responsibility for interpreting the law.[49] They interpret the law by deciding cases, which gives them great power because the power to interpret the law is the power to make the law, especially when no prior, similar cases are available to guide the judges.[50]

Another tradition that influences modern American law is **Puritan individualism**. The Puritans believed that the most important purpose of law was to protect individual freedom. They also believed that individuals should be free to choose how to live their lives and that government should not coerce them in those matters. By the same token, the Puritans held that people must accept the consequences of their choices; they should not expect government to rescue them from their own foolishness.[51]

The common-law tradition and Puritan individualism jointly produced a political/legal culture in which individuals and institutions revere their **rights**, are quick to hire lawyers to assert them, distrust legislative and executive institutions to guarantee them, but look to courts to protect them, in private disputes and in public controversies. In that culture, lawyers and judges resolve disputes by means of an **adversary system**. Under the adversary system, according to Professor Carrie Menkel-Meadow, "I take care of my side and you take care of yours and almost anything we do to win our 'rights' is justified."[52] The American political/legal culture assigns lawyers a prominent position in society, and it expects them to be aggressive advocates for their clients.[53] If, as one author has suggested, law has replaced religion as the most influential force in American life, then lawyers are indeed the "new high priests" of American society.[54]

Modern life has added a new ingredient to the American political/legal culture, namely, a demand for protection by government from a vast array of hazards and harms, whether financial, physical, or psychic. A sense of entitlement to protection from harm has replaced the self-reliance of Puritan individualism.[55] Yet Americans do not trust government to protect them, as befits their Puritan heritage, so they sue states and localities to compel those entities to enforce federal air-pollution or child-support standards, and they sue manufacturers to force them to produce safer products.[56] Thus, it is not surprising that the U.S. has one-third of the world's lawyers, and more lawyers per person than any other country.[57] "As the rule of law has extended," notes University of Wisconsin law professor Mark Galanter, "so has the rule of lawyers."[58]

The U.S. uses litigation to achieve results that could be achieved by government regulations. Americans' preference for litigation reflects their desire for "justice," their commitment to individual rights, and their distrust of government. Americans don't trust lawyers either, but lawyers are a necessary evil because they enable individuals to protect their rights and to obtain fair compensation for their injuries. Lawyers promote and perpetuate this preference for litigation, but they are largely consequences, not causes, of it; America's individualistic political/legal culture is the cause of it.

Practice

The diversity of law practice might be its most distinguishing characteristic. Washington, D.C., lawyer Robert Bennett, who represented President Clinton in *Clinton v. Jones*, charges $475 per hour for his services and earns more than $1 million annually as a partner at Skadden, Arps, Slate, Meagher and Flom, one of America's oldest, largest, and most prestigious law firms.[59] Bennett's hourly rate is several times that earned by lawyers in Aroostook County in northern Maine, where many clients are farmers and loggers and the payment for a half-hour consultation is often a handshake and a "thank you" or a sack of potatoes.[60] Figure 3.2 depicts the diversity of contemporary law practice.

Americans often fail to appreciate the diversity of law practice because they acquire their images of lawyers from televised depictions of courtroom

Type of Employment	Men No.	%	Women No.	%
Private Practice (Solo)	225,584	34	72,139	36
Private Practice (Firm)	265,356	41	71,395	35
Federal Courts	2,127	<1	810	<1
Other Federal Government	18,163	3	8,643	4
State/Local Courts	14,746	2	3,944	2
Other State/Local Government	25,609	4	13,214	7
Private Industry	53,882	8	17,468	9
Private Association	3,308	1	2,185	1
Legal Aid/Public Defender	4,938	1	3,561	2
Education	5,582	1	2,604	1
Retired/Inactive	36,328	6	6,345	3

FIGURE 3.2 Employment of Lawyers, 1995
Source: Clara N. Carson, *The Lawyer Statistical Report: The U.S. Legal Profession in 1995* (Chicago, Il.: American Bar Foundation, 1999), p. 10. Reprinted with permission.

advocacy, both actual and fictional, and usually in criminal cases. In reality, most lawyers do civil work, not criminal work, and they spend the bulk of their time in their offices trying to avoid or to settle litigation, not in court battling their adversaries. The legal profession is partly responsible, though, for the public's inaccurate image of lawyers' work. Lawyer/diplomat Sol Linowitz has observed that:

> The lawyer who wins in court is the publicized hero, but the lawyer who draws up the contract so carefully that the parties never wind up in court has performed a far greater service. Like the medical profession, the legal profession has organized itself to give the greatest rewards to the specialists, the people who handle the biggest troubles.[61]

The people who handle the biggest troubles in civil law usually work in large law firms located in major cities. They are only about 10 percent of the practicing lawyers in America, but their influence far exceeds their numbers because their firms are wealthy, prestigious, and often politically powerful.[62] That is why recent changes in large law-firm practice, and the consequences of those changes, have been the subjects of numerous books and articles. The changes have been reduced job security for partners, diminished client loyalty to any particular firm, and increased pressures on partners and associates to generate high fees for their firms. They have resulted from greater competition among law firms for the business of corporate clients who increasingly assign their legal work to in-house counsel in order to minimize their legal bills.

Partners in large law firms used to enjoy something like the "tenure" that many professors have. Firms typically hired several young associates every year who were fresh out of law school, trained them for five or six years, and then offered the best of them partnerships in the firm, which they would continue to enjoy until retirement. Partners' salaries rose by the same percentage annually, according to a seniority-based system of compensation. Those arrangements ended at many large law firms during the 1980s, when business conditions became increasingly competitive.

Today, the "eat what you kill" system of compensation for partners has replaced the seniority system; under the new system, the partner who obtains a client's business receives the financial reward from that business, even if another partner performs most of the work necessary to serve the client. The new system makes partners who are skilled at attracting clients ("rainmakers") more valuable to a firm than partners who do good work but who are not skilled at attracting clients. The latter are the partners who are most likely to lose their jobs when a law firm decides to "downsize." Thus, in large law firms, a "partnership" is no longer a personal relationship; instead, it is merely a legal form that is easily dissolved.[63]

Partners in large law firms are less secure today because their firms are less secure, and firms are less secure because clients are less loyal to firms than they used to be. By the mid–1980s, law firms could no longer take their clients' loyalty for granted. Corporations sought to cut their legal costs by hiring a law firm only when they faced a major lawsuit or a complex transaction.[64] When they hired law firms, they no longer hired one firm to perform all the necessary work; a corporation might hire one firm for the lawsuit and another for the transaction. The traditional arrangement, whereby a corporation paid a law firm an annual fee (a **retainer**) to perform all of the corporation's legal work during the year, had become the relic of a bygone era.

In this environment, both partners and associates feel pressure to bill many hours of work in order to earn money for their firms. Billing clients by the hour instead of charging an annual retainer and recording the time spent working on a client's business (**billable hours**) became standard practices for law firms during the 1950s. In the 1980s, because of the competition between law firms for clients, those practices became sources of considerable frustration for both partners and associates.[65] Boston lawyers expressed that frustration in a survey conducted in 1997 by the Boston Bar Association. Partners complained that the pressure to bill more than 2,000 hours annually while also attracting clients prevents them from working as carefully as they would like to and from properly supervising the associates who work for them.[66]

Associates complained that the pressures on partners often result in the "5 P.M. assignment," in which a partner assigns work to an associate at 5 P.M., insists that it be completed by 8 A.M. the next day, then returns to his own work or leaves the office without giving the associate any instructions. The associate cancels her plans for the evening and spends most of it in the firm's library trying to determine what the partner wants her to do.[67] She worries that if she spends too little time on the matter, she will not serve the client well, and that if she spends more time on it than the client will pay for, the assigning partner will be dissatisfied with her work. Both worries are justified in today's environment, where it is much harder than it used to be for associates to become partners.

In solo practices and small law firms, where the greatest number of lawyers works today, the burdens and benefits are quite different from those of large-firm practice. These lawyers, especially the solo practitioners, sacrifice financial security and professional prestige in return for personal and professional autonomy. No one tells a solo practitioner how to run her practice; if she wants to leave the office at 4 P.M. to train for a marathon, she can do so. If she wants to confine her practice to land use and zoning matters, she can do that too. That is why solo practitioners were among the most professionally fulfilled of the lawyers that the Boston Bar Association surveyed. They reported that their control over their professional lives was essential to their feelings of professional fulfillment.[68] Lawyers in small firms reported similar satisfaction with their professional lives; they enjoy slightly less autonomy but somewhat greater financial security than solo practitioners do.

Solo and small-firm lawyers pay a high price for their autonomy. Their personal incomes are often modest, and their paychecks can be irregular, especially during economic downturns. If they cannot afford to hire competent support staff, they must answer their own telephones, do their own clerical work, and perform the administrative tasks associated with running a small business, all of which reduce their billable hours.[69] They must decline cases that require larger amounts of time or money than they can spare.[70] They often struggle to pay bar association dues, do without legal periodicals because they cannot afford the subscription fees, and forego health, disability, life, and even malpractice insurance because the premiums are too high.[71] Under those conditions, it is fair to ask how much control such lawyers actually have over their lives. The answer for each lawyer undoubtedly depends upon his particular values, temperament, financial obligations, and family circumstances.

There are also distinct burdens and benefits associated with governmental practice, be it federal, state, or local, as reflected in the responses of federal and state government lawyers included in the Boston Bar Association survey. These lawyers reported that they were satisfied with their professional lives because they were doing work they believed in and they had considerable authority to manage cases as they saw fit. These lawyers also noted that, unlike their colleagues in private practice, they faced no pressure to bill hours, so senior lawyers took time to serve as mentors to less experienced lawyers who worked for them.[72] On the other hand, they complained that because of budgetary constraints, their offices were crowded and were not cleaned regularly, and that they could not afford to participate in professional activities, such as continuing legal education seminars.[73]

Those burdens are relatively minor compared to the burdens faced by government lawyers who serve poor clients, either as public defenders in criminal cases or as legal-aid lawyers in civil matters. A study of current and former public defenders in Chicago found that prosecutors, judges, and even clients often regarded public defenders as inferior lawyers and treated them as such. Several public defenders said that, as a group, they had "a reputation as crummy lawyers," which judges reinforced by treating them as second-class citizens.[74] Judges commonly heard cases in which a private lawyer represented the accused before they heard cases in which a public defender represented the accused. Accused persons recognized that bias, and often said to their public defenders: "I don't want a P.D. I want a real lawyer."[75]

The perception that public defenders are inferior lawyers probably results from their heavy caseloads and inadequate on-the-job training, which undoubtedly cause them to make mistakes early in their careers. One former Chicago public defender recalled that:

> I got trained by showing up [at the office] and they handed me a file and said, 'You are starting trials.' I had a partner for one week and then I was put on my own. It was crazy. We used to do fifteen bench trials a day and I had, on average, forty clients a day.[76]

The culprit in that scenario is not lawyer indifference or incompetence, but the public's and the politicians' choice not to support public defenders' offices adequately. Public defenders and their clients bear the burdens of that choice.

Legal-aid lawyers bear similar burdens. They represent poor people in civil matters such as landlord–tenant disputes, consumer-credit cases, and child-support enforcement efforts, and often help them to achieve improved housing, affordable credit terms, and the financial assistance to which they are entitled. Their caseloads are large, their work, especially in family-law matters, can be emotionally draining, and they frequently lose in court. To make matters worse, on January 1, 1996, the Congress cut the budget for the **Legal Services Corporation**, which is the largest source of funds for legal-aid offices nationwide, from $400 million to $278 million. Consequently, some legal-aid offices closed and others instituted layoffs, hiring freezes, and/or salary cuts.[77] As if that weren't bad enough, the Supreme Court ruled on June 15, 1998, that the interest on funds that lawyers hold temporarily for their clients, which states had been using to fund legal-aid offices, is the clients' private property.[78] It is unclear whether that means that states can no longer use those funds to support legal-aid programs. If that is the case, legal-aid programs nationwide will lose about $100 million, which they cannot afford to lose because of the 32 percent budget cut they suffered in 1996.

Public defenders and legal aid lawyers work for different rewards than private attorneys do. The public defender takes pride in forcing the state to prove guilt beyond a reasonable doubt by means of reliable evidence and by overcoming the presumption of innocence. The legal-aid lawyer takes pride in securing economic benefits for clients who cannot secure those benefits for themselves. Thus, law practice is a kind of all-you-can-eat buffet: it offers something that is likely to satisfy almost every taste.

Challenges

The legal profession faces three major challenges at the dawn of the twenty-first century. It must: (1) make legal services accessible to low- and moderate-income Americans; (2) improve the conditions of employment for lawyers, especially for women and minority lawyers; and (3) initiate an informed national conversation about America's much-criticized system of personal-injury compensation.

Learned Hand, who was a prominent legal thinker and judge early in the twentieth century, said: "If we are to keep our democracy, there must be one commandment: Thou shall not ration justice."[79] Unfortunately, modern America does ration justice, because low-income Americans and many moderate-income Americans cannot afford legal representation.

One indication of that is the recent aggressive promotion by credit card companies and some employee benefit plans of prepaid legal service plans. The United Auto Workers offers its members such a plan, and the American Telephone and Telegraph Company (AT&T) offers one to its employees. Both plans permit beneficiaries to choose a lawyer from among a preapproved list of lawyers, and the insurance plan administrator pays the lawyer a predetermined fee, just as an insurance company would pay a doctor who associates with a health maintenance organization (H.M.O.).[80] The result is affordable legal services for workers who might otherwise not be able to afford them.

Prepaid legal service plans could be available to more people if the American Bar Association and state bar associations encouraged employers to offer them as an option to their employees. A state bar association could maintain a panel of lawyers who have agreed to represent beneficiaries at fixed rates for routine tasks, such as real estate closings, wills, and uncontested divorces, and at predetermined hourly rates for more complex matters or specialized services.[81] Bar associations could also make legal services more accessible by requiring their members to either perform a minimum number of hours of **pro bono** (i.e., free) legal work annually or donate a minimum amount of money annually to fund the pro bono work of other lawyers. Many state bar associations require their members to attend continuing legal education seminars each year in order to maintain their law licenses; there is no reason why they could not also require members to either perform or support pro bono work in order to maintain their licenses.

Even if these programs remain voluntary, law firms could promote them by making the performance or the support of pro bono work a consideration in evaluating candidates for partnerships.[82] They could also open a branch office in a low-income neighborhood, as one Richmond, Virginia, firm did, establish a department in the firm that specializes in pro bono work, as a Washington, D.C., firm did, and/or offer their lawyers periodic "sabbaticals" to do pro bono work, as one Seattle firm does.[83] Congress could help by establishing a "legal service corps" of recent law school graduates who would work for modest salaries for several years in legal aid, public defenders', and prosecutors' offices, or in state or local government agencies in return for the forgiveness or the reduction of their loan debt.[84] All of these actions would reaffirm the professional duty of lawyers, as **officers of**

the court, to ensure the effective administration of justice. Lawyers are not "hired guns" whose only duty is to clients who pay them.

Neither should lawyers be indentured servants to their employers; leaders in the legal profession must encourage legal employers to carefully examine their expectations of their lawyers and the adverse consequences of those expectations. A study conducted in 1991 by researchers at Johns Hopkins University found that lawyers were the most depressed employment group among the 12,000 workers surveyed.[85] In April 1993, *Working Woman* magazine reported on two surveys of women lawyers, one from 1967 and another from 1992. The survey questionnaire asked the women lawyers whether they would have chosen a legal career if they had known ten years earlier what they knew at the time of the survey. In 1967 94 percent of the women surveyed answered "yes," but in 1993 only 54 percent answered "yes."[86] It is not surprising, then, that an estimated 40,000 lawyers leave the practice of law every year.[87]

Many of those lawyers are women who find the simultaneous demands of the law and of motherhood extremely stressful. The University of California—Davis School of Medicine tracked the post-law school lives of 584 female graduates of that university's law school, and discovered that those who practiced law more than forty-five hours per week were three times more likely to have had a miscarriage than those who practiced less than thirty-five hours per week. Of the lawyers who exceeded forty-five hours a week, 63 percent indicated that they were tense much, most, or all of the time.[88] These statistics are a clarion call to the legal profession to change its culture. One necessary change is the substitution of annual retainers, fixed fees, and **contingency fees** (the lawyer's fee is a percentage of the amount the client wins at trial or obtains by settlement) for hourly billing, because the pressure to bill hours creates stress and tempts lawyers to bill clients for more hours than they actually work. Another necessary change is greater use of mediation as an alternative to litigation, because litigation is contentious and time-consuming, therefore stressful. That could also reduce the incivility between opposing lawyers that is increasingly common in litigation. Law firms must devise alternatives to the traditional associate-to-partner progression too, such as permitting parents of young children to step off the partnership track temporarily, work shorter hours while their children are young, and then increase their hours when their children are older.

All legal employers must eliminate cultural assumptions and behaviors that make women and minorities feel like outsiders in a white men's club. A male judge is unlikely to ask a female attorney nowadays, "Are you a lawyer, little lady,?"[89] but, according to women lawyers who participated in the Boston Bar Association's 1997 survey, he might well address her by her first name instead of as "Attorney" or as "Ms."[90] Those women lawyers also reported that in a meeting of lawyers, the men often ignored a recommendation made by a woman until a man made the same recommendation.[91]

In the same survey, a black woman lawyer complained that judges often treated her as if she were invisible and that court employees often mistook her for a criminal defendant or for the court reporter.[92] Black lawyers often feel invisible in large law firms too; they report difficulty in finding mentors among the white partners, partly because the partners assume that they are less interested in corporate work than white associates are, and that they will leave for government jobs after a few years. It is not surprising, therefore, that in 1995, blacks were just 2.4 percent of the lawyers and only 1 percent of the partners in large law firms nationwide.[93]

The American Bar Association and state bar associations should join with management specialists and with industrial psychologists to offer instructional seminars that will help legal employers adjust to an increasingly diverse workplace. State bar associations should give continuing legal education credit to lawyers who attend those seminars and favorable publicity to law firms that put their lessons into practice.

Last but not least, the legal profession must lead a national conversation that tries to determine the most effective means of compensating individuals who suffer personal injuries as a result of negligence by others. Until that conversation occurs, too many Americans will believe that our tort system is a perverse lottery that routinely makes greedy lawyers and their undeserving clients rich, bankrupts businesses, and makes American products less competitive than they should be in the global marketplace. That view exaggerates Americans' propensity to sue, disregards the growing prevalence of alternative methods of dispute resolution, and ignores the cultural roots of our tort system. It also fails to recognize that business litigation is increasing faster than tort litigation is.[94] Businesses are suing each other at a faster rate than individuals are suing businesses, which suggests that businesses do not necessarily dislike litigation, but that they dislike having to compensate tort victims.

The American tort system is an easy target for criticism because its costs are so visible; newspaper reports publicize large damage awards to plaintiffs, and explain that their lawyers will receive one-third of those awards.[95] Opponents of our tort system seize on such reports to support their view that the system requires major reform. Neither the headlines nor the tort reformers mention, though, that it is expensive to compensate injury victims in Europe too, but that the costs of compensation are less visible there than here because they are addressed through tough regulations on businesses, national health insurance, and generous social security disability benefits, all of which American businesses oppose.[96] Indeed, the surest way to reduce tort litigation in America and the attorneys' fees that accompany it would be for Congress to enact a national health insurance program that would cover all of a tort victim's medical and hospital expenses. Ironically, the same businesspeople and politicians who call for tort reform vehemently oppose national health insurance. Absent national health insurance, victims of personal injuries must look to the tort system to compensate them for expenses that their insurance policies do not cover.

The legal profession, through bar association-sponsored public-education programs, must explain to Americans that the tort system is the product of their values, and that they have the power to change it, provided that they can make the value shift necessary to that change. Otherwise, they will have to be satisfied with the existing system, which is risky, slow, and expensive. The legal profession should also inform Americans that our tort system has one advantage over the European method of compensating injury victims, namely, the capacity to both deter defendants from future misconduct and to compensate plaintiffs for their injuries.[97] American juries can award an injured plaintiff not only **compensatory damages** that repay her for the costs of her injuries, but also **punitive damages**, which are designed to deter the defendant from committing future torts.[98] If government-financed benefits replaced the tort system as the primary means of compensating injury victims, government would have to devise an alternative to punitive damages in order to induce businesses to provide safe products and services.

The legal profession should provide the information necessary to enable Americans to make an informed choice about how best to compensate injury victims. Perhaps it would enhance its public image in the process.

CONCLUSION

Law is everywhere in modern America. Americans use law and courts to resolve disputes that are large and small, public and private. The legal profession shapes relations between individuals and institutions in this country today, as it has for more than 200 years.

There have been enormous changes in the legal profession since 1789. During the nineteenth century, law practice emphasized courtroom advocacy by solo practitioners, but by the end of the century it emphasized the counseling of corporate clients by lawyers who practiced in firms. During the twentieth century, law practice became more diversified, and the legal profession became more diverse, as minorities and women entered its ranks in unprecedented numbers.

Americans use litigation to achieve ends that other countries achieve by administrative means, which has conferred a lofty status on American lawyers. Despite that status, the legal profession faces formidable challenges as the twenty-first century dawns. America rations justice based on one's ability to afford legal counsel. Many legal employers impose excessive human costs on their lawyers, especially on women and minorities. Americans think that our system for compensating injury victims rewards undeserving plaintiffs and greedy lawyers, and hurts America's economic competitiveness.

Only time will tell if the legal profession can meet these challenges. If it can, it is likely to improve both the quality of American justice and its own public image. One source of public dissatisfaction with lawyers is their solicitation of potential personal-injury clients. The case reprinted below addresses that issue. After reading the case, identify the competing values involved, and try to determine whether the decision struck a proper balance between them.

Epilogue: Client Solicitation and Free Speech

Florida Bar v. Went For It, Inc.
115 S. Ct. 2371 (1995)

JUSTICE O'CONNOR delivered the opinion of the Court.

Rules of the Florida Bar prohibit personal injury lawyers from sending targeted direct-mail solicitations to victims and their relatives for 30 days following an accident or disaster. This case asks us to consider whether such rules violate the First and Fourteenth Amendments of the Constitution. We hold that in the circumstances presented here, they do not.

I

[Editor's Note: Two rules of the Florida Bar were at issue in this case. Rule 4.7–4(b)(1) prohibited a lawyer from sending a letter to an accident victim or to a relative of an accident victim, within 30 days of the accident, that offered to represent the victim or the relative in a personal injury case arising out of the accident. Rule 4.7–8(a) prohibited a lawyer from accepting a referral of work from a lawyer referral service that mailed such solicitations within 30 days of an accident.] Together, these rules create a brief 30-day blackout period after an accident during which lawyers may not, directly or indirectly, single out accident victims or their relatives in order to solicit their business.

… Went For It, Inc. [a lawyer referral service] filed this action … in the U.S. District Court for the Middle District of Florida challenging Rules 4.7–4(b)(1) and 4.7–8 as violative of the First and Fourteenth Amendments to the Constitution. [Editor's Note: The district court agreed with Went For It, Inc., and the Eleventh Circuit Court of Appeals affirmed that decision; the Florida Bar appealed, and the Supreme Court granted cert.]

II

It is now well established that lawyer advertising is commercial speech and, as such, is accorded a measure of First Amendment protection. Such First Amendment protection, of course, is not absolute. We have always been careful to distinguish commercial speech from speech at the First Amendment's core. Commercial speech enjoys a limited measure of protection, commensurate with its subordinate position in the scale of First Amendment values, and is subject to modes of regulation that might be impermissible in the realm of noncommercial expression.

Mindful of these concerns, we engage in "intermediate" scrutiny of restrictions on commercial speech, analyzing them under the framework set forth in *Central Hudson Gas & Electric Corp. v. Public Service Commission of N.Y.*, 447 U.S. 557 (1980). Under *Central Hudson*, the government may freely regulate commercial speech that concerns unlawful activity or is misleading. Commercial speech that falls into neither of those categories, like the advertising at issue here, may be regulated if the government satisfies a test consisting of three related prongs: first, the government must assert a substantial interest in support of its regulation; second, the government must demonstrate that the restriction on commercial speech directly and materially advances that interest; and third, the regulation must be narrowly drawn.

The Florida Bar asserts that it has a substantial interest in protecting the privacy and tranquility of personal injury victims and their loved ones against intrusive, unsolicited contact by lawyers. The regulation, then, is an effort to protect the flagging reputations of Florida lawyers by preventing them from engaging in conduct that, the Bar maintains, is universally regarded as deplorable and beneath common decency because of its intrusion upon the special vulnerability and private grief of victims or their families.

We have little trouble crediting the Bar's interest as substantial. On various occasions we have accepted the proposition that States have a compelling interest in the practice of professions within their boundaries, and ... as part of their power to protect the public health, safety, and other valid interests they have broad power to establish standards for licensing practitioners and regulating the practice of professions. Our precedents also leave no room for doubt that the protection of potential clients' privacy is a substantial state interest. In other contexts, we have consistently recognized that the State's interest in protecting the well-being, tranquility, and privacy of the home is certainly of the highest order in a free and civilized society.

Under *Central Hudson's* second prong, the State must demonstrate that the challenged regulation advances the Government's interest in a direct and material way. The Florida Bar submitted a 106-page summary of its 2-year study of lawyer advertising and solicitation to the District Court. That summary contains data— both statistical and anecdotal—supporting the Bar's contentions that the Florida public views direct-mail solicitations in the immediate wake of accidents as an intrusion on privacy that reflects poorly upon the profession. Fifty-four percent of the general population surveyed said that contacting persons concerning accidents or similar events is a violation of privacy. The study summary also includes page upon page of excerpts from complaints of direct-mail recipients. In light of this showing,... we conclude that the Bar has satisfied the second prong of the *Central Hudson* test.

Passing to *Central Hudson's* third prong, we examine the relationship between the Florida Bar's interests and the means chosen to serve them. The Bar's rule is reasonably well-tailored to its stated objective of eliminating targeted mailings whose type and timing are a source of distress to Floridians, distress that has caused many of them to lose respect for the legal profession. Our lawyer advertising cases have afforded lawyers a great deal of leeway to devise innovative ways to attract new business. Florida permits lawyers to advertise on prime-time television and radio as well as in newspapers and other media. They may rent space on billboards. They may send untargeted letters to the general population, or to discrete populations thereof. There are, of course, pages upon pages devoted to lawyers in the Yellow Pages of Florida telephone directories. These listings are organized alphabetically and by area of specialty. In fact, the record contains considerable empirical survey information suggesting that Floridians have little difficulty finding lawyers when they need one. Finding no basis to question the commonsense conclusion that the many alternative channels for communicating necessary information about attorneys are sufficient, we see no defect in Florida's regulation.

III

We believe that the Florida Bar's 30-day restriction on targeted direct-mail solicitation of accident victims and their relatives withstands scrutiny under the three-part Central Hudson test that we have devised for this context.

The judgment of the Court of Appeals, accordingly, is *reversed*.

JUSTICE KENNEDY with whom **JUSTICES STEVENS, SOUTER**, and **GINSBURG** join, dissenting.

Attorneys who communicate their willingness to assist potential clients are engaged in speech protected by the First and Fourteenth Amendments. The Court today undercuts this guarantee ... and unsettles leading First Amendment precedents, at the expense of those victims most in need of legal assistance.

I

... [T]he first of the *Central Hudson* factors to be considered is whether the interest the State pursues in enacting the speech restriction is a substantial one. The State says two different interests meet this standard. The first is the interest in protecting the personal privacy and tranquility of the victim and his or her family.

As [the Court] sees the matter, the substantial concern is that victims or their families will be offended by receiving a solicitation during their grief and trauma. But we do not allow restrictions on speech to be justified on the ground that the expression might offend the listener. And in *Zauderer v. Office of Disciplinary Counsel of Supreme Court of Ohio*, 471 U.S. 626 (1985), where we struck down a ban on attorney advertising, we held that the mere possibility that some members of the population might find advertising ... offensive cannot justify suppressing it.

We have applied this principle to direct mail cases as well as with respect to general advertising, noting that the right to use the mails is protected by the First Amendment. It is only where an audience is captive that we will assure its protection from some offensive speech. The occupants of a household receiving mailings are not a captive audience, and the asserted interest in preventing their offense should be no more controlling here than in our prior cases. All the recipients of objectional mailings need do is take the short, though regular, journey from mail box to trash can.

[The second interest cited by the State and the Court majority is] protecting the reputation and dignity of the legal profession. The fact is, however, that direct solicitation may serve vital purposes and promote the administration of justice, and to the extent the bar seeks to protect lawyers' reputations by preventing them from engaging in speech some deem offensive, the State is doing nothing more than manipulating the public's opinion by suppressing speech that informs us how the legal system works. This … is censorship pure and simple; and censorship is antithetical to the first principles of free expression.

II

Even were the interests asserted substantial, the regulation here fails the second part of the *Central Hudson* test, which requires that the dangers the State seeks to eliminate be real and that a speech restriction or ban advance that asserted State interest in a direct and material way. Here, what the State has offered falls well short of demonstrating that the harms it is trying to redress are real, let alone that the regulation directly and materially advances the State's interests. The most generous reading of [the 106 pages of documentary evidence submitted by the State] permits identification of 34 pages on which direct mail solicitation is arguably discussed. Of these, only two are even a synopsis of a study of the attitudes of Floridians towards such solicitations. Our cases require something more than a few pages of self-serving and unsupported statements by the State to demonstrate that a regulation directly and materially advances the elimination of a real harm when the State seeks to suppress truthful and non-deceptive speech.

III

The insufficiency of the regulation to advance the State's interest is reinforced by the third inquiry necessary in this analysis…. [T]he relationship between the Bar's interests and the means chosen to serve them is not a reasonable fit. The Bar's rule creates a flat ban that prohibits far more speech than necessary to serve the purported state interest. Even assuming that interest were legitimate, there is a wild disproportion between the harm supposed and the speech ban enforced.

To begin with, the ban applies with respect to all accidental injuries, whatever their gravity.

With regard to lesser injuries, there is little chance that for any period, much less 30 days, the victims will become distraught upon hearing from an attorney. It is at this precise time that sound legal advice may be necessary and most urgent.

Even as to more serious injuries, the State's argument fails, since it must be conceded that prompt legal representation is essential where death or injury results from accidents. The accident victims who are prejudiced to vindicate the State's purported desire for more dignity in the legal profession will be the very persons who most need legal advice, for they are the victims who, because they lack education, linguistic ability, or familiarity with the legal system, are unable to seek out legal services.

Nothing in the record shows that these communications do not in the least serve the purpose of informing the prospective client that he or she has a number of different attorneys from whom to choose, so that the decision to select counsel, after an interview with one or more interested attorneys, can be deliberate and informed.

IV

There is no authority for the proposition that the Constitution permits the State to promote the public image of the legal profession by suppressing information about the profession's business aspects.

Today's opinion is a serious departure, not only from our prior decisions involving attorney advertising, but also from the principles that govern the transmission of commercial speech.... [U]nder the First Amendment the public, not the State, has the right and the power to decide what ideas and information are deserving of their adherence. By validating Florida's rule, today's majority is complicit in the Bar's censorship. For these reasons, I dissent from the opinion of the Court and from its judgment.

QUESTIONS FOR DISCUSSION

1. What do the two Florida Bar rules at issue in this case say?
2. What is Went For It, Inc., and on what constitutional ground does it challenge those rules?
3. What type of speech is lawyer advertising, and is it entitled to constitutional protection?
4. What must the government demonstrate in order to regulate speech such as lawyer advertising?
5. Does the Court majority conclude that the Florida Bar has demonstrated a substantial interest that justifies the challenged rules? If so, what is that interest?
6. Does the Court majority conclude that the challenged rules directly and materially advance that interest? Why or why not?
7. Does the Court majority conclude that the challenged rules are sufficiently narrow to accomplish their stated purpose without unduly restricting lawyer advertising? Why or why not?
8. Why do the dissenters conclude that the Florida Bar fails to demonstrate a substantial interest that justifies the challenged rules?
9. Why do the dissenters conclude that even if the Florida Bar had demonstrated a substantial interest, the challenged rules would not directly and materially advance that interest?
10. Why do the dissenters conclude that the challenged rules are not sufficiently narrow to accomplish their stated purpose without unduly restricting lawyer advertising?
11. What are the two competing values that underlie this case?
12. Whom do you think resolved the conflict between those values correctly, the majority or the dissenters? Why?

NOTES

1. Robert A. Kagan, "American Lawyers, Legal Culture, and Adversarial Legalism," in Lawrence M. Friedman and Harry N. Scheiber, *Legal Culture and the Legal Profession* (Boulder, Colo.: Westview Press, 1996), p. 12.
2. Reuters News Agency, "Ex-Cheerleader Sues on Back Pain," *Boston Sunday Globe*, November 9, 1997, p. A15.
3. Tom Kunz, "Word for Word: Girl Trouble—Sugar and Spite and a Legal Mess Not Nice," *The New York Times*, December 7, 1997, Section 4, p. 7.
4. Dan Billin, "It's Unconstitutional," *The Valley News*, December 18, 1997, p. A1.
5. Lawrence M. Friedman, *A History of American Law*, second edition (New York: Simon & Schuster, 1985), p. 101.
6. Kermit L. Hall, William M. Wiecek, and Paul Finkelman, *American Legal History: Cases and Materials* (New York: Oxford University Press, 1991), p. 305.
7. Friedman, *A History of American Law*, pp. 96–97.
8. *Id.*, p. 304.
9. *Id.*, p. 306.
10. *Id.*, p. 319.
11. *Id.*, p. 609
12. *Id.*, p. 612.
13. *Id.*, p. 615.
14. *Id.*, p. 617.
15. Wayne K. Hobson, "Symbol of the New Profession: Emergence of the Large Law Firm," in Gerard W. Gawalt, ed., *The New High Priests: Lawyers in Post-Civil War America* (Westport, Conn.: Greenwood Press, 1984), pp. 6–8.
16. Kermit L. Hall, *The Magic Mirror: Law in American History* (New York, N.Y.: Oxford University Press, 1989), p. 217.
17. *Id.*, pp. 217–218.
18. *Bradwell v. The State*, 83 U.S. (16 Wall) 130 (1873).
19. *Id.*, p. 141. Myra Bradwell was finally admitted to the practice of law in Illinois in 1890, after many years of distinguished service as the editor of a legal newspaper in Chicago.
20. Karen Berger Morello, *The Invisible Bar: The Woman Lawyer in America, 1638 to the Present* (New York: Random House, 1986), p. 38.
21. *Id.*, pp. 96–97.
22. *Id.*, p. 100.
23. Kenneth Jost, *The Supreme Court Yearbook, 1996–1997* (Washington, D.C.: CQPress, 1998), p. 307.
24. *Id.*, p. 316.
25. Morello, *The Invisible Bar*, p. 248.
26. Hall, *The Magic Mirror*, p. 219.
27. *Id.*, p. 155.
28. *Id.*, p. 162.
29. U.S. Bureau of the Census, *Statistical Abstract of the United States: 1997* (Washington, D.C.: U.S. Government Printing Office, 1997), p. 410.
30. *Id.*
31. Rick L. Morgan and Kurt Snyder, *Official American Bar Association Guide to Approved Law Schools, 1999 Edition* (New York, N.Y.: Macmillan, 1998), p. 458.

32. *Id.*, p. 48.

33. As of August 1998, there were twenty-nine law schools in the United States that lacked A.B.A. accreditation. Many states prohibit graduates of those law schools from taking their bar exams; often, graduates of the unapproved law schools can take only the bar exam of the state in which their law school is located.

34. American Bar Association and National Conference of Bar Examiners, *Comprehensive Guide to Bar Admission Requirements 1997–98* (Chicago: A.B.A. and N.C.B.E., 1997).

35. Chris Goodrich, *Anarchy and Elegance: Confessions of a Journalist at Yale Law School* (Boston: Little, Brown, 1991), pp. 32–33.

36. W. Scott Van Alstyne, Jr., Joseph R. Julin, and Larry D. Burnett, *The Goals and Missions of Law Schools* (New York: Peter Lang, 1990), pp. 119–126.

37. Karl E. Klare, "The Law School Curriculum in the 1980's: What's Left?" in Martin Lyon Levine, ed., *Legal Education* (New York: New York University Press, 1993), p. 392.

38. For a good discussion of the boot camp analogy, see Robert Granfield, *Making Elite Lawyers: Visions of Law at Harvard and Beyond* (New York: Routledge, 1992), p. 41.

39. *Id.*, p. 113.

40. *Id.*, pp. 113–114.

41. In 1998, the starting salaries for new associates at the top New York City law firms reached $101,000, a 16 percent increase from 1997. Law firms in other large cities usually do not match New York salaries, but the increase in New York is likely to raise starting salaries in other big cities too. Terry Carter, "Superstars or Falling Stars?," *American Bar Association Journal,* August 1998, p. 28.

42. Morgan and Snyder, *American Bar Association Guide to Approved Law Schools,* p. 457.

43. National Association for Law Placement, *Selected Class of 1997 Employment Report and Salary Findings* (Washington, D.C.: National Association for Law Placement, 1998), p. 1.

44. *Id.*

45. *Id.*

46. Only Indiana, Louisiana, and Washington State do not administer "the Multistate," as it is commonly known. The Indiana bar exam is comprised entirely of essay questions. A.B.A. and N.C.B.E., *Comprehensive Guide to Bar Admission Requirements,* pp. 28–29.

47. Theodore F.T. Plucknett, *A Concise History of the Common Law,* Fifth Edition (Boston: Little, Brown, 1956), p. 13.

48. Arthur R. Hogue, *Origins of the Common Law* (Hamden, Conn.: Archon Books, 1974), p. 179.

49. *Id.*, p. 190.

50. Brian L. Porto, *The Craft of Legal Reasoning* (Forth Worth, Tex.: Harcourt Brace College Publishers, 1998), pp. 100–101.

51. *Id.*, pp. 103–104.

52. Carrie Menkel-Meadow, "Portia Redux: Another Look at Gender, Feminism, and Legal Ethics," in Stephen Parker and Charles Sampford, eds., *Legal Ethics and Legal Practice: Contemporary Issues* (Oxford: Clarendon Press, 1995), p. 40. Carrie Menkel-Meadow is a professor of law at the University of California at Los Angeles (U.C.L.A.).

53. Indeed, the preamble to the American Bar Association's **Model Rules of Professional Conduct**, which govern lawyers' conduct in most states, says in part that "as advocate, a lawyer zealously asserts the client's position under the adversary system". A.B.A. Center for Professional Responsibility, A.B.A. *Compendium of Professional Responsibility Rules and Standards* (Chicago: American Bar Association, 1997), p. 13.

54. Gerard W. Gawalt, ed., *The New High Priests: Lawyers in Post-Civil War America* (Westport, Conn.: Greenwood Press, 1984), p. vii.
55. Lawrence M. Friedman, "Are We a Litigious People?," in Lawrence M. Friedman and Harry N. Scheiber, *Legal Culture and the Legal Profession* (Boulder, Colo.: Westview Press, 1996), pp. 65–67.
56. Robert Kagan, "American Lawyers, Legal Culture, and Adversarial Legalism," in Friedman and Scheiber, *Legal Culture and the Legal Profession*, p. 16.
57. John Heilemann, "The Legal Profession," *The Economist*, July 18, 1992, pp. 3–18.
58. *Id.*
59. Nina Burleigh, "The Man to See," *American Bar Association Journal*, September 1994, pp. 50–53.
60. Steven Keeva, "Northern Composure," *American Bar Association Journal*, October 1997, pp. 52–60.
61. Sol M. Linowitz, *The Betrayed Profession: Lawyering at the End of the Twentieth Century* (Baltimore: Johns Hopkins University Press, 1994), p. 189.
62. Mary Ann Glendon, *A Nation Under Lawyers: How the Crisis in the Legal Profession Is Transforming American Society* (New York: Farrar, Strauss and Giroux, 1994), p. 87.
63. *Id.*, p. 26.
64. *Id.*, p. 34.
65. *Id.*, p. 29.
66. Boston Bar Association, *Professional Fulfillment: Expectations, Reality and Recommendations for Change* (Boston, MA: Boston Bar Association, 1997), p. 5.
67. *Id.*, p. 10.
68. *Id.*, p. 3.
69. Carol Seron, "The Business of Practicing Law: The Work Lives of Solo and Small-Firm Attorneys," in Richard L. Abel, ed., *Lawyers: A Critical Reader* (New York: The New Press, 1997), p. 39.
70. Boston Bar Association, *Professional Fulfillment*, p. 12.
71. *Id.*
72. *Id.*, p. 15.
73. *Id.*, p. 16.
74. Lisa J. McIntyre, "The Public Defender: The Practice of Law in the Shadows of Repute," in Richard L. Abel, ed., *Lawyers: A Critical Reader* (New York: The New Press, 1997), p. 262.
75. *Id.*, p. 263.
76. *Id.*
77. David Barringer, "Downsized," *American Bar Association Journal*, July 1996, pp. 60–66.
78. *Phillips v. Washington Legal Foundation*, 118 S. Ct. 1925 (1998).
79. Linowitz, *The Betrayed Profession*, p. 222.
80. *Id.*, p. 150.
81. *Id.*, pp. 152–153.
82. *Id.*, p. 202.
83. *Id.*, p. 203.
84. *Id.*, p. 133.
85. *Id.*, p. 242.
86. *Id.*
87. *Id.*, p. 192.

88. Laura Gatland, "Dangerous Dedication," *American Bar Association Journal*, December 1997, pp. 28–30.

89. That is the question that federal district judge Julius Hoffman of Chicago asked Mary Ann Glendon, who is now a professor at Harvard Law School, when she argued a case in his courtroom in the early 1960s. Glendon, *A Nation Under Lawyers*, p. 61.

90. Boston Bar Association, *Professional Fulfillment*, p. 25.

91. *Id.*, p. 24.

92. *Id.*

93. David B. Wilkins and G. Mitu Gulati, "Why Are There So Few Black Lawyers in Corporate Law Firms? An Institutional Analysis," in Abel, ed., *Lawyers: A Critical Reader*, p. 102.

94. John Heilemann, "The Legal Profession."

95. It is customary in personal injury (i.e., tort) suits for the plaintiff's lawyer to receive a contingency fee. The lawyer receives a percentage (usually one-third) of any money **damages** that the jury awards to the plaintiff or of the amount for which the opposing parties settle the case. If, however, the plaintiff loses the case, the plaintiff owes the lawyer only the amount of the lawyer's expenses in the case. Thus, the lawyer's fee is *contingent* upon the plaintiff receiving damages for his injuries. A contingency fee is usually higher than the fee that the lawyer would receive if she billed the client hourly, because the lawyer takes the risk that her client will lose at trial and that she will receive no fee at all.

96. *Id.*, p. 13.

97. David Luban, "Speculating on Justice: The Ethics and Jurisprudence of Contingency Fees," in Stephen Parker and Charles Sampford, eds., *Legal Ethics and Legal Practice: Contemporary Issues* (Oxford: Oxford University Press, 1995), p. 97.

98. The business community wants Congress to put a cap (e.g., $250,000) on punitive damages in personal-injury lawsuits against businesses that arise out of injuries caused by defective products (**products liability** suits). To date, Congress has not complied with that wish. Nevertheless, since 1994, Congress has: (1) prohibited product liability suits involving airplanes that were more than eighteen years old; (2) made it harder for private investors to sue companies that fail to disclose certain information about their operations; and (3) protected volunteers, such as Little League coaches, from lawsuits by persons injured in activities that the volunteers supervise. T. R. Goldman, "Tort Reform: Back in Business?," *Legal Times*, June 15, 1998, p. 1. Moreover, nine states have enacted caps on noneconomic (including "pain and suffering" and punitive) damage awards in all personal-injury cases, and fifteen states have done so in medical malpractice cases. James Podgers, "Throwing Caps out of the Ring," *American Bar Association Journal*, August 1996, pp. 48–49.

Chapter 4

JUDICIAL SELECTION AND REMOVAL

LAW, POLITICS, AND JUDICIAL NOMINATIONS

Judicial nominations demonstrate that law and politics are closely related but are not identical. The politics of **judicial selection** are most evident in the states, where political parties nominate lawyers to run for elected judgeships. Politics are equally important but more subtle in the federal system because federal judges are appointed by the President rather than elected. Recently, the politics of judicial selection have become more visible than ever before, in the states and in the federal system, as politicians, organized groups, and the public have shown a heightened interest in judicial nominees. The higher the court, the greater is the interest, especially in controversial nominees. President Bush's 1991 nomination of Clarence Thomas and President Reagan's 1987 nomination of Robert Bork to the Supreme Court (see Chapter 1) are the most prominent examples of that interest.

Americans' interest in judicial nominees reflects their growing awareness that courts, especially appellate courts, make important public policy decisions and that judges' values and personal politics affect the ways in which they resolve cases. It can make an enormous difference, therefore, whom a President or a governor appoints to the bench.

For example, after California voters rejected Chief Justice Bird and Justices Reynoso and Grodin in 1986 (see Chapter 1), Governor George Deukmejian appointed to the state supreme court judges who shared his support for capital punishment. A great change resulted. From 1977 until 1986, the California Supreme Court affirmed only four of the eighty-six death sentences (6 percent) it reviewed; between 1986 and 1990, though, it affirmed eighty-four of the 109 death sentences (77 percent) it reviewed.[1] That change reflected the crime-weariness of California voters, who, by 1986, wanted their highest court to protect victims, not criminals.

Nevertheless, Americans expect more from judges than just political account-ability. They expect integrity, competence, and appropriate professional experi-ence too. That is why the public generally and lawyers particularly protested President Richard Nixon's nomination of Judge G. Harrold Carswell of Florida to the Supreme Court in 1970. Judge Carswell had a closet full of skeletons. In 1948, when he ran for a seat in the Georgia legislature, he professed his "vigorous belief in the principles of white supremacy"; in 1953, while practicing law in Tallahas-see, Florida, he drafted incorporation papers for a whites-only sports-booster club for Florida State University; in 1956, while serving as the **U.S. Attorney** for northern Florida, the federal government's chief law-enforcement officer there, he drafted papers that transformed a public golf course into a private club in order to evade a Supreme Court decision that outlawed racial segregation in public facil-ities.[2] Civil rights lawyers who had appeared in his court told the Senate Judiciary Committee that Judge Carswell was openly hostile to them and to their black clients, and research revealed that the Court of Appeals for the Fifth Circuit (which then included Florida) had reversed nearly 60 percent of his decisions, including 17 civil rights decisions.[3]

Leaders of the legal profession and many ordinary citizens spoke out against the Carswell nomination. Louis H. Pollak, Dean of the Yale Law School, observed that Carswell presented "more slender credentials than any Supreme Court nom-inee put forth in this century."[4] Lawyers across America signed letters that opposed Carswell on the ground that his appointment would tarnish the integrity of the federal judiciary. More than 500 professionals from ten departments of the federal government released a petition that asked the Senate to reject Carswell because of his "utter lack of qualifications as a jurist."[5] Senators eventually reached the same conclusion; on April 9, 1970, they rejected the Carswell nomination by a vote of 51 to 45.[6]

Thus, both law and politics influence judicial selection. Legislators and the public expect governors and presidents to nominate their political allies for judge-ships, but they also expect the nominees to be competent, ethical lawyers who reject extreme views. There is an unresolved tension in judicial selection between independence (law) and accountability (politics). Americans want judges to be impartial, to resist partisan political influences, and to decide cases on the basis of the law and the facts, but they also want judges to reflect mainstream values. The next section will show the different ways in which the states have sought to balance independence and accountability in selecting their judges.

JUDICIAL SELECTION IN THE STATES

Introduction

The states use four methods of judicial selection, including election, appointment, appointment-plus-election, and legislative selection. Some states use one method to choose both trial and appellate judges, while other states use one method to choose trial judges and another to choose appellate judges. Those choices reflect the states' respective judgements about the relative importance of independence and accountability among judges.

Election

Most states require at least some of their judges to win election to the bench. Nineteen states choose some or all of their trial judges in **partisan** elections.[7] Ten states choose some or all of their appellate judges in partisan elections.[8] Eighteen states choose some or all of their trial judges in **nonpartisan** elections,[9] and thirteen states choose some or all of their appellate judges in nonpartisan elections.[10] In partisan elections, the candidates' names and political party affiliations appear on the ballot, whereas in nonpartisan elections, only their names appear on the ballot.

Supporters of judicial elections argue that because judges make important public policy decisions that can affect life, liberty, and property, they should be accountable to the public by means of regular elections.[11] Opponents of judicial elections believe that it is more important that judges decide cases according to their interpretations of the law than that the public have regular opportunities to judge their performances in office. The election opponents argue that elections encourage judges to decide cases in conformity with public passions rather than with their reading of the law.

It is impossible to resolve that debate here. It is worthwhile, though, to examine the evidence for and against judicial elections so that you can decide for yourself which side has the stronger argument. Ironically, both sides neglect an important aspect of judicial selection in the "election" states, which is that many of the judges in those states ascend to the bench not by election, but by appointment by the governor to fill the unexpired terms of judges who retire before their terms of office end. In California, for example, despite a nonpartisan election system, almost 90 percent of trial judges receive appointments by the governor to fill the unexpired terms of their predecessors.

That is because judges prefer to retire when a governor of their political party is in office, in order to give another lawyer of their political party a chance to be appointed to the bench. When the unexpired term ends, the appointee runs unopposed in a **retention election**. The voters' choice in a retention election is to retain the judge or to force her off the bench; the appointee is likely to be retained because she is the incumbent, and voters almost always retain incumbent judges. As a result, judges have more independence in some "election" states than the opponents of judicial elections recognize; judges are also less accountable to the voters in those states than supporters of judicial elections would like.

Another barrier to political accountability in judicial elections is the American Bar Association's **Model Code of Judicial Conduct**, which prohibits judicial candidates from making campaign promises other than that they will faithfully and impartially carry out the duties of the office, and from taking positions on cases or issues that are likely to reach their courts.[12] Consequently, voters sometimes have so little information that their choices in judicial elections reflect a candidate's gender, race, ethnicity, or political party affiliation (partisan elections only) rather than his professional qualifications or issue positions. That is especially likely in metropolitan areas, where candidates for numerous judgeships are on the ballot and voters are hard-pressed to draw meaningful distinctions between them. Thus, an incumbent judge is likely to be reelected, if for no other reason than the voters' familiarity with her name, unless a scandal or a highly unpopular decision erases that advantage.

That does not mean that all judicial elections are dull, one-sided affairs, or that they necessarily fail to make judges accountable to the voters. Several factors can turn judicial elections into close contests, including the presence of presidential candidates on the ballot, a high state murder rate, generally close competition between the two major political parties in a state, the absence of incumbent judges on the ballot, and a shift in the public's views (e.g., on the death penalty or the insanity defense) in the years since a judge went on the bench.[13] In other words, judicial elections are not immune to the political forces at work nationally or statewide; voters can use judicial elections to ensure political accountability, just as they can use gubernatorial or congressional elections for that purpose.

For example, a study of elected state supreme court justices in Louisiana, North Carolina, Kentucky, and Texas found that justices who generally voted *for* the defendant's position in criminal cases, a minority view on all four courts, nevertheless voted *against* the defendant's position in death penalty cases (a majority view on each court): (1) during the last two years of their terms; (2) if they had run for reelection before; and (3) if they received a lower percentage of the vote in their previous reelection bid than they had received in an earlier election.[14]Justices whom one would have expected to vote against imposing a death sentence in most cases nevertheless voted for imposing it, presumably to satisfy the pro-death-penalty voting majorities in their states and keep their jobs. Thus, judicial elections appear to make state supreme court justices accountable to the voters in Louisiana, North Carolina, Kentucky, and Texas in death-penalty cases.

The voters pay a price for that accountability, though. The price is the appearance, and sometimes the reality, of corruption that results when judicial candidates receive financial contributions for their campaigns from persons who later appear in court before them as lawyers and as parties to litigation. Most states permit judges to accept campaign contributions from lawyers without requiring the judges to disqualify themselves from cases in which lawyers who contributed to their campaigns participate. Those conditions enabled lawyers, between 1989 and 1994, to contribute a total of $5.3 million, or more than $1 million per year, to the campaign funds of the members of the supreme courts of Texas and Alabama.[15] Indeed, lawyers for Texaco and Pennzoil, during a multi-billion-dollar lawsuit between those two companies, donated a total of almost $400,000 ($315,000 by lawyers for Texaco and $72,000 by lawyers for Pennzoil) to the campaign funds of the justices of the Texas Supreme Court when the case was there on appeal.[16]

Such contributions create ethical dilemmas for judges, from whom parties to litigation expect fairness, impartiality, and objectivity. Lawyers' contributions to judicial campaigns are potentially corrosive to public confidence in the judiciary. They are also corrosive to the judiciary itself when they deter talented lawyers from pursuing elected judgeships because of the ethical dilemmas associated with accepting campaign contributions from fellow lawyers.[17]

Several states and localities have adopted reform measures to remedy the appearance of corruption that taints judicial elections. The Philadelphia Bar Association raises campaign funds, primarily from lawyers, and distributes an equal amount to each judicial candidate in that city without informing the candidates who contributed the money. That arrangement reduces the potential that a judge will issue a decision that rewards a political supporter for a past contribution, and it liberates judicial candidates from having to raise campaign funds.[18] Oregon prohibits judicial candidates from personally requesting campaign contributions; instead, judicial candidates who wish to raise campaign funds must establish campaign committees that are authorized to request contributions on behalf of their respective candidates.[19] Other states have limited spending and/or campaign contributions in judicial elections. In 1995, the Texas legislature placed caps on contributions in judicial elections, which range from $5,000 by an individual donor to $30,000 by a law firm for a candidate in a statewide election.[20] In 1996, the Ohio Supreme Court adopted a rule that imposed a mandatory $75,000 spending limit in trial-court elections.[21] These measures seek to reform but not to replace judicial elections. They reflect the disagreement that exists between opponents and supporters of judicial elections, and they represent a compromise position: namely, retain judicial elections, but regulate them more vigorously in the future than they have been regulated in the past.

Appointment

In eight states, the governor appoints some or all appellate judges.[22] The governor appoints some or all trial judges in fifteen states.[23] Appointed judges usually serve terms of between four and twelve years in office, after which they are eligible for reappointment; only Massachusetts and New Hampshire give judges lifetime appointments.[24] Court reformers have long argued that states should substitute appointment for partisan elections as a means of choosing judges, in order to reduce the importance of politics and to increase the importance of professional competence in the judicial selection process. Legislators in the partisan-election states have largely ignored the court reformers, though, because most legislators want to preserve the influence that political parties and voters have over judicial selection in those states.

Supporters of judicial elections argue, correctly, that the appointment of judges does not remove political considerations from the judicial selection process. Governors are political people, and they typically appoint judges who share their political party affiliations and their views about major legal issues, especially issues of criminal justice. Therefore, it would be naive to think that political factors are less influential in judicial selection in states that appoint judges than in states that elect judges. That is true even in states that require the governor to select a nominee from a list of candidates compiled by a judicial nominating commission.

For example, in November 1996, Governor Howard Dean of Vermont, a moderate Democrat, received from his state's **Judicial Nominating Board** a list of candidates whom the board considered to be qualified to succeed Frederic Allen, the retiring Chief Justice of the Vermont Supreme Court. Dean rejected the list because it excluded one of his cabinet secretaries, whom he wished to appoint, and because it included the names of only two people, both of whom were liberal justices whom the moderate governor did not wish to elevate to chief justice.[25] The board had refused to consider applicants who lacked judicial experience, a qualification that was important to board members but not to the governor. Governor Dean's action forced the board to call for new applications, one of which came from Attorney General Jeffrey Amestoy, a moderate Republican whom Vermonters had elected to that post six times, which caused reporters to dub him the "Eternal General." Dean liked Amestoy's centrist record, which was pro-consumer and tough on crime; Dean therefore crossed party lines in January 1997 and appointed the popular attorney general to the chief justiceship.[26]

Howard Dean's appointment of Jeffrey Amestoy was no less "political" than the election of a chief justice in another state. It was untainted by campaign contributions, though, which is a major advantage of appointment. Chief Justice Amestoy will not feel constrained in his decision making by the need to please past campaign contributors in order to receive their support in a reelection bid several years from now. He will have to satisfy the Vermont Senate in 2003 that he is worthy of reappointment for another six-year term, which is designed to make him politically accountable, but he will not face the ethical dilemma that results when judges accept campaign contributions from lawyers and litigants.

Another benefit of appointment is that it can hasten the achievement of a demographically diverse state judiciary. For example, in California, where the governor appoints new judges to fill unexpired terms, Governor Jerry Brown greatly diversified that state's judiciary between 1975 and 1981. Brown appointed 86 African-Americans, 73 Hispanics, 33 Asians, and 132 women to the California courts; indeed, 40 percent of Brown's appointees were minorities and women. Among those appointees were the first woman, the first African-American, and the first Hispanic to sit on the California Supreme Court.[27]

Despite such advantages, there is no movement among states today to replace election with appointment as their principal means of judicial selection. Some states, though, have combined election and appointment in order to balance political accountability and judicial independence.

Appointment-and-Election

The combined appointive-elective mechanism is known as the **Missouri Plan** because it originated in Missouri in 1940, although some lawyers and scholars refer to it as the **Merit Plan**.[28] Sixteen states choose their appellate court judges by this method,[29] and ten states use it to choose their trial court judges.[30] In Missouri Plan states, judicial nominating commissions, which consist of judges, lawyers, and ordinary citizens, screen applicants for judicial vacancies and recommend several qualified candidates to the governor, who then appoints one of those candidates. After the appointee serves for a designated period of time, she faces the voters in a **retention election** in which a ballot question asks the voters: "Shall Judge _____ be retained as a judge of the _____ court?" Voters cast their votes by indicating "Yes" or "No"; therefore, the judge runs against her record, but not against another candidate.

In Wyoming, the judicial nominating commission is comprised of three lawyers elected by the members of the bar, three non-lawyers appointed by the governor, and the chief justice of the state supreme court, who serves as chair.[31] The commission nominates three candidates for each vacancy and forwards the nominees' names and files to the governor. The commission must submit its list of nominees to the governor within sixty days of the announcement of the vacancy. The governor has thirty days from receipt of the list to appoint one of the candidates. The governor must select a name from the commission's list; the governor cannot add names to the list nor ask the commission to nominate other persons. If the governor fails or refuses to fill the vacancy, the chief justice will do so by choosing one of the names on the commission's list.[32] Whether the governor or the chief justice fills the vacancy, the new judge will serve for one year, after which he will face the voters in a retention election during the next general election. If retained, the judge will then serve his term of years, at the end of which he will face another retention election.[33]

The vast majority of judges in Missouri Plan states enjoy both job security and independence from politics. They usually do not have to worry about the ethics of hearing a case in which a campaign contributor is counsel for one of the parties, because their retention elections typically attract neither public attention nor campaign contributions. Neither do they have to worry about being defeated at the polls, as voters reject judges in only about 1 percent of retention elections nationwide in any given election year. Voters also customarily retain sitting judges by large margins. A study of 645 retention elections found that the average vote in favor of retention was 73.6 percent.[34] The rare rejections of sitting judges that occur in retention elections usually result from a public controversy that foreshadows the retention vote. A public clamor for enforcement of the death penalty in California preceded the defeats of Justices Bird, Grodin, and Reynoso in 1986. Controversy also preceded the defeat in 1984 of a Wyoming trial court judge who had suspended all but sixty-one days of the sentence of a convicted child molester, yet had sentenced a teenage boy to 5–15 years in prison for killing his abusive father.[35]

The infrequency of defeats in retention elections does not mean that the Missouri Plan always balances judicial independence and political accountability properly, or that judges who have lost their seats necessarily got what they deserved. The Missouri Plan is not perfect. Indeed, the Missouri Plan's major weakness is retention elections, which sometimes sacrifice judicial independence on the altar of political accountability. They are susceptible to the influence of organizations that are committed to a particular position on a particular political issue, such as gun control, the death penalty, or abortion. Such groups, especially when they are well funded, can turn a retention election into a referendum on a judge's vote in *one case*.

Recall from Chapter 1 that pro-death penalty forces and the Tennessee Republican Party engineered the defeat of Justice Penny White of the Tennessee Supreme Court in 1996 because she voted to grant a new death-sentencing hearing for a convicted murderer.[36] Justice White's critics were well funded, and they produced television commercials critical of her, to which there was no effective response because the Code of Judicial Conduct prohibited Justice White from discussing her decisions in public. The critics ignored her overall performance, and even her reasoning in the crucial case, focusing instead on the result of that reasoning. They also ignored the possibility that at the court-ordered rehearing, prosecutors would prove that the murder in question was "heinous, atrocious or cruel," which would reinstate the death sentence.[37] The critics prevailed, in part because it was much easier, in thirty-second television commercials, to convince Tennesseans to support the death penalty than to convince them of the value of judicial independence.

Legislative Selection

The least commonly used method of choosing judges in the states is **legislative selection**, which exists today only in Connecticut, South Carolina, and Virginia. In Connecticut, the legislature *appoints* both appellate and trial judges from nominations that the governor submits to the legislature after the governor considers a list of candidates compiled by the **Judicial Selection Commission**. When judges' eight-year terms are complete, the legislature has the power to reappoint them, subject to the recommendations of the **Judicial Review Council**.[38] In Virginia, the legislature also appoints and reappoints both appellate and trial judges. In South Carolina, though, the legislature *elects* both appellate and trial judges, and can reelect them when their terms end.[39]

The selection of judges by legislators honors judicial independence by not requiring judges to face the voters in periodic elections. It also respects political accountability by requiring judges to obtain the support of legislators in order to retain their seats on the bench. Reappointment or reelection by the legislature works like retention elections do in Missouri Plan states; absent major controversy, legislators regularly reappoint or reelect judges when their terms end.

Nevertheless, legislative selection is out of favor in modern America because it offers neither the direct political accountability of judicial elections nor the emphasis on professional qualifications of the Missouri Plan. Bar associations and court reformers dislike the tendency of legislators to appoint to the bench retired or defeated legislators, even when more qualified candidates are available. Thus, legislative selection seems not to be "political" enough for advocates of political accountability, and to be too political for proponents of professionalism and judicial independence. Consequently, it is likely to remain confined to a few states.

Conclusion

The presence of four different methods of judicial selection (five if you count partisan and nonpartisan elections separately) in the states underscores the disagreement among politicians, legal professionals, and voters about which method is best. Disagreement persists partly because no single method seems to be more likely than the others to recruit to the bench the best legal talent that a state has to offer. Professor Sheldon Goldman, a scholar of judicial selection, observed in 1982 that:

> As it stands now, there is no basis for concluding that any one selection system is clearly superior to any other in producing candidates with the qualities that make for good judges or persons whose on-the-bench performance is adjudged to be of high caliber.[40]

Professor Goldman's observation is as true today as it was in 1982.

That does not mean that it is irrelevant which method of judicial selection a state uses. There is some evidence that partisan, nonpartisan, and retention elections can encourage judges to accommodate voters' views on high-profile issues such as the death penalty. Recall that an approaching retention election and a disappointing showing in the previous retention election influenced usually pro-defendant judges to uphold death sentences in states where the voters strongly supported the death penalty.[41] Moreover, the various judicial selection mechanisms do not balance judicial independence and political accountability in the same way. Appointment, especially if accompanied by lengthy terms in office, favors judicial independence, and election, especially if accompanied by shorter terms in office, favors political accountability. A state's preference for one method over another reflects a decision about the relative importance of those two values. Figure 4.1 depicts the various methods that states use to select judges for their trial courts. Figure 4.2 depicts the various methods that states use to select judges for their appellate courts.

Partisan Election	Nonpartisan Election
Alabama	Arkansas
Arizona	California
Arkansas	Florida
Georgia	Georgia
Illinois	Idaho
Indiana	Kentucky
Maine (Probate only)	Louisiana
Connecticut (Probate only)	Michigan
Kansas	Minnesota
Missouri	Montana
Mississippi	Nevada
New Mexico	North Dakota
New York	Ohio
North Carolina	Oklahoma
Ohio	Oregon
Pennsylvania	South Dakota
South Carolina	Washington
Tennessee	Wisconsin
Texas	Utah (Part of Justice Court only)
Utah (Part of Justice Court only)	Wyoming (Justices of the Peace only)
Vermont (Probate only)	
West Virginia	

Appointment	Missouri Plan	Legislative Selection
Arizona	Alaska	Connecticut
Delaware	Colorado	South Carolina
Hawaii	Idaho	Virginia
Maine	Iowa	
Maryland	Kansas	
Massachusetts	Missouri	
Montana (Worker's Compensation Court only)	Nebraska	
Nebraska	Pennsylvania	
New Hampshire	Utah	
New Jersey	Wyoming	
New York		
Oklahoma (Worker's Compensation Court only)		
Rhode Island		
South Carolina (Probate and Magistrate's Courts only)		
Vermont		

FIGURE 4.1 Selection Methods for State Trial Judges*
*Note: Some states use more than one method to select trial judges.
Source: David B. Rottman et al., State Court Organization, 1993 (Washington, D.C.: U.S. Department of Justice., Bureau of Justice Statistics, 1995).

Partisan Election	Nonpartisan Election
Alabama	Georgia
Arkansas	Idaho
Illinois	Kentucky
Mississippi	Louisiana
New Mexico	Michigan
North Carolina	Minnesota
Pennsylvania	Montana
Tennessee (Supreme Court only)	Nevada
Texas	North Dakota
West Virginia	Ohio
	Oregon
	Washington
	Wisconsin

Appointment	Missouri Plan	Legislative Selection
Delaware	Alaska	Connecticut
Hawaii	Arizona	South Carolina
Maine	California	Virginia
Massachusetts	Colorado	
New Hampshire	Florida	
New Jersey	Indiana	
New York	Idaho	
Vermont	Iowa	
	Kansas	
	Missouri	
	Nebraska	
	Oklahoma	
	Rhode Island	
	South Dakota	
	Tennessee (Court of Appeals and Court of Criminal Appeals only)	
	Utah	
	Wyoming	

FIGURE 4.2 Selection Methods for State Appellate Judges

Source: David B. Rottman et al., *State Court Organization, 1993* (Washington, D.C.: U.S. Department of Justice, Bureau of Justice Statistics, 1995).

DISCIPLINE AND REMOVAL OF STATE JUDGES

Just as the states use different methods to select judges, they also use different methods to discipline or remove judges.

Forty-six states provide for the **impeachment** of state judges for "treason, bribery, or other high crimes and misdemeanors," for "malfeasance or misfeasance in the conduct of official duties," for "willful neglect of duty or corruption in office," for "any offense involving moral turpitude," or for the "commission of a felony."[42] If the lower house of the state legislature, usually known as the **House** of **Representatives**, votes to impeach a judge, that is the equivalent of an **indictment** in a criminal court, which means that there is sufficient evidence of wrongdoing to justify holding a trial. The upper house of the state legislature, usually known as the **Senate**, then conducts a trial; if, after the trial, two-thirds of the senators vote to remove the judge, the judge is removed from office and cannot hold any public office in the state. The judge would also be subject to prosecution in a state criminal court. States rarely use impeachment to remove judges from office because most judicial misconduct does not rise to the level of an impeachable offense, and because impeachment is a divisive and time-consuming process that most state legislators dread.

Another rarely used method of removal is **legislative address**, which exists in twelve states in one form or another. In nine states, the governor can remove a judge from office if both houses of the state legislature pass a resolution that requests the governor to remove the judge; four states require a two-thirds vote of each house before the governor can act.[43] In New York, the governor's recommendation, followed by a two-thirds vote of the Senate, can remove a judge, and in Ohio and Tennessee, a resolution passed by both houses of the state legislature can do so.[44]

Five states also remove judges by means of **recall elections**, in which a ballot question asks the voters whether a particular judge should be removed from office. The question can only qualify for the ballot if a sufficient number of voters signs a petition to place it on the ballot. At the next general election, if a majority of voters answers that ballot question in the affirmative, the judge is removed. In 1977, voters recalled a Wisconsin trial judge named Archie Simonson, who sentenced two teenage boys who had sexually assaulted a teenage girl to a year at home under court supervision instead of to confinement in a residential treatment center, which the prosecutor had requested. Judge Simonson pronounced from the bench his view that the sexual permissiveness of the times and provocative women's clothing had encouraged the assault.[45]

States rarely use impeachment, legislative address, or recall elections to remove judges today. Instead, every state has a formal administrative process for investigating complaints of misconduct made against judges, which can lead to removal, involuntary retirement, suspension, or reprimand.[46] States usually define misconduct according to the Model Code of Judicial Conduct, which they often supplement with specific statutes and/or constitutional provisions.[47] The process begins with the filing of a complaint against a judge by another judge, a lawyer, or an ordinary citizen, followed by consideration of the complaint by a board or commission on judicial conduct. The complaint might contain allegations of corruption, such as the receipt of a bribe or services in return for a favorable court decision. It might allege instead the receipt of gratuities, such as liquor or tickets to sporting events, that create the appearance of impropriety, or it could allege that the judge exhibits bias in court against prosecutors, female lawyers, or out-of-state corporations.

In most cases, after the board reviews a complaint against a judge, it asks the judge for an explanation, and the explanation satisfies the board that no misconduct occurred. The board therefore takes no further action on the complaint. If, however, the board's investigation reveals that the complaint has merit, the board can impose a penalty, which could be a private letter of **reprimand**; a private or public **censure**, which might have a fine or other punishment attached to it; a forced retirement if the judge has reached retirement age; or removal. The board can forcibly retire judges for medical reasons as well as for misconduct; it can also encourage a judge to retire voluntarily, which would end the investigation and spare the judge the embarrassment of a forced retirement. The board's investigation of a complaint is confidential in every state, but beyond the investigatory stage, confidentiality ends earlier in some states than in others. In some states, confidentiality continues until the punishment is announced. The state's highest court announces the punishment after it reviews the results of the board's investigation and the board's recommendations, which it can accept or reject. The high court's decision is not designed to "make the judge pay" for his misconduct, but instead, to counter any public perception that might exist that the justice system in that particular state is "for sale" or otherwise unfair. Thus, judicial disciplinary proceedings are extremely important because they enable state judiciaries to preserve their most valuable assets, namely, integrity and the public support that results from it.

SELECTION OF FEDERAL JUDGES

Introduction

The sole mechanism of federal judicial selection is presidential appointment, subject to the advice and consent of the U.S. Senate. The Constitution authorizes the President to appoint persons to the Supreme Court and to the lower federal court judgeships that Congress creates. Presidential appointments to the federal courts are for life, provided that the appointee demonstrates "good behavior" on the bench. Despite the lifetime appointment, district judges and courts of appeals judges commonly accept **senior status** at age 70, which enables them to work part-time in return for a full salary. Supreme Court justices, however, frequently work full-time long past age 70.

The Founding Fathers chose appointment as the sole method for selecting federal judges in order to shelter the judges from the winds of public opinion, so that their decisions would respond to law and facts, not public passions. For the same reason, the Founding Fathers gave federal judges lifetime job security and prohibited the lowering of their salaries.[48] Federal judges are therefore only indirectly accountable to the people; Congress can remove them from office for impeachable offenses, and they usually share the party affiliation and the values of their appointers, whom, after all, the voters elected. Nevertheless, the shifting tides of presidential and senatorial elections have generally made the federal courts sensitive to the national mood throughout American history.[49]

The Lower Federal Courts

Vacancies occur on the district and appellate benches because of deaths, resignations, and retirements, and because Congress periodically creates new judgeships in response to increased caseloads. Approximately fifty vacancies occur annually because of deaths, resignations, and retirements.[50] Increased caseloads in the federal courts generate recommendations from the Judicial Conference of the United States to Congress to create new judgeships.[51] Congress is more likely to create new judgeships when the President belongs to the political party that enjoys a majority of the seats in Congress. A Democrat-controlled Congress prefers to create new judgeships when the President who will fill them is also a Democrat.

When a vacancy occurs on the district or the appellate bench, White House and Department of Justice (DOJ) personnel consider candidates to fill the vacancy. The candidates come from the ranks of state court judges, lawyers who are in private practice, state and federal government lawyers, law school faculty members, and, for the court of appeals, judges who already sit on the district bench. Numerous sources will contribute names to the pool of candidates to be considered; those sources include the president, the White House staff, lawyers who work at DOJ, senators, representatives, governors, state and local political party officials, state and local bar associations, individuals who would like to be considered, and individuals who wish to see their friends and colleagues considered.[52]

The Reagan Administration created a joint White House–DOJ committee, chaired by the White House Counsel, to oversee the judicial selection process. Presidents Bush and Clinton retained this committee. In the Clinton Administration, the joint committee assigns each candidate to a DOJ lawyer, who examines the candidate's professional credentials, including any decisions the candidate has rendered as a state court judge or as a federal district judge. Simultaneously, lawyers who work in the Office of White House Counsel screen the candidate's political credentials. If Senator Orrin Hatch (R-Utah), the chair of the Senate Judiciary Committee, objects to a potential nominee, President Clinton will not nominate that person because the President does not want to risk a bitter and lengthy confirmation battle in the Republican-controlled Senate.[53] The F.B.I. and the American Bar Association's **Committee on Federal Judiciary** also evaluate potential federal judges; the F.B.I. is concerned with possible criminal behavior or security risks, while the A.B.A. committee is concerned with the candidate's professional competence as a lawyer.

The A.B.A. committee is a fifteen-member panel comprised of prominent lawyers who represent each of the appellate circuits. It has participated in the federal judicial selection process for more than forty years, during which it has evaluated candidates on the basis of their age, number of years in law practice, trial experience, academic credentials, and personal character. The result of that evaluation is a rating of "not qualified," "qualified," or "well-qualified," which the committee makes available to the DOJ and to the Senate Judiciary Committee. The committee's influence has increased and decreased as the presidency has changed hands; some presidents have been more respectful of its evaluations than others have. Recently, other organizations that are interested in federal judicial selection have publicly questioned why the American Bar Association, which represents only about half of this nation's practicing lawyers, should have a formal role in choosing federal judges. Liberal critics have long charged that the committee over-represents wealthy, conservative white male corporate lawyers, while conservatives have charged more recently that unfavorable ratings by the committee forced President Reagan to abandon plans to nominate conservatives to the federal bench.[54] Conservatives are still angry at the committee because in 1987, a minority of its members rated Robert Bork "unqualified" for the Supreme Court.[55]

Therefore, the committee no longer has the influence that it once had with the Senate Judiciary Committee; indeed, one of its most vocal critics is Senator Hatch, who chairs the Judiciary Committee. Nevertheless, President Clinton and the A.B.A. committee appear to be on the same wavelength, as 64 percent of the district court nominees and 83 percent of the courts of appeals nominees during Mr. Clinton's first term in office received a rating of "well-qualified."[56] That is more important to the committee than its loss of influence with some senators is because the committee's chief advisee has always been the president. That is why it has periodically accommodated a president's wishes in order to retain its role in the judicial selection process. During the Carter Administration, it reduced from fifteen to twelve the number of years of law practice that it required for potential federal judges in order to allow President Carter to nominate a large number of African-Americans and women to the federal bench.[57] It also modified that requirement during the Reagan Administration because 10 percent of President Reagan's nominees to the courts of appeals were less than forty years old, and had practiced law for less than fifteen years.[58] Thus, the committee's major role is to prevent ill-advised nominations; once the president nominates a candidate, the committee does not actively oppose confirmation even if it rated the nominee "not qualified."

When the president selects a nominee, the Senate Judiciary Committee considers the nomination and votes on it. If the Judiciary Committee approves the nomination, the full Senate then votes on it; a majority vote is necessary to confirm the nominee. When the Judiciary Committee receives a nomination, counsel for the committee sends **blue slips** to the two senators from the nominee's state. If either senator returns the blue slip marked "objection," the custom, known as **senatorial courtesy**, is that no hearing will take place and the nomination will die. If, however, both senators return the blue slips marked "no objection," the counsel, with the approval of the chair of the committee, will schedule a hearing on the nomination.[59] The hearing is likely to be short and superficial, lasting five minutes or less, and it is usually a foregone conclusion that the Senate will vote to confirm the nominee. That is especially true of nominees to the district courts because senatorial courtesy governs the selection of district judges; if the nominee is acceptable to the home-state senators, the Senate will almost always vote to confirm.

Senatorial courtesy does not apply to nominations for the courts of appeals, but it is customary for senators from each state in a circuit in which a vacancy occurs to submit names of potential candidates to the president. Moreover, there is an unwritten rule that at least one judge from each state in a circuit ought to serve on the court of appeals for that circuit. Therefore, if only one judge from South Dakota sat on the Court of Appeals for the Eighth Circuit and that judge resigned or retired, the president would probably nominate a South Dakotan to fill the vacancy. The hearing for an appellate nominee may be more elaborate than the hearing for a district court nominee, but the Senate is likely to confirm if the nominee is acceptable to senators and has reasonably good professional credentials.[60]

If the Judiciary Committee fails to act on a nomination, the nomination dies at the end of the current session of Congress unless senators approve a motion to carry it over to the next session. Absent a carryover motion, the president must renominate the candidate for consideration during the next Congress. If the Senate confirms a nominee, the president must sign the judicial commission that officially appoints the president's choice to the federal bench. The new judge's seniority on the bench begins on the date that the president signs the commission.[61]

Political considerations are highly influential in the selection of federal judges. One of those is partisanship, that is, membership and participation in the political party of the appointer. Griffin Bell, who was a federal district judge in Georgia before he became U.S. Attorney General in the Carter Administration, acknowledged the influence of partisanship when he observed that:

> Becoming a federal judge wasn't very difficult. I managed John F. Kennedy's presidential campaign in Georgia. Two of my oldest friends were the senators from Georgia. And I was campaign manager and special counsel for the governor.[62]

Federal judges usually belong to the same political party as the president who appointed them, and, like Griffin Bell, they were often politically active before being appointed. When President Nixon, a Republican, took office in January 1969, 70 percent of the federal judges were Democrats; by the time President Ford finished President Nixon's second term in January 1977, as a result of Nixon–Ford appointees, more than half of the federal judges were Republicans.[63] Most of the people whom President Nixon and President Ford appointed to the lower federal courts had been active in politics.[64] Political activity that can lead to a federal judgeship includes service as the chair of a state or local political party organization, an unsuccessful campaign for public office, and/or financial contributions to a political party and its candidates.

Partisanship also dictates federal judges' retirement and resignation decisions; a judge is likely to leave the bench when her political party controls the White House. For example, 66 percent of the federal judges who retired or resigned during the Carter Administration were Democrats, and almost 60 percent of the federal judges who retired or resigned during the Nixon Administration were Republicans.[65]

Another political consideration that influences the selection of federal judges is the president's agenda. President Carter's agenda included the appointment of women and members of racial minority groups to the federal bench, which he achieved in record numbers. President Carter appointed fourteen Hispanics to the district courts and two Hispanics to the courts of appeals.[66] He also appointed twenty-eight African-Americans to the district courts and nine African-Americans to the courts of appeals. President Carter appointed twenty-nine women to the lower federal courts, including the district courts in twenty states, the District of Columbia, and Puerto Rico, and seven appellate circuits. By January 1981, when the Carter Administration ended, the percentage of women judges on the federal bench had increased from 1.4 percent to 6.9 percent.[67]

President Reagan's goal, on the other hand, was to appoint conservatives to the federal bench, that is, judges who shared his passions for a smaller federal government, more authority for state and local governments, and less federal regulation of business. Therefore, the Reagan Administration did not proceed with a nomination to the federal bench, especially to the court of appeals, unless it felt certain that the nominee shared its conservative political philosophy. That caution helped President Reagan to remake the lower federal courts to his liking; resignations, retirements, and the **Judgeships Bill** of 1984 (which created eighty-five new judgeships) helped too, because they enabled Reagan to appoint 47 percent of the federal district and appellate judges between 1981 and 1989, more than any of his predecessors.[68]

President Clinton, like President Carter, has been more interested in appointing women and minorities to the federal bench than in reshaping the bench to reflect his political philosophy.

He has appointed a record number of women and minorities to the federal courts; as a result, at the beginning of 1997, more than one in four federal judges was a woman, a minority, or both, an increase from about one in five when Clinton took office. There were more women and minorities serving on the federal bench during the Clinton Administration than there had been at any previous time in American history.[69]

The final political consideration that influences judicial selection is the relationship between the White House and the Senate. Judicial selection during the Clinton Administration illustrates how a change in that relationship can affect the President's capacity to fill vacancies on the federal bench. During his first two years in office, when the Democrats controlled the Senate, President Clinton submitted 118 nominations for district judgeships, and the Senate confirmed 107 (91 percent) of them.[70] He also submitted twenty-one nominations for appellate judgeships, and the Senate confirmed eighteen (86 percent) of them.[71] In 1995 and 1996, though, the Republicans controlled the Senate, and President Clinton's nominees faced a more difficult confirmation process. The Senate confirmed sixty-two of his eighty-five nominees to the district courts (73 percent) and eleven of his eighteen nominees to the courts of appeals (61 percent) during that period.[72]

The confirmation process became especially tough for President Clinton's nominees in 1996. Senate Majority Leader Robert Dole was President Clinton's Republican opponent in the presidential election that year, and, until he resigned from the Senate to campaign full-time, Dole postponed Senate consideration of Clinton's judicial nominees. During the 1996 campaign, Dole attacked Clinton's appointments to the lower federal courts, and warned that if Clinton were reelected, he would appoint liberal judges. According to Senator Dole, that would mean:

> More Federal intrusion in the lives of average Americans. More centralized power in Washington. Less freedom of religious expression. More rights for criminals. And more arrogant disregard of the rights of law-abiding citizens.[73]

Shortly after President Clinton's reelection in 1996, Senator Hatch promised that the Senate Judiciary Committee would give Mr. Clinton's future judicial nominees "especially careful scrutiny."[74]

Republican opposition to President Clinton's judicial appointments is ironic because the "Clinton judges" are hardly liberal activists. Instead, they are decidedly moderate, as a 1996 study revealed. The data showed that 48 percent of the opinions that Clinton's district court appointees wrote and 36 percent of the opinions that his appellate appointees wrote could be classified as "liberal." The comparable figures for President Carter's district and appellate appointees, whom Republican senators did not routinely criticize as "liberal," were 53 percent and 43 percent, respectively.[75] Republican senators' determination to scrutinize President Clinton's judicial nominees therefore probably resulted not from the liberalism of his first-term appointees, but from a desire to ensure that he would continue to appoint moderates in his second term.

Thus, federal judicial selection operates at the crossroads of law and politics. Partisanship, political philosophy, and the relationship between the President and the Senate, as well as the nominees' merit, influence the appointment of judges to the lower federal courts. The same factors influence the appointment of Supreme Court justices, which is the subject of the following section.

The Supreme Court

The nomination of a Supreme Court justice is one of the most important decisions a president makes. If confirmed, the nominee will join an institution that wields enormous power, and will probably serve for many years after the president who appointed that justice has left office. Therefore, presidents usually take great care in selecting their nominees. Unlike potential nominees to the lower federal courts, potential nominees to the Supreme Court usually meet with the president, who then chooses the nominee. The importance of the nomination spurs the president to get to know his choice and to think about why he wants to put that person on the Supreme Court.

Much work occurs, however, before the president interviews "finalists" and selects a nominee. Usually, the assistant attorney general in charge of the DOJ's **Office of Legal Policy** will compile a list of candidates from among names recommended by White House staff members, Members of Congress, governors, state and local bar associations, and interest-group leaders. The president's top advisors will narrow that list to a "short list" of two or three names, which the advisors will then submit to the F.B.I., which investigates the potential nominees for prior criminal behavior or possible security risks.[76] Some presidents permit the A.B.A. committee to assist in the selection of the short list by prescreening potential nominees, while others do not. President Nixon permitted the committee to prescreen the first two of his four nominations to the Court and President Ford permitted the committee to prescreen his lone nomination, but Presidents Reagan and Bush did not permit prescreening.[77] If the president's advisors receive favorable reports from the F.B.I. and the A.B.A. committee, the advisors will send their recommendation to the president; if the president approves that choice, he will send the nominee's name to the Senate.

President Bush's nomination of Clarence Thomas is illustrative. Besides Bush, the primary participants in the selection of Thomas were Attorney General Dick Thornburgh, White House Chief of Staff John Sununu, and White House Counsel C. Boyden Gray. Thornburgh, Sununu, and Gray interviewed Thomas and another federal judge, Emilio Garza; President Bush had interviewed the third finalist, Judge Edith Jones, the previous year, when he had nominated David Souter to the Court. Bush tentatively chose Thomas, and invited him to the Bush family's summer home in Kennebunkport, Maine, for discussions; after those discussions, President Bush nominated Judge Thomas to the Supreme Court.[78]

The customary criteria that cause Presidents to nominate certain individuals to the Court are: (1) objective merit; (2) personal friendship; (3) "representativeness" on the basis of race, religion, gender, or geography; and (4) ideological compatibility. Occasionally, one candidate stands out as the best person for the job, as in 1932 when President Herbert Hoover, a Republican, chose Democrat Benjamin Cardozo to replace the retiring Oliver Wendell Holmes.[79] Sometimes, several well-qualified candidates are available, and personal friendship becomes the deciding factor, as in 1965, when President Lyndon Johnson chose Abe Fortas to succeed Arthur Goldberg on the High Court.[80] Gender was the key criterion in 1981, when President Ronald Reagan nominated Sandra Day O'Connor to be the Court's first female justice; ten years later, race was crucial when President Bush nominated Clarence Thomas to replace Thurgood Marshall, the Court's first African-American justice. Geography was important to Bush's first nomination, in 1990, when he chose David Souter of New Hampshire. Two years earlier, candidate Bush's victory in the New Hampshire Presidential Primary had propelled him toward the Republican presidential nomination and the presidency. President Bush paid his political debt to New Hampshire by nominating one of its native sons to the Supreme Court.

Old-fashioned luck plays a role too, as Justice O'Connor observed in a speech in May, 1993. She said:

> While there are many supposed criteria for the selection of a Justice, when the eventual decision is made, as to who the nominee will be, that decision from the nominee's viewpoint is probably a classic example of being the right person in the right spot at the right time. Stated simply, you must be lucky. That certainly is how I view my nomination....[81]

Just as good luck can make Supreme Court nominations, bad luck can break them; sometimes, the nominee is qualified to serve on the Court, but finds himself in the wrong spot at the wrong time. The Senate has refused to confirm 30 of the 144 nominees that Presidents have submitted to it since 1789; it has rejected 17 and has declined to act on 11 others.[82] Among the Senate's reasons for refusing to confirm nominees have been: (1) opposition to the president who made the nomination; (2) opposition to the nominee's political philosophy generally or to his stance on a particular issue; (3) opposition to decisions of the Court that the nominee supported; (4) senatorial courtesy; (5) a perception that the nominee was unqualified to serve on the Court; (6) opposition to the nominee by influential interest groups; and (7) fear that the nominee would shift the ideological balance of the Court in an undesirable direction.[83]

In 1795, the Senate rejected President George Washington's nominee for Chief Justice, John Rutledge, because Rutledge had opposed the Jay Treaty, which the United States had signed with England the previous year.[84] In 1968, the Senate declined to vote on President Lyndon Johnson's nomination of Associate Justice Abe Fortas to be chief justice because some senators were angry at the Court for its liberal decisions in civil rights and criminal justice matters, and they took out their anger on Fortas, who had not even participated in many of the decisions to which his opponents objected.[85] President Johnson had already announced that he would not run for reelection, so senators did not fear presidential revenge for their refusal to vote on the Fortas nomination.[86] In 1987, as noted in Chapter 1, the Senate rejected President Reagan's nomination of Judge Robert Bork, even though it had unanimously approved his nomination to the federal appellate bench several years earlier, because of a fear that Bork's addition would make the Court too conservative. Thus, the Supreme Court confirmation battle occurs on two fronts: the partisan front pits Democrats against Republicans, and the institutional front pits the Senate against the President.

Judge Bork lost on both fronts. He lost on the partisan front because Democrats outnumbered Republicans in the Senate in 1987, and Democratic senators feared that Bork's vote would make the Supreme Court hostile to the interests of women and minorities. Under those conditions, President Reagan gambled when he nominated Judge Bork, an outspoken conservative, to succeed Lewis Powell, a moderate, and his gamble failed. Judge Bork lost on the institutional front because of the timing of his nomination, which occurred just six months before the start of President Reagan's final year in office. The Senate has historically been less likely to confirm nominees whom the president has chosen during his final year in office.[87] President Reagan either misunderstood or ignored the partisan and institutional dynamics of Supreme Court nominations when he nominated Bork.[88]

President Reagan was defiant after the Senate rejected Bork; he promised to select a nominee who would upset Senate liberals "just as much" as Bork had.[89] Ironically, Mr. Reagan's next nominee, Judge Douglas Ginsburg, upset conservatives as much as liberals. Liberals disliked Ginsburg's politics and his decision to work on a cable broadcasting case when he was a lawyer at the DOJ, even though he held $140,000 worth of stock in a cable television company at the time. Conservatives were outraged that Ginsburg had smoked marijuana, not only while he was a student at Cornell University, but even when he was a law professor at Harvard.[90] Amidst a crescendo of Senate criticism, Judge Ginsburg asked President Reagan to withdraw his nomination, and the President complied. Reagan lost the institutional battle over Ginsburg because late in his presidency, when his party was the minority in the Senate, he nominated someone whom senators, who hate to publicly oppose a Supreme Court nominee on ideological grounds, could safely oppose on ethical grounds.[91]

Successful Supreme Court nominees have been a homogeneous lot, that is, usually native-born, white Anglo-Saxon Protestant males aged 50–55 who grew up in metropolitan areas and were the first-born children of upper-middle-class or upper-class, civic-minded, and politically-active parents. They have held bachelor's degrees and law degrees from prestigious colleges and universities, have served in government prior to being nominated to the Court, and have lived in populous states.[92] For many years, the only demographic diversity on the Court, other than geographic, was religious. President Andrew Jackson's appointment of Roger Taney to the chief justiceship in 1836 initiated what came to be the "Catholic seat" on the Court. Presently, three Catholics, including Clarence Thomas, Antonin Scalia, a 1986 Reagan appointee, and Anthony Kennedy, a 1988 Reagan appointee, sit on the Court; Justice Scalia was also the Court's first Italian-American appointee. President Woodrow Wilson's appointment of Louis Brandeis in 1916 created the "Jewish" seat on the Court, which has remained occupied during most of the years since then. The current Court has two Jewish justices, Ruth Bader Ginsburg and Stephen Breyer, whom President Clinton appointed in 1993 and 1994, respectively. President Johnson's appointment of Thurgood Marshall in 1967 created a seat on the Court for African-Americans, and President Reagan's 1981 appointment of Sandra Day O'Connor did the same for women. Today, societal pressures to appoint women and members of racial minorities to the Court far exceed pressures to appoint Catholics and Jews, who hold many positions of power in the United States. Therefore, the African-American and female seats on the Court are more secure than is either one of the religious seats.

Ideologically, justices will probably continue to confound the Presidents who appoint them. Noted Supreme Court scholar Charles Warren wrote that "nothing is more striking in the history of the Court than the manner in which the hopes of those who expected a judge to follow the political views of the President appointing him are disappointed."[93] Perhaps the most famous example of a justice who confounded a president was Earl Warren, whom President Eisenhower appointed Chief Justice in 1953 on the assumption that Warren, the former governor of California, was moderately conservative. For the next sixteen years Chief Justice Warren presided over the most liberal Court in American history; the "Warren Court" desegregated public schools, outlawed prayer in those same schools, and expanded the rights of persons accused of crimes.

If the unpredictability of Supreme Court nominees has not changed since 1789, the degree of public attention their nominations receive surely has changed. Indeed, the confirmation of a Supreme Court nominee can take on the look and feel of a campaign for elective office, as supporters and opponents vie for public support in order to influence the votes of senators. That was precisely what happened when President Reagan nominated Robert Bork. Anti-Bork forces sprang into action shortly after they received word of the nomination, and pro-Bork forces responded to that challenge. Within weeks, more than 250 opinion pieces, for and against Bork, appeared on the editorial pages of more than 200 newspapers. Interest groups, most of them Bork opponents, produced more than fifteen reports about him, and distributed them to newspaper editorial boards throughout the country. **People for the American Way**, a liberal group, launched a $2 million media campaign against the nomination, and the **National Conservative Political Action Committee** (NCPAC) countered with a $1 million media campaign in favor of it. Anti-abortion groups and conservative Christian groups flooded Senate offices with letters and telephone calls in support of Judge Bork.[94] Confirmation hearings in the Senate Judiciary Committee lasted for three weeks.[95]

The degree of press and public attention that attends Supreme Court nominations today demands that the President make a politically savvy choice, especially late in his presidency and/or when his party is the minority in the Senate. President Bush's choice of David Souter was politically savvy for several reasons. First and foremost, it enabled Bush to pay his political debt to New Hampshire and to its former governor, John Sununu, for their electoral support in 1988. Second, Souter had splendid academic and professional credentials. He held a bachelor's degree and a law degree from Harvard, and he had won a Rhodes Scholarship to Oxford University. He had been New Hampshire's Attorney General, and had served on that state's superior and supreme courts.

Third, Souter had neither spoken nor written publicly about "hot button" constitutional issues such as abortion, affirmative action, or church–state relations. Therefore, President Bush reasoned, Souter would not fall victim to his own public statements and published writings, as Bork had done. Bush also reasoned that because Souter was largely unknown outside New Hampshire, he would be safely confirmed and would be trying on his new robe at the Supreme Court before anyone could discover anything damaging about him.

The President's reasoning was sound. Judge Souter's lack of a public record on abortion enabled him to claim credibly during his confirmation hearings that he had not made up his mind on that issue, and that he would approach it objectively. The opinions he wrote as a member of the New Hampshire Supreme Court did not address the federal constitutional issues that he would face on the U.S. Supreme Court, so it was difficult for senators to challenge his judicial philosophy. That prompted some observers to dub Souter the "stealth nominee," after the fighter plane that supposedly can avoid enemy radar.[96] Nevertheless, Souter impressed the Senate Judiciary Committee with his encyclopedic knowledge of constitutional law, and he won over the members with his gracious manners and dry Yankee wit. Souter's wit and wisdom did not convince groups that support abortion rights to endorse him, but their opposition did not prevent his confirmation. Two weeks after confirmation hearings began, the committee voted 13–1 to confirm Judge Souter; shortly thereafter, the Senate voted 90–9 to confirm him, and David Souter became America's 105th Supreme Court justice. Like his predecessors, Justice Souter owes his seat on the Court to talent, politics, and luck. Figure 4.3 depicts the membership of the Supreme Court during its 1998–99 term.

Justice	Year Appointed	Appointing President	Political Party Affiliation	Age at Appointment
William Rehnquist	1971	Nixon	Republican	48
John Paul Stevens	1975	Ford	Republican	55
Sandra Day O'Connor	1981	Reagan	Republican	50
Antonin Scalia	1986	Reagan	Republican	50
Anthony Kennedy	1988	Reagan	Republican	51
David Souter	1990	Bush	Republican	50
Clarence Thomas	1991	Bush	Republican	43
Ruth Bader Ginsburg	1993	Clinton	Democrat	60
Stephen Breyer	1994	Clinton	Democrat	55

FIGURE 4.3 The U.S. Supreme Court, 1998–1999

DISCIPLINE AND REMOVAL OF FEDERAL JUDGES

Federal judges are subject to disciplinary actions, including removal from office. They are removable, though, only by **impeachment** by a majority vote of the House of Representatives, followed by a trial in the Senate and a vote by a two-thirds majority of the Senate for removal. Until 1980, there was no mechanism short of impeachment for disciplining federal judges; Congress established that mechanism in the **Judicial Councils Reform and Judicial Conduct and Disability Act**, the second part of which set up a procedure for filing complaints against federal judges.[97] A complainant (including a fellow judge) can file a written complaint with the clerk of the appellate circuit within which the complained-of judge sits. The chief judge of that circuit will review the complaint, and, if it appears to be valid, the chief judge must appoint a committee to investigate the complaint. The investigative committee includes the chief judge and an equal number of district judges and appellate judges. When the investigation is complete, the committee must report its findings to the judicial council for its particular circuit. The council can: (1) determine that the complaint is unfounded, and exonerate the judge; (2) remove the offender from office if he is a magistrate or a bankruptcy (i.e., Article I) judge; or, if he is an Article III judge, (3) issue a private reprimand or a public reprimand, censure him (public reprimand plus a penalty short of removal, such as a fine), certify that he is disabled, request his voluntary resignation, or prohibit him from receiving any new case assignments. If the council determines that the complained-of conduct "might constitute" grounds for impeachment, it must notify the Judicial Conference of the United States, which, in turn, can transmit the matter to the House of Representatives for possible impeachment proceedings.

The impeachment of federal judges has been a rare event in American history. The Founding Fathers anticipated that when they restricted impeachment to "treason, bribery, or other high crimes and misdemeanors."[98] Since 1789, the House of Representatives has begun impeachment proceedings against only thirteen judges, although about that same number resigned before such proceedings began. Only seven of those thirteen cases resulted in impeachment plus removal from office after a Senate trial.[99] Three of the seven occurred during the 1980s. In 1986, the Senate removed from office district judge Harry Claiborne of Nevada for willfully underpaying his 1979 and 1980 income taxes. Then, within a two-week period in 1989, the Senate removed district judge Alcee Hastings of Florida for lying during a criminal trial in which he was cleared of bribery charges, and district judge Walter Nixon of Mississippi for lying to a grand jury.[100]

Thus, although federal judges are not directly accountable to ordinary Americans at the ballot box, they do not have unlimited power either. When circumstances warrant, both statutory and constitutional mechanisms are available to judge the judges.

CONCLUSION

Political considerations, especially partisanship and political ideology, affect who sits on state and federal courts. It would be impossible to eliminate political considerations from the selection and removal of American judges, and it would be a mistake to do so because political accountability is essential to the preservation of democracy. It would also be a mistake to abandon judicial independence in favor of political accountability because democracy requires courts to protect the rights of the minority, not to ratify the will of the majority. Thus, the challenge in judicial selection and removal is to appreciate the importance of both judicial independence and political accountability to democratic government, and to balance them in order to preserve both. Neither law without politics nor politics without law is appropriate in the selection of judges.

The case reprinted below concerns a legal issue raised by Louisiana's preference for political accountability over judicial independence. That issue is whether the federal Voting Rights Act of 1965, which prohibits racial discrimination in voting, applies to judicial elections because judges are "representatives" within the meaning of the Act. After reading the case, try to decide whether the Court read the Act correctly, in light of its language and of Louisiana's method of judicial selection.

Epilogue: Voting Rights and Judicial Elections

Chisom v. Roemer
501 U.S. 380 (1991)

JUSTICE STEVENS delivered the opinion of the Court.

In 1982, Congress amended § 2 of the Voting Rights Act to make clear that certain practices and procedures that *result* in the denial or abridgement of the right to vote are forbidden even though the absence of proof of discriminatory intent protects them from constitutional challenge. The question presented by this case is whether this "results test" protects the right to vote in state judicial elections. We hold that the coverage provided by the 1982 amendment is coextensive with the coverage provided by the Act prior to 1982 and that judicial elections are embraced within that coverage.

I

[The plaintiffs] represent a class of approximately 135,000 black registered voters in Orleans Parish, Louisiana. They brought this action against the Governor and other state officials to challenge the method of electing justices of the Louisiana Supreme Court from the New Orleans area.

The Louisiana Supreme Court consists of seven justices, five of whom are elected from five single-member Supreme Court Districts, and two of whom are elected from one multimember Supreme Court district. Each of the seven members of the court must be a resident of the district from which he or she is elected and must have resided there for at least two years prior to election. The one multimember district, the First Supreme Court District, consists of the parishes [counties] of Orleans, St. Bernard, Plaquemines, and Jefferson. Orleans Parish contains about half of the population of the First Supreme Court District and about half of the registered voters in that district. More than one-half of the registered voters of Orleans Parish are black, whereas more than three-fourths of the registered voters in the other three parishes are white.

[The plaintiffs] allege that the present method of electing two Justices at-large [i.e., candidates run districtwide] from the New Orleans area impermissibly dilutes minority voting strength in violation of § 2 of the Voting Rights Act. [They] seek a remedy that would divide the First District into two districts, one for Orleans Parish and the second for the other three parishes. If this remedy were adopted, the seven members of the Louisiana Supreme Court would each represent a separate single-member judicial district, and each of the two new districts would have approximately the same population. According to [the plaintiffs], the New Orleans Parish district would also have a majority black population and majority black voter registration.

II

[T]his case presents us solely with a question of statutory construction. That question involves only the scope of the coverage of § 2 of the Voting Rights Act as amended in 1982.

It is ... undisputed that § 2 applied to judicial elections and that § 5 of the amended statute continues to apply to judicial elections. Moreover, there is no question that the terms "standard, practice, or procedure" are broad enough to encompass the use of multimember districts to minimize a racial minority's ability to influence the outcome of an election covered by § 2. The only matter in dispute is whether the test for determining the legality of such a practice, which was added to the statute in 1982, applies in judicial elections as well as in other elections. [**Editor's Note**: a district court ruled in this case that § 2 of the Voting Rights Act did not apply to judicial elections because it applied only to elections for "representatives," and judges are not representatives. Section 2(b) of the Voting Rights Act states that a violation of the Act occurs if members of a particular race "have less opportunity than other members of the electorate to participate in the political process and to elect representatives of their choice." While this case was on appeal, the Fifth Circuit, sitting *en banc* in another case, held that § 2 did not apply to judicial elections.]

III

The text of § 2 of the Voting Rights Act as originally enacted read as follows:

"SEC. 2. No voting qualification or prerequisite to voting, or standard, practice, or procedure shall be imposed or applied by any State or political subdivision to deny or abridge the right of any citizen of the United States to vote on account of race or color."

[**Editor's Note**: In 1982, Congress amended the Voting Rights Act, and replaced the phrase "to deny or abridge" with the phrase "in a manner which *results* in a denial or abridgement of" in § 2 of the amended Act. That "results" test is the focus of this case.]

Under the amended statute, proof of intent is no longer required to prove a § 2 violation. Now plaintiffs can prevail under § 2 by demonstrating that a challenged election practice has resulted in the denial or abridgement of the right to vote based on color or race....

V

[The Governor relies] on Congress' use of the word "representatives" instead of "legislators" in the phrase [in § 2(b)] "to participate in the political process and to elect representatives of their choice." When Congress borrowed the phrase from [the Supreme Court's opinion in *White v. Regester* [412 U.S. 755 (1973)], it replaced "legislators" with "representatives...."

[The Supreme Court majority said in *League of United Latin American Citizens Council No. 4434 v. Clements*, 914 F. 2d 620 (1990)] that "judges need not be elected at all," and that ideally public opinion should be irrelevant to the judge's role because the judge is often called upon to disregard, or even to defy, popular sentiment. The Framers of the Constitution had a similar understanding of the judicial role, and as a consequence, they established that Article III judges would be appointed, rather than elected, and would be sheltered from public opinion by receiving life tenure and salary protection. Indeed, these views were generally shared by the States during the early years of the Republic. Louisiana, however, has chosen a different course. It has decided to elect its judges and to compel judicial candidates to vie for popular support just as other political candidates do.

The fundamental tension between the ideal character of the judicial office and the real world of electoral politics cannot be resolved by crediting judges with total indifference to the popular will while simultaneously requiring them to run for elected office.

When each of several members of a court must be a resident of a separate district, and must be elected by the voters of that district, it seems both reasonable and realistic to characterize the winners as representatives of that district. Indeed, at one time the Louisiana Bar Association characterized the members of the Louisiana Supreme Court as representatives for that reason: "Each justice and judge now in office shall be considered as a representative of the judicial district within which is situated the parish of his residence at the time of his election...."

VII

The judgment of the Court of Appeals is reversed and the case is remanded [to the district court] for further proceedings consistent with this opinion.

It is so ordered.

JUSTICE SCALIA, with whom **THE CHIEF JUSTICE [REHNQUIST]** and **JUSTICE KENNEDY** join, dissenting.

Section 2 of the Voting Rights Act is not some all-purpose weapon for well-intentioned judges to wield as they please in the battle against discrimination. It is a statute. I thought we had adopted a regular method for interpreting the meaning of language in a statute: first, find the ordinary meaning of the language in its textual context; and second, using established canons of construction, ask whether there is any clear indication that some permissible meaning other than the ordinary one applies. If not—and especially if a good reason for the ordinary meaning appears plain—we apply that ordinary meaning....

Today, however, the Court adopts a method quite out of accord with that usual practice. It begins not with what the statute says, but with an expectation about what the statute must mean absent particular phenomena ("*we are convinced* that if Congress had ... an intent [to exclude judges] Congress would have made it explicit in the statute, or at least some of the Members would have identified or mentioned it at some point in the unusually extensive legislative history"); and the Court then interprets the words of the statute to fulfill its expectation. Finding nothing in the legislative history affirming that judges were excluded from the coverage of § 2, the Court gives the phrase "to elect representatives" the quite extraordinary meaning that covers the election of judges.... In my view, that reading reveals that § 2 extends to vote dilution claims for the election of representatives only, and judges are not representatives.

There is little doubt that the ordinary meaning of "representatives" does not include judges, see Webster's Second New International Dictionary 2114 (1950). The Court's feeble argument to the contrary is that "representatives" means those who "are chosen by popular election." On that hypothesis, the fan-elected members of the baseball All-Star teams are "representatives"—hardly a common, if even a permissible, usage. Surely the word "representative" connotes one who is not only *elected by* the people, but who also, at a minimum, *acts on behalf of* the people. Judges do that in a sense—but not in the ordinary sense....

As I said at the outset, this case is about method. The Court transforms the meaning of § 2, not because the ordinary meaning is irrational, or inconsistent with other parts of the statute, but because it does not fit the Court's conception of what Congress must have had in mind. Our highest responsibility in the field of statutory construction is to read the laws in a consistent way, giving Congress a sure means by which it may work the people's will. We have ignored that responsibility today. I respectfully dissent.

QUESTIONS FOR DISCUSSION

1. What practices and procedures does § 2 of the Voting Rights Act, as amended in 1982, prohibit?

2. Does § 2 require a plaintiff to prove that an intent to discriminate motivated the use of those practices and procedures? Explain.

3. What question must the Court answer in this case concerning the applicability of § 2?

4. Who are the plaintiffs, and what practice or procedure do they challenge?

5. On what grounds do the plaintiffs allege that the practice they challenge is racially discriminatory? What remedy do they seek?

6. According to the majority, is the use of multimember electoral districts to minimize the voting power of a racial minority a "standard, practice, or procedure" within the meaning of § 2?

7. Why must the Court determine whether judges are "representatives" in order to resolve this case?

8. Does the majority conclude that judges are "representatives"? What is the reasoning for the majority's conclusion?

9. What evidence does the majority opinion cite to indicate that Louisiana regards its judges as "representatives"?

10. Why does the dissent argue that the majority has misinterpreted the plain meaning of § 2?

11. What requirement does the dissent establish for a "representative" that the majority opinion does not?

12. Who do you think reached the correct result, the majority or the dissenters? Why?

NOTES

1. Harry P. Stumpf and John H. Culver, *The Politics of State Courts* (New York: Longman, 1992), p. 50.
2. Richard Harris, *Decision* (New York: E. P. Dutton, 1971), p. 18.
3. *Id.*, pp. 96–101. Florida is now in the Eleventh Circuit, which also includes Alabama and Georgia.
4. Henry J. Abraham, *Justices and Presidents: A Political History of Appointments to the Supreme Court*, Third Edition (New York: Oxford University Press, 1992), p. 17.
5. *Id.*, p. 106.
6. *Id.*, p. 17.
7. David B. Rottman et al., *State Court Organization, 1993* (Washington, D.C.: U.S. Department of Justice, Bureau of Justice Statistics, 1995), pp. 32–43.
8. *Id.*, pp. 48–67.
9. *Id.*, pp. 32–43.
10. *Id.*, pp. 48–67.
11. Madison B. McClellan, Note, "Merit Appointment Versus Popular Election: A Reformer's Guide to Judicial Selection Methods in Florida," *Florida Law Review* 43 (1991): 529–560; National Center for the Public Interest, *State Judiciaries and Impartiality* (Washington, D.C.: National Legal Center for the Public Interest, 1996), p. 15.
12. National Legal Center for the Public Interest, *State Judiciaries and Impartiality*, p. 45, note 3.
13. Melinda Gann Hall, "Competition in Judicial Elections, 1980–1995," presented at the 1998 Annual Meeting of the American Political Science Association, Boston, Mass., September 3–6, 1998, p. 11.
14. Melinda Gann Hall, "Electoral Politics and Strategic Voting in State Supreme Courts," *Journal of Politics* 54 (1992): 427–446.
15. National Legal Center for the Public Interest, *State Judiciaries and Impartiality*, p. 26.
16. *Id.*, p. 25.
17. Robert Moog, "Campaign Financing for North Carolina's Appellate Courts," *Judicature* 76 (August/September 1992): 76.
18. Stumpf and Culver, *The Politics of State Courts*, p. 44.
19. *Id.*, p. 45.
20. Mark Hansen, "A Run for the Bench," *American Bar Association Journal,* (October 1998): 68–72.
21. *Id.* That rule is the subject of a lawsuit that has reached the U.S. Court of Appeals for the Sixth Circuit. That court is considering whether the $75,000 spending limit is unconstitutional in light of the U.S. Supreme Court's decision in *Buckley v. Valeo* (424 U.S. 1, 1976), which invalidated spending limits in congressional campaigns as a violation of the freedom of speech guaranteed by the First Amendment.
22. Rottman et al., *State Court Organization, 1993*, pp. 32–43.
23. *Id.*, pp. 48–67.
24. Stumpf and Culver, *The Politics of State Courts*, p. 39. In both Massachusetts and New Hampshire, a "lifetime" appointment means an appointment until the age of 70. Massachusetts and New Hampshire judges must retire at age 70.
25. Christopher Graff, "Amestoy on High Court List," *Burlington Free Press*, January 9, 1997, p. 1B.

26. Jeffrey Good and Adam Lisberg, "Dean Taps Amestoy for Chief Justice," *Burlington Free Press*, January 11, 1997, p. 1A.
27. Stumpf and Culver, *The Politics of State Courts*, p. 48.
28. *Id.*, p. 41.
29. Rottman et al., *State Court Organization, 1993*, pp. 32–43. The most recent convert to the Missouri Plan is Rhode Island, which adopted it in 1994 for choosing the justices of the state's supreme court.
30. *Id.*, pp. 48–67.
31. Lawrence H. Averill, Jr., "Observations on the Wyoming Experience with Merit Selection of Judges: A Model for Arkansas," *University of Arkansas—Little Rock Law Review* 17 (1994): 281-327.
32. *Id.*, p. 293.
33. *Id.*, pp. 293–294.
34. Larry T. Aspin and William K. Hall, "Retention Elections and Judicial Behavior," *Judicature* 77 (May/June 1994): 306–315.
35. Stumpf and Culver, *The Politics of State Courts*, p. 41.
36. John Gibeault, "Taking Aim," *American Bar Association Journal*, (November 1996): 51–55.
37. *Id.*, p. 53.
38. Council of State Governments, *The Book of the States, 1998–99 Edition* (Lexington, Ky.: Council of State Governments, 1998), p. 135.
39. *Id.*, p. 136.
40. Sheldon Goldman, "Judicial Selection and the Qualities That Make a 'Good' Judge," *Annals of the American Academy of Political and Social Science* 462 (July 1982): 112–124.
41. Hall, "Electoral Politics and Strategic Voting in State Supreme Courts," p. 438.
42. Council of State Governments, *The Book of the States, 1998–1999 Edition*, pp. 138–145.
43. The states where legislative address exists are Arkansas, Connecticut, Maine, Maryland, Massachusetts, Michigan, Mississippi, New Hampshire, New York, Ohio, Tennessee, and Wisconsin. *Id.*
44. *Id.*
45. Stumpf and Culver, *The Politics of State Courts*, p. 51.
46. In Hawaii, Indiana, North Carolina, and Oregon, this administrative process is the only means of removing judges.
47. James D. Miller, "State Disciplinary Proceedings and the Impartiality of Judges," in National Legal Center for the Public Interest, *State Judiciaries and Impartiality*, p. 119.
48. Article III, Section 1 of the Constitution provides that federal judges' salaries "shall not be diminished during their continuance in office."
49. David M. O'Brien, *Judicial Roulette: Report of the Twentieth Century Fund Task Force on Judicial Selection* (New York: Priority Press Publications, 1988), p. 97.
50. Ronald Stidham, Robert A. Carp, and Donald R. Songer, "The Voting Behavior of President Clinton's Judicial Appointees," *Judicature* 80 (July/August 1996): 16–20.
51. Deborah J. Barrow, Gary Zuk, and Gerard S. Gryski, *The Federal Judiciary and Institutional Change* (Ann Arbor, Mich.: University of Michigan Press, 1996), p. 67.
52. Sheldon Goldman, *Picking Federal Judges: Lower Court Selection from Roosevelt Through Reagan* (New Haven, Ct.: Yale University Press, 1997), pp. 9–10.
53. Robert A. Carp and Ronald Stidham, *The Federal Courts*, Third Edition (Washington, D.C.: CQ Press, 1998), p. 81.

54. Henry J. Abraham, "Beneficial Advice or Presumptuous Veto? The A.B.A.'s Committee on Federal Judiciary Revisited," in National Legal Center for the Public Interest, *Judicial Selection: Merit, Ideology, and Politics* (Washington, D.C.: National Legal Center for the Public Interest, 1990), p. 69.

55. Terry Carter, "A Conservative Juggernaut," *American Bar Association Journal,* (June 1997): 32–35.

56. Carp and Stidham, *The Federal Courts*, Third Edition, p. 84.

57. O'Brien, *Judicial Roulette*, p. 89.

58. *Id.*, p. 90.

59. Goldman, *Picking Federal Judges*, p. 12.

60. Carp and Stidham, *The Federal Courts*, p. 87.

61. Goldman, *Picking Federal Judges*, p. 12.

62. Quoted in O'Brien, *Judicial Roulette*, p. 37.

63. Goldman, *Picking Federal Judges*, p. 235.

64. *Id.*, p. 232.

65. *Id.*, p. 77.

66. *Id.*, p. 283.

67. *Id.*, p. 282.

68. *Id.*, p. 336.

69. Sheldon Goldman and Elliott Slotnick, "Clinton's First Term Judiciary: Many Bridges to Cross," *Judicature* 80 (May/June 1997): 254–273.

70. *Id.*, p. 255.

71. *Id.*

72. *Id.*

73. Quoted in Goldman, *Picking Federal Judges*, p. 2, note 6.

74. Henry J. Reske, "Withholding Consent," *American Bar Association Journal,* (February 1997): 28–29.

75. Stidham et al., "The Voting Behavior of President Clinton's Judicial Nominees."

76. David M. O'Brien, *Storm Center: The Supreme Court in American Politics*, Third Edition (New York: W. W. Norton, 1993), p. 74.

77. Lawrence Baum, *The Supreme Court*, Fourth Edition (Washington, D.C.: CQ Press, 1992), p. 32.

78. *Id.*, p. 39.

79. Abraham, *Justices and Presidents*, p. 5.

80. *Id.*, p. 6.

81. *Id.*, p. 344.

82. *Id.*, p. 39; Carp and Stidham, *The Federal Courts*, p. 87.

83. Abraham, *Justices and Presidents*, p. 39.

84. *Id.*, p. 41.

85. *Id.*, pp. 43–44. See also Laura Kalman, *Abe Fortas: A Biography* (New Haven, Ct.: Yale University Press, 1990), p. 356.

86. Kalman, *Abe Fortas: A Biography*, p. 333.

87. Jeffrey Segal, "Senate Confirmation of Supreme Court Justices: Partisan and Institutional Politics," *Journal of Politics* 49 (1987): 998–1015.

88. When he nominated Bork, President Reagan was politically weak not only because his term was drawing to a close, but because his leadership was under fire at home and overseas. He had been embarrassed by recent revelations that his aides had devised an illegal plan to sell missiles to Iran, and to use the proceeds of those sales to fund a guer-

rilla war against the government of Nicaragua. Therefore, it is surprising that Mr. Reagan chose to risk his limited supply of good will with senators on a controversial Supreme Court nomination. See Abraham, *Justices and Presidents*, p. 358.

89. John Massaro, *Supremely Political: The Role of Ideology and Presidential Management in Unsuccessful Supreme Court Nominations* (Albany: State University of New York Press, 1990), p. 193.
90. *Id.*, p. 194.
91. *Id.*, p. 197.
92. Abraham, *Justices and Presidents*, p. 61.
93. Quoted in Abraham, *Justices and Presidents*, p. 69.
94. O'Brien, *Judicial Roulette*, p. 101.
95. *Id.*, p. 104.
96. Warren B. Rudman, *Combat: Twelve Years in the U.S. Senate* (New York: Random House, 1996), p. 171; see also David J. Garrow, "Justice Souter Emerges," *The New York Times Magazine*, September 25, 1994, p. 36.
97. Carp and Stidham, *The Federal Courts*, p. 107.
98. U.S. Constitution, Article II, Section 4.
99. Carp and Stidham, *The Federal Courts*, p. 106.
100. *See generally* Mary L. Volcansek, *Judicial Impeachment: None Called for Justice* (Urbana, Ill.: University of Illinois Press, 1993).

Chapter 5

Norm Enforcement—The Criminal Justice Process

Introduction

A principal function of courts in America (see Chapter 1) is to enforce social norms in favor of certain types of behavior and against other types of behavior. Courts perform that function most directly in the criminal justice process, where they punish antisocial behavior commonly known as **crime**. A crime is an act or a failure to act that violates a law that forbids or commands it.[1] A criminal case, as its name suggests, is a dispute between a state or the United States, on the one hand, and the accused, on the other. *State v. Johnson*, the hypothetical case to be presented in this chapter, is a dispute between the State of New Hampshire and Stan Johnson; if it were a dispute between the United States and Mr. Johnson, it would be titled *United States v. Johnson*.

Statutes (i.e., laws passed by Congress and by the state legislatures) define most crimes today. For example, statutes typically define **murder** as: (1) an act or a failure to act (when one has a duty to act); (2) by one who has a "malicious" state of mind (e.g., an intent to kill or do serious bodily harm); (3) that is the direct cause of the death of a living human being; (4) within one year and one day after the defendant's conduct caused the victim's fatal injury.[2] A prosecutor must prove each of those elements **beyond a reasonable doubt** in order to win a conviction in a murder case.

Both federal courts and state courts have jurisdiction over crimes (see Chapter 2), but state courts resolve most of the criminal cases that arise in the United States. Criminal cases raise issues of **substantive criminal law** and/or issues of **procedural criminal law**. Substantive criminal law declares what conduct is criminal and prescribes the punishment for that conduct.[3] The elements of murder, described above, are an example of substantive criminal law. Procedural criminal law describes the steps that a criminal proceeding must follow, from investigation through punishment, to satisfy **due process**, which is the constitutional require-ment of fairness.[4] Procedural criminal law attempts to protect the rights of indi-viduals accused of crimes without unreasonably hampering law enforcement.[5]

A substantive legal issue arises when it is not clear that all of the elements of a crime are present. If, for example, it is unclear whether a witness was properly sworn (i.e., placed under oath) before she lied in her trial testimony, a prosecutor would probably not charge her with **perjury**.[6] Some crimes, such as murder, require a specific result in order for all their elements to be met; for example, unless and until the victim dies, a prosecutor can charge the assailant with **aggravated assault** or even with **attempted murder**, but not with murder.

A substantive legal issue also arises when the elements of a crime are present, but the accused offers a defense for his actions. One valid defense is **entrapment**, which applies when a law enforcement officer encourages a person to commit a crime and thereby influences one to break the law who would otherwise have obeyed it.[7] Entrapment is a valid defense because it demonstrates the absence of the *mens rea* ("guilty mind") that a defendant must have in order to be punished for her actions.[8]

A procedural legal issue arises when a defendant alleges that police officers illegally searched his apartment, and argues that the court should prohibit the prosecutor from using against him the incriminating evidence discovered during that search. Still another procedural issue emerges when a defendant claims that he is a victim of **selective prosecution**, that is, that the prosecutor chose to pros-ecute him for who he is, rather than for what he did.

The selective prosecution defense illustrates the discretion that police offi-cers, prosecutors, and judges exercise during the criminal justice process. For exam-ple, prosecutors choose not to prosecute many people who have committed crimes and whose guilt they could establish beyond a reasonable doubt. Official discre-tion is often necessary, though. That is because legislatures fail to provide suffi-cient resources to permit enforcement of all criminal laws against all offenders.[9] Therefore, police officers and prosecutors enforce some criminal laws more vigor-ously than others. Prosecutors are elected in forty-five states, so public opinion can influence their choices about how to allocate the limited resources that are available to them.[10]

Official discretion can be a good thing, too. Officials should exercise discre-tion when the substantive criminal law conflicts with the realities of everyday life. Plea bargaining (see Chapter 2) is perhaps the most visible example of the need to overcome a poor fit between law and life. The substantive criminal law often assigns a lengthy **mandatory minimum sentence** to a particular offense, such as drug trafficking, in response to public pressure to "get tough" on crime or to "declare war" on drugs.[11] Therefore, the prosecutor might offer and the trial judge might approve a plea of guilty by the defendant to a lesser charge in the belief that the plea bargain adjusts the punishment to the crime more fairly than the law on the books does.[12] Thus, discretion can wisely separate law from politics when pol-itics makes bad law.

State v. Johnson, which appears below, will illustrate many of the principles discussed above, as they would apply in an actual prosecution. Read carefully the following paragraphs that describe the facts and the trial of *State v. Johnson*. Then consider (1) whether law enforcement authorities acted improperly in this case, thereby justifying a dismissal, and (2) even if they acted properly, whether they proved the defendant's guilt beyond a reasonable doubt.

STATE V. JOHNSON: FACTS

On January 29, 1999, Stan Johnson was twenty-two years old and a student at Grayson College in Grayson, New Hampshire. Grayson College is a private liberal arts college of 3,000 students. The town of Grayson is a picturesque New England village with a population of 7,500 that is nestled in the shadows of the White Mountain National Forest in north-central New Hampshire. Stan Johnson's life changed permanently on January 29, 1999, when three Grayson police officers arrested him for the possession of cocaine with intent to sell and for the sale of cocaine.

The series of events that led to Stan's arrest began on November 25, 1998, when Mike Halloran, the lone detective on the eight-member Grayson police force, and Marie Leveau, a Grayson College security officer, met for an early-morning run. Halloran and Leveau discussed their work while running that morning, and Leveau informed Halloran that she had heard rumors from several students that Stan was selling cocaine to his classmates. Leveau added that she had informed the Dean of Students of the rumors in hopes that the college would investigate them and, if necessary, would discipline Stan without reporting his alleged activities to the police. To Leveau's dismay, the college took no action and the rumors persisted; she therefore decided to alert Halloran to the rumors so that the Grayson Police Department could investigate them. Halloran promised Leveau that he would look into the matter.

On January 29, Detective Halloran obtained permission from his supervisor to organize an undercover operation to investigate Stan Johnson's alleged drug dealing. Halloran borrowed Trooper Steve Cummings of the New Hampshire State Police for the operation. Trooper Cummings was twenty-one years old, he looked like a college student, and he normally worked in western New Hampshire, so Stan would not recognize him. Therefore, he was the perfect person to "buy" cocaine from Stan.

He did precisely that early in the evening of January 29. At about 6 P.M., Trooper Cummings parked his own car in front of the house in which Stan's apartment was located and walked up the pathway to the house. He was wearing a "body wire" that enabled Detective Halloran and two other officers, who were in a van that was parked across the street from Stan's house, to listen to any conversation that might occur between Cummings and Stan.

When he reached the house, Trooper Cummings knocked on the door to an enclosed porch that was attached to the main part of the building. There was no answer, so he opened the exterior door of the porch, crossed the porch, and knocked on the interior door, which opened into the house. A male voice said, "Come in." Trooper Cummings opened the interior door and entered the kitchen of the down-stairs apartment that Stan shared with his roommate. In the kitchen, a tall, dark-haired, athletic-looking young man greeted Trooper Cummings, who said, "Hi. I'm looking for Stan." The dark-haired man said, "I'm Stan. What's up?" "A couple of guys told me that you could sell me some coke," said Trooper Cummings. "Sure," Stan responded, and he invited Cummings to sit at the kitchen table.

Stan asked, "How much do you want?" "A fifty-dollar bag," answered Trooper Cummings. Stan turned and went into another room while Cummings remained seated at the kitchen table. When Stan returned to the kitchen, he handed Cum-mings a plastic bag that was marked "$50." It contained nearly one-sixteenth of an ounce of cocaine. Cummings handed Stan two twenty-dollar bills and a ten-dollar bill, said "Thanks," and got up to leave. Stan then asked Cummings: "Who told you I could sell you coke?" Cummings replied: "Some guys my girlfriend knows. She goes to school here." Stan nodded and told Cummings to "have a good time," and Cummings left the house.

Trooper Cummings then drove to the Grayson Police Department, where he gave the plastic bag to Detective Halloran, who field-tested its contents. The result was a positive test for cocaine. Detective Halloran completed an application for a search warrant, and directed another officer to take the application to District Court Judge Margaret Levesque, who lived near the police station, in order to obtain per-mission to search Stan's apartment. Judge Levesque signed the warrant, which authorized Grayson police officers to execute a search between midnight and 2 A.M.

Shortly after 1 A.M., Detective Halloran and two fellow officers arrested Stan outside his apartment as he returned home from an off-campus party. Their sub-sequent search of the apartment revealed a shoebox full of plastic bags that appeared to contain drugs and a second shoebox that contained approximately $1,500 in cash and a small notepad that listed the names and addresses of drug suppliers and the amounts that Stan had purchased from them. When the search was finished, the officers escorted Stan to the police station, where he telephoned his parents, who lived in upstate New York. Shortly thereafter, a **bail commis-sioner**, who was also a Grayson police officer, set bail for Stan because no court was in session at that hour.[13] The bail commissioner released Stan **on his own rec-ognizance**, that is, Stan's promise to appear for future court proceedings, the first of which would occur on Monday, February 1.[14] The police then released him.

STATE V. JOHNSON: PARTICIPANTS

The Defendant

The most important participant in *State v. Johnson* was the defendant, Stan John-son. Stan was no ordinary college student. He had been a member of the U.S. Alpine Ski Team since he was seventeen years old. Early in 1998, he won a gold medal in the downhill event and a silver medal in the giant slalom event at the Winter Olympics at Nagano, Japan. Those triumphs made Stan an instant celebrity; photographers loved to take his picture, and his smiling face graced cereal boxes across America. It seemed too good to be true.

It was. On May 20, 1998, Stan was running on a rural highway near the Olympic Training Center at Colorado Springs, Colorado. He was determined to maintain the form he had demonstrated at Nagano and to win two gold medals in 2002. Unfortunately, a drunk driver ended Stan's dreams of future Olympic success when his car swerved out of control and hit Stan, leaving him with a permanent back injury that made ski racing impossible.

Stan tried to make the best of his new circumstances. His rehabilitation program had sparked an interest in sports medicine. Stan decided to enroll at Grayson College because it had a prestigious pre-med program and because the college agreed to waive tuition for him in return for his service as the assistant coach of its ski team. Free tuition, however, did not ease Stan's transition from celebrity athlete to college student. His celebrity ended as fast as it had begun, his classmates seemed immature, and he missed ski racing. Only cocaine eased his emotional pain and bridged the social gap between his classmates and himself. Selling cocaine and marijuana bridged that gap even more. By late November 1998, when Detective Halloran and Officer Leveau went for their morning run, it was common knowledge among the undergraduates at Grayson College that Stan sold drugs.

Stan was even more unusual as a criminal defendant than he was as an undergraduate. Like most defendants in rural New Hampshire, Stan was young, male, and white, but that was where his similarities to them ended. Stan, unlike most defendants anywhere in America, was the son of an architect and a business executive who could afford to hire a private lawyer to represent their son. Therefore, he did not have to rely on an overworked public defender to represent him; nor did he have to accept the first plea bargain that the prosecutor might offer. Indeed, he did not have to accept a plea bargain at all, because he was confident that his lawyer would be an effective advocate for him at trial. Thus, Stan could afford to be the rare criminal defendant whose case would go to trial (see Chapter 2).

The Defense Attorney

Gene Jefferson, Stan's lawyer, was an unusual man. He was a black man and a Democrat in overwhelmingly white, staunchly Republican New Hampshire. Jefferson loved to puncture stereotypes, and he reveled in the outdoor life of rural New Hampshire. Jefferson had grown up in Boston and arrived in New Hampshire in 1974, when he received a football scholarship to the University of New Hampshire. He was an all-conference running back in 1977 and 1978, but no professional team drafted him. He took his degree in criminal justice home to Boston, where he attended the police academy, then joined the Boston Police Department as a patrolman in 1979.

In 1984, Gene began to attend law school in the evenings at Northeastern University, where he earned excellent grades while continuing to work as a police officer. After law school, he joined the Suffolk County (Ma.) District Attorney's Office, where he worked until 1990. In 1990, Gene, his wife, and two young children left Boston and moved to Graniteville when an old college friend who had set up a solo law practice there called Gene and asked him to "come aboard." He looked forward to enjoying clean air and mountains and to spending more time with his children.

Gene passed the New Hampshire Bar Exam and quickly became a respected member of the Bar and a prominent criminal defense attorney. He also dabbled in Democratic Party politics. In 1992, he worked as a volunteer in the presidential campaign of Senator Bob Kerry of Nebraska, where he met Janet Johnson, Stan's mother. Janet Johnson was grateful for Gene Jefferson's friendship early on the morning of January 30, 1999, when she got off the phone with Stan, who had called her from the police station. Janet called Gene, and asked him to represent Stan, which he quickly agreed to do.

The Prosecutor

The only New Hampshire native who played a prominent role in *State v. Johnson* was the prosecutor, Granite County Attorney Kevin Quinlan, a "hometown boy" who had grown up in Grayson. Kevin Quinlan was born to be a prosecutor. One could see that even during his high school years, when Kevin was both the scrappy point guard on a state-champion basketball team and his school's best debater. He took those skills to Grayson College, thanks to a scholarship designed to benefit a local resident, and again distinguished himself in debate and on the basketball court. His excellent college record won him admission to Boston College Law School, from which he graduated in 1988. Several prestigious Boston law firms offered Kevin a job after graduation, but he chose to become a deputy prosecutor in the office of the Granite County Attorney. In 1996, when his boss retired, the voters overwhelmingly elected Kevin Granite County Attorney.

Kevin won in part because of his name recognition and his Republican Party affiliation, but also because he had promised during the campaign to prosecute vigorously any Grayson College students who sold or possessed drugs. That promise resonated with many voters, especially the residents of Grayson, who were tired of the late-night noise, the automobile accidents, and the property damage that had resulted from the students' "partying." They believed that the college, the police, and the county attorney's office had winked at the students' drug use for too long, and they were thrilled that Kevin seemed determined to change things.

The Judge

Judge Mary Romano was sitting in Granite County Superior Court when *State v. Johnson* landed on the docket there. Her participation in the case was coincidental, because superior court judges in New Hampshire rotate periodically among several counties. Judge Romano was a rising star on the trial bench, and members of the Bar speculated that she would soon ascend to the state supreme court or even to a federal judgeship. Nobody was more surprised by that speculation than Mary, who still thought of herself as "a little Italian girl from Queens."

Mary was the youngest of Sal and Rose Romano's five children, and the student in the family. She was the valedictorian of her high school class and graduated *summa cum laude* from Manhattanville College in suburban Westchester County, New York, in 1974. After college, she taught history and government at a Catholic high school for girls in Queens until 1979. In the fall of that year, Mary entered Fordham University Law School in New York City, just as the doors of law schools nationwide were opening to large numbers of women. She graduated near the top of her class, and earned a position on the editorial board of the *Fordham Law Review* during her final year of school.

After law school, Mary worked as deputy counsel to the New York City Board of Education for three years and in the litigation department of a medium-sized Queens law firm for two years. Then a ski trip to New Hampshire in 1987 changed her life. Mary and her husband, John LoScalzo, "fell in love" with New Hampshire and decided to move there. Six months and a bar exam later, they moved to New Hampshire, and Mary went to work for a politically connected law firm in Concord. Mary quickly established herself as a first-rate lawyer, and she worked tirelessly for Republican candidates for state and local offices. In 1996, just eight years after Mary moved to New Hampshire, the Republican governor appointed her a superior court judge.

STATE V. JOHNSON: PROCESS

Pretrial

Every state has a multistage pretrial process that is designed to give persons accused of crimes some form of hearing on issues such as the legality of their arrests, whether they are entitled to be released pending court proceedings, and whether the police had **probable cause** (i.e., legal grounds) to arrest them. Those processes vary considerably among states; *State v. Johnson* will follow New Hampshire's procedures, but the discussion will identify alternatives that other states use. It will also compare state and federal procedures when necessary.

Arraignment

On February 1, 1999, Stan Johnson appeared for his **arraignment** before New Hampshire District Court Judge Nathan Cody at the Grayson County Courthouse. In New Hampshire, district court judges preside over pretrial proceedings in felony cases, while superior court judges preside at trial. The purposes of the arraignment were to: (1) inform Stan of the charges against him and (2) offer him an opportunity to enter a **plea** to those charges.[15] In some states, an arraignment does not occur until after there has been a **preliminary hearing**, also known as a **probable cause hearing**, which determines whether there are reasonable grounds to believe that a crime occurred and that the defendant committed it. In New Hampshire, though, an arraignment must occur within twenty-four hours of an arrest, excluding Saturdays and Sundays; therefore, an arraignment precedes a preliminary hearing in New Hampshire.[16]

Stan's lawyer, Gene Jefferson, appeared in court with Stan. The Sixth Amendment to the U.S. Constitution entitles a defendant to be represented by a lawyer at all critical stages of the criminal justice process, of which the arraignment is one.[17] Had Stan been unable to afford a lawyer, Judge Cody would have appointed one for him at his arraignment; the Sixth Amendment requires a state court to appoint a lawyer for a defendant who cannot afford one when that defendant makes her first court appearance. The U.S. Supreme Court has held that the defendant's first appearance in court must occur within forty-eight hours of arrest.[18]

Judge Cody informed Stan that he was charged with the possession of a controlled drug with intent to sell and with the sale of a controlled drug, both of which are felonies under New Hampshire law. Stan had allegedly violated R.S.A. (Revised Statutes Annotated) 318–B:2, which makes it a felony for any person to "…possess, have under his control, sell,…or possess with intent to sell any controlled drug…." Cocaine is a "controlled drug" within the meaning of this statute. Cody also informed Stan of the constitutional rights to which he, like all criminal defendants, was entitled. Those rights are the so-called **Miranda rights**, which the Supreme Court announced in *Miranda v. Arizona* in 1966.[19] They are contained in the Fifth and Sixth Amendments to the Constitution and they entitle a defendant to: (1) remain silent; (2) stop answering police officers' questions at any time; (3) the assistance of a lawyer; and (4) the assistance of a court-appointed lawyer if the defendant cannot afford to hire a lawyer.

Judge Cody asked Stan if he understood the charges against him, to which Stan responded, "Yes, I do." Then, Judge Cody asked Stan how he wished to plead, to which Stan answered, "Not guilty, Your Honor." Had Stan said nothing or refused to enter a plea, Judge Cody would have considered that a plea of "not guilty."[20]

Alternatively, Stan could have entered a plea of guilty or of *nolo contendere* ("I do not contest this"). Either plea would have resulted in an immediate conviction. Nevertheless, the two pleas are not identical. The defendant who pleads guilty admits guilt, but the defendant who pleads *nolo contendere* does not admit guilt; he merely chooses not to contest the charges against him. Unlike the defendant who pleads guilty, the defendant who pleads *nolo contendere* will not see that plea used against him in a subsequent civil lawsuit in which the plaintiff seeks monetary compensation for injuries caused by the defendant's behavior (e.g., drunk driving).[21]

Judge Cody next considered the issue of bail for Stan. Judge Cody had the power to continue or to revoke the bail commissioner's decision to release Stan on his own recognizance. He reasoned that Stan was not a threat to flee or to commit a crime during pretrial release, so he continued Stan's release on recognizance (ROR), which freed Stan based on his written promise to appear for future court proceedings.[22] Courts increasingly use ROR instead of **bail**; under the bail system, the defendant typically pays a **bail bondsman** 15 percent of his bail, in return for the bondsman's pledge to the court that the defendant will appear for future court proceedings. If the defendant fails to appear, the bondsman must pay the bail amount to the court, which gives the bondsman a powerful incentive to find the fugitive and return him to court.[23] Alternatively, if a judge concludes that a defendant is a threat to flee and/or to commit crimes during pretrial release, she can order the defendant jailed pending trial. That practice, which seems to conflict with the **presumption of innocence**, is known as **preventive detention**.[24]

Judge Cody concluded Stan Johnson's arraignment by setting a date for his next court appearance. On February 15, 1999, Stan would appear for his preliminary hearing. Stan's temporary freedom was a small consolation to him in the days that followed his arraignment. The Grayson College skiing coach fired him from his job as an assistant coach, which cost Stan his tuition-free education. When the Dean of the College upheld that decision, Stan withdrew from Grayson College and returned to his parents' home to await his next court appearance.

Preliminary Hearing

Stan's **preliminary** (or **probable cause**) **hearing** also took place before Judge Cody in district court. The purposes of the preliminary hearing were to determine whether: (1) there was probable cause to believe that a crime had occurred and (2) there was probable cause to believe that Stan had committed it.[25] Prosecutor Quinlan argued that there was undisputed evidence that Stan sold cocaine to Trooper Cummings in Stan's kitchen, which established probable cause to believe that Stan had possessed cocaine with intent to sell and that he had, in fact, sold it.

Defense Attorney Jefferson countered that the "drug buy" that occurred in Stan's kitchen was an **unreasonable search and seizure** in violation of the Fourth Amendment to the U.S. Constitution because: (1) it shattered the reasonable expectation of privacy that Stan enjoyed in his home; and (2) there was no basis for it other than a rumor that Stan was a drug dealer, which did not amount to the probable cause that is required for a valid search. Probable cause is knowledge of relevant facts and circumstances that is sufficient to cause a prudent person to believe that a search would produce evidence of a crime.[26] According to the defense, the evidence that the State had obtained against Stan resulted from an illegal search and seizure; therefore, the **exclusionary rule** made it inadmissible in court, which meant that Judge Cody ought to dismiss the charges against Stan. The exclusionary rule prohibits the use in court of evidence that the police obtain by illegal means.[27]

County Attorney Quinlan responded that the "drug buy" in Stan's kitchen was a constitutionally permissible search and seizure because: (1) Stan invited Trooper Cummings into his kitchen in order to sell cocaine to him, whereby he waived any expectation of privacy he might otherwise have had in his home; and (2) Stan's invitation to Trooper Cummings amounted to **consent** to a search, and consent eliminates the need for probable cause and a search warrant. That is because consent is an exception to the Fourth Amendment's requirement that police officers conduct searches pursuant to warrants that are based on probable cause.[28] Thus, the "drug buy" was a constitutionally permissible search, and the evidence that resulted from it established probable cause to prosecute Stan Johnson.

The arguments that the prosecutor and the defense attorney presented at Stan's preliminary hearing reflect the **adversary system of justice** that operates in American courts. The adversary system makes every criminal trial both a competition and a search for the truth. The philosophy of the adversary system holds that the truth is most likely to emerge when the State and the defendant argue their respective causes aggressively, within the bounds of the law and professional ethics, before an impartial jury.[29] The wisdom of that philosophy is open to debate, and it is not clear that truth always triumphs in court. For example, it is not clear that truth triumphed in 1995, when a California jury acquitted former football star O. J. Simpson of a double murder despite seemingly powerful evidence of his guilt. Nevertheless, the adversary system remains in effect in the United States, which is why a defense attorney who is sure that his client is guilty still tries to present the strongest defense possible for that client.[30] The adversary system is not a "no-holds-barred brawl," though. Each side is entitled to know what evidence the opponent will present at trial, and the prosecutor is required to disclose to the defendant evidence that suggests he is innocent.[31]

Judge Cody considered the lawyers' arguments, and concluded that there was probable cause to conclude that a crime had occurred and that Stan had committed it. He therefore ruled that Stan would remain free on his own recognizance to await a decision whether there was sufficient evidence for a trial in superior court.

Indictment

Two weeks after Stan's preliminary hearing, a **grand jury** met in Granite County and considered whether or not to return an **indictment** against him on the charges that the prosecutor had filed. An indictment is a decision by a grand jury that the prosecutor has presented sufficient evidence of criminal behavior to justify taking a case to trial.[32] A grand jury is a group of citizens that is usually selected from automobile and/or voter registration lists; in New Hampshire, it can have from twelve to twenty-three members, although it can have as few as five members in some states.[33] A federal grand jury has between sixteen and twenty-three members.[34] A grand jury can **subpoena** (i.e., command) a witness to appear before it, and it can offer the witness **immunity** from prosecution in return for her testimony.[35] A witness who refuses to testify despite a grant of immunity is subject to a **contempt citation**, which can send the witness to jail until he testifies or the grand jury's term ends.[36]

A grand jury proceeding is unlike a trial. There is no judge; only the prosecutor, the grand jurors, and the witness are present in the room. The prosecutor guides the proceeding, and the grand jurors hear only the prosecution's case; no defendants or defense witnesses appear before the grand jurors. Therefore, the prosecutor usually gets the indictment that she seeks; lawyers are fond of saying that a grand jury would indict a ham sandwich if a prosecutor asked it to do so. After it considers the evidence, the grand jury votes; if a majority (e.g., twelve of twenty-three federal grand jurors) votes to indict, it issues a **true bill**, which becomes the basis for prosecution in a trial court. If a majority votes not to indict, it issues **no bill**, which prevents the case from going forward.[37]

When the grand jury met in *State v. Johnson*, prosecutor Quinlan began the hearing by reading the indictment against Stan. He then explained the elements of the crimes with which Stan was charged and the principles of search-and-seizure law that governed the case, and answered the grand jurors' questions about both matters. Next, he called Detective Halloran and Trooper Cummings, respectively, as witnesses, and asked them numerous questions about the "drug buy" at Stan's apartment and about events that occurred immediately before and after the "buy." Several grand jurors also questioned the officers. Finally, Quinlan left the room and the grand jurors reviewed the evidence. After forty-five minutes of discussion, a majority voted to indict Stan on charges of selling a controlled drug and of possessing a controlled drug with the intent to sell it.

Not all states use the grand jury indictment as a means of deciding that there is sufficient evidence for a trial. Indeed, in approximately thirty states, a prosecutor achieves the same end by filing an **information** against a defendant and by obtaining judicial approval of the information. An information is a document in which a prosecutor argues that there is sufficient evidence of criminal behavior to warrant prosecution in a particular case. If the prosecutor's case against the defendant survives judicial scrutiny at the preliminary hearing, the prosecutor will obtain judicial approval for his information.[38]

Plea Bargain

Stan Johnson's case could have ended without a trial had he accepted Kevin Quinlan's offer of a plea bargain. Quinlan's offer would have required Stan to plead guilty to a felony charge of the sale of cocaine, but it would have sentenced him to probation and community service instead of to jail. Stan rejected the offer because he wanted to avoid the stigma of a felony conviction and because he was confident that his claim of police misconduct would prevail at trial.

That decision alone made Stan Johnson an unusual criminal defendant. More than 90 percent of criminal defendants in the United States plead guilty, after accepting the prosecutor's offer of a plea bargain (see Chapter 2). Recall that in a plea bargain, the defendant agrees to plead guilty in exchange for favorable consideration by the State, which usually means a lesser charge or a recommendation for a reduced sentence. Prosecutors offer plea bargains because they are under administrative and political pressure to resolve cases and to obtain convictions as efficiently as possible. Defendants accept plea bargains because they fear that if they go to trial, the jury will convict them of the original charges against them and they will receive long prison sentences.[39]

A judge is not required to honor a plea bargain unless she participated in the plea negotiations and promised that she would fulfill the terms of the bargain.[40] Yet a judge must, before she accepts a plea bargain, make sure that the defendant entered into it intelligently and voluntarily. That means that the judge who conducts the arraignment must ask the defendant whether: (1) he understands the elements of the bargain, including that he will give up his right to a jury trial; and

(2) the prosecutor or his lawyer coerced him into agreeing to the bargain.[41] The arraignment judge must also determine that the charge to which the defendant has pled guilty is reasonably related to the facts of the case.[42] For example, it would be reasonable, in the case of a bar fight in which the defendant's punch killed the victim, to reduce a charge of **second-degree** (not premeditated) **murder** to **manslaughter** (an unintentional killing), but not to **misdemeanor assault** because the facts warrant a felony charge. A failure by the judge to adequately determine that a defendant entered into a plea bargain intelligently and voluntarily can result in a reversal of that defendant's conviction on appeal.

Motions

After Stan rejected a plea bargain, both sides began preparations for trial; for the defense, preparations included the filing of several pretrial **motions**. A motion is a request that a party to a lawsuit makes to a judge for a ruling that favors that party, such as a ruling that evidence that the party wishes to exclude at trial is inadmissible. Gene Jefferson submitted a **motion to suppress** (i.e., exclude at trial) the evidence obtained from the "drug buy" and the subsequent search of Stan's apartment; he also submitted a **memorandum of law** in support of his motion that presented his search-and-seizure argument in detail. Jefferson also submitted a **motion to dismiss** the case against Stan on the ground that Stan was a victim of **selective prosecution**. The motion charged that the State had impermissibly singled Stan out for more severe treatment than it ordinarily applied to $50 cocaine sales because he was famous and County Attorney Quinlan wanted to make an example of him.

Finally, Attorney Jefferson filed a motion for a **change of venue**, which sought to transfer *State v. Johnson* to a superior court in another New Hampshire county. The motion noted that the Sixth Amendment to the Constitution guarantees a criminal defendant a trial by an **impartial jury**. The motion argued that it would be impossible to select an impartial jury of Granite County residents for Stan's trial because Stan's fame had generated massive media coverage of the case. Reporters had solicited the opinion of almost every Granite County resident about the case, and hardly anyone seemed to be neutral about what the outcome should be.

State v. Johnson was now in superior court because the grand jury had indicted Stan on felony charges; therefore, Judge Mary Romano considered Gene Jefferson's motions, each of which the State opposed. Judge Romano denied the motion to suppress the testimony of Trooper Cummings about the drug sale because she rejected the argument that the undercover operation violated Stan's reasonable expectation of privacy in his home. Judge Romano wrote that:

> When the Defendant invited a stranger into his kitchen for the clear purpose
> of buying cocaine and then removed the alleged cocaine from its storage place,
> the Defendant surrendered any reasonable expectation of privacy that he might
> otherwise have had.[43]

That view was consistent with the well-established principle that, despite a reasonable expectation of privacy in one's home, one does not have a reasonable expectation of privacy in whatever one willingly exposes to the public, even if the exposure occurs in one's home.[44]

Judge Romano granted that part of Stan's motion that sought to suppress the results of the electronic surveillance that occurred during the "drug buy." She reasoned that New Hampshire law required a police officer who wishes to conduct electronic surveillance to first obtain authorization from a county attorney (plus the written approval of the State's attorney general), the attorney general, or the deputy attorney general. Then the officer must obtain a written order from a superior court judge that approves the officer's request.[45] The Grayson police officers had not obtained either administrative authorization or judicial approval for their electronic surveillance of Stan's conversation with Trooper Cummings. Therefore, the prosecution could not introduce in court the tape recording that the officers had made of that conversation, or the drugs, cash, and notepad that they had seized in their search of Stan's apartment.

That was good news for the defense because it meant that the State could only prosecute Stan for the sale and the possession of $50 worth of cocaine, and not for the possession with intent to sell the ten additional bags of cocaine that the police search had yielded. On the other hand, Trooper Cummings's testimony, which presumably would be identical to the recording, was admissible in court, and it could be enough evidence for the jury to convict Stan.

Judge Romano denied Stan's motion to dismiss his case on the ground of selective prosecution. She noted that in order to prove selective prosecution, Stan would have to show that: (1) the State had chosen to prosecute him even though it had not prosecuted others for the same offense; and (2) the decision to prosecute him was intentionally based on an arbitrary choice by the State to single him out for harsh treatment.[46] Furthermore, Stan would have to show that the State had selected him for prosecution on the basis of an improper criterion such as his race, religion, gender, national origin, or an equivalent.[47]

Judge Romano concluded that Stan had failed to demonstrate selective prosecution. First, it was irrelevant whether Stan was the only Grayson College student whom Granite County had ever prosecuted for selling drugs. The relevant comparison was to the numerous people whom Granite County *had* prosecuted for selling drugs; that comparison indicated that the decision to prosecute Stan was not arbitrary. Second, Stan had not established that the State had selected him for prosecution on an impermissible basis; neither race, religion, gender, nor national origin affected the decision to prosecute him. Nothing prohibited the county attorney from prosecuting Stan in order to deter others from selling drugs in Granite County.

Finally, Judge Romano granted Stan's motion for a change of venue. She had reviewed the numerous newspaper clippings and tapes of radio and television broadcasts that Gene Jefferson had submitted in an effort to demonstrate that pretrial publicity about the case would make it impossible to impanel an impartial jury in Granite County.[48] Judge Romano concluded that the pretrial publicity in this case was so pervasive and the hostility of local residents toward Stan was so great that it would be extraordinarily difficult to select an impartial jury. She therefore moved the case to neighboring Pine County, New Hampshire's northernmost and least populous county.

Trial

Defendant's Right to a Speedy Trial

Like all criminal defendants, Stan Johnson was entitled to receive a **speedy trial**. The Sixth Amendment guarantees speedy trials for both state and federal defendants. That does not mean that the trial must proceed quickly; instead, it means that the trial must occur within a reasonable time after an indictment is returned or an information is filed. Many states also have speedy trial statutes, which usually set limits of ninety days or 120 days between accusation (information or indictment) and the start of trial.[49] If a judge concludes that the State has denied a defendant a speedy trial, he must dismiss the case **with prejudice,** which means that the State cannot attempt to reprosecute the defendant.[50] Judges rarely reach that conclusion because they are reluctant to dismiss criminal cases on the basis of what the public often considers to be "legal technicalities."

The **Federal Speedy Trial Act of 1974**, which applies in federal court only, permits judges to dismiss criminal charges in cases in which the government fails to seek an indictment within thirty days of arrest or trial does not begin within seventy working days after the grand jury returns an indictment.[51] That is no guarantee against lengthy litigation, though, because dismissal requires proof of *intentional* delay by the prosecutor; bureaucratic sluggishness is insufficient to justify dismissal.[52]

Jury Selection

When *State v. Johnson* went to trial in Pine County Superior Court, the first order of business was jury selection, which lawyers call *voir dire*. *Voir dire* ("to see what is said") is a process of questioning a pool of potential jurors, known as a *venire*, in order to reduce it to the number of persons required for the trial, or *petit* jury.[53] Most states select the *venire* at random from voter and/or automobile registration lists in order to ensure that the *venire* will be a cross section of the community from which it is drawn, as the Sixth Amendment requires. There is no constitutional requirement, though, that each trial jury be a cross section of the community from which it is drawn.[54]

Voir dire is the principal device that the court and the lawyers use to ensure that a jury will be impartial. Each lawyer would prefer to have a jury that is partial to her side; that is why she will sometimes hire a **jury consultant,** usually a sociologist or a psychologist, to help her pick a jury. Typically, though, she must be satisfied with a jury that has assured her of its impartiality.

In some states, the lawyers conduct *voir dire*. They try to learn potential jurors' attitudes toward a case by asking them questions that are designed to elicit those attitudes. In New Hampshire, however, the judge conducts *voir dire* in felony cases, except capital and first-degree murder cases.[55] In *State v. Johnson*, Judge Romano asked the potential jurors two questions that she was required by statute to ask: whether (1) they believed that, because Stan was on trial for a crime, he was probably guilty and must prove his innocence; and if so, (2) that belief would prevent them from following the court's directions concerning the presumption of innocence and the State's burden of proof.[56] No potential juror answered "Yes"; Judge Romano could have removed from the *venire* anyone who did. She also asked whether any member(s) of the *venire* had expressed or formed opinions about the case, and whether they were prejudiced to any degree about it.[57]

Judge Romano concluded *voir dire* by asking several questions that the lawyers had submitted, which New Hampshire judges can, but are not required, to do. First, she asked questions that the State had submitted, for example:

1. Have you formed an opinion concerning the legalization or the decriminalization of drugs?
2. If the police receive information that someone is selling drugs, do you think that it would be unfair or a dirty tactic for the police to send an officer to the suspect's house to "buy" drugs?

Then she asked questions that the defense had submitted, for example:

1. Do you think that people who use drugs aren't hurting anyone but themselves, and that the police spend too much time pursuing drug dealers?
2. Have you had any experiences with college students that would make it difficult for you to be impartial in this case?

Judge Romano removed one member of the *venire* based on his answers to the supplementary questions. She pronounced the remaining members qualified to serve on the jury.

Then the lawyers began to exercise **challenges for cause** and **peremptory challenges**. A challenge for cause is a claim by a lawyer that a prospective juror cannot be impartial for a particular reason, such as service on a grand jury that investigated the same crime.[58] It is a means of removing persons whose biases or likely biases are open and obvious. In *State v. Johnson*, Gene Jefferson successfully challenged for cause a man who had served on a jury that had convicted a college-age male of selling cocaine.

A peremptory challenge requires no reason for removing a potential juror. A lawyer may use it to remove a person who exhibits no obvious bias, but whose background or appearance suggests that he could be hostile to that lawyer's cause,[59] so long as he does not use it to exclude the members of a particular race from a jury.[60] In *State v. Johnson*, Kevin Quinlan removed by peremptory challenge a young woman whose purse bore a large button that said: "Question Authority." A lawyer can make an unlimited number of challenges for cause, in both state courts and federal courts, but there is a limit on peremptory challenges in state courts and in federal courts.[61] For example, Judge Romano allotted the lawyers in *State v. Johnson* three peremptory challenges each, pursuant to New Hampshire court rules.[62]

When jury selection was complete in *State v. Johnson,* the clerk of the court swore in the twelve jurors who would hear the evidence at trial. New Hampshire courts use twelve-member juries in felony cases,[63] but states can use juries with as few as six members in criminal cases, and many states, including New Hampshire, do so in misdemeanor matters.[64] Federal courts always use twelve-member juries in criminal cases. Judge Romano decided not to **sequester** the jury in a hotel because she anticipated a short trial, which would diminish the likelihood that a juror would discuss the case with others or would read or hear news reports about it. Instead, before excusing the jurors for the day, she gave them a stern warning to avoid media accounts of the trial and to refrain from discussing the trial with anyone, even each other, until further notice.

Opening Statements

The trial phase of *State v. Johnson* began in earnest the following morning, when Judge Romano entered the courtroom promptly at 9 A.M. She wished everyone present a "good morning," and then asked the lawyers if they were ready to proceed. Both lawyers indicated that they were ready. Judge Romano swore in the jury. Then she introduced the jurors to the case and instructed them about their role in it. She explained that the indictment that the grand jury had returned against Stan was merely a set of allegations, and that it was not evidence of guilt. She also explained that the State had the burden of proving guilt **beyond a reasonable doubt**. She reminded the jurors to presume that Stan was innocent unless and until the State proved him guilty. She instructed them to determine the facts from the testimony and other evidence that both sides introduced during the trial. They were to disregard any evidence that she instructed them to disregard during trial and anything they had read or heard about the case before trial. Finally, they were not to discuss the case among themselves until both sides had presented all of their evidence.

Judge Romano's statement to the jurors focused on their role at trial, but it also illustrated her role. The jury decides what the facts are in a case, but the judge decides what the law is, by choosing whether to admit certain evidence and to **sustain** (i.e. allow) or to **overrule** (disallow) certain questions or categories of question that opposing counsel ask witnesses. A judge's rulings about evidence are especially important because they can strengthen or weaken a prosecutor's case. A judge evaluates evidence according to its **relevance** to the case at hand, its **probative value** (i.e., capacity to prove or disprove a proposition that is at issue in the case), and its potential to **prejudice** the jury against the defendant.[65] Evidence can be relevant and probative, but inadmissible because its potential to prejudice the jury outweighs its probative value. In other words, the evidence would likely cause the jury to convict the defendant on the basis of his past behavior instead of on the facts of the present case.

For example, in a rape trial, if the prosecutor sought to introduce an affidavit sworn to by a woman who claimed that the defendant had sexually assaulted her several years earlier, the affidavit would be relevant and it might be probative, but it would be inadmissible if the judge concluded that its potential for prejudice out-weighed its probative value.[66] When a judge admits prejudicial information into evidence and the jury convicts, the defendant will undoubtedly urge an appellate court to reverse his conviction and to grant him a new trial in which the preju-dicial information will be inadmissible.[67]

When Judge Romano had finished her statement to the jury, she said to the prosecutor, "You may begin, Mr. Quinlan." Quinlan greeted the jurors and intro-duced himself; then he began his **opening statement**. Quinlan reiterated the charges against Stan and indicated that he would prove them during the trial. That was in keeping with the purposes of an opening statement, which are to inform the jurors about what the lawyer intends to prove and about how he intends to prove it.[68] Quinlan then recounted the facts of the case, stressing that Stan was on trial not because he was famous or a college student, but because he "knowingly sold a controlled drug, cocaine, to another person." Quinlan cited only evidence that he believed would be introduced at trial.[69] It is "professional mis-conduct" for a lawyer to cite in an opening statement evidence that she knows will not be presented at trial.[70] Kevin Quinlan concluded his opening statement by telling the jurors:

> I am confident that, once you have heard all of the evidence in this case, you will be convinced beyond a reasonable doubt that the Defendant knowingly sold cocaine to Steve Cummings. Don't let anybody put the police or the Town of Grayson or Grayson College on trial here. Stan Johnson and only Stan Johnson is the Defendant in this case. Please remember that. Thank you.

Then it was Gene Jefferson's turn to make an opening statement. He greeted the jurors, introduced himself, and explained his view of the case, which was dra-matically different from the State's view. Jefferson told the jurors that Stan sold cocaine to Trooper Cummings because the Grayson police entrapped him by means of "unlawful and overzealous tactics." In other words, the Grayson police "manufactured a cocaine sale in order to catch the Defendant in their trap." Entrapment was the best defense available to Jefferson after Judge Romano refused to suppress Trooper Cummings's testimony and to dismiss the case because of selec-tive prosecution. Jefferson noted that Trooper Cummings had told Stan a false story that friends of Cummings's girlfriend had referred him to Stan, and then Cummings made an unsolicited request to purchase cocaine from Stan. Thus, Jef-ferson concluded:

> The issue for you to decide is not whether Stan Johnson sold cocaine to an under-cover police officer, but whether the police used unlawful methods that induced him to sell that cocaine. I believe that when you hear the evidence, you will con-clude that what happened in this case was an example of the improper use of gov-ernmental power against an individual. The evidence will show that the Grayson police entrapped Stan Johnson to sell cocaine. That is why Stan Johnson is not guilty of the charges against him. Thank you.

That completed the opening statements. It was time for both sides to pre-sent their evidence.

Presentation of Evidence

The presentation of evidence began with the **direct examination** by Mr. Quinlan of Detective Mike Halloran of the Grayson Police Department. Direct examination occurs when a lawyer questions a witness whom he has called to testify. In criminal cases, the presentation of evidence begins with a direct examination of a witness by the prosecutor. Quinlan asked Halloran to describe how the "drug buy" unfolded on January 30, and Halloran recited the events that led to Stan's arrest. He identified a bag of cocaine in a photograph that Quinlan displayed as the cocaine that Stan had sold to Cummings; that was the same cocaine that Halloran had field-tested at the police station after the sale, before he sent it to the State Police Laboratory for further tests. Halloran also explained how the Grayson police placed confiscated drugs in sealed bags, marked the bags, and stored them in an evidence room so that the State could prove at trial that nobody had tampered with the evidence between arrest and trial. Finally, Halloran identified Stan Johnson as the person whom he had arrested in the early hours of January 30, 1999. That concluded the direct examination; Quinlan thanked Halloran for his testimony.

Then Gene Jefferson cross-examined Detective Halloran. **Cross-examination** occurs when a lawyer questions a witness whom opposing counsel has called to testify. The witness's testimony during direct examination is likely to have been adverse to the interests of the cross-examiner's cause, so cross-examination can be unpleasant for the witness. The cross-examiner often tries to **impeach**, or call into question, the witness's credibility by identifying discrepancies between the witness's courtroom testimony and her pretrial statements to the police or to the lawyers. The other main difference between direct examination and cross-examination is that during cross-examination, a lawyer may ask a witness **leading questions**, which presume their own answers. Any question that begins with the phrase, "Isn't it true that ..." is a leading question. Leading questions are prohibited during direct examination.

Cross-examination is not only a custom in criminal trials; it is a constitutional right of the defendant. The Sixth Amendment to the U.S. Constitution guarantees a criminal defendant's right "to be confronted with the witnesses against him," which includes the opportunity to cross-examine those witnesses. The Sixth Amendment also guarantees a criminal defendant the related right "to have compulsory process for obtaining witnesses in his favor," which means he can compel defense witnesses to testify and he can obtain documents or other materials that will bolster his defense. Thus, the Sixth Amendment in general, and cross-examination in particular, equalize the trial contest between the State and the individual.

Gene Jefferson's goal in cross-examining Detective Halloran was to emphasize for the jury what Jefferson believed was the insufficient basis for the attempt by the Grayson police to make a "drug buy" at Stan's apartment. First, Jefferson asked Halloran about his conversation with Officer Leveau. The questions and answers were as follows:

Q.   Did you ask Officer Leveau what the basis was for her information?

A.   I believe she said that she had heard it from students at Grayson College.

Q.   And did you ask her who those students were?

A.   No.

Q.   Why not?

A.   I don't know why not.

Q   So the information that Officer Leveau gave you was a totally unsubstantiated rumor, is that correct?

A.   Yes.

Q.   You had no idea where Officer Leveau got her information?

A.   That's correct.

Q   And you never asked her where she got this information, did you?

A.   I can't remember asking her, no.

Q.   You didn't even ask her when she received this information, did you?

A.   No, I did not.

When the cross-examination was over, Prosecutor Quinlan conducted a brief **redirect examination** of Halloran. Lawyers can conduct several redirect and **recross** examinations of witnesses, until they have asked and the witnesses have answered all their questions. Quinlan wanted the jury to know that it was customary for police officers to conduct undercover drug operations on the basis of unsubstantiated rumors, and that this case was not unusual. His exchange with Halloran was as follows:

Q.   Detective Halloran, in your experience with the Grayson Police Department, have you conducted undercover drug operations, before or since this case, based on unsubstantiated rumors?

A.   Yes, both before and since this case.

Q.   Is it standard procedure in the Grayson Police Department to conduct undercover drug operations based on unsubstantiated rumors?

A.   If we think the rumor could have some validity to it, yes, it is standard procedure.

When Quinlan finished, the defense had no more questions for Detective Halloran, so Judge Romano excused him. The prosecution called its next witness, Trooper Steve Cummings. Cummings testified that he became aware of Stan Johnson in late January, 1999, when Detective Halloran recruited him to "buy" drugs from Stan. Cummings testified that, on January 29, he met with his boss, Lieutenant Ted Yates of the New Hampshire State Police, and with Halloran, and that they instructed him what to do during the "buy." Cummings also described his trip to Stan's apartment, his conversation with Stan, and his purchase of cocaine from Stan. Quinlan showed Cummings a photograph of a small bag of cocaine, and Cummings identified the bag in the photograph as the same bag that Stan had sold him. Finally, Cummings identified Stan Johnson as the person who had sold him cocaine.

Then Gene Jefferson cross-examined Trooper Cummings. Jefferson wanted to elicit answers that would convince the jury that Cummings had induced Stan to commit a crime that he would not otherwise have committed. A portion of the cross-examination appears below.

Q. When you went to the Defendant's house on January 30, you entered and asked for Stan, is that right?

A. Yes.

Q. And Stan identified himself?

A. Yes.

Q. Did he invite you in?

A. Yes.

Q. And you told him that you were a student?

A. Yes.

Q. That wasn't true, was it?

A. No.

Q. And you told him that some friends of your girlfriend had told you that you could buy cocaine from him; is that right?

A. Yes.

Q. That wasn't true, was it?

A. No.

Q. You also told him that your girlfriend was a student at Grayson College; is that right?

A. Yes.

Q. That wasn't true either, was it?

A. No.

Q. You were the first one to raise the subject of buying drugs, right?

A. Yes.

Q. Were you friendly toward the Defendant while you were in his apartment?

A. Yes.

Q. Approximately how long were you in the Defendant's apartment?

A. Ten or fifteen minutes.

Q. And you had a friendly conversation with the Defendant for ten or fifteen minutes?

A. Yes.

A brief redirect by the prosecutor followed. Quinlan wanted to make the point that Stan had sold cocaine to Trooper Cummings voluntarily. The redirect was as follows:

Q. Trooper Cummings, where were you in the apartment when the subject of drugs came up?

A. At the entrance to the kitchen.

Q. Were you standing or sitting?

A. Sitting.

Q. What happened immediately after the Defendant said, "I'm Stan?"

A. I told him that friends of my girlfriend said I could buy coke from him.

Q. So the Defendant knew before he invited you to sit at his kitchen table that you had come there to buy cocaine from him?

A.   Yes.
Q.   Had you discussed with Detective Halloran and Lieutenant Yates what you would do if the Defendant had said, "I don't sell drugs?"
A.   Yes, I would have left.

When the redirect ended, it was nearly 5 P.M. Judge Romano adjourned the trial for the day, and reminded the jurors not to discuss the case with anyone while court was adjourned. The next morning, Kevin Quinlan called his final witness, Margerie McCloud, a chemist who worked at the New Hampshire State Police Crime Laboratory. McCloud was an **expert witness**, whose education and experience qualified her to express her professional opinion in court about technical matters relevant to the case. The purpose of her testimony was to help the jury understand those matters. McCloud testified that she had conducted hundreds of tests on confiscated drugs during her employment at the crime lab, and that she had conducted a test in this case. She described the testing procedure at length, especially the security measures that she and her colleagues employed to protect evidence against tampering or contamination at the lab. She identified the substance that Stan had sold to Trooper Cummings as being the same substance that she had tested, and she indicated that the test showed that it was cocaine. Finally, Ms. McCloud explained the security measures that she took after testing the cocaine to make sure that it would not be contaminated prior to its use in court. She said that it remained in the same condition that it was in when she tested it at the lab.

Gene Jefferson briefly cross-examined Margerie McCloud. He asked her to open the bag that contained the sample she had tested so that the jury could see how small an amount one-sixteenth of an ounce is. That prompted a redirect from the prosecutor, who did not want the jurors to literally weigh the evidence against Stan according to the amount of cocaine that he had sold. Quinlan therefore asked McCloud if one-sixteenth of an ounce was a "typical" amount that she tested in her lab in drug prosecutions, and she responded that it was.

Then the State rested its case. The defense could have called witnesses of its own, including Stan, but Gene Jefferson chose instead to rest his case too. The heart of the defense's case was that the police had induced Stan to sell cocaine, and Jefferson believed that he had shown that inducement during his cross-examinations of Detective Halloran and Trooper Cummings, respectively. It was pointless for Stan to testify because Stan did not deny that he had sold cocaine to Trooper Cummings. Besides, if any jurors resented Stan's fame or his student status, his testimony could prejudice his case. Thus, instead of presenting witnesses, Gene Jefferson made a motion to the court for a **directed verdict**; the motion asked Judge Romano to find Stan not guilty because the State had not introduced sufficient evidence to justify a jury verdict against him.[71] Defense attorneys routinely move for directed verdicts (a.k.a. **judgments of acquittal**) when all the evidence has been presented. Judge Romano denied the motion. Jefferson also moved to strike Trooper Cummings's testimony from the trial record because it was the product of an unlawful search and seizure. Judge Romano denied that motion too.

Closing Arguments

Then it was time for the lawyers to present their **closing arguments**. Closing arguments provide an opportunity for each lawyer to review and interpret the evidence presented at trial in an effort to persuade the jurors to decide in his favor. A lawyer will quote favorable testimony, refer to helpful exhibits, and draw jurors' attention to inconsistencies in the opponent's evidence during a closing argument.[72]

Gene Jefferson began his closing statement by thanking the jurors for their time and their attention.[73] He then told them that the issue in this case was not whether Stan had sold cocaine to Trooper Cummings, but instead, whether the police had induced Stan to sell cocaine. Jefferson reminded the jurors that the police had based their undercover operation against Stan on a rumor and that they had designed the operation to induce Stan to sell cocaine. He said:

> The police used Steve Cummings in this undercover operation because he was about the same age as Stan and he appeared to be a fellow student, which increased the likelihood that if Stan had any drugs and Cummings asked for a small amount, Stan would sell the drugs to him. Don't forget that Cummings raised the subject of a drug sale when he and Stan had a conversation in Stan's kitchen. In other words, the police created the drug sale that is the subject of this case; the police induced Stan to do what he would not have done without that inducement.

Finally, Jefferson reminded the jurors that they had the option to find Stan not guilty of the sale of a controlled drug, but guilty of the lesser crime of possession of a controlled drug, which was the only real offense that Stan had committed on January 30, 1999. That verdict, Jefferson concluded, "would punish Stan for possessing cocaine, but it would also punish the police, and they deserve to be punished for their outrageous conduct in this case. Thank you."

Kevin Quinlan also began his closing argument by thanking the jurors for their time and attention. He told them that they make the adversary system of justice work. Then he said:

> The State must prove that the Defendant knowingly sold a controlled drug, cocaine, to Trooper Steve Cummings. The State has met its burden of proof. The substance that changed hands was cocaine, as Ms. McCloud testified. Trooper Cummings paid the Defendant $50, and the Defendant handed Trooper Cummings a bag of cocaine. The bag was marked for sale. Trooper Cummings identified the Defendant as the person who sold the cocaine to him.

Turning to entrapment, Quinlan told the jurors:

> You also have to decide whether the police acted in a manner that induced the Defendant to commit a crime that he would not otherwise have committed, and whether, if the police acted in that manner, the Defendant should leave this courtroom a free man. Ladies and gentlemen, Trooper Cummings did not force the Defendant to sell him cocaine. The Defendant invited Trooper Cummings to sit in his kitchen while the Defendant retrieved a bag of cocaine that he then sold to Trooper Cummings. Trooper Cummings operated undercover, but that is

necessary. If not for undercover work, it would be impossible to investigate drug dealers. So there is no evidence that the police induced the Defendant to commit a crime that he would not otherwise have committed. Thus, the only fair verdict in this case is a guilty verdict. Thank you.

Finally, Quinlan told the jurors that it would not be sufficient to find Stan guilty of possession because the bag of cocaine that Stan had sold to Trooper Cummings was marked for sale. Stan intended to sell the cocaine in that bag, not consume it.

Jury Instructions

When the prosecutor finished his closing argument, Judge Romano instructed the jury about the law that governed the case. She read a list of written **jury instructions**. Jury instructions are designed to (1) clarify the issues in the case and (2) help the jurors to understand the questions that they must answer in order to resolve the case.[74] The lawyers can recommend instructions to the judge, but the judge decides which instructions to give to the jurors. The instructions remind jurors about: (1) their duty to consider only evidence that the lawyers presented; (2) their duty to consider that evidence objectively and impartially; (3) the elements of the alleged offense, as defined by statute; (4) the State's burden of proof; and (5) the requirement that the State prove guilt beyond a reasonable doubt.[75]

The key elements of Judge Romano's instructions were:

1. If the Defendant proves to you by a **preponderance** (i.e., a majority) **of the evidence** (a defendant's burden of proof in demonstrating entrapment) that police officers induced or encouraged him to sell a controlled drug, by methods that created a substantial risk that a person who was otherwise not disposed to sell drugs would sell them, then you must find the Defendant not guilty of the offense of sale of a controlled drug. If the Defendant fails to prove to you that he was entrapped, the State still must prove to you beyond a reasonable doubt that the Defendant's conduct met all the elements of the offense of sale of a controlled drug.

2. If you find that the Defendant is not guilty of the sale of a controlled drug, either because the State has failed to prove each element of that offense beyond a reasonable doubt or because the Defendant has proved entrapment by a preponderance of the evidence, then you may consider whether the Defendant is guilty of the lesser included offense of possession of a controlled drug.

3. In order to prove possession, the State must show, beyond a reasonable doubt, that on the date and at the location alleged, the Defendant knowingly possessed a controlled drug; specifically, a $50 bag of cocaine.

Verdict

The jurors retired to the jury room to deliberate at 2:28 P.M. New Hampshire law required them to reach a unanimous verdict, although the U.S. Supreme Court has held that the federal Constitution requires unanimous verdicts only in cases in which the defendant could receive the death penalty.[76] At 4:49 P.M., the jurors informed the deputy sheriff who was stationed outside the jury room that they had reached a verdict, and the deputy sheriff informed Judge Romano. The trial participants returned to the courtroom. A brief conversation followed between the clerk of the court and the **foreman** of the jury, whose fellow jurors had selected her to preside over their deliberations. The conversation was as follows:

Q. Has the jury reached a verdict on the sale of a controlled drug?
A. Yes, we have.
Q. What is your verdict?
A. Guilty.
Q. So say you all?
A. (All) Yes.

Gene Jefferson asked Judge Romano to poll each juror; she complied, and the result was still a guilty verdict. Judge Romano thanked the jurors for their service and excused them. The trial was over. Stan Johnson was guilty of the sale and of the possession of a controlled drug.

Sentencing

On July 27, 1999, Judge Romano convened a **sentencing hearing** in *State v. Johnson.* Sentencing is the imposition of a penalty on one who has been convicted of a crime. It is the judge's job in most criminal cases, although juries sentence when the defendant is eligible for the death penalty. Sentences usually consist of **imprisonment**, **probation** (supervised release with restrictions), a **fine**, or some combination of those penalties; most states and the federal government, however, impose **death** as the penalty for some crimes, such as the murder of a law enforcement officer.[77] Sentencing is a risk-management device that seeks to punish offenders for their crimes and to deter others from committing similar crimes, while also giving offenders an opportunity to rehabilitate themselves.[78]

Some states and the federal government use **determinate sentencing**, which establishes a particular punishment for a particular crime.[79] For example, everyone convicted of first-degree burglary would receive the same sentence. The judge would have little or no discretion to modify the sentence.[80] Determinate sentencing removes the variation between sentences for the same crime that occurs when judges have discretion in sentencing. It also eliminates the reductions in sentences that result from an offender's good behavior in prison or his enrollment in work or study programs there.[81] Thus, determinate sentencing offers "truth in sentencing."

New Hampshire generally uses **indeterminate sentencing**, which establishes relatively general penalties for offenses and gives judges considerable discretion to choose the penalty and to set the upper and lower limits on prison sentences.[82] Indeterminate sentencing sets sentences based on characteristics of the crime and the offender, and it reduces prison time as a reward for positive behavior in prison. It rewards offenders when appropriate in order to encourage them to participate in their own rehabilitation.[83] Thus, Judge Romano had discretion to choose the sentence that she believed was appropriate for Stan Johnson.

Judge Romano considered the **sentencing memorandum** that Gene Jefferson had submitted and the **presentence report** that the Granite County Probation

Office had submitted before she imposed Stan's sentence. The sentencing memorandum recommended that Stan be sentenced to a period of probation and community service. It noted that he had lived an exemplary life since his arrest; he was attending college in New York State and had completed a drug treatment program.

The presentence report was not nearly so forgiving. A presentence report is the product of a **presentence investigation** of the offender's background, and the investigator's recommendations often influence sentencing decisions, especially in states that use indeterminate sentencing.[84] It attempts to recommend a penalty that matches an offender's crime and the prospects for his rehabilitation. Those prospects are brighter if the offender can show a good employment record, strong family ties, regular church attendance, psychological stability, and that his crime was nonviolent.[85] The presentence report on Stan Johnson acknowledged that he was attending college, had strong family ties, and had completed drug treatment. It also noted, though, that the sale of cocaine required premeditation (i.e., acquisition, weighing, packaging, sale) and that Stan could not or would not explain why he had become a drug dealer. Therefore, the report recommended that the court impose a jail sentence of from three to six months to force Stan to see the gravity of his mistake.

The sentence that Judge Romano imposed reflected a balance between these factors. The statutory penalty in New Hampshire for the sale of less than one-half ounce of cocaine was three-and-one-half to seven years in jail.[86] Judge Romano sentenced Stan to serve three-and-one-half to five years in the Granite County House of Correction, but **suspended** all but three months, which meant that he would serve three months in jail. He could serve his sentence during the summer, so that it would not interrupt his education. After his release, Stan would have to perform 250 hours of community service speaking to schoolchildren about the dangers and consequences of drug use. He would also have to pay a $1,500 fine or make a $1,500 contribution to a nonprofit corporation that assisted recovering drug addicts in New Hampshire. Having pronounced sentence, Judge Romano banged her gavel and rose from the bench; the sentencing hearing was over.

CONCLUSION

The criminal justice process illustrates the norm-enforcement function of courts, which occurs when courts punish acts and failures to act that violate criminal statutes. Criminal courts not only enforce social norms, though; they also resolve disputes between the people of a state or of the United States and the defendant(s). They make public policy, too; for example, sentences reflect policy judgments about how best to protect public safety, deter and punish crime, and rehabilitate criminals.

State v. Johnson showed a state court performing all of those functions. It also showed prosecutorial discretion, the difference between substantive and procedural criminal law, and the ways in which a defendant's socioeconomic circumstances can affect his case. Furthermore, it showed how politics influences who will prosecute, what crimes will be prosecuted, and who will preside at criminal trials.

The case discussed below shows how politics and public sentiment can combine to deny a defendant a fair trial. It is perhaps the definitive example of how a judge should *not* conduct a criminal trial. It is also a favorite subject of the entertainment industry, having inspired a 1990s film, *The Fugitive*, and a 1960s television series by the same name. After reading the U.S. Supreme Court's decision in this case, try to decide: (1) whether the Court correctly reversed the defendant's murder conviction; and (2) if so, what the trial judge should have done to protect the defendant's right to a fair trial.

Epilogue: Dr. Sheppard's Trial

Sheppard v. Maxwell
384 U.S. 333 (1966)

JUSTICE CLARK delivered the opinion of the Court.

This federal habeas corpus application involves the question whether Sheppard was deprived of a fair trial in his state conviction for the second-degree murder of his wife because of the trial judge's failure to protect Sheppard sufficiently from the massive, pervasive and prejudicial publicity that attended his prosecution. We have concluded that Sheppard did not receive a fair trial consistent with the Due Process Clause of the Fourteenth Amendment and, therefore, reverse the judgment.

I

Marilyn Sheppard, petitioner's pregnant wife, was bludgeoned to death in the upstairs bedroom of their lakeshore home in Bay Village, Ohio, a suburb of Cleveland.

From the outset officials focused suspicion on Sheppard. After a search of the house and the premises on the morning of the tragedy, Dr. Gerber, the Coroner, is reported—and it is undenied—to have told his men, "Well, it is evident the doctor did this, so let's go get the confession out of him." He proceeded to interrogate and examine Sheppard while the latter was under sedation in his hospital room.

Throughout this period the newspapers emphasized evidence that tended to incriminate Sheppard and pointed out discrepancies in his statements to authorities. The newspapers also delved into Sheppard's personal life. Articles stressed his extramarital love affairs as a motive for the crime. [**Editor's Note**: Trial testimony revealed one such affair, not the numerous affairs that the newspapers suggested had occurred].

On July 28, an editorial entitled "Why Don't Police Quiz Top Suspect?" demanded that Sheppard be taken to police headquarters.

A front-page editorial on July 30 asked: "Why Isn't Sam Sheppard in Jail?" It was later titled "Quit Stalling—Bring Him In."

II

With this background the case came on for trial two weeks before the November general election at which the chief prosecutor was a candidate for common pleas judge and the trial judge, Judge Blythin, was a candidate [for reelection]. Twenty-five days before the case was set, 75 veniremen were called as prospective jurors. All three Cleveland newspapers published the names and addresses of the veniremen. As a consequence, anonymous letters and telephone calls, as well as friends, regarding the impending prosecution were received by all of the prospective jurors.

… After the trial opened, the witnesses, counsel, and jurors were photographed and televised whenever they entered or left the courtroom. Sheppard was brought to the courtroom about 10 minutes before each session began; he was surrounded by reporters and extensively photographed for the newspapers and television. A rule of court prohibited picture-taking in the courtroom during the actual sessions of the court, but no restraints were put on photographers during recesses, which were taken once each morning and afternoon, with a longer period for lunch.

All of these arrangements with the news media and their massive coverage of the trial continued during the entire nine weeks of the trial.

The jurors themselves were constantly exposed to the news media. Every juror, except one, testified at voir dire to reading about the case in the Cleveland papers or to having heard broadcasts about it. As the selection of the jury progressed, individual pictures of prospective members appeared daily. During the trial, pictures of the jury appeared over 40 times in the Cleveland papers alone. The court permitted photographers to take pictures of the jury in the box, and individual pictures of the members in the jury room.

While the jury was being selected, a two-inch [newspaper] headline asked: "But Who Will Speak for Marilyn?" [T]he author—through quotes from detective Chief James McArthur—assured readers that the prosecution's exhibits would speak for Marilyn. "Her story," McArthur stated, "will come into this courtroom through our witnesses."

On November 19, a Cleveland police officer gave testimony that tended to contradict details in the written statement Sheppard made to the Cleveland police. Two days later, in a broadcast heard over [radio] Station WHK in Cleveland, [the announcer] likened Sheppard to a perjurer…. Though defense counsel asked the judge to question the jury to ascertain how many heard the broadcast, the court refused to do so. The judge also overruled the motion for continuance based on the same ground.

On November 24, a [newspaper] story appeared under an eight-column headline: "Sam Called A 'Jekyll-Hyde' By Marilyn, Cousin To Testify." It was related that Marilyn had recently told friends that Sheppard was a "Dr. Jekyll and Mr. Hyde" character. No such testimony was ever produced at the trial. Defense counsel made motions for change of venue, continuance and mistrial, but they were denied. No action was taken by the court.

The principle that justice cannot survive behind walls of silence has long been reflected in the "Anglo-American distrust for secret trials." *In re Oliver*, 333 U.S. 257 (1948). A responsible press has always been regarded as the handmaiden of effective judicial administration, especially in the criminal field. The press does not simply publish information about trials but guards against the miscarriage of justice by subjecting the police, prosecutors, and judicial processes to extensive public scrutiny and criticism. This Court has, therefore, been unwilling to place any direct limitations on the freedom traditionally exercised by the news media....

But the Court has also pointed out that "[l]egal trials are not like elections, to be won through the use of the meeting-hall, the radio, and the newspaper." *Bridges v. California*, 314 U.S. 252 (1941).

The undeviating rule of this Court was expressed by Mr. Justice Holmes over half a century ago in *Patterson v. Colorado*, 205 U.S. 454 (1907):

> "The theory of our system is that the conclusions to be reached in a case will be induced only by evidence and argument in open court, and not by any outside influence, whether of private talk or public print."

The carnival atmosphere at [Sheppard's] trial could easily have been avoided since the courtroom and courthouse premises are subject to the control of the court. [T]he presence of the press at judicial proceedings must be limited when it is apparent that the accused might otherwise be prejudiced or disadvantaged. Bearing in mind the massive pretrial publicity, the judge should have adopted stricter rules governing the use of the courtroom by newsmen, as Sheppard's counsel requested.

And it is obvious that the judge should have further sought to alleviate this problem by imposing control over the statements made to the news media by counsel, witnesses, and especially the Coroner and police officers. The prosecution repeatedly made evidence available to the news media which was never offered in the trial. Much of the "evidence" disseminated in this fashion was clearly inadmissible. The exclusion of such evidence in court is rendered meaningless when news media make it available to the public.

More specifically, the trial court might well have proscribed [out-of-court] statements by any lawyer, party, witness, or court official which divulged prejudicial matters, such as the refusal of Sheppard to submit to interrogation or take any lie detector tests; any statement made by Sheppard to officials; the identity of prospective witnesses or their probable testimony; any belief in guilt or innocence; or like statements concerning the merits of the case.

Due process requires that the accused receive a trial by an impartial jury free from outside influences. Of course, there is nothing that proscribes the press from reporting events that transpire in the courtroom. But where there is a reasonable likelihood that prejudicial news prior to trial will prevent a fair trial, the judge should continue the case until the threat abates, or transfer it to another county not so permeated with publicity. In addition, sequestration of the jury was something the judge should have raised [voluntarily] with counsel. If publicity during the proceedings threatens the fairness of the trial, a new trial should be ordered. The courts must take such steps by rule and regulation that will protect their processes from prejudicial outside interferences.

Since the state trial judge did not fulfill his duty to protect Sheppard from the inherently prejudicial publicity which saturated the community and to control disruptive influences in the courtroom, we must reverse [the federal district court's] denial of the habeas petition. The case is remanded to the District Court with instructions to issue the writ [of habeas corpus to Maxwell, the Warden of the Ohio State Penitentiary] and order that Sheppard be released from custody unless the State [tries] him … again within a reasonable time.

It is so ordered.

JUSTICE BLACK dissented but did not write an opinion.

QUESTIONS FOR DISCUSSION

State v. Johnson

1. Did the police act improperly in this case? Should the court have dismissed the charges against Stan Johnson?
2. Assuming the police acted properly, did the State prove Stan's guilt beyond a reasonable doubt?
3. If you agree with the verdict in this case, do you also agree with the sentence? If not, what aspect of the sentence do you oppose, and why?

Sheppard v. Maxwell

1. What two fundamental constitutional rights were in conflict in this case?
2. Why did Sheppard argue that he was entitled to be released from prison and to receive a new trial?
3. Why did Sheppard argue that he had not received a fair trial?
4. What evidence did Sheppard introduce to show that he had not received a fair trial?
5. How did politics influence Sheppard's trial? How might the local authorities have minimized the influence of politics in the *Sheppard* case?
6. Why had the Supreme Court long been reluctant to restrict media coverage of criminal trials?
7. When, according to Justice Clark, are restrictions on media coverage of criminal trials justified?
8. What steps could the trial judge have taken before the *Sheppard* trial to minimize the adverse effects of pretrial publicity on the jury? What restrictions could the trial judge have imposed on media coverage once the trial began?
9. Was the Supreme Court correct to grant Sheppard's petition for *habeas corpus*? Explain.

NOTES

1. Frank Schmalleger, *Criminal Justice Today*, Third Edition (Englewood Cliffs, N.J.: Prentice-Hall, 1995), p. 118.
2. Wayne R. LaFave and Austin W. Scott, Jr., *Substantive Criminal Law*, Volume Two (St. Paul, Minn.: West Publishing Company, 1986 and 1999 Supplement), p. 190.

3. Wayne LaFave and Austin W. Scott, Jr., *Substantive Criminal Law*, Volume One (St. Paul, Minn.: West Publishing Company, 1986 and 1999 Supplement), p. 8.

4. *Id.*, p. 2.

5. Charles H. Whitebread and Christopher Slobogin, *Criminal Procedure: An Analysis of Cases and Concepts*, Third Edition (Westbury, N.Y.: The Foundation Press, 1993), p. 9.

6. One is guilty of perjury if she makes a false statement under oath in any official proceeding, or swears to the truth of a statement previously made, when the statement is material to the issue or point in question, and she does not believe that statement to be true.

7. LaFave and Scott, *Substantive Criminal Law*, Volume One, p. 596.

8. *Id.*, p. 296.

9. *Id.*, p. 28.

10. Schmalleger, *Criminal Justice Today*, Third Edition, p. 320.

11. Heightened enforcement of drug laws and tougher sentences for drug offenses have had dramatic consequences in the United States in recent years. In 1994, 31 percent of the felony convictions in state courts were for drug offenses, particularly drug trafficking, which resulted in 165,430 convictions, or 19 percent of the total convictions in state courts that year. Brian J. Ostrom and Neal B. Kauder, *Examining the Work of State Courts, 1996: A National Perspective*, from the Court Statistics Project (Williamsburg, Va.: National Center for State Courts, 1997), p. 67. Between 1989 and 1995, drug offenders comprised approximately one-third of the offenders sent to prison in the United States annually, an increase from less than 10 percent in the early 1980s. *Id.*, p. 96.

12. *Id.*, p. 29.

13. Richard McNamara, *New Hampshire Practice: Criminal Practice and Procedure*, Third Edition, Volume One (Charlottesville, Va.: Lexis Law Publishing, 1997 and 1998 Supplement), p. 377.

14. *Id.*

15. McNamara, *New Hampshire Practice: Criminal Practice and Procedure*, Third Edition, Volume One, pp. 399–400; Schmalleger, *Criminal Justice Today*, p. 309.

16. *Id.*, pp. 376–377.

17. Schmalleger, *Criminal Justice Today*, p. 323; McNamara, *New Hampshire Practice: Criminal Practice and Procedure*, Third Edition, Volume One, p. 401.

18. See *County of Riverside v. McLaughlin*, 111 S. Ct. 1661 (1991).

19. 384 U.S. 436.

20. Schmalleger, *Criminal Justice Today*, p. 311.

21. *Id.*

22. Schmalleger, *Criminal Justice Today*, p. 305.

23. *Id.*

24. Whitebread and Slobogin, *Criminal Procedure*, p. 505.

25. Schmalleger, *Criminal Justice Today*, p. 308.

26. Whitebread and Slobogin, *Criminal Procedure*, p. 75.

27. Schmalleger, *Criminal Justice Today*, p. 248.

28. *Id.*, p. 254.

29. *Id.*, p. 341.

30. *Id.*

31. Whitebread and Slobogin, *Criminal Procedure*, p. 592. See also *Brady v. Maryland*, 373 U.S. 83 (1963).

32. Schmalleger, *Criminal Justice Today*, p. 309.

33. McNamara, *New Hampshire Practice: Criminal Practice and Procedure*, Third Edition, Volume One, p. 491; Whitebread and Slobogin, *Criminal Procedure*, p. 548.

34. Whitebread and Slobogin, *Criminal Procedure*, p. 548.

35. *Id.*, p. 547.

36. *Id.*

37. Schmalleger, *Criminal Justice Today*, p. 309; Whitebread and Slobogin, *Criminal Procedure*, p. 546.

38. Whitebread and Slobogin, *Criminal Procedure*, p. 547.

39. Michael J. Gorr and Sterling Harwood, eds., *Controversies in Criminal Law: Philosophical Essays on Responsibility and Procedure* (Boulder, Colo.: Westview Press 1992), p. 243.

40. Whitebread and Slobogin, *Criminal Procedure*, p. 635.

41. *Id.*, p. 640.

42. *Id.*

43. In court documents, lawyers and judges spell "Defendant" with an uppercase "D" when they refer to the "Defendant" in the case at hand. This book will honor that convention.

44. Whitebread and Slobogin, *Criminal Procedure*, p. 136.

45. McNamara, *New Hampshire Practice: Criminal Practice and Procedure*, Third Edition, Volume One, pp. 151–152.

46. *Id.*, p. 515.

47. *Id.*

48. *Id.*, p. 335.

49. Schmalleger, *Criminal Justice Today*, p. 345.

50. Whitebread and Slobogin, *Criminal Procedure*, p. 622.

51. Schmalleger, *Criminal Justice Today*, p. 342.

52. Whitebread and Slobogin, *Criminal Procedure*, p. 615.

53. *Id.*, p. 671.

54. *Id.*, p. 672.

55. McNamara, *New Hampshire Practice: Criminal Practice and Procedure*, Volume Two (Charlottesville, Va.: Lexis Law Publishing, 1997 and 1998 supplement), pp. 382–383.

56. *Id.*, pp. 385–386.

57. *Id.*, p. 385.

58. *Id.*, p. 686.

59. Schmalleger, *Criminal Justice Today*, p. 345.

60. Whitebread and Slobogin, *Criminal Procedure*, p. 697.

61. Schmalleger, *Criminal Justice Today*, p. 346.

62. McNamara, *New Hampshire Practice: Criminal Practice and Procedure*, Third Edition, Volume Two, p. 393.

63. *Id.*, p. 396.

64. See the Supreme Court's decision in *Williams v. Florida*, 399 U.S. 78 (1970), in which the Court held that the Constitution does not require twelve-member juries in criminal cases.

65. Schmalleger, *Criminal Justice Today*, p. 351.

66. In the much-publicized 1991 rape trial of William Kennedy Smith, a Florida judge ruled two such affidavits inadmissible because she concluded that their potential for prejudice outweighed their probative value.

67. Schmalleger, *Criminal Justice Today*, p. 352.

68. *Id.*, p. 350.

69. *Id.*

70. See *United States v. Dinitz*, 424 U.S. 600 (1976).

71. McNamara, *New Hampshire Practice: Criminal Practice and Procedure*, Third Edition, Volume Two, pp. 436–437.
72. Schmalleger, *Criminal Justice Today*, p. 356.
73. In criminal trials in New Hampshire, unless the court orders otherwise, the defense attorney delivers the first closing argument and the prosecutor follows. McNamara, *New Hampshire Practice: Criminal Practice and Procedure*, Third Edition, Volume Two, p. 440.
74. *Id.*, pp. 477–478.
75. *Id.*
76. *Id.*, p. 498; see also *Apodaca v. Oregon*, 406 U.S. 404 (1972) and *Johnson v. Louisiana*, 406 U.S. 356 (1972).
77. Schmalleger, *Criminal Justice Today*, p. 367.
78. *Id.*, p. 387.
79. The federal government began to use determinate sentencing in 1984, when Congress enacted the **Sentencing Reform Act** [see 18 U.S.C. § 3551 and 28 U.S.C. sections 991–998], which delegated to the **United States Sentencing Commission** authority to establish sentencing guidelines for federal crimes. The guidelines established a grid composed of offense (e.g., bank robbery, committed with gun, $2,500 stolen) and offender (e.g., one prior conviction, not resulting in imprisonment) categories and prison terms of various lengths. A judge must sentence an offender to the term of imprisonment that the grid specifies for the offender and offense categories present in the case at hand. The judge can depart from the guidelines if she finds aggravating or mitigating factors in the case that the guidelines do not address, but she must state in writing her reason(s) for imposing a sentence that is different from the one that the guidelines specify. See Brian L. Porto, *The Craft of Legal Reasoning* (Fort Worth, Tex.: Harcourt Brace College Publishers, 1998), p. 142.
80. *Id.*, p. 374.
81. *Id.*, p. 372.
82. McNamara, *New Hampshire Practice: Criminal Practice and Procedure*, Third Edition, Volume Two, p. 514.
83. *Id.*
84. *Id.*, p. 383.
85. *Id.*
86. N.H. R.S.A. 318-B:26.

Chapter 6

Dispute Resolution— The Civil Justice Process

Introduction

The civil justice process illustrates courts' dispute-resolution function. Civil cases present disputes between individuals, between institutions (e.g., corporations or organizations), and between individuals and institutions that arise because one party's actions have injured the other party's physical or financial health, property, or reputation. Civil justice compensates injured parties, thereby discouraging them from seeking retribution directly from the injurer. Retribution often produces more injuries rather than resolution. Civil justice also encourages responsible behavior by penalizing individuals and institutions that behave irresponsibly.

A dispute becomes a civil case when an injured party seeks a resolution that a court can authorize, such as compensation for an injured skier's medical expenses and lost wages. A lawyer who concludes that a dispute is winnable will fit his client's grievance into an appropriate legal category, such as the negligent operation of business premises, and will present it to a court as a lawsuit.[1] One type of dispute that is likely to become a civil case features serious and costly bodily injuries that motivate the plaintiff to sue, and enough doubt about who was responsible for those injuries to prevent the defendant from accepting a settlement.[2] In such circumstances, each side is likely to believe that it can convince a jury to find in its favor. The hypothetical case in this chapter presents such circumstances, which are rare. The rarity of those circumstances is why more than 90 percent of civil suits end by means of out-of-court settlements rather than by jury verdicts (see Chapter 2). Nevertheless, civil justice generally and jury verdicts particularly have been the subjects of enormous press attention in recent years. Private disputes have spawned public controversy and political debate.

Critics of the civil justice process are known as "tort reformers" because their principal target is **tort** (i.e., personal injury) litigation. Tort reformers charge that civil juries are biased against defendant corporations in personal injury cases and that they award large amounts of money to plaintiffs in frivolous lawsuits against those corporations merely because the corporations have "deep pockets."[3] They also charge that litigation has had catastrophic consequences for the American economy.[4] Walter Olson maintains that litigation "clogs and jams the gears of commerce, sowing friction and distrust between the productive enterprises on which material progress depends and all who buy their products, work at their plants and offices, and join in their undertakings."[5] He adds that lawsuits, both actual and potential, cause American corporations to discontinue producing or not to produce products that were or that would have been desirable alternatives to their available competitors.[6] There has been a receptive audience for such charges among physicians, manufacturers, insurance executives, and other business people.

Supporters of the civil justice process, who include plaintiffs' lawyers, Democratic politicians, and consumer advocates, disagree that litigation reduces America's economic competitiveness. Professor Marc Galanter notes that domestic relations cases, especially divorce cases, are largely responsible for the increased civil court caseloads in recent years, and that those cases do not make American companies less competitive.[7] He adds that civil cases result not only from plaintiffs' claims, but also from defendants' unwillingness to satisfy those claims.[8] Moreover, civil litigation can benefit society by: (1) depriving an irresponsible defendant of funds that it might otherwise have used to continue irresponsible behavior; (2) deterring a defendant from behaving irresponsibly again for fear of the financial consequences; or (3) changing a defendant's values so that its irresponsible behavior ends.[9]

Finally, supporters of the civil justice process argue that civil juries are not necessarily pro-plaintiff. They cite survey results that show that jurors perceive a litigation explosion, and feel duty-bound to combat it by not awarding plaintiffs large amounts of money.[10] For example, a 1994 study found that the probability that tort plaintiffs would receive financial compensation at trial had declined steadily nationwide, from 63 percent in 1989, to 58 percent in 1990, 57 percent in 1991, and 52 percent in 1992.[11]

The tort reform debate will probably continue in the new century, partly because of two 1999 verdicts. One verdict required cigarette maker Philip Morris to pay a smoker $51.5 million for causing her to become addicted to cigarettes.[12] Another required several handgun manufacturers to pay a shooting victim $560,000 for failing to act reasonably to prevent their products from injuring him.[13]

Tort reformers favor federal legislation to change civil justice nationwide, but President Clinton did not, at least not as of the early spring of 1999.[14] Consequently, federal legislation will probably depend on who controls the White House and the Congress after 2000.[15] Law and politics are cousins in civil justice, just as they are in criminal justice.

Keep the tort reform debate in mind as you read *Peterson v. Big Pine Mountain Ski Corporation*, which follows. That debate is the backdrop for *Peterson*, which results from an alpine skiing accident. After reading *Peterson*, consider: (1) whether the court should assign the financial costs of the skier's injuries to the skier or to the ski corporation, and (2) the consequences for society of each alternative.

PETERSON V. BIG PINE MOUNTAIN SKI CORPORATION: FACTS

December 31, 1998, was supposed to be a terrific day for Shannon Peterson, a sophomore at Grayson College in Grayson, New Hampshire. She planned to ski with friends during the day and to attend a New Year's Eve party that night. Early in the morning of December 31, she left her parents' home in Madbury, New Hampshire, and drove two-and-a-half hours north to the Big Pine Mountain Ski Resort, where she met her friends at the Base Lodge. The group soon took to the slopes, where everyone skied for several hours until it was time for lunch. After lunch, the friends returned to the slopes for more skiing; they were pleasantly tired by 3:45 P.M. when they entered the chair lift and rode up the mountain to begin their last "run" of the day. There would be time for one more "run" before dusk fell and resort personnel turned on the snowmaking "guns" to get the trails ready for the following day.

Shortly before 4 P.M., Shannon, who was an intermediate skier, led her friends down an intermediate trail that she had skied comfortably earlier in the day. Five minutes later, an unexpected encounter with artificial snow startled Shannon. Snowmaking had begun earlier than usual that day to get the slopes ready for an expected large crowd on New Year's Day. The blowing snow distracted Shannon and obscured a large patch of ice that lay before her on the trail. When her skis hit the icy patch, she lost her balance, fell hard, slid downhill 150 feet, and crashed into one of the steel towers that supported the cables along which the chair lifts travel.

Shannon suffered a severe concussion, a broken collarbone, crushed vertebra, broken ribs, and numerous cuts and abrasions as a result of the fall and the collision. Her injuries caused her to miss a semester of classes, and they ended her college soccer career. Today, more than two years after her accident, Shannon suffers from periodic double vision that prevents her from driving a car, a permanent lower-back injury that has cancelled her plans for a career in physical therapy, and bouts of depression that result from her injuries and her diminished career prospects.

On June 17, 1999, Shannon's lawyer, Gene Jefferson of Graniteville, New Hampshire, filed suit in Pine County Superior Court against Big Pine Mountain Ski Corporation (Big Pine), the owner of the resort where Shannon was injured. The suit sought compensation from Big Pine for Shannon's injuries on the ground that Big Pine was legally responsible for those injuries.

PARTICIPANTS

The Plaintiff

Plaintiff Shannon Peterson was nineteen years old on the day of her accident. Like many plaintiffs in personal injury cases, Shannon saw her life change forever that day because she sustained permanent damage to her back, which prevents her from being the physically active person she was before the accident. She can no longer ski, play recreational softball, or play varsity soccer at Grayson College, all of which she loved to do. Swimming and walking are her only recreational options now.

Shannon's career prospects as a physical therapist have dimmed considerably because her weak back prevents her from standing for long periods of time and from lifting patients. She dreads the prospect of being "chained to a desk, pushing papers" instead of doing the "hands-on" type of work that she would prefer. Shannon's diminished physicality and career potential have weighed heavily on her mind since the accident, and have caused her to suffer from depression, which has triggered weight loss, sleeplessness, irritability, and a loss of appetite.

Shannon holds Big Pine responsible for her injuries. She hopes that a jury will do the same, to compensate her for the reduced quality of her life, but also to "send a message" to ski area operators that if they needlessly put skiers at risk of injury, they will pay dearly when injuries occur. Money is rarely able to compensate an accident victim adequately for her injuries, but it is the best means of compensation that the civil justice process can offer.

The Plaintiff's Lawyer

Shannon and her parents agreed that Big Pine was responsible for Shannon's injuries and that it ought to compensate her accordingly. A family friend referred the Petersons to Attorney Gene Jefferson of Graniteville, who met with them and agreed to represent Shannon in a suit against Big Pine. You will recall Mr. Jefferson from Chapter 5, where he represented the defendant in *State v. Johnson*.

Jefferson enjoys representing plaintiffs in personal injury cases. He is sympathetic to them because of the physical and emotional pain they have suffered, and because of the extent to which their injuries have disrupted their lives. Like many plaintiff's attorneys, he resents defendants, especially corporate defendants, which, he believes, bully plaintiffs into settling for much less money than their injuries warrant. He resents the ski industry most of all because he believes that it uses the popularity of skiing to force the state legislature to write laws that make it extremely difficult to win a personal injury lawsuit against a ski area operator. Thus, Jefferson looked forward to locking horns with Big Pine.

The Defendant

The **defendant**, Big Pine Mountain Ski Corporation, is a New Hampshire-based corporation that owns and operates the resort where Shannon Peterson was injured. That is also where the corporation's offices are located. The founder and chief executive officer of the corporation is Klaus Waldmeier, who won an Olympic gold medal in alpine skiing for Austria in 1972 and then emigrated to the United States, where, by 1992, he had become the fabulously wealthy owner of six ski resorts, two each in Maine, New Hampshire, and Vermont.

Ski operators fear warm weather, rain, and lawsuits above all else. Waldmeier had adjusted to New England's quirky winters over the years, but he could not adjust to lawsuits, which he saw as threats to his livelihood and as a windfall for plaintiffs. In Waldmeier's view, Americans seemed not to realize that alpine skiing was inherently risky, and that it was neither possible nor his responsibility to guarantee their safety on the slopes. He shook with anger when he received a copy of the court papers that Gene Jefferson had filed against Big Pine. Waldmeier threw the papers on his desk, swore in German and in English, then called his lawyer. Lawsuits were war to Waldmeier, and he wanted to make sure that his lawyer was ready to fight.

The Defendant's Lawyer

Nobody could have been more different from Klaus Waldmeier than his easy-going lawyer, Payson Parker. Payson was a fifth-generation New Hampshire native and the heir to a banking fortune. After prep school, he earned a B.A. from Princeton and a law degree from Harvard before returning to New Hampshire in 1991, where he joined the Manchester office of Howe and Davis, a prestigious Boston law firm. Among the firm's clients were several New England ski operators.

Parker expected Klaus Waldmeier's call on June 17, 1999, because he had received a copy of the court papers in the *Peterson* case earlier that day. He looked forward to representing Big Pine, despite Waldmeier's temper, because skiing was crucial to the economy of northern New Hampshire, where winters were long, jobs were scarce, and incomes were low. Parker believed that the successful defense of lawsuits was as important as cold weather and snowmaking to the ski industry in New Hampshire. He told Waldmeier that he would mount an aggressive defense, but Waldmeier was skeptical. Parker hung up the phone convinced that he was in for a long battle, with Waldmeier and with Jefferson.

The Judge

When Gene Jefferson filed *Peterson v. Big Pine Mountain Ski Corporation* in Pine County Superior Court, the presiding judge there that month was the Honorable Mary Romano. You will recall Judge Romano from Chapter 5, where she presided in *State v. Johnson*.

PROCESS

Pretrial

Complaint

Shortly after he agreed to represent Shannon Peterson, Gene Jefferson prepared to file suit against Big Pine. It would be necessary to file suit on or before December 31, 2001, because New Hampshire law requires a plaintiff to file a suit that arises from an alpine skiing injury within two years of her injury.[16] Otherwise, the plaintiff would violate the **statute of limitations**, which would mean that no court would have jurisdiction in the case. The two-year statute of limitations on suits like Shannon's reflects the New Hampshire legislature's desire to protect ski area operators in New Hampshire against lawsuits by injured skiers. The best evidence of that intent is that in New Hampshire, the statute of limitations on personal injury lawsuits unrelated to alpine skiing is three years.

Jefferson would file suit in superior court because that court had subject matter jurisdiction in major civil cases in New Hampshire. Specifically, he would file suit in the superior court in Pine County, where the accident occurred. New Hampshire law requires that a lawsuit that arises from an accident that involves a chair lift used by skiers be heard in the county in which the accident occurred.[17] Pine County Superior Court had personal jurisdiction over both Shannon and Big Pine because both parties were residents of New Hampshire. The parties' common residency prevented Shannon from filing a diversity-of-citizenship suit in federal court, and it prohibited Big Pine from removing the case to federal court (see Chapter 2). Nor would it be necessary to invoke New Hampshire's **long-arm statute**, which permits state courts there to exercise jurisdiction over civil defendants who are not residents of New Hampshire.[18]

Gene's first task, in filing suit, was to prepare a **complaint.** Besides starting the lawsuit, the complaint would: (1) state the basis for the court's jurisdiction; (2) indicate the nature of Shannon's claim against Big Pine; (3) show that she was entitled to compensation for her injuries; and (4) demand a decision by the court awarding her such compensation.[19] The complaint recited the pertinent facts, namely, that Shannon had lost her balance when startled and distracted by blowing artificial snow, and that she had fallen, slid, and then crashed into a lift tower, sustaining injuries to her head, collarbone, ribs, and back. The complaint alleged that Big Pine was responsible for those injuries because of its **negligent operation of business premises** and its **negligent infliction of emotional distress** on Shannon. The complaint demanded **damages** (monetary compensation) in an unspecified amount that would be within the jurisdictional limits of the court. Finally, the complaint requested a jury trial.[20]

Gene arranged for a deputy sheriff to deliver the complaint to a corporate officer of Big Pine. This delivery is known as **service of process.** Service of process establishes a court's personal jurisdiction over the defendant because it notifies her about the lawsuit and directs her to appear in court and to defend the suit, or risk a **default**, which would mean an automatic victory for the plaintiff.[21] Absent service of process, a court cannot exercise personal jurisdiction over a defendant.

The deputy sheriff served process on Big Pine's corporate secretary by hand delivery of two copies of the complaint and of a **summons**, a separate document, signed by the clerk of the Pine County Superior Court, that stated a date by which Big Pine had to respond to the complaint, under penalty of default.[22] The corporate secretary kept one copy of the papers and the deputy sheriff signed the back of the second copy of the complaint, which certified that service of process was complete. The deputy delivered this **certificate of service** to Gene Jefferson, who copied it and sent the original to the clerk of the Pine County Superior Court, along with the complaint and the **entry** (or **filing**) **fee** necessary to have the case placed on the court's docket.[23] It would remain on the docket until there was a settlement or a verdict. *Peterson v. Big Pine Mountain Ski Corporation* was underway.

Answer/Motion to Dismiss

Payson Parker responded to Shannon's lawsuit within thirty days, as superior court rules required him to do, by filing a **general appearance** and an **answer**; the former is specific to New Hampshire, but the latter is standard procedure throughout the United States. The general appearance notified the court that Parker would represent Big Pine and that Big Pine would submit to the court's exercise of jurisdiction.[24] It also enabled Big Pine to avoid default, and it entitled Payson Parker to receive copies of any documents Gene Jefferson filed that requested court action in his client's favor.[25]

An answer is a defendant's reply to each statement of fact and each allegation made in a complaint. It identifies for the parties and for the judge the issues that are in dispute in a case.[26] In its answer to Shannon's complaint, Big Pine agreed with Shannon that she fell on ice and that her injuries were the result of that fall and of a collision with a lift tower. Yet, Big Pine disagreed that her fall was the result of Big Pine having prematurely activated its snowmaking equipment. Instead, the answer declared, Shannon fell because she lost her balance on ice, and ice is an inherent danger of skiing for which an injured skier cannot hold a ski area operator responsible. Furthermore, Shannon's head and back injuries resulted from her collision with a lift tower, another inherent risk of skiing for which an injured skier cannot hold a ski area operator responsible. Thus, the answer concluded, Big Pine was not **liable** (legally responsible) for Shannon's injuries, and the court ought to dismiss her suit.

Big Pine filed a **motion to dismiss** along with its answer. A motion to dismiss asks a judge to dismiss a case because the plaintiff has failed to state a claim for which the law grants a remedy, or because the plaintiff's claim is in some other way legally deficient. Big Pine's motion cited a New Hampshire law that listed ice and lift towers as risks that the skier, not the ski area operator, must bear. Therefore, Shannon's suit failed to state a claim that entitled her to compensation, and the court should dismiss the suit.[27] Within ten days, as court rules required, Gene Jefferson filed an **objection** to Big Pine's motion, requested a **hearing**, and Judge Romano granted his request.[28] During the hearing, the lawyers argued orally for and against dismissal, respectively. Two weeks later, Judge Romano denied Big Pine's motion because Shannon's claim that negligence in snowmaking had caused her fall, if proved, would make Big Pine liable for at least some of her injuries. In other words, Shannon had stated a claim that *potentially* entitled her to compensation, which defeated Big Pine's motion to dismiss and enabled her suit to proceed.

Discovery

The **discovery** phase of the *Peterson* case began after Judge Romano denied Big Pine's motion to dismiss. Discovery is a systematic exchange of information that enables the parties to a civil suit to learn all of the relevant facts.[29] It is especially important today, when the civil justice process features many more settlements than trials, because it produces the information on which parties base their settlement offers and negotiations. Indeed, some commentators have suggested that discovery has replaced the trial as the most critical stage in civil litigation.[30] The purposes of discovery are to: (1) preserve information and evidence for trial (e.g., the videotaped testimony of a terminally ill witness); (2) clarify the issues that are in dispute between the parties when the complaint and the answer are vague; and (3) permit each party to gather information that might lead to admissible evidence, thereby avoiding surprise at trial.[31]

Parties can discover any information that is **relevant** to the subject matter of their case and that is not protected from disclosure by a **privilege**, such as those that exist between attorney and client, physician and patient, or priest and penitent. Information is "relevant" if it is reasonably likely to lead to the identification of admissible evidence.[32] For example, Shannon Peterson is entitled to discover the identity of the Big Pine employee who activated the snowmaking guns on the day of her accident, because that could lead to admissible evidence that snowmaking began while skiers were still on the slopes.

Parties are obligated to exchange discoverable information; early in a case, they must disclose the names of their potential witnesses and of persons likely to have relevant information.[33] Later on, they must make available for inspection and copying relevant documents and related materials (e.g., medical records pertaining to Shannon's injuries, Big Pine's Operations Manual, including safety procedures) that the opposing party seeks in a **request to produce**. Parties must also disclose to each other the names and addresses of their respective expert witnesses, the experts' education and professional experience, the nature of the experts' expected testimony at trial, and the reason(s) for the experts' conclusions.[34] Finally, as the trial date approaches, parties must identify for each other the evidence that they expect to offer during trial.[35]

A party must respond to discovery requests honestly, fully, and responsibly. She must refresh her recollection of events relevant to the case, find out what information is in her records and what her employees know, and try to give her opponent the information and materials requested. She need not volunteer information not requested, but she should not be evasive either.[36] In New Hampshire and in other states, a requesting party whose opponent fails to disclose the requested information within thirty days can file a **motion to compel** that asks the judge to order the recipient party to comply with the request. The recipient party can object to the motion, and the judge will decide whether compliance is necessary.[37] A recipient party can also file a **motion for a protective order** that asks the judge to prohibit or limit discovery of particular information, or to limit the number of persons who may participate in discovery of that information or who may learn about it.[38]

Despite the duty to disclose, motions to compel and motions for protective orders are common because many lawyers use discovery to bully, harass, distract, or frustrate opposing counsel in some way that will advantage the aggressor lawyers' clients. Increased economic competition among law firms and the impersonality of legal practice in big cities probably have intensified discovery battles (see Chapter 3), but those battles are products of the adversary system too. The adversary system of justice operates not only in American criminal courts (see Chapter 5), but also in American civil courts.

The adversary system requires the parties to a civil lawsuit to begin the suit, define the issues, gather evidence that supports their respective arguments, and present that evidence in court.[39] It assumes that the best way to resolve civil disputes is for the parties to argue their own causes as vigorously as possible within legal and ethical bounds.[40] The parties **move** the case forward by making **motions** on which the judge rules; the judge's role in the investigation and the presentation of the case is reactive and limited.[41] A lawyer's primary duty is to represent his client, not to serve the best interests of society.[42] The parties' control over the gathering and the presentation of evidence has two major consequences. One is that a party who seeks to use discovery to mislead, confuse, or delay can succeed, especially when his lawyer is more skilled than opposing counsel and/or when he is wealthier than his opponent. The other consequence is that judges and juries can resolve civil cases without necessarily having determined the truth.

The principal alternative to the adversary (or **accusatorial**) system is the **inquisitorial** system, which most European countries use. The inquisitorial system assigns the primary responsibility for the discovery of relevant evidence in civil cases to judges instead of to the parties. Judges gather evidence by conducting investigations and questioning witnesses.[43] Judges gather evidence in civil cases in the inquisitorial system because the major goal of that system is to serve the public good by finding the truth.[44] Judges, who are public servants, are presumably more attentive to the public good than private lawyers are. In contrast, the adversary system aims to protect private rights while it resolves private disputes, so it permits the parties to gather their own evidence.[45]

Both systems have burdens and benefits. The inquisitorial system, as it exists in Germany, for example, avoids the slow pace, the nastiness, the complexity, and the incentives to distort evidence that plague American civil litigation.[46] The judge actively seeks the truth, which can make up for a mismatch between the parties' lawyers.[47] America's adversary system, however, assigns the gathering and the presentation of evidence to the persons who have the greatest incentives to perform those tasks effectively. That arrangement protects the parties from the consequences of a sloppy inquiry by a lazy or biased judge.[48] It also reflects Americans' skepticism toward government and their passionate devotion to individual rights.

Discovery began in *Peterson* two weeks after Judge Romano denied Big Pine's motion to dismiss. Gene Jefferson drafted and mailed to Payson Parker written questions, called **interrogatories**, which court rules obligated Parker to answer and return within thirty days.[49] Jefferson directed the questions to Big Pine, but he knew that Parker would answer them himself, after consultation with Klaus Waldmeier, and that Waldmeier would sign them and swear to their accuracy. That is customary nationwide. The questions were designed to find out whether: (1) Big Pine had safe snowmaking procedures in place; (2) its employees followed those procedures on December 31, 1998; (3) its lift towers met industry safety standards; and (4) it would argue that it was not liable for Shannon's injuries because they were the result either of her own negligence or of an unforeseeable accident. One question asked:

Was snowmaking equipment on the premises at Big Pine as of December 31, 1998? If so, please indicate:

a. the type of equipment present on that date, the model name, and the name, address, and telephone number of its manufacturer;

b. the procedures in place for snowmaking operations, including schedule, maintenance of the equipment, training of employees; and procedures for preventing injuries to customers and employees;

c. the name(s), address(es), and telephone number(s) of the person(s) responsible for directing and executing snowmaking operations at Big Pine on December 31, 1998;

d. the precise time at which snowmaking began at Big Pine on December 31, 1998.

Another question asked for similar information about the lift towers at Big Pine. Still another question asked:

Do you contend that Big Pine is not liable for the injuries that the Plaintiff sustained on December 31, 1998? If so, please indicate whether:

a. Big Pine did not have a duty to the Plaintiff to protect her against the kinds of injuries she suffered;

b. Big Pine had such a duty to the Plaintiff, and it took sufficient precautions to prevent the kinds of injuries she suffered;

c. the Plaintiff's own negligence caused her injuries.

Two months later, after he had answered Jefferson's interrogatories, Payson Parker drafted interrogatories for Gene Jefferson to answer on Shannon's behalf. Parker's interrogatories aimed to learn: (1) the circumstances, the severity, and the consequences of Shannon's injuries; (2) whether she was partly or wholly responsible for her injuries; and (3) the bases on which she would argue that Big Pine's negligence was responsible for her injuries. One question asked:

Between December 31, 1998, and the present, have there been days when you were unable to attend college classes because of your injuries? If so, please indicate:

a. each day that you missed the entire day of classes;

b. each day that you missed a portion of the school day.

Another question asked:

Did you consume any alcohol on December 31, 1998, prior to your accident? Did you use any drugs on December 31, 1998, prior to your accident? If so, please identify the alcohol and/or drugs used and the amount(s) consumed.

A third question asked:

Do you claim that a Big Pine employee negligently inflicted emotional distress upon you? If so, please indicate:

a. which employee(s) of Big Pine inflicted such emotional distress;

b. the specific act(s) the employee(s) engaged in that caused such emotional distress;

c. when the employee(s) acted so as to cause you emotional distress;

d. what physical symptoms of emotional distress you experienced as a result of the negligent behavior of the Big Pine employee(s).

Both lawyers attached to their interrogatories requests to produce relevant documents and personal property items, as they were entitled to do. Jefferson requested copies of Big Pine's operations manual, employee handbook, and maintenance logs. Parker requested copies of the medical records concerning Shannon's injuries, and he asked to examine the skis, boots, and poles that Shannon was using when her accident occurred.

Both lawyers were dissatisfied with, but not surprised by, the answers they received to their interrogatories. Responses to interrogatories tend to reflect the adversarial atmosphere in which they exist; they interpret questions as narrowly as they can in order to provide as little information to the questioner as possible.[50] Lawyers frequently refuse to respond to particular questions on the grounds that those questions seek irrelevant information, require burdensome research, or ask for information to which the questioner is not entitled, such as a lawyer's "theory of the case."[51] For example, Parker's answer to Jefferson's question about snowmaking equipment was "see attached operations manual and maintenance logs"; Jefferson would have to search those materials for the answers he sought. Jefferson's answer to Parker's question about the act(s) that caused Shannon's emotional distress was "defendant's negligent operation of snowmaking equipment and negligent maintenance of lift towers," which did not give Parker any new or specific information. Similarly, Jefferson's answer to Parker's question about the symptoms of Shannon's emotional distress was "see attached medical records." Fortunately for both lawyers, interrogatories were not the only discovery tool available to them.

On September 10, 1999, Judge Romano convened a **structuring conference** between the parties, as superior court rules required her to do. Federal courts, and state courts outside New Hampshire, also convene such meetings, which they call

pretrial conferences or **discovery conferences**. The chief purpose of these meetings is to set dates for the completion of discovery and for the parties to participate in alternative dispute resolution (A.D.R.). The lawyers for both parties must attend.[52] In New Hampshire, after the structuring conference, the superior court will issue a **structuring conference order** that can include deadline dates, not only for discovery and A.D.R., but also for motions, additional conferences, jury selection, and the start of trial.[53]

Discovery continued in *Peterson* after the structuring conference. Gene Jefferson requested from Big Pine and received permission to examine the location where Shannon's accident occurred, accompanied by the **accident reconstruction expert** whom he had hired to assist him. Payson Parker requested from Shannon and received permission to have a physician and a psychotherapist hired by Big Pine examine her in order to determine her physical and emotional health. Both examinations were permissible because Shannon's claims that she had suffered physical and emotional injuries as a result of Big Pine's negligence were central issues in the case.[54]

Each party also took the **depositions** of the opponent's principal witnesses. Lawyers can take depositions orally or by means of written questions, but they almost always do so orally.[55] Depositions usually occur in the office of a lawyer for one of the parties, and the attendees typically include the lawyers for the parties, a court reporter who records the testimony (which can also be videotaped), and the witness (**deponent**), who can also have her own lawyer present if she is not a party to the case.[56]

A deposition consists chiefly of the questioning of a witness, who is under oath, by a lawyer for a party. Opposing counsel or the witness may object to a question, and the witness may refuse to answer a question after he states the reason(s) for that refusal.[57] When the **deposing attorney** finishes questioning the witness, opposing counsel may question the witness; thereafter, the lawyers alternate questioning the witness until both sides have asked all their questions.[58] The party who takes the deposition pays all of its costs, including the witness's fee and mileage, the court reporter's fee, and the respective fees for recording the testimony, preparing a written transcript, and distributing one copy of that transcript to each party in the case.[59]

In *Peterson*, Gene Jefferson took the depositions of Big Pine's operations manager, one of its snowmakers, and the accident reconstruction expert who would testify for Big Pine at trial. Payson Parker took the depositions of Shannon Peterson, a physician and a psychologist who had treated her, and Shannon's accident reconstruction expert. Like interrogatories, depositions exist in an adversarial atmosphere. Lawyers instruct their clients to answer questions asked of them in depositions as narrowly as possible, and not to volunteer any information for which the questioner has not asked. The *Peterson* case was no exception. Shannon stated that she fell because blowing artificial snow distracted and blinded her, while Big Pine's operations manager stated that she probably fell because the trail was icy. Shannon's expert supported Shannon's version of the events that led to her injuries, and Big Pine's expert supported the operations manager's version.

A.D.R.

While discovery was in progress, the date arrived for the parties to submit their dispute to A.D.R. New Hampshire court rules offered them a choice between: (1) neutral evaluation; (2) mediation; (3) nonbinding arbitration; and (4) binding arbitration. Those procedures are also available in the federal courts, as are **summary jury trials**. In a summary jury trial, lawyers make short arguments to a six-member advisory jury, which makes a nonbinding decision, after which the lawyers try to settle the case, using that decision as a guide.[60]

Neutral evaluation (or early neutral evaluation) includes an opening statement by the evaluator and presentations by the lawyers for the parties. The evaluator then: (1) identifies matters about which the parties agree; (2) assesses the strengths and weaknesses of the parties' arguments; and (3) estimates the likelihood that a jury will find the defendant liable and the amount of compensation that it will award.[61] The premise that underlies neutral evaluation is that parties will be more likely to settle when they receive such information early in a case.[62]

Mediation features an impartial mediator who tries to assist the parties to reach an agreement that will resolve their case. Both sides state their positions, which the mediator helps them to clarify; then, with the mediator's help, they try to identify alternative solutions and to reach agreement on one of the alternatives. Only the parties can resolve the case; the mediator cannot impose a solution.[63] An arbitrator, in contrast, hears opening and closing statements by both parties and the testimony of witnesses, reads the documents the parties submit, and then renders a decision.[64] That decision might or might not obligate the parties, depending on whether they chose binding or nonbinding arbitration beforehand.[65]

The parties in *Peterson* chose nonbinding arbitration. They did not want to be bound by the result, but they preferred arbitration to mediation because they knew it was unlikely that they would resolve the case by means of a mutual agreement.[66] The arbitrator ruled in Big Pine's favor on the grounds that New Hampshire law required skiers to assume the inherent risks of alpine skiing and that Shannon's injuries resulted from two of those risks, namely, a fall on an icy trail and a collision with a lift tower. The decision of the arbitrator convinced Klaus Waldmeier that Big Pine would win at trial, and he instructed Payson Parker to refuse any settlement offer that Gene Jefferson might make.

Waldmeier's reaction to the arbitration decision put Shannon Peterson in a difficult position. She began to favor a settlement because she feared that a jury might decide the case in the same way that the arbitrator had decided it. Waldmeier refused to settle for the same reason, which meant that the case would proceed to trial, where Shannon might not recover any compensation for her injuries. Worse still, she would have to reimburse Gene Jefferson for the expenses he had incurred, such as the expert witness fees and the fee of the court reporter who recorded the depositions Jefferson had taken.

Reimbursement was one of the provisions of the **contingent fee agreement** that Shannon had signed when Jefferson agreed to represent her. Contingent fee agreements are standard in personal injury cases. They typically provide that the plaintiff's lawyer will pay the expenses of the lawsuit from discovery through trial, if necessary. When the case is resolved, the lawyer will receive one-third of any amount that the plaintiff obtains from a settlement or a verdict, plus reimbursement for expenses. If the plaintiff loses at trial, the lawyer is still entitled to reimbursement for expenses incurred. This arrangement enables low- and moderate-income people who have suffered injuries to file lawsuits that they could not otherwise afford to file. It also gives lawyers a financial incentive to represent those people in lengthy litigation against wealthy corporate defendants.

That is why corporate defendants and tort reformers dislike contingent fees. They would end contingent fees if they could, and they would introduce to American courts the **English Rule**, which requires the loser in a civil case to pay the winner's litigation expenses.[67] Those changes would reduce civil caseloads, but they would also leave some injured people without a legal remedy. That would be cause for particular concern in the United States, which lacks the low-cost national health insurance program that England has.[68] For Americans like Shannon Peterson, personal injury lawsuits are a risky but potentially lucrative substitute for government-funded medical insurance.

Summary Judgment

The arbitration decision in the *Peterson* case convinced Payson Parker that he could win an early victory for Big Pine by filing a **motion for summary judgment** right away. A motion for summary judgment asks a judge to decide a case for the moving party because: (1) there are no **material facts** in dispute, and (2) the law favors the moving party in that particular case.[69] In other words, there are no facts for a jury to determine that could affect the outcome of the case, so there is no need for a trial. The judge can decide the case based on the **pleadings** (i.e., complaint, answer, and supporting memoranda) that the parties have filed.[70] Summary judgment is a great idea in appropriate circumstances, because it shortens civil litigation considerably.

On October 25, 1999, Parker filed a motion for summary judgment, to which he attached a twenty-page **memorandum of law** that presented Big Pine's arguments in favor of summary judgment. On November 15, Gene Jefferson responded with a motion in opposition to Parker's motion, to which he attached a memorandum of law that presented arguments against summary judgment. Judge Romano heard oral arguments from both lawyers and denied the motion. Her reasoning appeared in a brief **order** issued on December 6, which stated:

> The Defendant's argument in favor of summary judgment fails because there is a factual dispute in this case that is appropriate for a jury to resolve. The Plaintiff claims that the Defendant's negligence caused her injuries, but the Defendant argues that the cause of those injuries was ice, for which the Defendant is not responsible. As long as this fact is in dispute, the Defendant cannot show conclusively that the law is on its side. Thus, this court must deny the Defendant's motion for summary judgment.

Judge Romano's decision meant that the *Peterson* case was headed for trial. On January 25, 2000, Judge Romano held a **trial management conference** with the parties and their lawyers.[71] This conference was more formal and more adversarial than the structuring conference held earlier in the case.[72] The parties were required to bring all of their evidence to court and to allow opposing counsel to examine it.[73] Judge Romano began a settlement discussion, but she soon realized from the parties' comments that a trial was much more likely than a settlement. Therefore, several days after the conference, she issued a written **final pretrial order** that summarized the issues to be litigated at trial.[74]

Federal courts also conduct a conference among the parties and their lawyers shortly before trial, which is known as a **final pretrial conference**. During the conference, the lawyers must devise a plan for the conduct of the trial, which includes identifying the information, documents, and other materials that they will seek to admit into evidence.[75] Like its New Hampshire counterpart, this conference aims to make trials more efficient by narrowing and clarifying beforehand the issues to be litigated.

Trial

The Right to a Jury Trial

The parties in the *Peterson* case were entitled to a jury trial. The right to a jury trial is not restricted to criminal cases; it extends to most civil cases too. Indeed, the civil jury is a cornerstone of the Anglo-American legal tradition. It existed in England for several hundred years before the first colonists brought it to North America in the early seventeenth century. Jury trials were available for all civil cases in Virginia by 1624 and in the Massachusetts Bay Colony by 1628. All thirteen colonies eventually adopted jury trials in civil cases.[76]

After independence, Virginia was the first state to include in its constitution the right to a jury trial in civil cases. Most of the other states quickly did the same.[77] Part I, Article 20, of the New Hampshire Constitution of 1784, as amended in 1988, protects the right to a jury trial in civil cases when the amount in controversy exceeds $1500.[78] The right to a civil jury trial in federal court has existed since 1791, when the Seventh Amendment became part of the Constitution. The Seventh Amendment guarantees a jury trial when the amount in controversy exceeds $20. [79]

Jury Selection

Jury selection in the *Peterson* case began on February 1, 2000. That was the first day of a new court term, so the clerk of the court selected a pool of potential jurors (*venire*) from among New Hampshire residents who held either a driver's license or a "Safety I.D. Card" issued by the state's Department of Safety.[80] Judge Romano instructed them about the responsibilities of jurors and administered their oath. The clerk randomly selected twelve members of the *venire* to serve on the initial jury.[81] *Voir dire* began shortly thereafter.

You will recall from Chapter 5 that *voir dire* is questioning of potential jurors that is designed to select an impartial jury. Lawyers conduct *voir dire* in some states, but the judge usually conducts it in New Hampshire. Judges also usually conduct *voir dire* in the federal courts.[82] In *Peterson*, Judge Romano, pursuant to court rules, asked the jurors whether any one of them: (1) expected to gain or lose from the outcome of the case; (2) was related to either party; (3) was the employer or the employee of either party; (4) had advised or assisted either party; or (5) was currently a client of one of the lawyers or of a partner of one of the lawyers in the case.[83] None of the potential jurors answered "Yes"; Judge Romano could have removed from the *venire* anyone who did. Then, again pursuant to court rules, Judge Romano asked the potential jurors whether any of them had expressed or formed opinions about the case, and whether they were prejudiced to any degree about it.[84] No one answered "Yes."

Judge Romano proceeded to ask several questions that the lawyers had submitted, which New Hampshire judges can do if they wish.[85] First, she asked questions that Gene Jefferson had submitted, which included:

1. Have you formed an opinion about personal injury lawsuits and whether they help or harm society?

2. Has anyone ever sued you and claimed that he or she suffered an injury on your property or because of your action or inaction? If so, what was the outcome?

Then she asked questions that Payson Parker had submitted, which included:

1. Have you ever sued a business owner or a manufacturer because you suffered an injury on the owner's property or when using the manufacturer's product?

2. Have you had any experiences with a ski resort or with the skiing industry that would make it difficult for you to be impartial in this case?

Judge Romano removed one woman from the *venire* based on her answers to the supplementary questions. She pronounced the remaining members qualified to serve on the jury.

The lawyers then exercised their **challenges for cause** and **peremptory challenges.** A challenge for cause means that a lawyer believes that a prospective juror cannot be impartial for a particular reason, such as racial prejudice, political ideology, or religious convictions (see Chapter 5). There is no limit in New Hampshire courts to the number of jurors that a lawyer may challenge for cause, but the challenge must be based on specific facts.[86] The same rule applies in the federal courts.[87] In *Peterson*, Payson Parker successfully challenged for cause a biologist who worked for the New Hampshire Waterways Council. The Council had publicly criticized Big Pine for taking too much water from the Pine River for snowmaking.

A peremptory challenge permits a lawyer to remove a potential juror for no reason other than that the juror's background or appearance suggest hostility to the lawyer's cause (see Chapter 5). A lawyer cannot, however, use peremptory challenges to remove members of a particular race or gender from the jury.[88] New Hampshire courts permit lawyers for each side to exercise up to three peremptory challenges.[89] The same general rule applies in the federal courts, although the judge can permit additional peremptory challenges.[90] In *Peterson*, Gene Jefferson used a peremptory challenge to remove from the jury the president of a company that manufactured equipment used in pole-vaulting, high-jumping, and gymnastics for fear that he would favor Big Pine.

When jury selection was complete in *Peterson*, the clerk of the court swore in the twelve jurors and two alternates who would hear the evidence at trial. New Hampshire courts typically use twelve-member juries in civil cases, but a lesser number is permissible if the parties agree.[91] Federal courts also typically use twelve-member juries in civil cases. If one of the regular *Peterson* jurors became incapacitated, died, or was disqualified during the trial, Judge Romano would replace the departed juror with an alternate.[92] Judge Romano chose not to sequester the jurors in a hotel because she expected the trial to last less than a week, which convinced her that jurors would refrain from discussing the case and that they would avoid media reports too. Instead, before she excused them for the day, she warned them not to discuss the trial with anyone, including each other, and not to pay attention to media reports about the trial until further notice.

Opening Statements

The trial began the following morning. Judge Romano entered the courtroom at 9 A.M., wished everyone a "good morning," and then asked the lawyers if they were ready to proceed. The lawyers indicated that they were ready. Judge Romano swore in the jurors. Then she summarized the case for them and told them what role they would play in the trial. The facts were as follows: Shannon alleged that Big Pine's failure to observe its snowmaking schedule or to warn her that snowmaking had begun, and its failure to place protective padding around its lift towers had caused Shannon to suffer serious injuries in a fall at Big Pine on December 31, 1999. Big Pine's defense was that the cause of Shannon's injuries was not Big Pine's action or inaction, but rather, a fall on an icy trail, which is an inherent danger in alpine skiing for which Big Pine was not responsible.

Shannon, as the plaintiff, had to prove that: (1) Big Pine had a **duty of care** (legal responsibility) to Shannon to protect her from injury; (2) Big Pine **breached** (violated) that duty; (3) Big Pine's breach of its duty was the **proximate cause** of Shannon's injuries, which means that, absent Big Pine's breach of duty, the injuries would not have occurred; and (4) as a result of Big Pine's breach of duty, Shannon suffered injuries that entitled her to damages. Shannon had to prove all four elements of her case by **a preponderance** (majority) **of the evidence** in order to recover damages from Big Pine.

Judge Romano advised the jurors to determine the facts from the testimony and the other evidence that the lawyers introduced during the trial. Jurors were to disregard any evidence that she told them to disregard during trial and anything that they had read or heard about the case before trial. They were not to discuss the case among themselves until all the evidence was in and it was time for them to deliberate and reach a verdict.

In civil cases, as in criminal cases, the jury decides what the facts are, but the judge decides what the law is. The judge chooses to admit or exclude evidence and to sustain or overrule lawyers' efforts to obtain information from witnesses.

Those choices can affect the outcome of a case. A judge evaluates evidence according to three criteria (see Chapter 5). Evidence must be **relevant,** which means that it is offered to prove or disprove a proposition that could determine the outcome of the case. Evidence must have **probative value,** which means power to prove or disprove that proposition. Evidence must not **prejudice** the jury against a party, though. It will be inadmissible, despite being relevant and probative, if its potential to prejudice the jury outweighs its probative value.

Suppose, for example, that in the *Peterson* case, Gene Jefferson sought to introduce evidence that Big Pine began to pad its lift towers after Shannon's accident, to prove that Big Pine admitted that it should have padded its towers before Shannon's accident. Payson Parker could object that this evidence was irrelevant because it did not tend to prove that Big Pine admitted responsibility for Shannon's injuries. Parker could also object that this evidence was not probative because there were alternative explanations for Big Pine's decision to pad its towers after Shannon's accident, such as the availability of new technology or changing safety standards in the ski industry. Finally, Parker could object that this evidence was prejudicial because it could cause the jury to hold Big Pine liable to Shannon because of events that occurred *after* her accident. Judge Romano would have sustained any or all of those objections.

When Judge Romano had finished her statement to the jury, she said to Gene Jefferson, "You may begin, Mr. Jefferson." Jefferson thanked Judge Romano, greeted the jurors, and introduced himself; then he began his opening statement. In New Hampshire courts, the opening statement of the plaintiff's lawyer precedes the opening statement of the defendant's lawyer.[93] In a twenty-minute statement, Jefferson recounted the facts of the case and indicated that he would prove during trial that Big Pine's **negligence**, or failure to take reasonable precautions to prevent accidents, had caused Shannon's injuries. He would show that Big Pine's decision to begin snowmaking before all skiers were off the slopes, its failure to warn skiers that snowmaking had begun, and its failure to pad its lift towers breached a duty of care to Shannon and resulted in injuries for which she deserved compensation. Jefferson concluded his opening statement by telling the jurors:

> It will become clear to you during this trial that Shannon Peterson sustained a permanent injury because the defendant failed to act reasonably to prevent an accident that was foreseeable. There are inherent risks in alpine skiing, but they did not cause Shannon's injuries; the defendant's negligence did, and the evidence will prove that to you. Thank you.

Then it was Payson Parker's turn to make an opening statement. He greeted the jurors, introduced himself, and presented his view of the case. Parker told the jurors that Shannon's injuries were tragic, but that they were not the result of negligence by Big Pine. Instead, they were the result of a fall on an icy trail and of a collision with a lift tower, both of which New Hampshire law identifies as inherent risks of skiing for which a ski area operator cannot be held liable.[94] Both the fall and the collision resulted from Shannon's loss of balance on ice, for which Big Pine was not legally responsible. Big Pine did not have a duty of care to protect Shannon from injuries caused by the inherent risks of skiing. Thus, Parker concluded:

The issue for you to decide is not whether Shannon Peterson's injuries are serious or permanent, but instead, whether they resulted from her failure to negotiate an icy ski trail. I believe that after you hear the evidence, you will conclude that loss of balance due to ice was the cause of her injuries, which means that Big Pine is not liable to Ms. Peterson. Thank you.

That completed the opening statements. It was time for both parties to present their evidence.

Presentation of Evidence

Fourteen witnesses testified during a four-day trial in *Peterson*. This section will discuss the testimony of four key witnesses. Gene Jefferson began the presentation of evidence by a direct examination of Shannon Peterson. In civil cases, the presentation of evidence begins with a direct examination of a witness by the lawyer for the plaintiff because the plaintiff has the burden of proof. Jefferson asked Shannon to describe the events that led to her injuries on December 31, 1999. Shannon explained that at 3:45 P.M., she and her friends decided to ski their last "run" of the day. They entered the chair lift and rode to the top of the mountain, where they saw a sign that said: "This lift closes at 4 P.M." It was 3:55 P.M. The group decided to ski "Black Forest," an intermediate trail that they had skied earlier that day. About five minutes later, Shannon emerged from a grove of trees and encountered blowing snow, which surprised and distracted her. She looked to see if a snow "gun" was operating, and fell, after which she slid until she hit the lift tower. The next thing she remembered was waking up in the hospital and asking a nurse what had happened.

This exchange between Gene Jefferson and Shannon followed:

Q. Why did you look to see if a snow "gun" was on?
A. The weather was clear, so I thought that the snow must have come from a snow "gun."
Q. Did you ski regularly before your accident?
A. Yes; at least ten times every winter since I was twelve years old.
Q. Had you ever seen a snow "gun" operating before while you were skiing?
A. Yes, but in those cases, there were signs that said: "Snowmaking in Progress."
Q. Before you fell, did you see a patch of ice on the trail in front of you?
A. No. I couldn't see clearly because of the blowing snow.

That concluded the direct examination; Jefferson thanked Shannon for her testimony.

Then Payson Parker cross-examined Shannon. He wanted to show that Shannon's injuries occurred because she lost her balance on ice, which was an inherent risk in alpine skiing. The questions and answers were as follows:

Q. Did you know when you took your last "run" shortly before 4 P.M. that the trail might be icy?
A. Sure. Ice is always possible at that time of day.

Q. But you took another "run" anyway?

A. Yes. The lift was still open. Besides, I didn't know for sure that there *was* ice on the trail.

Q. But you knew that there was a risk of encountering ice on the trail at that time of day?

A. Yes.

Q. Did you fall on ice?

A. Yes.

Q. How do you know that?

A. Because when I hit the ground, it hurt a great deal, and I figured that I must have fallen on ice.

After the cross-examination, Gene Jefferson conducted a brief redirect examination. He wanted to remind the jurors that Big Pine's ill-timed snowmaking was responsible for Shannon's fall. His exchange with Shannon was as follows:

Q. Shannon, when were you first aware of ice on the trail?

A. When I fell.

Q. Why were you not aware of ice before that?

A. Because the blowing snow prevented me from seeing the ice on the trail.

When Jefferson finished, Parker had no more questions for Shannon, so Judge Romano excused her. Jefferson called his next witness, Joe Beliveau, who was in charge of snowmaking at Big Pine on December 31, 1999.

During direct examination, Beliveau testified that he was a native of Quebec who had emigrated to the United States in 1985. He had worked in New Hampshire for nearly fifteen years as a carpenter in the summer and as a chairlift operator and snowmaker in the winter. He presently lived in Caribou, Maine, where he was a self-employed cabinetmaker. On December 31, 1999, he was responsible for snowmaking at Big Pine, where he reported to Fred Monkton, the operations manager. Beliveau testified that snowmaking ordinarily began no earlier than one half-hour after the chairlifts closed. Occasionally, when skier traffic was heavy, he would make snow to repair trails while skiers were still on the slopes. In those instances, he would place warning signs on the affected trails. Beliveau testified that on December 31, 1999, Fred Monkton told him to begin snowmaking when the lifts closed in order to prepare the slopes for the large crowd expected the following day. This exchange between Jefferson and Beliveau followed.

Q. Did you question Mr. Monkton's orders?

A. Yes. I told him it was dangerous to start so early, and that I would have to put up warning signs first.

Q. Did Mr. Monkton respond to you?

A. Yes. He said: "Forget the signs, Joe. Just make snow."

Q. What happened then?

A. I turned on the "guns" a minute or two after 4 o'clock.

Q. Did you warn skiers that snowmaking had started?

A. No.

That concluded direct examination, and cross-examination followed. Payson Parker sought to impeach, or raise doubts about, Beliveau's credibility. The following exchange occurred:

Q.   Mr. Beliveau, were you ever fired from your job at Big Pine?
A.   Yes, I was.
Q.   When were you fired?
A.   In 1987.
Q.   Who fired you.
A.   The operations manager at that time. I don't remember his name.
Q.   Why did he fire you?
A.   I falsified some papers, and said that I had inspected lift equipment that I hadn't inspected.
Q.   Why did you falsify the inspection reports?
A.   Because I hadn't done my job, but I didn't want anybody to know.

On redirect, Gene Jefferson tried to rehabilitate Joe Beliveau's credibility. The questions and answers were as follows:

Q.   Mr. Beliveau, how old were you when you were fired at Big Pine?
A.   Twenty.
Q.   Why had you not performed the inspections you were supposed to perform?
A.   Because I was a stupid kid. I left work early a couple of times to party with my friends.
Q.   Were you rehired at Big Pine?
A.   Yes, Mr. Waldmeier rehired me a couple of weeks after I was fired.
Q.   After Mr. Waldmeier rehired you, how long did you work at Big Pine?
A.   Until the spring of 2000.
Q.   Did you leave voluntarily?
A.   Yes.

When redirect ended, Payson Parker had no further questions for Joe Beliveau. It was nearly 4:30 P.M., so Judge Romano warned the jurors to avoid discussions and media reports about the trial, and excused them until the following morning.

When the trial resumed the following morning, Gene Jefferson called Fred Monkton to testify. Monkton was Big Pine's operations manager on December 31, 1999; he supervised snowmaking and directed the maintenance of its chairlifts and lift towers.[95] During direct examination, Monkton testified that he had written Big Pine's operations manual, which prescribed the safety procedures to be followed during snowmaking. Ordinarily, snowmaking could not begin until one half-hour after the chairlifts closed. If necessary, snowmaking could begin earlier, but not until warning signs appeared on the affected trails. Those procedures prevented collisions between skiers and snowmaking equipment. Monkton acknowledged that they could also prevent falls that resulted from poor visibility in blowing snow.

Then the following exchange occurred between Jefferson and Monkton:

Q. Did you tell Mr. Beliveau to start making snow when the lifts closed
    on December 31, 1999, without posting warning signs?
A. I don't recall, but I doubt it. I just didn't do that sort of thing. I fol-
    low the safety procedures, and I expect our employees to follow
    them too. Joe Beliveau knew that.
Q. Did you have any conversation with Mr. Beliveau about snowmak-
    ing on December 31, 1999?
A. I don't recall. I might have, but I don't recall.

That concluded the direct examination. Payson Parker had no questions for Fred
Monkton, so Judge Romano excused him. Gene Jefferson then called as a witness
Dr. Kathleen Barnett, his accident reconstruction expert.

Dr. Barnett was a professor of civil engineering and a former international ski
racer who designed ski trails. Gene Jefferson had hired her as an **expert witness**.
Recall that an expert witness is a witness who, by virtue of education and/or experience, possesses specialized knowledge about a subject relevant to a case that
enables her to assist the jury to understand that subject and its effect(s) on the
case. Recall too that an expert witness is not neutral. Each side in a personal injury
case hires one or more experts, and an expert's testimony will support the arguments of the lawyer who hired her. In *Peterson*, Dr. Barnett's job was to explain to
the jury how Big Pine's failure to take reasonable precautions caused Shannon's
injuries. Dr. Barnett was the second expert witness whom Jefferson had called to
testify during the trial. Dr. Antonio Rojas, a psychiatrist, had testified earlier about
Shannon's emotional injuries and the physical symptoms that accompanied them.

Now it was Dr. Barnett's turn. During direct examination, she stated that it
was standard practice in the ski industry either to wait until all skiers were off the
slopes before beginning to make snow or to post signs that warned skiers that
snowmaking was in progress. Therefore, Big Pine violated industry practice when
it began snowmaking early, and without warning, on December 31, 1999. That
violation caused Shannon's fall because the blowing artificial snow startled her,
distracted her, and obscured the icy trail, which resulted in her loss of balance. Dr.
Barnett also testified that Big Pine could have prevented, or reduced the severity
of, Shannon's injuries by placing protective padding around the bases of its lift
towers, as other ski areas had done. Gene Jefferson's direct examination of Dr. Barnett concluded as follows:

Q. In your opinion, Dr. Barnett, were Shannon Peterson's injuries
    inherent risks of skiing, or were they preventable?
A. They were preventable.
Q. Do you have any doubt about that?
A. No, I do not.

Payson Parker then cross-examined Dr. Barnett. Parker and Barnett sparred
about whether the volume of artificial snow that Shannon encountered on the
Black Forest trail was sufficient to limit her visibility and obscure the icy trail.
Their exchange follows:

Q. Isn't it true that skiers often find it hard to see ice on a ski trail, even when snowmaking is not occurring?

A. Yes. It can be hard to see ice while you are skiing.

Q. So you can't be sure that Shannon Peterson didn't just ski too fast and slip on the ice, right?

A. I am sure that she was not skiing too fast. I am also sure that she did not have a chance to see the ice because the blowing snow prevented her from seeing it.

Parker then addressed Shannon's collision with the lift tower.

Q. Is there an industry requirement that ski areas pad their lift towers?

A. No, not at this time.

Q. So Big Pine did not violate an industry standard by not padding its lift towers, right?

A. That's right.

Q. Isn't it true that skiers have been injured in collisions with lift towers even when those towers were padded?

A. Yes, but their injuries usually were less severe because of the padding.

Q. Are you a physician, Dr. Barnett?

A. No, I am not.

Q. Then you cannot say for certain that Shannon Peterson's injuries would have been less severe if she had hit a padded lift tower, can you?

A. No, I cannot.

Kathleen Barnett was Gene Jefferson's final witness. When Payson Parker had finished cross-examining her, Gene Jefferson rested his case. Parker then announced that he would move for a directed verdict. Judge Romano excused the jurors temporarily, and the lawyers argued the motion. Parker argued that, based on the evidence presented, no reasonable jury could conclude that Shannon was entitled to a verdict in her favor.[96] Jefferson countered that a reasonable jury could conclude that Big Pine had caused Shannon's fall by beginning snowmaking too soon, and that Big Pine had made her injuries worse by not padding its lift towers. Judge Romano agreed with Jefferson, and observed that: "There is enough doubt about what the right result is in this case that the jury should resolve it." By then, it was 4:45 P.M., so Judge Romano adjourned the trial for the day.

The following day, Payson Parker called several witnesses, the last of whom was Frank McGuane, an accident reconstruction expert. McGuane, a mechanical engineer, was a safety consultant to ski area operators and other recreation providers. He testified during direct examination that Shannon fell because of ice, not blowing snow, as the snow "guns" at Big Pine did not produce a blinding "storm" of artificial snow. It was more likely that Shannon lost her concentration, which caused her to fall on the ice. Otherwise, she would have seen the ice because snowmaking had just begun and the artificial snow had not yet covered the trail. McGuane testified further that a padded lift tower would not have prevented Shannon's injuries because the length of her slide and the steepness of the slope, not the steel tower, caused those injuries to be severe.

Gene Jefferson cross-examined Frank McGuane. Part of that cross-examination appears below:

Q. Could Shannon's surprise at seeing a snow "gun" operating, without seeing a warning sign, have caused her to lose concentration?
A. I don't know. Perhaps.
Q. It could have, right?
A. I suppose so. But she might just have gotten tired or careless.
Q. Is it customary nowadays for ski areas to pad their lift towers?
A. Well, it is not required. Some do, and some don't.
Q. Is padding more common than it was five or ten years ago?
A. Yes. I suppose so.
Q. What is the purpose of the padding?
A. Presumably, to prevent injuries or to reduce their severity.

That ended the cross-examination of McGuane and the presentation of evidence. Judge Romano warned the jurors not to discuss the case, and she adjourned court for the day.

Closing Arguments

The trial resumed the next morning with the lawyers' closing arguments. Payson Parker closed first, because the defense usually closes first in civil trials in New Hampshire.[97] He thanked the jurors for their time and attention. Then he told them that Big Pine was not legally responsible for Shannon's injuries. Shannon's fall on an icy trail is an inherent risk in alpine skiing for which ski area operators are not responsible. Legal responsibility for such risks would make it prohibitively expensive to operate a ski area, which would force most ski areas to close. That would damage New Hampshire's economy, and it would deprive moderate-income people of the chance to ski. Thus, Parker concluded:

> The law requires ski area operators to minimize risks that they can control, such as by marking trails according to their degrees of difficulty. It exempts ski area operators from liability for risks that they cannot control, including icy trails and collisions with lift towers. Therefore, Big Pine is not responsible for the Plaintiff's injuries. The verdict should reflect that. Thank you.[98]

Gene Jefferson also began his closing argument by thanking the jurors for their participation. Then he said that Big Pine was liable for Shannon's injuries. Big Pine had a duty to protect Shannon from risks it could control, including its snowmaking operations and its lift towers. Jefferson said:

> New Hampshire law requires ski area operators to take reasonable precautions to prevent injuries that are preventable. The injuries that Shannon Peterson suffered were preventable. Big Pine should have delayed its snowmaking until all skiers were off the slopes. Alternatively, it should have warned skiers that snowmaking had begun. Finally, it should have padded its lift towers. Big Pine failed to act reasonably to prevent injuries that it could have prevented. Big Pine must therefore compensate Shannon for her injuries. Thank you.

Jury Instructions

When Gene Jefferson finished his closing argument, Judge Romano instructed the jurors about the law that governed the case and about the factual issues that they had to resolve to reach a verdict. The instructions stated that:

1. Negligence is the failure to use reasonable care, which means the degree of care that a reasonably careful person would use under similar circumstances. Negligence means doing something that a reasonably careful person would not do, or failing to do something that a reasonably careful person would do under similar circumstances.[99]

2. All landowners have a duty to use reasonable care in the maintenance and the operation of their properties. You must decide whether Big Pine exercised reasonable care in the maintenance and operation of its ski area. If it failed to do so and that failure was a cause of the plaintiff's injuries, Big Pine would be legally responsible for those injuries.[100]

3. The Plaintiff claims that she has suffered emotional distress as a result of her accident. The Plaintiff can recover damages for emotional distress resulting from the Defendant's negligence only if she proves that the emotional distress has manifested itself through physical symptoms. The Plaintiff must use expert testimony to prove that she experienced physical symptoms due to emotional injury.[101]

4. If you find for the Plaintiff, you should award her fair compensation for her injuries. In determining fair compensation, you may consider the costs of medical care, services, and supplies, the Plaintiff's lost wages, present and future, and her pain, discomfort, and emotional distress.[102]

Verdict

The jurors retired to the jury room to deliberate at 1:02 P.M. New Hampshire law required them to reach a unanimous verdict,[103] and prohibited them from awarding **punitive damages**. Punitive damages punish a civil defendant financially for injuring a plaintiff intentionally or **recklessly**, which means without regard for the plaintiff's safety.[104] The jurors could award only **compensatory damages**, which would reimburse Shannon for expenses, pain, and suffering, but they could "enhance" the award if they concluded that Big Pine had acted recklessly.[105] At 4:41 P.M., the jury foreman told the deputy sheriff who guarded the jury room that the jury had reached a verdict, and the deputy sheriff informed Judge Romano and the lawyers. The trial participants returned to the courtroom, and the clerk of the court conversed briefly with the foreman. That conversation appears below:

Q. Has the jury reached a verdict on the claim of negligence in the operation of business premises?

A. Yes, we have.

Q. What is your verdict?

A. We find the Defendant liable to the Plaintiff in the amount of $375,000.

Q. Has the jury reached a verdict on the claim of negligent infliction of emotional distress?

A. Yes, we have.
Q. What is your verdict?
A. We find the Defendant liable to the Plaintiff in the amount of
$100,000.

Payson Parker asked Judge Romano to poll each juror; she complied, and the result remained the same. Judge Romano thanked the jurors and discharged them. The trial was over. Big Pine's negligence had caused Shannon's injuries, and Big Pine would have to pay her $475,000.

CONCLUSION

The civil justice process illustrates courts' dispute-resolution function. Civil courts do not just resolve disputes, though. They also enforce social norms about proper personal and business relations. They make public policy, too, as when tort verdicts decide who should bear the cost for the risks of modern life. The *Peterson* case showed that those decisions can affect individuals, businesses, and communities. It also showed that politicians try to protect important industries against the uncertainties of the civil justice process.

The case below concerns punitive damages, a major issue in the "tort reform" debate. Read the U.S. Supreme Court's opinion, and try to decide whether punitive damages were justified in light of the defendant's conduct and the harm that the plaintiff suffered.

Epilogue: Dr. Gore's Windfall

B.M.W. of North America, Inc. v. Gore
517 U.S. 559 (1996)

JUSTICE STEVENS delivered the opinion of the Court.

The Due Process Clause of the Fourteenth Amendment prohibits a State from imposing a grossly excessive punishment on a [tort defendant]. The wrongdoing involved in this case was the decision by a national distributor of automobiles not to advise its dealers, and hence their customers, of predelivery damage to new cars when the cost of repair amounted to less than 3 percent of the car's suggested retail price. The question presented is whether a $2 million punitive damages award to the purchaser of one of these cars exceeds the constitutional limit.

I

In January, 1990, Dr. Ira Gore, Jr. purchased a black BMW sports sedan for $40,750.88 from an authorized BMW dealer in Birmingham, Alabama. After driving the car for approximately nine months, and without noticing any flaws in its appearance, Dr. Gore took the car to "Slick Finish," an independent detailer, to make it look "snazzier than it normally would appear." Mr. Slick, the proprietor, detected evidence that the car had been repainted. Convinced that he had been cheated, Dr. Gore brought suit against BMW of North America, the American distributor of BMW automobiles. Dr. Gore alleged ... that the failure to disclose that the car had been repainted constituted suppression of a material fact. The complaint [sought] compensatory and punitive damages, and costs.

At trial, BMW acknowledged that it had adopted a nationwide policy in 1983 concerning cars that were damaged in the course of manufacture or transportation. If the repair cost did not exceed 3 percent of the suggested retail price,... the car was sold as new without advising the dealer that any repairs had been made. Because the $601.37 cost of repainting Dr. Gore's car was only about 1.5 percent of its suggested retail price, BMW did not disclose the damage or repair to the Birmingham dealer.

Dr. Gore asserted that his repainted car was worth less than a car that had not been refinished. To prove his actual damages of $4,000, he relied on the testimony of a former BMW dealer, who estimated that the value of a repainted BMW was approximately 10 percent less than the value of a new car that had not been damaged and repaired. To support his claim for punitive damages, Dr. Gore introduced evidence that since 1983, BMW had sold 983 refinished cars as new, including 14 in Alabama, without disclosing that the cars had been repainted before sale at a cost of more than $300 per vehicle. Using the actual damage estimate of $4,000 per vehicle, Dr. Gore argued that a punitive award of $4 million would provide an appropriate penalty for selling approximately 1,000 cars for more than they were worth.

The jury returned a verdict finding BMW liable for compensatory damages of $4,000. In addition, the jury assessed $4 million in punitive damages, based on a determination that the nondisclosure policy constituted "gross, oppressive or malicious" fraud.

[**Editor's Note:** On appeal, the Alabama Supreme Court reduced the award to $2 million, but only because the jury had computed the $4 million figure incorrectly, not because that figure violated the Constitution. The Supreme Court granted *certiorari* in order to clarify the standards for a constitutionally excessive punitive damages award.]

II

Punitive damages may properly be imposed to further a State's legitimate interests in punishing unlawful conduct and deterring its repetition. In our federal system, States necessarily have considerable flexibility in determining the level of punitive damages that they will allow in different classes of cases and in any particular case. Only when an award can fairly be characterized as "grossly excessive" in relation to [the States' interests] does it enter the zone of arbitrariness that violates the [Constitution]. We therefore focus our attention first on the scope of Alabama's legitimate interests in punishing BMW and deterring it from future misconduct.

No one doubts that a State may protect its citizens by prohibiting deceptive trade practices and by requiring automobile distributors to disclose presale repairs that affect the value of a new car. But the States need not, and in fact do not, provide such protection in a uniform manner.

... A State may not impose economic sanctions on violators of its laws with the intent of changing [their] lawful conduct in other States. Alabama may insist that BMW adhere to a particular disclosure policy in that State. Alabama does not have the power, however, to punish BMW for conduct that was lawful where it occurred and that had no impact on Alabama or its residents. Nor may Alabama impose sanctions on BMW in order to deter conduct that is lawful in other [states]. [**Editor's Note**: BMW's conduct was lawful in 25 states.]

The Alabama Supreme Court therefore properly [rejected] reliance on BMW's out-of-state conduct and based its [reduced] award solely on conduct that occurred within Alabama. The award must be analyzed in the light of the same conduct, with consideration given only to the interests of Alabama consumers, rather than those of the entire Nation. When the scope of the interest in punishment and deterrence that an Alabama court may appropriately consider is properly limited, it is apparent—for reasons that we shall now address—that this award is grossly excessive.

III

Perhaps the most important [indicator] of the reasonableness of a punitive damages award is the degree of reprehensibility of the defendant's conduct.... This principle reflects the accepted view that some wrongs are more blameworthy than others....

In this case, none of the aggravating factors associated with particularly reprehensible conduct is present. The harm BMW inflicted on Dr. Gore was purely economic in nature. The presale refinishing of the car had no effect on its performance or safety features, or even its appearance for at least nine months after his purchase. BMW's conduct evinced no indifference to or reckless disregard for the health and safety of others. To be sure, infliction of economic injury, especially when done intentionally through affirmative acts of misconduct or when the target is financially vulnerable, can warrant a substantial penalty. But this observation does not convert all acts that cause economic harm into torts that are sufficiently reprehensible to justify a significant sanction in addition to compensatory damages.

We accept, of course, the jury's finding that BMW suppressed a material fact which Alabama law obligated it to communicate to prospective purchasers of repainted cars in that State. But the omission of a material fact may be less reprehensible than a deliberate false statement, particularly when there is a good-faith basis for believing that no duty to disclose exists.

… Because this case exhibits none of the circumstances ordinarily associated with egregiously improper conduct, we are persuaded that BMW's conduct was not sufficiently reprehensible to warrant imposition of a $2 million [punitive] damages award.

The second and perhaps most commonly cited [indicator] of an unreasonable or excessive punitive damages award is its ratio to the actual harm inflicted on the plaintiff…. Our [prior decisions have] endorsed the proposition that a comparison between the compensatory award and the punitive award is significant.

… [T]he proper inquiry is whether there is a reasonable relationship between the punitive damages award and *the harm likely to result* from the defendant's conduct as well as the harm that actually has occurred.

The $2 million in punitive damages awarded to Dr. Gore by the Alabama Supreme Court is 500 times the amount of his actual harm as determined by the jury. Moreover, there is no suggestion that Dr. Gore or any other BMW purchaser was threatened with any additional potential harm by BMW's nondisclosure policy. The disparity in this case is thus dramatically greater than those considered in [prior cases].

Of course, we have consistently rejected the notion that the constitutional line is marked by a simple mathematical formula…. When the ratio [between compensatory damages and punitive damages] is a breathtaking 500 to 1, however, the [punitive damages] award must surely raise a suspicious judicial eyebrow.

Comparing the punitive damages award and the civil or criminal penalties that could be imposed for comparable misconduct provides a third [indicator] of excessiveness…. In this case the $2 million economic sanction imposed on BMW is substantially greater than the statutory fines available in Alabama and elsewhere for similar malfeasance.

The maximum civil penalty authorized by the Alabama Legislature for a violation of its Deceptive Trade Practices Act is $2,000; other States authorize more severe sanctions, with the maxima ranging from $5,000 to $10,000. None of these [state] statutes would provide an out-of-state distributor with fair notice that the first violation—or, indeed the first 14 violations—of its provisions might subject an offender to a multimillion dollar penalty.

IV

[W]e are not prepared to draw a bright line marking the limits of a constitutionally acceptable punitive damages award. [H]owever, we are fully convinced that the grossly excessive award imposed in this case transcends the constitutional limit. Whether the appropriate remedy requires a new trial or merely an independent determination by the Alabama Supreme Court of the award necessary to vindicate the economic interests of Alabama consumers is a matter that should be addressed by the state court in the first instance. The judgment is reversed and the case is remanded for further proceedings not inconsistent with this opinion.

It is so ordered.

[**Editor's Note**: Justice Breyer wrote a concurring opinion that Justice O'Connor and Justice Souter joined. It stated that: (1) the punitive damages in this case resulted from a process that gave jurors and judges unlimited discretion, and (2) those damages were excessive considering Alabama's objectives in awarding them.

Justice Scalia wrote a dissent in which Justice Thomas joined. It stated that "the Constitution does not make [the size of punitive damages awards] any of [the Supreme Court's] business"; therefore, "the Court's activities in this area are an unjustified incursion into the province of state governments...."].

JUSTICE GINSBURG, with whom **CHIEF JUSTICE REHNQUIST** joins, dissenting.

The Court, I am convinced, unnecessarily and unwisely ventures into territory traditionally within the States' domain, and does so in the face of reform measures recently adopted or currently under consideration in legislative arenas. The Alabama Supreme Court, in this case, endeavored to follow this Court's prior instructions; and, more recently, [it] has installed further controls on awards of punitive damages. I would therefore leave [its] judgment undisturbed, and resist unnecessary intrusion into an area dominantly of state concern.

II

B

The Court finds Alabama's $2 million award not simply excessive, but grossly so, and therefore unconstitutional. The decision leads us further into territory traditionally within the States' domain, and commits the Court, now and again, to correct misapplication of a properly stated rule of law.... The Court is not well equipped for this mission. Tellingly, the Court repeats that it brings to the task no "mathematical formula," ... no "bright line." It has only a vague concept of substantive due process, a "raised eyebrow" test, as its ultimate guide.

For the reasons stated, I dissent from this Court's disturbance of the judgment the Alabama Supreme Court has made.

QUESTIONS FOR DISCUSSION

1. What constitutional question does the Supreme Court face in this case?
2. What conduct by BMW caused Dr. Gore to sue BMW? What legal injury did Dr. Gore suffer because of BMW's conduct?
3. What amount of damages did the jury award Dr. Gore at trial?
4. What happened to that award on appeal? Why?
5. According to Justice Stevens, did the Alabama Supreme Court properly disregard the impact of BMW's nondisclosure policy in other states when it reviewed the jury award? Why or why not?
6. Does Justice Stevens acknowledge that states have legitimate objectives in awarding punitive damages? What are those objectives?
7. What criteria does Justice Stevens use to measure the reasonableness of an award of punitive damages?

8. Does the punitive damages award to Dr. Gore satisfy those criteria? Why or why not?
9. Does Justice Stevens establish clear limits for a constitutionally acceptable punitive damages award?
10. What is the significance for Justice Stevens of the 500:1 ratio between the punitive damages and the compensatory damages that the jury awarded to Dr. Gore?
11. What evidence does Justice Ginsburg cite for her conclusion that the Supreme Court is "not well-equipped" to judge the constitutionality of punitive damages awards? Who does she think should decide whether those awards are reasonable?
12. Who do you think reached the correct result in this case, the majority or the dissenters? Why?

NOTES

1. Marc Galanter, "Reading the Landscape of Disputes: What We Know and Don't Know (And Think We Know) About Our Allegedly Contentious and Litigious Society," *U.C.L.A. Law Review* 31 (1983): 4–71.
2. *Id.*, p. 29.
3. Valerie P. Hans and William S. Lofquist, "Jurors' Judgments of Business Liability in Tort Cases: Implications for the Litigation Explosion Debate," *Law and Society Review* 26 (1992): 85–115.
4. Critics have published several books that present their views of the civil justice process. Those books include: (1) Patrick M. Garry, *A Nation of Adversaries: How the Litigation Explosion is Reshaping America* (New York: Plenum Press, 1997); (2) Philip K. Howard, *The Death of Common Sense: How Law is Suffocating America* (New York: Random House, 1994); and (3) Walter K. Olson, *The Litigation Explosion: What Happened When America Unleashed the Lawsuit* (New York: Dutton, 1991).
5. Olson, *The Litigation Explosion: What Happened When America Unleashed the Lawsuit*, p. 2.
6. *Id.*, pp. 6–7.
7. Marc Galanter, "The Day After the Litigation Explosion," *Maryland Law Review* 46 (1986): 3–39.
8. *Id.*, p. 7.
9. *Id.*, p. 33.
10. Valerie P. Hans and William S. Lofquist, "Jurors' Judgments of Business Liability in Tort Cases: Implications for the Litigation Explosion Debate," *Law and Society Review* 26 (1992): 85–115.
11. Henry J. Reske, "Stingier Jurors Doling out Fewer Awards," *American Bar Association Journal* (September 1994), p. 20.
12. Associated Press, "Mounting Tobacco Suits Seen," *The Boston Globe*, February 12, 1999, p. A 22.
13. Fred Kaplan, "Jury Finds Gun Firms Negligent," *The Boston Globe*, February 12, 1999, p. A 1.
14. See T. R. Goldman, "Tort Reform: Back in Business?," *Legal Times*, June 15, 1998, p. 1.
15. For a discussion of state tort reforms, see James Podgers, "Throwing Caps out of the Ring," *American Bar Association Journal* (August 1996): 48–49.

16. See New Hampshire Revised Statutes Annotated (N.H.R.S.A.) 225-A:25, IV.
17. *Id.*
18. The New Hampshire long-arm statute, N.H.R.S.A. 510:4(I), which is comparable to those that exist in other states, says:

> Any person who is not an inhabitant of this state and who, in person or through an agent, transacts business within this state, commits a tortious act within this state, or has the ownership, use, or possession of any real or personal property situated in this state submits himself, or his personal representative, to the jurisdiction of the courts of this state as to any cause of action arising from or growing out of the acts enumerated above.

19. Larry L. Tepley and Ralph U. Whitten, *Civil Procedure* (Westbury, N.Y.: Foundation Press, 1994), p. 498. I use the term **complaint**, even though New Hampshire lawyers call this document a **writ**, because lawyers in most states refer to it as a complaint.
20. Richard Wiebusch, *New Hampshire Practice: Civil Practice and Procedure*, Second Edition (Charlottesville, Va.: Lexis Law Publishing, 1997), p. 180.
21. Tepley and Whitten, *Civil Procedure*, p. 219.
22. Richard Wiebusch, *New Hampshire Practice: Civil Practice and Procedure*, Second Edition, Volume 4, pp. 291–292.
23. *Id.*, p. 297.
24. *Id.*, p. 328.
25. *Id.*, pp. 332–333.
26. *Id.*, p. 209.
27. *Id.*, pp. 264–265; Tepley and Whitten, *Civil Procedure*, p. 511.
28. Wiebusch, *New Hampshire Practice: Civil Practice and Procedure*, Second Edition, Volume 4, p. 266.
29. Geoffrey C. Hazard, Jr., and Jan Vetter, *Perspectives on Civil Procedure* (Boston: Little, Brown, 1987), p. 124.
30. Lief Carter, Austin Sarat, Mark Silverstein, and William Weaver, *New Perspectives on American Law* (Durham, N.C.: Carolina Academic Press, 1997), p. 13.
31. *Id.*, p. 36.
32. Tepley and Whitten, *Civil Procedure*, p. 711.
33. *Id.*, p. 717.
34. *Id.*; see also Wiebusch, *New Hampshire Practice: Civil Practice and Procedure*, Second Edition, Volume 4, pp. 526–527.
35. Tepley and Whitten, *Civil Procedure*, p. 717.
36. Wiebusch, *New Hampshire Practice: Civil Practice and Procedure*, Second Edition, Volume 4, p. 541.
37. *Id.*, p. 544.
38. *Id.*
39. Tepley and Whitten, *Civil Procedure*, p. 9.
40. Stephan Landsman, *Readings on Adversary Justice: The American Approach to Litigation* (St. Paul, MN.: West, 1988), p. 2.
41. Tepley and Whitten, *Civil Procedure*, p. 10.
42. Carter, Sarat, Silverstein, and Weaver, *New Perspectives on American Law*, p. 6.
43. *Id.*, p. 7.
44. *Id.*
45. *Id.*
46. John H. Langbein, "The German Advantage in Civil Procedure," *University of Chicago Law Review* 52 (1985): 823–866.

47. *Id.*, p. 843.
48. *Id.*, p. 848.
49. Wiebusch, *New Hampshire Practice: Civil Practice and Procedure*, Second Edition, Volume 4, p. 559.
50. Hazard and Vetter, *Perspectives on Civil Procedure*, p. 130.
51. Wiebusch, *New Hampshire Practice: Civil Practice and Procedure*, Second Edition, Volume 4, p. 561.
52. Wiebusch, *New Hampshire Practice: Civil Practice and Procedure*, Second Edition, Volume 5 (Charlottesville, Va.: Lexis Law Publishing, 1997), p. 2; see also Tepley and Whitten, *Civil Procedure*, pp. 729–730.
53. Wiebusch, *New Hampshire Practice: Civil Practice and Procedure*, Second Edition, Volume 5, pp. 2–3.
54. *Id.*, p. 572.
55. Tepley and Whitten, *Civil Procedure*, pp. 748–749.
56. Wiebusch, *New Hampshire Practice: Civil Practice and Procedure*, Second Edition, Volume 4, p. 595.
57. *Id.*
58. *Id.*
59. *Id.*, p. 597; see also Tepley and Whitten, *Civil Procedure*, p. 736.
60. Tepley and Whitten, *Civil Procedure*, p. 21.
61. *Id.*
62. David I. Levine, Donald L. Doernberg, and Melissa L. Nelken, *Civil Procedure Anthology* (Cincinnati, Oh.: Anderson, 1998), p. 516.
63. Wiebusch, *New Hampshire Practice: Civil Practice and Procedure*, Second Edition, Volume 5, p. 259.
64. Tepley and Whitten, *Civil Procedure*, p. 20.
65. John W. Cooley, "Arbitration vs Mediation—Explaining the Differences," *Judicature* 69 (February–March 1986): 263–269.
66. *Id.*
67. Herbert M. Kritzer, "The English Rule," *American Bar Association Journal* (November 1992), pp. 55–58.
68. *Id.*, p. 56.
69. Wiebusch, *New Hampshire Practice: Civil Practice and Procedure*, Second Edition, Volume 5, p. 29.
70. Tepley and Whitten, *Civil Procedure*, pp. 782–783.
71. Wiebusch, *New Hampshire Practice: Civil Practice and Procedure*, Second Edition, Volume 5, pp. 7–8.
72. *Id.*, p. 8.
73. *Id.*
74. *Id.*, p. 9.
75. Tepley and Whitten, *Civil Procedure*, p. 773.
76. Levine, Doernberg, and Nelken, *Civil Procedure Anthology*, p. 336.
77. *Id.*, p. 339.
78. Wiebusch, *New Hampshire Practice: Civil Practice and Procedure*, Second Edition, Volume 5, p. 273.
79. Landsman, *Readings in Adversarial Justice: The American Approach to Litigation*, p. 123.
80. Wiebusch, *New Hampshire Practice: Civil Practice and Procedure*, Second Edition, Volume 5, p. 285.
81. *Id.*, p. 288.

82. Tepley and Whitten, *Civil Procedure*, p. 798.

83. *Id.*

84. *Id.*, pp. 288–289.

85. *Id.*, p. 289.

86. *Id.*, p. 290.

87. Tepley and Whitten, *Civil Procedure*, pp. 798–799.

88. See *J.E.B. v. Alabama ex rel T.B.*, 511 U.S. 127 (1994), and *Edmonson v. Leesville Concrete Company*, 500 U.S. 614 (1991).

89. Wiebusch, *New Hampshire Practice: Civil Practice and Procedure*, Second Edition, Volume 5, p. 291.

90. Tepley and Whitten, *Civil Procedure*, p. 799.

91. Wiebusch, *New Hampshire Practice: Civil Practice and Procedure*, Second Edition, Volume 5, p. 286.

92. *Id.*, p. 292.

93. *Id.*, p. 308.

94. See N.H.R.S.A. 225-A:24(I)(a) and (d).

95. The tort-law doctrine of *respondeat superior* holds employers responsible for the tortious acts that their employees commit on the job. Therefore, in this case, as in most personal injury cases, the defendant is the employer, not the specific employee(s) who allegedly committed the tortious act(s) that injured the plaintiff.

96. Wiebusch, *New Hampshire Practice: Civil Practice and Procedure*, Second Edition, Volume 5, p. 331.

97. *Id.*, p. 308.

98. See N.H.R.S.A. 225-A:24,I; see also *Nutbrown v. Mt. Cranmore, Inc.*, 140 N.H. 675 (1996).

99. Hon. Walter L. Murphy and Daniel C. Pope, *New Hampshire Civil Jury Instructions*, Third Edition (Charlottesville, Va.: Lexis Law Publishing, 1997), p. 6–2.

100. *Id.*, p. 11–2.

101. *Id.*, p. 9–7.

102. *Id.*, pp. 9–4, 9–6.

103. Wiebusch, *New Hampshire Practice: Civil Practice and Procedure*, Second Edition, Volume 5, p. 362.

104. Murphy and Pope, *New Hampshire Civil Jury Instructions*, Third Edition, p. 9–13.

105. *Id*

Chapter 7

POLICY MAKING— THE APPELLATE PROCESS

INTRODUCTION

The appellate process is fundamentally different from the trial process because trials and appeals have different functions. The function of trials is to determine whether a criminal defendant is guilty or innocent and whether a civil defendant is liable to the plaintiff, based on the consideration of **questions of fact**. It was a question of fact whether the substance that Stan Johnson sold to a state trooper was cocaine; it was also a question of fact whether Shannon Peterson fell while skiing because of ice or because of blowing snow from a snowmaking "gun."

The functions of appeals are to correct legal errors that somehow made the trial unfair to the losing party, and to "make policy" by devising rules of law that will guide lawyers and trial courts in future cases.[1] Appellate courts perform both functions by considering **questions of law** that the parties' lawyers present to the court. For example, it was a question of law whether the "controlled buy" in which Stan Johnson sold cocaine to a state trooper violated constitutional protections against unreasonable searches and seizures. If the "buy" was unconstitutional, then Judge Romano erred when she admitted the trooper's testimony and the cocaine into evidence, and an appellate court should reverse her decision.

The focus on questions of law makes appeals dramatically different from trials. One difference is that appellate courts accept the factual determinations that the jury made at trial. Neither juries nor witnesses appear in appellate courts because the trial established the facts. Another difference is that lawyers' arguments on appeal lack the emotional elements that their arguments to juries often contain. Appellate arguments emphasize instead why one legal rule is better than another. For example, one lawyer might argue that ski area operators should not be liable for injuries that result from icy trails, while opposing counsel might argue for liability when the ski area operator caused or aggravated the plaintiff's injuries.

Still another difference is that lawyers cannot raise on appeal legal issues that they did not address at trial, because appellate courts cannot consider any issue that did not appear in the trial **record**.[2] The record includes the written transcript of the trial and the motions and memoranda of law that the parties submitted during trial. Appellate courts confine themselves to issues that appear in the record because they wish to review the fairness of the trial as it actually was, not as it might have been. They also refuse to decide issues that have not been "heat tested" via direct and cross-examination at trial.[3] For example, a lawyer cannot argue on appeal that police officers searched her client's house illegally if she failed to argue that at trial.

The most important difference between trials and appeals is that appellate courts make policies that affect not only the parties to a particular case, but also families, schools, businesses, and communities. For example, a decision that a ski area operator was liable for injuries suffered by a skier who fell and hit a lift tower might force operators to make alpine skiing safer, such as by padding lift towers. The cost of additional safety equipment, however, could force some operators out of business, thereby causing unemployment. The remaining ski area operators would pass the cost of the new equipment on to skiers in the form of higher prices for lift tickets, which could make skiing less popular and increase unemployment.

Appellate judges, then, are policy makers who choose between competing visions of the good society when they decide cases. Their own visions of how society should work influence those choices. In other words, "the law" (i.e., statutes and prior cases) and the record are not the only factors that influence appellate court decisions. The judges' backgrounds, experiences, and philosophies (i.e., public policy preferences) influence those decisions too.[4]

This does not mean that the judges' public policy preferences influence all, or even most, appellate decisions. Indeed, most cases have no consequences for society; they are important only to the parties involved. In those cases (e.g., tax cases), judges are likely to rely on "the law" as the basis for their decisions, and to agree on the result or, at least, to refrain from dissenting because their disagreement is not passionate.[5] In other cases, (e.g., freedom-of-speech or search-and-seizure matters), though, there are societal consequences, the judges' policy preferences are influential, and dissents are more likely.[6] Dissents occur often in the U.S. Supreme Court, which decides many controversial and consequential cases.

Another reason why judges' public policy preferences do not influence every case is the collegial nature of appellate courts. Appellate judges work in **panels** of three, and they must work together for years despite differences in temperament and philosophy. They therefore seek smooth working relationships, by modifying their writing styles or by joining a colleague's opinion despite the wish to dissent.[7] Furthermore, appellate judges honor institutional norms, such as respect for jurisdiction and precedent, which limit their discretion.[8] Institutional norms reduce the influence of policy preferences, and produce consensus, or narrow dissents based on alternative views of the facts or the precedents, in most cases.[9] Philosophically based dissents are the exception, not the rule.

Thus, the public policy preferences of appellate judges do not decide most cases, but they often influence outcomes in significant cases. Even then, policy preferences mix with the facts, the judges' desire for collegiality, and institutional norms in order to produce results.[10] The remainder of this chapter will show how that process works.

STATE V. JOHNSON ON APPEAL

Post-Verdict Motions

When the jury announced its verdict in *State v. Johnson* (see Chapter 5), Stan Johnson's lawyer, Gene Jefferson, decided to file a post-verdict motion that asked Judge Romano to overturn the verdict. If the motion was unsuccessful, he would file an appeal in the New Hampshire Supreme Court.[11] Jefferson filed a **motion to set aside the verdict**. Pursuant to superior court rules, he submitted the motion to Judge Romano within seven days after the verdict.[12] The motion argued that the verdict was legally incorrect because (1) Stan had not consented to a warrantless search of his apartment and (2) he was a victim of selective prosecution based on his fame. Prosecutor Quinlan filed an opposing motion. Judge Romano conducted a brief hearing in which the lawyers presented arguments for and against setting the verdict aside. A week later, Judge Romano issued a six-page order that denied Jefferson's motion. The order stated that "Defendant has presented no evidence, concerning either his apprehension or his prosecution, that the verdict in this case was contrary to law."

Notice of Appeal

When Gene Jefferson had finished reading Judge Romano's order, he began to plan an appeal to the New Hampshire Supreme Court. His first task was to convince the court to hear the appeal, because the court was not required to hear it. The court could refuse to consider the case or it could **affirm** the verdict **summarily**—that is, without offering the parties a chance to present written or oral arguments.[13] New Hampshire is the only state that does not guarantee to all criminal defendants in felony cases a chance to present written arguments to an appellate court.[14] The Court would decide whether or not to hear Stan's appeal after reviewing his **notice of appeal**. Court rules required Gene Jefferson to file a notice of appeal within thirty days of the date on which Judge Romano denied his motion to set aside the verdict.[15] Failure to do so would mean the loss of an opportunity to appeal.

In New Hampshire, a lawyer files a notice of appeal with the Clerk of the Supreme Court, but in most states and in the federal system, a lawyer files with the clerk of the trial court, who then submits the notice of appeal to the appellate court.[16] In every state and in the federal system, there is a prescribed time period within which one must file, which ranges from ten days to thirty days after the verdict or judicial decision that one wishes to appeal. Failure to file within the prescribed time period precludes an appeal because the appellate court's jurisdiction in a case depends on a timely notice of appeal.[17]

In criminal cases, it is usually the lawyer for the defendant who must file a notice of appeal, because the law permits a prosecutor to appeal in only a few instances.[18] A prosecutor can appeal a judge's order that grants a motion to: (1) dismiss an indictment; (2) suppress evidence; (3) set aside a guilty verdict; (4) grant a new trial; or (5) vacate a sentence.[19] A prosecutor cannot appeal an acquittal in hopes of securing a reversal and a retrial of the defendant, because the retrial would violate the prohibition against **double jeopardy** (being tried twice for the same crime) in the Sixth Amendment to the federal Constitution.

The purpose of the notice of appeal in *State v. Johnson* was to persuade the New Hampshire Supreme Court to permit the parties to present written and oral arguments to the Court. Gene had laid the foundation for the notice of appeal during pretrial and trial by submitting to the Court motions to suppress and to dismiss, respectively, which he knew would present issues for a potential appeal. Those issues would not be available on appeal had Gene not raised them either before or during trial.[20]

He stressed that *State v. Johnson* presented a new question of law in New Hampshire, and that the Court ought to resolve it in order to clarify the law and to guide the trial courts.[21] The question was whether the consent exception to the constitutional requirements of probable cause and a search warrant applied when a police officer, pursuant to a rumor, initiated a controlled drug "buy" in a suspect's home. Jefferson explained why the consent exception did not apply in such circumstances, and he cited cases that supported his view. He hoped that the Court would accept *State v. Johnson* in order to answer the consent question for the benefit of the trial courts and the bar.

When the notice of appeal was ready, Jefferson's secretary mailed an original and fifteen copies to the Court, as its rules required.[22] She also mailed a copy to the clerk of the trial court and another copy to the Attorney General of New Hampshire, whose office would represent the State during the appeal.[23] Three months later, Jefferson received a **scheduling order** from the Court, which indicated that the Court had accepted Stan's appeal, and that Jefferson's **brief** was due in thirty days.[24] The order also requested the preparation of a full trial transcript. Jefferson, as the lawyer for the **appellant** (the party who appeals), was responsible for ordering a copy of the transcript from the court reporter who had produced the original and for making sure that the Supreme Court received the copy.[25]

Jefferson was pleased to receive the scheduling order. He knew that, when deciding whether or not to accept an appeal, the New Hampshire Supreme Court considers the importance of the question(s) presented in the notice of appeal, whether the trial court decision conflicts with one of the Court's own precedents, and whether the error alleged requires correction in order to prevent an injustice.[26] He suspected that the Court had accepted the case because the trial courts needed guidance on the scope of the consent exception. He hoped that the Court would reverse Stan's conviction as the product of a search that lacked probable cause, a warrant, and consent. It was time to begin work on his brief.

Briefs

Appellant

An appellate brief is a written statement of the reasons why an appellate court should affirm or reverse a decision of a lower court.[27] Gene Jefferson looked forward to writing the brief despite the thirty to forty hours that would be necessary to research and write it. There was an intellectual challenge in trying to persuade the five justices, who were highly intelligent, experienced lawyers, of the correctness of one's position on an important issue of law and public policy. If that was not sufficient motivation, Court rules required Gene to file a brief if he wished to present an oral argument to the Court, which he did.[28]

Gene read the **New Hampshire Rules of Appellate Procedure** carefully before he began the research for his brief. Those rules govern practice in the New Hampshire Supreme Court, and they reminded Gene about the information that his brief must include, the maximum length permitted (fifty pages, excluding the table of contents), and that he had to submit an original and fifteen copies to the Court.[29] Gene followed the rules closely as he prepared his brief, and he kept track of its due date. He knew that the Court enforced its rules more strictly now than in past years, imposing penalties for violations, because its workload had increased significantly during the 1990s.

Court rules governed the substance of Gene Jefferson's brief as much as they governed its form. Substantively, Gene was careful to discuss fully in his brief every issue that he had raised in his notice of appeal. He knew that the Court could refuse to consider an issue that he raised in the notice of appeal but either ignored or barely mentioned in the brief. The Court could decide that he had **waived** his right to a judicial resolution of that issue.[30] Gene was also careful to comply with the rules that governed the form of his brief, because he knew that the failure to file a brief in the proper form can influence judges' evaluations of its substantive merits.[31]

In New Hampshire, appellants' briefs must contain certain preliminary material, including: (1) a **title page** (which identifies the case, the party who filed the brief, and the party's lawyer); (2) a **table of contents** (which identifies the contents of the brief); (3) a **table of cases** (which lists all cases cited in the brief); (4) a **table of statutes and other authorities** (which lists statutes, administrative regulations, and constitutional provisions cited in the brief); and (5) the **question(s) presented**.[32] Gene Jefferson stated the questions presented in *State v. Johnson* as follows:

1. Did the trial court err when it denied the Defendant's motion to suppress evidence, thereby violating rights that Part I, Article 19, of the New Hampshire Constitution guarantees to him, because the "controlled buy" of cocaine that occurred in the Defendant's home lacked probable cause, a search warrant, and the Defendant's consent?

2. Did the trial court err when it denied the Defendant's motion to dismiss, thereby violating rights that Part I, Article 15, of the New Hampshire Constitution guarantees to him, because the State selectively prosecuted him as a result of his fame?

Jefferson relied on the New Hampshire Constitution because it sometimes furnishes greater protection for individual rights, including the rights of criminal defendants, than the federal Constitution does. American federalism permits states to provide more, but not less, protection for individual rights than the federal government provides. Therefore, the New Hampshire Constitution was a more promising basis for Jefferson's arguments than the federal Constitution was.

Appellants' briefs in New Hampshire must also contain: (1) a **statement of the case**; (2) a **statement of the facts**; (3) a **summary of the argument(s)**; (4) the **argument(s)**; (5) a **conclusion**; (6) the date of the brief and the signature of its author; (7) a statement indicating that the author has sent a copy to opposing counsel; and (8) a request for, or a waiver of, oral argument.[33] A statement of the case recounts a case's procedural history. In *State v. Johnson*, it noted that a jury had convicted Stan of the sale and the possession of a controlled drug, that Judge Romano had denied part of his motion to suppress evidence, that she had denied his motion to dismiss, and that he now appealed those denials.

A statement of the facts recounts a case's factual history. In *State v. Johnson*, that required an account of the "controlled buy" at Stan's apartment and of his subsequent arrest and trial. Gene Jefferson stated the facts in a neutral fashion, as Court rules required, but he also stated that a rumor was the basis for the "buy," that Trooper Cummings had gone to Stan's apartment uninvited, and that Cummings initiated a conversation with Stan about buying cocaine, but that Judge Romano concluded that Stan consented to Cummings's entry into his apartment. Gene knew that appellate judges respect lawyers who can state facts fairly and accurately but still identify trial court error(s).[34]

The argument is the heart of any appellate brief, and Gene worked hard on his argument. He recalled the cardinal rules of appellate writing, which state that briefs should be short, clear, and to the point. Brevity and clarity are crucial because appellate judges do not have the time to reread clumsy or confusing sentences. The Colorado Supreme Court, for example, hears oral arguments in six or seven cases per day for four days each month. It usually receives three briefs (appellant's brief, appellee's brief, and, frequently, appellant's reply brief) in each case, which means that the justices must read up to 84 briefs per week in order to prepare for oral arguments.[35] Similarly, Judge Alex Kozinski of the U.S. Court of Appeals for the Ninth Circuit estimates that he reads 3500 pages worth of briefs each month.[36]

Brevity and clarity are not enough, though; above all, an appellate argument must be persuasive. It must furnish the raw materials, namely, accurate facts and compelling legal reasoning, from which the court can write an opinion that favors the author's client.[37] The written argument is the most powerful tool that a lawyer can wield in the appellate process. That partly reflects the American legal tradition, which emphasizes written, rather than oral, communications between lawyers and appellate judges.[38] It also reflects an increase in appellate court caseloads in recent years, which has made briefs more significant and oral argument less significant, and less frequent. Indeed, the U.S. Court of Appeals for the Eleventh Circuit hears oral arguments in only one-third of its cases because of its heavy caseload.[39] Thus, appellate judges rely on briefs to introduce them to cases before oral argument, to help them decide cases at post-argument conferences, and to help them justify their decisions in the opinions that they write.[40]

Gene knew about the pressures of appellate caseloads, so he limited his argument to two major issues. They were whether (1) the search of Stan's apartment violated a constitutional guarantee against unreasonable searches and seizures, and (2) the decision to prosecute Stan violated a constitutional guarantee against selective prosecution. Gene introduced each issue with a heading that summarized his argument and that invoked the responsibility of an appellate court to correct trial court errors.

The headings were as follows:

I. When the trial court denied the Defendant's motion to suppress evidence, it violated his freedom from unreasonable searches and seizures, as guaranteed by Part I, Article 19, of the New Hampshire Constitution, because the "controlled buy" of cocaine that occurred in his home occurred without probable cause, a search warrant, or his consent.

II. When the trial court denied the Defendant's motion to dismiss, it violated his freedom from selective prosecution, as guaranteed by Part I, Article 15, of the New Hampshire Constitution, because the State selectively prosecuted him as a result of his fame as an Olympic athlete.

In other words, when Judge Romano denied Stan's motions, she committed **reversible error**. Reversible error affects the outcome of a case and warrants a **reversal** by an appellate court of a trial court's decision. Courts distinguish reversible error from **harmless error** (e.g., misspelling the defendant's name on an indictment), which does not require the reversal of a conviction because it did not influence the verdict.[41]

In alleging reversible error, Gene was careful to remind the Court of the **standard of review** it should apply to Judge Romano's rulings. A standard of review is the degree of scrutiny that an appellate court should use in evaluating a trial court decision; appellate judges care about standards of review, and reject arguments that ignore them or misapply them.[42] Different standards of review apply to different types of trial court decisions. Rulings on motions to suppress and motions to dismiss are exercises of discretion, so the standard of review in *State v. Johnson* was **abuse of discretion**: the appellate court had to decide whether Judge Romano had abused her discretion when she denied Stan's motions.[43] Abuse of discretion can occur when a judge: (1) fails to consider a relevant factor that deserves considerable weight in a decision; (2) gives considerable weight to an irrelevant factor; or (3) weighs only and all the relevant factors, but nevertheless makes an error in judgment.[44] Standards of review, including abuse of discretion, give trial courts leeway to apply the law as they see fit, prior to and during trial. Consequently, about 80 percent of civil appeals and 90 percent of criminal appeals are unsuccessful, and the appellate courts' decisions in most of those cases are unanimous.[45]

In Gene Jefferson's view, Judge Romano abused her discretion when she denied Stan's motions. Moreover, the two denials, taken together, reflected a dangerous tolerance for abusive law enforcement practices. Gene first challenged the denial of the motion to suppress because that was his strongest argument. He wrote that Judge Romano failed to consider that there was no probable cause for a search of Stan's apartment and that Trooper Cummings had initiated the drug sale, and she misinterpreted Stan's friendliness to Cummings as "consent" to a search. Gene also believed that Judge Romano abused her discretion when she denied Stan's motion to dismiss. She failed to consider that Stan was the first Grayson College student to be prosecuted for selling drugs, instead of being disciplined exclusively by the College, and the only student-dealer who was famous.

There were no prior decisions by the New Hampshire Supreme Court that supported Gene's "consent" argument, nor was there a decision by a supreme court in another state that had found that "consent" was lacking in similar circumstances. Worse yet, there was a decision by the U.S. Supreme Court in *Lewis v. United States* (1966), in which the High Court held that the "purchase" of drugs in the seller's home by an undercover police officer did not violate the protection against unreasonable searches and seizures in the Fourth Amendment to the federal Constitution.[46] Furthermore, Gene knew that most members of the New Hampshire Supreme Court were political conservatives who favored the State in criminal cases and rarely overturned a conviction. Two of the justices had begun their legal careers as prosecutors.

Gene therefore presented a narrow, technical argument that emphasized the differences between *Lewis* and *Johnson*. He stated that *Lewis* should not govern the outcome in *Johnson* for two reasons. First, the Supreme Court decided *Lewis* pursuant to the federal Constitution, which may provide less protection for individual freedom than does the New Hampshire Constitution, which governs *State v. Johnson*. Gene cited a decision of the New Hampshire Supreme Court that said the New Hampshire Constitution provides at least as much protection for individual freedom as the federal Constitution does.[47] He also cited a decision of that Court that said the search warrant requirement of the New Hampshire Constitution is "particularly stringent" when police enter a private home, where there is a "strong expectation of privacy and protection from government intrusion."[48]

Second, in *Lewis*, the undercover officer had telephoned the defendant and asked if he could buy marijuana from the defendant, who then *expressly invited* the officer to his home to make the sale. That invitation was the defendant's consent to entry of his house, and it gave the officer probable cause to believe that illegal activity was about to occur there. No such consent or probable cause existed in *State v. Johnson*; Trooper Cummings arrived unexpectedly, and based on a rumor, not an invitation. Thus, Gene Jefferson **distinguished** *Lewis* from *Johnson*, which meant that the former should not control the latter. In so doing, he tapped into the Court's passion for individual freedom and its skepticism about government. He concluded:

> In New Hampshire, where our State Constitution zealously protects the privacy of the home, a police officer who would enter a private home under cover in order to solicit the resident's participation in a crime must, pursuant to that constitution, first obtain a search warrant that is based on probable cause. If the resident "consents" merely by admitting a police officer who appears to be a fellow college student, then the only limit to the government's ability to gather information about our private lives will be the ingenuity of its agents in disguising themselves.

There were no prior decisions by the New Hampshire Supreme Court or by supreme courts in other states that supported Gene's "selective prosecution" argument either. Moreover, two federal appellate courts had held that in order to prove selective prosecution, a defendant must show that the police singled him out for prosecution on the basis of race, religion, or a desire to prevent his exercise of constitutional rights.[49]

Gene reiterated that the New Hampshire Constitution contains as least as much protection for individual rights, including the rights of criminal defendants, as does the federal Constitution, and he cited a decision by the Court to that effect.[50] Then he argued that such protection should extend to this case, in which Granite County authorities prosecuted Stan Johnson for selling drugs, an offense for which they had not prosecuted other Grayson College students, in order to deter other students from selling drugs. The argument concluded as follows:

> The prosecution of Stan Johnson occurred not because of *what he had done*, for the record indicates that other Grayson College students have sold drugs, but they were neither arrested nor prosecuted. The prosecution of Stan Johnson occurred because of *who he was*, namely, an Olympic champion. That is as unacceptable to the spirit, if not the letter, of our State Constitution as is prosecution based on one's race, religion, or political beliefs.

Gene concluded his brief by asking the Court for the **relief** that his client sought. He requested a dismissal of the indictment because of selective prosecution, which would end the case, or a new trial in which Trooper Cummings's testimony and the cocaine he "bought" from Stan would not be evidence. The latter decision would end the prosecution too, because there would be no case against Stan without Cummings's testimony and the cocaine. Gene revised his brief four times before he was satisfied with it. Then his secretary proofread it for grammar, style, and punctuation. When it was finally finished, Gene signed it, and his secretary mailed the original and fifteen copies to the Court and one copy to opposing counsel.

Appellee

In *State v. Johnson*, the State was the **appellee**, that is, the party that responds to the appeal. The lawyer for the State was Assistant Attorney General Karen Rasmussen, who had practiced law in New Hampshire for five years. Karen was a native of Fort Dodge, Iowa, who had come to New Hampshire in 1988 to attend Dartmouth College, from which she graduated in 1992. In 1995, after graduation from law school at the University of Iowa, Karen returned to New Hampshire to join her fiancé, a Concord psychologist who had been her classmate at Dartmouth. She passed the bar exam and joined the attorney general's staff.

Karen read Gene's brief carefully when it arrived at her office, and she thought of counterarguments as she read. Then, after consulting with Kevin Quinlan, who had argued the case at trial (see Chapter 5), Karen began to write her brief. Karen followed the same format as Gene had, except that because she represented the appellee, she could exclude from her brief a statement of the case and the question(s) presented.[51] Karen's job was to convince the Court that it should affirm Judge Romano's denials of Stan's motions to suppress and to dismiss, respectively, because Judge Romano had applied the law to the facts correctly. Karen was optimistic because she knew that most of the justices were not only *political* conservatives who rarely reversed criminal convictions, but also *judicial* conservatives who were reluctant to second-guess a trial judge who had seen the witnesses and heard the evidence.

Karen presented her arguments in the same order that Gene had presented his; she first addressed the constitutionality of Trooper Cummings's entry into Stan's apartment. She argued that the entry was constitutional because Stan had used his apartment for illegal drug trafficking. The *Lewis* decision stated that a householder who used his residence in that way forfeited any expectation of privacy that he might otherwise have. In other words, Stan was entitled to no more privacy while selling cocaine in his apartment than he would have been while selling it on the street. Thus, Trooper Cummings's entry into Stan's apartment for undercover work did not violate the New Hampshire Constitution, and Judge Romano had properly denied Stan's motion to suppress.

Karen also argued that Judge Romano had properly denied Stan's motion to dismiss because the State had not engaged in selective prosecution. She noted that Granite County had not prosecuted previous student drug dealers because the College had disciplined them itself instead of reporting them to the police. Granite County *had* prosecuted, however, nonstudents who had sold cocaine, so Stan's prosecution was by no means unique. Moreover, even if Granite County prosecuted Stan to deter others from selling drugs, that was permissible because *United States v. Peskin* and *United States v. Berrios* established that selective prosecution is unconstitutional only when it is based on the defendant's race or religion, or on a desire to prevent her exercise of constitutional rights.[52] Karen acknowledged that *Peskin* and *Berrios* had interpreted only the federal Constitution, but she added that Stan had not shown that the New Hampshire Constitution defined selective prosecution differently. Thus, Judge Romano's denial of Stan's motion to dismiss should stand.

Reply

Pursuant to Court rules, Gene Jefferson received a copy of Karen's brief in the mail. When he had read it, he decided not to file a **reply brief**. The appellant is entitled, but is not required, to file a reply brief. A reply brief is a good idea when the appellee's brief makes an argument or cites cases that the appellant's opening brief did not address, and that are important enough to merit a rebuttal.[53] Gene did not find any surprises in Karen's brief, so he chose not to reply. Instead, he worked on other cases while he waited for the Court to set a date for oral argument.

Oral Argument

Oral argument in *State v. Johnson* occurred on January 4, 2000. *State v. Johnson* was the third and final case that the Court heard during its morning session; it would hear three more cases in the afternoon. As usual, the courtroom was nearly empty, except for the justices, the lawyers, and a law clerk who tape-recorded the proceedings. Only two law students and a political science professor sat in the seats reserved for the public. At 11:15 A.M., Chief Justice Bronson Davis said to Gene Jefferson, who was seated at the appellant's counsel table: "You may proceed, counsel." Gene stood up, walked to the podium that faced the judges' bench, and began his oral argument as follows:

> May it please the Court. My name is Eugene Jefferson, and I represent the appellant, Mr. Johnson. We would like to reserve five minutes for rebuttal. We ask this Court to reverse the trial court's denials of our motion to suppress and our motion to dismiss. I will address the motion to dismiss first.

That was as far as Gene got before Justice Donald Sawyer interrupted him with a question. Part of Sawyer's exchange with Jefferson appears below:

Q. Mr. Jefferson, you argue in your brief that there is a distinction between using a telephone to invite an undercover officer to your house to buy drugs, as occurred in the *Lewis* case, and inviting him into your kitchen for the same purpose when he appears at your door, as occurred in this case. Is that a distinction without a difference?

A. No, Your Honor. There is a big difference between those two cases. In *Lewis*, the defendant expressly invited the officer to his home to buy drugs, which established both consent to the officer's entry and probable cause to believe that a drug sale would occur in the home. In this case, there was no probable cause, just an unsubstantiated rumor, and there was no consent because the officer appeared in my client's kitchen uninvited.

Q. Didn't your client consent when he offered the trooper a chair while he retrieved the cocaine from his closet?

A. No, Your Honor. Unlike the defendant in *Lewis*, my client had no chance to consent; the trooper was already in my client's kitchen when my client discovered him. Moreover, the trooper had no right to be in that kitchen because there was no probable cause to believe that my client would sell drugs there.

Then Chief Justice Davis interjected with a question. Part of his exchange with Jefferson appears below:

Q. Mr. Jefferson, what rule are you telling us should govern this case?

A. The rule should be that a police officer can enter a private home undercover in order to solicit the resident's participation in a crime only after obtaining a warrant supported by probable cause.

Q. What if the resident consents to the entry?

A. Consent is an exception, but it must be voluntary.

Q. Was your client's consent involuntary?

A. My client did not consent. A young man who seemed to be a college student appeared in my client's kitchen; my client never had a chance to consent to the man's entry into his home.

The final justice to question Jefferson was Nikki Panos, the Court's only woman and only Democrat. Part of her conversation with Jefferson appears below:

Q. Mr. Jefferson, must a defendant formally invite an undercover officer into his home, as in *Lewis*, in order to consent to the officer's entry, or can circumstances short of a formal invitation constitute consent?

A. There can be consent without a formal invitation, but it must be voluntary. The defendant must have a chance to refuse entry.

Q. Suppose that Trooper Cummings had knocked on the front door, and your client spoke briefly with him, then admitted him. Would that have been consent?

A. The State's argument for consent would be stronger in that case, but Trooper Cummings would still have not had a right to be there without a warrant supported by probable cause.

That was the extent of Gene Jefferson's argument. No sooner had he answered Justice Panos's last question than the red light on the podium flashed, which meant that his time was up. He had spent thirteen of the past fifteen minutes answering questions. He would have five minutes for rebuttal after Karen Rasmussen finished her argument.

When Jefferson sat down, Karen Rasmussen began her argument as follows:

May it please the Court. My name is Karen Rasmussen, and I represent the State in this case. The State requests this Court to affirm the trial court's denials of the Defendant's motions to suppress and to dismiss, respectively. I will address the motion to suppress first. The trial court correctly denied it because the Defendant consented to Trooper Cummings's entry into his apartment. Mr. Jefferson draws a false distinction between the *Lewis* case and this case. In both cases, the defendant admitted an undercover officer into his home in order to sell drugs to the officer. It is irrelevant that, in *Lewis*, the invitation occurred on the telephone, whereas in this case it occurred in the Defendant's kitchen. In each case, the defendant acted knowingly and voluntarily.

Then Justice Carter Derrick interrupted her with a question. Part of their exchange appears below:

Q. Ms. Rasmussen, if we were to find in favor of the State, what limit would there be to the State's ability to gain warrantless entry into the private homes of its citizens?

A. Nothing would change if this Court decided this case in favor of the State, Your Honor. The State could still gain warrantless entry into private homes only by means of a resident's consent. The resident would be as free then as he is today to deny entry to anyone he did not wish to admit.

Q.   If we decide in favor of the State, won't we give police officers a green light to devise all kinds of ingenious disguises that they can use to gain entry to private homes?

A.   Police officers already use disguises in undercover operations, Your Honor. A decision for the State in this case won't increase that use dramatically. More important, a decision for the State won't change the police practice of acting on tips from reliable sources. The trooper went to the defendant's home in this case because he had reliable information that the defendant was selling drugs. There is no reason to believe that, if this Court finds for the State in this case, undercover officers will knock on doors at random in New Hampshire in hopes of discovering crime.

Then the Court fell silent. Karen did not raise the selective prosecution issue because the Court had not raised it with Gene, which probably meant that the Court saw no reversible error there. Instead, although she had five minutes of argument time left, Karen merely repeated the State's request to affirm the trial court, thanked the justices for their attention, and sat down before her time was up. In short, Karen quit while she was ahead, which was a sign of an experienced (and confident) appellate advocate.

When Karen sat, Gene rose, returned to the podium, and delivered his rebuttal. He tried to use the Court's conservatism to his advantage by arguing that a decision for his client would preserve the integrity of the consent exception, whereas a decision for the State would destroy it. If the State won, the consent exception would become so broad that trial courts would almost always find that defendants had "consented" to warrantless entries into their homes. Many sloppy undercover operations, without probable cause or a search warrant, would result. New Hampshire could avoid that result if the Court reversed Judge Romano's denial of Stan's motion to suppress. Then Gene thanked the justices and sat down. Oral argument was over.

The law students and the professor enjoyed listening to the argument in *State v. Johnson* because it reinforced three key points from classroom discussions. First, oral argument can clarify the positions that the lawyers took in their briefs, and can alert the judges to the likely consequences of the result that each lawyer seeks.[54] Justice Sawyer's question to Gene Jefferson whether *State v. Johnson* was distinct from *Lewis v. United States* sought clarification. Justice Derrick's question to Karen Rasmussen whether a decision for the State would unleash a flood of warrantless searches of private homes aimed to identify the potential consequences of her argument. Second, lawyers must be prepared to modify their arguments if the judges steer them away from their planned presentations.[55] Neither Gene nor Karen discussed selective prosecution, even though they were prepared to do so, because the judges showed no interest in it. Karen ended her argument early rather than discuss selective prosecution because she sensed that she had won on that issue.

Third, appellate courts prefer gradual change to dramatic change, so lawyers should not ask them to change an area of law in one fell swoop. That is why both lawyers told the Court that it needed only to honor the consent exception's requirement of "voluntariness" in order to reach the correct result.[56]

Decision Conference

Oral arguments ended at 3:30 P.M. on January 4, 2000. Shortly thereafter, the justices gathered in their conference room for a **decision conference**, during which they decided the cases argued that day.[57] The discussion of *State v. Johnson* lasted only ten minutes because all the justices favored affirming Judge Romano's denials of Stan Johnson's motions to suppress and dismiss, respectively. They were convinced that the circumstances of *State v. Johnson* were enough like those of *Lewis v. United States* that *Lewis* should govern the outcome in *Johnson*.

Nevertheless, Justices Panos and Derrick feared that the Court would encourage sloppy police work unless it emphasized that the only reason for its conclusion was that Stan had invited Trooper Cummings into his apartment. They did not want this decision to signal a relaxation of the constitutional rule that, absent valid consent, searches require warrants and probable cause. Their views were not lost on Justice Arthur Jorgensen, who would write the opinion in *Johnson*. He would try to preserve unanimity by incorporating the views of Justices Panos and Derrick into his opinion.[58]

Decision

The Court announced its decision in *State v. Johnson* on March 3, 2000. Justice Jorgensen, in a six-page opinion that all of the justices joined (as indicated by their signatures), affirmed Judge Romano's denials of Stan Johnson's motions. The opinion quickly disposed of Gene Jefferson's arguments, namely, that there was an illegal search of Stan's apartment, and that Stan was the victim of selective prosecution. Justice Jorgensen responded to the illegal search argument by stating:

> The evidence is clear that Trooper Cummings entered Defendant's home with Defendant's consent. Furthermore, when Cummings asked Defendant if Cummings could buy cocaine there, Defendant invited Cummings to sit at the kitchen table while Defendant retrieved the cocaine in order to make the sale. Based on these facts, we cannot conclude that an illegal search and seizure resulted from Cummings's entry into Defendant's home. Admittedly, it is open to question whether the police acted on the basis of probable cause in this case, and their undercover operation should not be considered a model for future drug investigations in this State. Nevertheless, probable cause and a search warrant are not necessary when, as occurred in this case, one who is authorized to consent to a search does so voluntarily.

Justice Jorgensen then turned to the selective prosecution issue. He wrote that:

> Defendant, in order to establish selective prosecution, must show that the State singled him out for prosecution, and that it did so based on his race, his religion, or on a wish to prevent his exercise of constitutional rights. Defendant fails this test. He has not shown that his fame motivated the State to prosecute him or that the State chose not to prosecute other students whom it suspected of selling drugs. Rather, the State did not pursue other student suspects because the College disciplined them itself and did not reveal their names to police or prosecutors.

Gene Jefferson and Karen Rasmussen received telephone calls from the Clerk of the Court on March 3, 2000, that announced the decision in *State v. Johnson*. The decision was not a surprise to either lawyer, but it was still a disappointment to Gene Jefferson, whose client would soon report to jail.

PETERSON ON APPEAL

Post-Verdict Motion

When the jury announced its verdict in *Peterson* (see Chapter 6), Payson Parker, who was the lawyer for Big Pine Mountain Ski Corporation, decided to file a post-verdict motion that asked Judge Romano to overturn the verdict. He filed a **motion for judgment notwithstanding the verdict (J.N.O.V.)**. Pursuant to court rules, Parker submitted his motion to Judge Romano within ten days after the jury announced the verdict.[59] The motion argued that, although trial procedures were adequate, the verdict was plainly contrary to the facts and the law; therefore, Judge Romano should enter a verdict for Big Pine without a new trial.[60] Shannon Peterson had fallen on ice and had collided with a lift tower, two inherent risks of skiing for which New Hampshire law expressly stated that ski area operators were not liable.[61] Gene Jefferson filed an opposing motion within ten days of receiving Parker's motion, as court rules required.[62]

Judge Romano held a hearing, during which the lawyers argued for and against overturning the verdict. Ten days later, she issued a five-page order that denied Parker's motion. The order stated that "Defendant has failed to show that this court should overturn the verdict because the jury completely misjudged the evidence or misunderstood the law, thereby reaching a verdict that was unreasonable. This court must therefore deny Defendant's motion."[63] Parker was not surprised by Judge Romano's decision. He knew that courts intentionally set a high standard for granting motions for J.N.O.V., and rarely grant them, in order to preserve the jury system.[64]

Notice of Appeal

When Payson Parker finished reading Judge Romano's order, he began to consider an appeal to the New Hampshire Supreme Court. Klaus Waldmeier, Big Pine's owner, was eager to appeal, but Parker felt duty-bound to remind Waldmeier that there were costs to an appeal. Big Pine would be responsible for additional attorney's fees whether it won or lost. If Big Pine lost, it would be responsible for its court costs (preparation of trial transcript; printing and binding of brief) and for Shannon's (printing and binding of brief), and it would owe Shannon $475,000 *plus* the interest (1 percent per month) that accrued on that amount between the date of the verdict and the conclusion of the appeal.[65] There was a fair chance that Big Pine would lose on appeal because it would have to show that no reasonable jury, after applying the facts to the law in this case, would have reached the verdict that the *Peterson* jury reached.[66]

Payson Parker discussed the costs and the risks of an appeal with Klaus Waldmeier, but Waldmeier remained adamantly in favor of an appeal. Parker therefore began to prepare a notice of appeal, in hopes of convincing the New Hampshire Supreme Court to review the *Peterson* verdict. The court could reject the case, accept it but not consider one or more issues raised in the notice of appeal, or dismiss it "summarily" (i.e., without benefit of briefs or oral argument) for lack of jurisdiction or for another "just cause."[67] The court could also summarily affirm or reverse the jury's verdict if it wished.[68]

Parker had laid a foundation for the notice of appeal during pretrial and trial by submitting to Judge Romano a motion to dismiss, a motion for summary judgment, and a motion for a directed verdict, all of which argued that Big Pine was not liable for injuries produced by the inherent risks of skiing. That argument would not have been available on appeal had Parker not raised it before or during trial. Parker emphasized that by deciding *Peterson*, the Court could clarify for the trial courts, the bar, the ski area industry, and skiers the circumstances in which New Hampshire ski area operators would be liable for skiers' injuries. That could reduce litigation and its costs to the ski industry, which would benefit skiers, ski area operators, and the New Hampshire economy.[69]

Parker argued that New Hampshire's ski liability statute protected ski area operators from liability for injuries that resulted from the "inherent risks" of skiing, including icy trails and collisions with lift towers.[70] He cited a recent case, *Nutbrown v. Mt. Cranmore, Inc.*, in which the Court had acknowledged that ski area operators are not liable for such injuries.[71] The Court should honor the legislature's intent and reaffirm *Nutbrown* by reversing the erroneous verdict in *Peterson*.

When Parker had finished the notice of appeal, his secretary mailed the original and fifteen copies, plus the filing fee, to the Clerk of the Court within thirty days of the date that was on the trial court's order that had formally notified him of the *Peterson* verdict.[72] The secretary also mailed a copy of the notice of appeal to Gene Jefferson and two copies to the clerk of the trial court.[73] The Court could have dismissed the appeal had Parker failed to file the notice of appeal on time or failed to enclose the filing fee.[74] Instead, by filing on time and by enclosing the fee, Parker not only preserved the appeal, but also delayed the date that the jury verdict would take effect until after the state supreme court had decided the appeal.[75] Similar filing and fee deadlines apply in the federal courts.[76]

Several months later, Parker was pleased to receive from the Clerk of the Court, a scheduling order that indicated that the Court would hear Big Pine's appeal, and that Parker's brief was due in thirty days. The order also requested the preparation of a full trial transcript, which it was Parker's responsibility, as the appellant's lawyer, to deliver to the Court.[77] He asked his **legal assistant (paralegal)** to order a copy of the transcript from the court reporter who had transcribed the trial, and to mail it to the Court. Then he began work on his brief.

Briefs

Appellant

Payson Parker reviewed the New Hampshire Rules of Appellate Procedure before he began to research and write his brief. Those rules are the same for civil and criminal cases, so the filing deadlines, the contents and length of briefs, and the numbers of copies to be filed that applied to *State v. Johnson* also applied to *Peterson*.[78] The rule that a brief can argue only those issues that the notice of appeal raised also applied in *Peterson*, as it had in *Johnson*. The Court will not consider an issue that the notice of appeal raised but that the brief failed to argue.[79]

Parker began to write his brief when he had finished reading the ski liability statute and relevant cases in his law firm's library. He wrote the "question presented" as follows:

> 1. Does R.S.A. 225-A:24 absolve ski area operators of liability for injuries that result from the inherent risks of skiing, including falls on icy trails and collisions with lift towers?

He then wrote a "statement of the case" that recounted Shannon's accident and subsequent suit, Judge Romano's denials of Big Pine's motion to dismiss, motion for summary judgment, and motion for a directed verdict, the jury's verdict for Shannon, Judge Romano's denial of Big Pine's motion for J.N.O.V., and Big Pine's notice of appeal. A "statement of facts" followed, in which Parker explained that Shannon fell while skiing when she failed to see a patch of ice on the trail because she was looking at a snow making "gun," and that she subsequently collided with a lift tower, which resulted in a permanent back injury. Parker tried to state the facts as objectively as possible because he knew that the Court disliked argumentative fact statements.

Parker next wrote his argument, which he revised several times in order to make it as clear, concise, and convincing as possible. He limited it to one issue, namely, whether R.S.A. 225-A:24 absolved ski area operators from liability for injuries that resulted from the inherent risks of skiing, including falls on icy trails and collisions with lift towers. He introduced that issue with a heading that telegraphed his argument. The heading was as follows:

> I. There was no evidence presented at trial from which a reasonable jury could conclude that the Appellant was liable for the Appellee's injuries because her injuries resulted from the inherent risks of skiing, and R.S.A. 225-A:24 absolves ski area operators of liability for such injuries.

In other words, the verdict was erroneous, and the Court, as part of its responsibility to correct errors, should reverse.

Payson Parker knew that the Court would not overturn a jury verdict unless the verdict were **unreasonable**, that is, completely contrary to the evidence presented. The standard of review required the Court to affirm any jury verdict for which there was a **rational basis**, which meant just enough evidence to make the verdict plausible.[80] He argued that the *Peterson* verdict was indeed unreasonable because it ignored both R.S.A. 225-A:24 and the Court's 1996 decision in *Nutbrown v. Mt. Cranmore, Inc.*, which interpreted that statute.[81] R.S.A. 225-A:24, I states:

> Each person who participates in the sport of skiing accepts as a matter of law, the dangers inherent in the sport, and to that extent may not maintain an action against the operator for any injuries which result from such inherent risks, dangers, or hazards. The categories of such risks, hazards, or dangers which the skier … assumes as a matter of law include but are not limited to the following: variations in … subsurface snow or ice conditions;… lift towers and components thereof; [and] collisions with other skiers or other persons or with any of the categories included in this paragraph.

In Parker's view, that language plainly indicated the legislature's intent to shield ski area operators from liability for the sorts of injuries that Shannon Peterson had sustained at Big Pine Mountain.

Moreover, the Court had acknowledged that intent in *Nutbrown*, when it stated that R.S.A. 225-A:24, I meant that:

> … a ski area operator owes its patrons no duty to protect them from inherent risks of skiing. To the extent that a skier's injury is caused by an inherent risk of skiing, the skier may not recover [damages] from the ski area operator. An injury entirely caused by an inherent risk of skiing is not actionable, and a suit based on such an injury should be dismissed.[82]

Thus, Parker concluded, both the intent of the legislature and the Court's recent acknowledgement of that intent in *Nutbrown* showed that the *Peterson* verdict was unreasonable, and that the Court should reverse it.

Payson Parker was satisfied with his brief after three drafts. He was also optimistic about his chances for success on appeal because most of the justices held conservative political and judicial philosophies. They favored business interests, and they read statutes narrowly in order to enforce the legislature's express intent. Their goal was dispute resolution, not social change. Parker's secretary proofread the brief, typed a final version, which Parker signed, then mailed the original and fifteen copies to the Court and one copy to Gene Jefferson.

Appellee

Shannon Peterson was the appellee in the case that bore her name. Gene Jefferson would represent her on appeal, as he had done at trial. Jefferson read Payson Parker's brief carefully when it arrived in the mail, and noted potential counterarguments on a legal pad as he read. Then he began to research and write his brief. It followed the same format as Parker's brief, except that because it was for the appellee, it did not include a statement of the case and the question presented.[83] Jefferson's task was to convince the Court to affirm the verdict because the jury had reached a reasonable conclusion in *Peterson*.

Jefferson's brief argued that the verdict was reasonable because Big Pine's negligence caused Shannon's injuries, and New Hampshire law did not absolve ski area operators from liability for negligence. The brief acknowledged that ski area operators were not liable for injuries that resulted from the inherent risks of skiing, but argued that Shannon's injuries had not resulted from such risks. Instead, Shannon's injuries had resulted from Big Pine's failures to warn skiers that snow making was in progress, and to pad its lift towers.

The failure to warn was negligent because R.S.A. 225-A:23, II(b) requires ski operators to "warn skiers ... by use of a trail board or otherwise, if applicable, that snow grooming or snow making operations are routinely in progress on the slopes and trails serviced by each [ski lift]." The failure to pad was negligent because collisions with lift towers are foreseeable, and padding is a reasonable precaution that could reduce the severity of the injuries that result. Big Pine was liable for its negligence because the Court stated in *Nutbrown* that R.S.A. 225-A:24, I does not free ski area operators from liability for injuries that result from their own negligence.[84] Thus, the jury's verdict in this case was reasonable in light of the facts and the law, and the Court should affirm it.

When Jefferson was satisfied with his brief, his secretary proofread it and typed a final copy, which Jefferson signed. He was cautiously optimistic about his chances for success. He knew that the Court was "pro-business" and that it honored "legislative intent," but he also knew that it honored precedent, and *Nutbrown* was a precedent that could work in his favor. Jefferson's secretary mailed the original and fifteen copies of the brief to the Court and one copy to Payson Parker within 45 days of receiving Parker's brief, as court rules required.[85]

Reply

Payson Parker received a copy of Gene Jefferson's brief in the mail, read it, and decided not to file a reply brief. Jefferson's brief was persuasive, but Parker had anticipated, and countered, its arguments in his opening brief, so there was no reason to submit a reply brief. Instead, he worked on other cases while he waited for the Court to set a date for oral argument.

Oral Argument

Oral argument in *Peterson* occurred on June 3, 2000. *Peterson* was the final case that the Court heard that afternoon. Klaus Waldmeier and two newspaper reporters who covered the ski industry were the only spectators. The Petersons chose not to attend. At 2:45 P.M., Chief Justice Bronson Davis said to Payson

Parker, "You may proceed, counsel." Parker rose, strode to the podium, and began his oral argument as follows:

> May it please the Court. My name is Payson Parker, and I represent the appellant, Big Pine Mountain Ski Corporation. We would like to reserve five minutes for rebuttal. We ask this Court to reverse the jury's verdict because there was no reasonable basis for it.

Then Justice Nikki Panos interjected a question. Part of her exchange with Parker appears below.

> Q. Mr. Parker, would Big Pine be liable to a skier for injuries sustained because Big Pine failed to groom its trails or left fallen limbs on the trails after an ice storm?
>
> A. The skier would have a strong case under those circumstances, Your Honor, because it is the ski area operator's responsibility to groom trails and to keep them free of obstructions.
>
> Q. Isn't it also the ski area operator's responsibility, under the statute [R.S.A. 225-A:23, II(b)], to warn skiers when snow making is in progress?
>
> A. Yes, but the ski area operator is not liable for the failure to warn about snow making unless injuries result from that failure. Ms. Peterson's injuries resulted instead from her fall on a patch of ice, for which the statute does not hold a ski area operator liable. This Court recognized in *Nutbrown v. Mt. Cranmore, Inc.* that the statute does not hold ski area operators liable for injuries that result from inherent risks of skiing.

Justice Arthur Jorgensen questioned Parker next. Part of their conversation appears below.

> Q. Wasn't there sufficient evidence to indicate that Ms. Peterson could have fallen because the snow making "gun" produced snow that startled her and limited her visibility? If so, that would make the verdict reasonable, would it not?
>
> A. The verdict would have been reasonable if the snow had blinded Ms. Peterson, but that is not what the evidence indicated. She was too far away from the "gun" for artificial snow to have blinded her.

Then Justice Carter Derrick changed the subject. Part of his exchange with Parker appears below.

> Q. Mr. Parker, let us assume that Ms. Peterson's fall was not the result of Big Pine's failure to warn her that snow making was in progress. Wasn't Big Pine still negligent for failing to pad its lift towers because that failure aggravated Ms. Peterson's injuries?
>
> A. No, Your Honor. The statute [R.S.A. 225-A:24, I] specifically includes collisions with lift towers among the inherent risks of skiing for which the ski area operator is not liable. Moreover, the evidence indicated that no amount of padding could have prevented

Ms. Peterson's injuries. The force with which she hit the tower was too great for padding to have helped her.

Q. Does that mean that the ski area operator need not try to reduce the likelihood of collisions with lift towers or the severity of the injuries that result?

A. Big Pine continually tries to reduce the likelihood of collisions and the severity of injuries, Your Honor. Lift towers, however, are necessary to alpine skiing, and they are inherently dangerous. No precautions could eliminate those dangers. That is why the legislature included lift towers among the inherent risks of skiing. This Court endorsed the legislature's intent in *Nutbrown*.

The red light on the podium lit up as Parker finished his answer to Justice Derrick's question. Now it was Gene Jefferson's turn to argue. Parker would have five minutes for rebuttal when Jefferson finished.

Gene Jefferson began his argument as follows:

May it please the Court. My name is Eugene Jefferson, and I represent the appellee, Shannon Peterson. My client requests this Court to affirm the jury's verdict because it was consistent with the law and with the facts of this case. My client's injuries resulted from Big Pine's negligence, and the legislature did not intend to absolve ski area operators from liability for injuries caused by their own negligence.

That was as far as Jefferson got before Justice David Sawyer asked him a question. Part of their conversation appears below.

Q. Mr. Jefferson, if we find for your client, won't we open the courts to every skier who falls and breaks her ankle because she was skiing too fast or on a trail that she should have avoided?

A. No, Your Honor, because my client's injuries did not result from her own negligence. Unlike the skier in *Nutbrown*, who skied off the trail on his own and was injured, my client was injured because of Big Pine's negligence. Big Pine failed to warn that snow making was in progress and failed to pad lift towers. Both of those failures were negligent, and they caused my client's injuries. This Court said in *Nutbrown* that the legislature did not immunize ski area operators for injuries that result from their negligence. Therefore, Big Pine is not immune from liability in this case.

Q. Your client fell on a patch of ice and slid into a lift tower. There will always be ice on ski trails, Mr. Jefferson, and there will always be lift towers. How can we hold ski area operators liable for such inherent risks?

A. My client fell on ice because blowing snow from a snow "gun," of which Big Pine had not warned her, reduced her visibility, and prevented her from seeing the patch of ice. The fall resulted in a collision with a lift tower, which Big Pine failed to pad, and the lack of padding made my client's injuries more serious than they would otherwise have been. We cannot hold Big Pine liable for ice, but we can hold it liable for a failure to warn about snow making that causes a fall on ice, with injuries resulting.

Then Chief Justice Davis interjected a question. Part of his conversation with Jefferson appears below.

Q. Would Big Pine be liable to your client if she had skied into an unpadded lift tower because she drank wine prior to skiing and her coordination was impaired?

A. Yes, but only to the extent that the lack of padding made her injuries worse than they would otherwise have been. Under those circumstances, my client would bear the primary responsibility for her injuries. Nevertheless, Big Pine would still be responsible for making its lift towers as safe as it reasonably could.

The red light on the podium flashed as Jefferson finished his answer. He thanked the justices and sat down as Parker rose and strode toward the podium to rebut.

Parker tried to tap into the Court's respect for both legislative intent and precedent. He told the justices that, contrary to Jefferson's assertions, the evidence indicated that Shannon was too far away from the snow "gun" for artificial snow to have blinded her and caused her to fall. The evidence also indicated that her injuries would not have been substantially less severe had the lift tower been padded. R.S.A. 225-A:24, I intended to include icy trails and lift towers among the inherent risks of skiing for which ski area operators could not be held liable. The Court had honored that intent in *Nutbrown*. Thus, the only reasonable conclusion that a jury could reach in this case was that Big Pine was not liable for Shannon Peterson's injuries. This Court, therefore, should overturn the verdict. Then Parker thanked the justices and sat down. Oral argument was over.

Decision Conference

The *Peterson* oral argument ended shortly before 3:30 P.M., and the justices adjourned to their conference room for a decision conference. The discussion of *Peterson* lasted twenty minutes. The justices agreed that Big Pine was negligent in failing to warn skiers that snowmaking was in progress, and that the jury could reasonably have concluded that Shannon's fall resulted from poor visibility caused by blowing artificial snow. They disagreed, however, about whether Big Pine's failure to pad its lift towers was negligent. Justices Sawyer and Jorgensen argued that R.S.A. 225-A:24, I absolved ski area operators from liability for injuries caused by collisions with lift towers. Nevertheless, all five justices agreed that the jury could reasonably have concluded that Shannon's collision with a lift tower, like her fall, resulted from Big Pine's failure to warn that snowmaking was in progress. Thus, the Court chose, unanimously, to affirm the *Peterson* verdict, but not to decide whether ski area operators could be held liable for failing to minimize an inherent risk of skiing. Justice Sawyer would try to preserve that unanimity as he wrote the Court's opinion.

Decision

The Court announced its decision in *Peterson* on August 17, 2000. Justice Sawyer, in a five-page opinion, explained not only what *Peterson* decided, but what it *did not* decide. He wrote:

> Today, we decide only that the jury's verdict was reasonable. There was sufficient evidence to conclude that Big Pine's failure to warn of snow making in progress caused Shannon Peterson's fall, which resulted in her injuries. We do not decide whether a ski area operator can be held liable for failure to minimize the inherent risks of skiing. We need not decide that larger issue in this case because Big Pine's failure to warn of snow making plainly breached its duty of care to Ms. Peterson. We leave the larger issue for another day.

Payson Parker and Gene Jefferson received telephone calls from the Court on August 17, 2000, that announced the Court's decision in *Peterson*. Parker was disappointed to learn that the Court had affirmed the verdict, but relieved that it had not required ski area operators to minimize the inherent risks of skiing. Jefferson was pleased that the Court had affirmed the verdict, but disappointed that it had not required ski area operators to minimize inherent risks, especially unpadded lift towers. Neither side had won all that it sought, which occurs often in litigation.

CONCLUSION

The *Johnson* and *Peterson* cases reflect error-correction and policy-making functions of appellate courts. In both cases, the appellant alleged that legal errors at trial had resulted in an unfair verdict, and asked the Court to correct those errors. The Court did not find reversible error in either case, so it affirmed the jury's verdict. The lawyers raised legal questions that offered the Court opportunities to make public policy. In *Johnson*, the Court held that there was consent to a police entry of a home when an officer appeared in a doorway disguised as someone whom the resident might reasonably have expected to call. That was a policy decision because it would affect future drug investigations and prosecutions. *Johnson* forced the Court to choose between crime control and personal privacy, and the Court chose crime control.

In *Peterson*, the Court decided the case strictly on its facts, and declined to consider whether ski area operators' duty of care to their customers required them to minimize inherent risks, such as by padding lift towers. That decision reflected preferences for gradualism in the law and unanimity on the Court, and it was a policy decision despite its narrow scope. It kept the existing policy (no liability for inherent risks) in place, and postponed a change indefinitely, which enabled ski area operators to avoid increased costs for equipment and insurance. It also reminded ski area operators that they must minimize risks that they can affect, such as by warning skiers of snowmaking in progress.

Appellate courts are not always reluctant to make major policy decisions. *State v. Kirchoff*, which follows, dramatically changed search-and-seizure law in Vermont.[86] *Pines v. Perssion*, which follows *Kirchoff*, fundamentally changed landlord–tenant law in Wisconsin.[87] Read both cases, and decide whether each Court reached the correct result.

Epilogue: Open Fields and a "Tumbledown" House

State v. Kirchoff
156 Vt. 1, 587 A.2d 988 (1991)

Morse, J. The sole issue in this appeal from a conviction for cultivating marijuana is the legality under the Vermont Constitution of a warrantless search of defendant's posted land. We hold that this search violated Chapter I, Article 11, of the Vermont Constitution, and accordingly reverse.

In 1982, defendant purchased thirty-nine acres of land, consisting of woods, swamp, and meadows, in an isolated part of Lincoln, Vermont. He put up several "no trespassing" signs where the road turned into his driveway and posted his land with signs that said, "POSTED Private Property. Hunting, Fishing, Trapping or Trespassing for Any Purpose Is Strictly Forbidden. Violators Will Be Prosecuted." ...

Acting on an informant's tip that marijuana was growing on defendant's land, a sheriff and another law enforcement officer went onto the land, without a warrant, in September of 1986. They first drove up defendant's driveway where they noticed the "no trespassing" signs, as well as one that read "Road Ends—Private Drive Ahead." The officers parked at a neighbor's house, crossed a fence, and walked along an old logging road toward defendant's house. They observed one or two old "no trespassing" signs as they walked. At some point, the officers left the road and walked through woods and a marsh, coming upon a marijuana patch about 100 yards from defendant's house. The marijuana plants were not visible from any road.

The officers left the area to obtain a search warrant. Later, after [obtaining a] warrant ..., the officers searched the house, finding more evidence of marijuana cultivation and seizing numerous plants.

Defendant moved to suppress the evidence gathered during the search on the ground that it was obtained in violation of the Vermont Constitution. The motion was denied, and the evidence was admitted over defendant's objection at trial.

I

We begin by acknowledging that this "walk-on" search would be permissible under the federal constitution. The United States Supreme Court has held that the Fourth Amendment permits the police to conduct a warrantless search of an area in which a person does not have a "reasonable expectation of privacy." *Katz v. United States*, 389 U.S. 347, 360 (1967). In *Oliver v. United States*, 466 U.S. 170, 179 (1984), that Court held that an expectation of privacy in "open fields" will not be deemed reasonable for Fourth Amendment purposes. That is, "an individual may not legitimately demand privacy for activities conducted out of doors in fields, except in the area immediately surrounding the home." *Id.* at 178. "Open fields" is a term of art ...; it refers generally to land that is unoccupied or undeveloped. Woods, in particular, may be open fields. As the warrantless search in this case was not of "the area immediately surrounding the home," an area known in law as "the curtilage," defendant's Fourth Amendment rights were not violated.

II

That the officers' conduct was permissible under the federal constitution does not, of course, end our inquiry. The Vermont Constitution may afford greater protection to individual rights than [the federal Constitution does]. *State v. Badger*, 141 Vt. 430, 450 A.2d 336 (1982). The issue is whether the "walk-on" search violated Chapter I, Article 11, of the Vermont Constitution.

[Chapter I, Article 11] protects persons, houses, papers, and **possessions** [from warrantless searches without probable cause], while the Fourth Amendment protects persons, houses, papers, and **effects**. Unfortunately, research into the possible significance of this textual difference sheds little light on the issue. [**Editor's Note:** the U.S. Supreme Court said in *Oliver* that, when the Constitution was drafted, "effects" meant personal property (e.g., books, clothes, furniture) only, not land. Therefore, the Fourth Amendment did not protect "open fields" from warrantless searches. The Vermont Supreme Court concluded, after some historical research, that it is unclear whether, when the Vermont Constitution was drafted, "possessions" included land. If it did, then Chapter I, Article 11, would protect "open fields" from warrantless searches.]

Our decision, however, need not rest on the drafters' choice of one word over another. Even if we cannot say with confidence that the scope of the term "possessions" mandates a right of privacy in real estate, it certainly does not rule out such a right. We strive to honor not merely the words but the underlying purposes of constitutional guarantees, and to give meaning to the text in light of contemporary experience. In the case of Fourth Amendment–Article 11 jurisprudence, the value traditionally protected is "freedom from unreasonable government intrusion into ... legitimate expectations of privacy." *Oliver*, 466 U.S. at 187.

We believe Article 11 embraces the core value of privacy discarded in *Oliver* [when the U.S. Supreme Court held that the Fourth Amendment does not protect "open fields" from warrantless searches].

The [U.S. Supreme] Court reasoned [in *Oliver*] that society does not recognize a reasonable expectation of privacy in open fields because they "do not provide the setting for those intimate activities that the [Fourth] Amendment is intended to shelter from government interference or surveillance." 466 U.S. at 179.

III

While generally there is not an expectation of privacy in unoccupied lands, such is not the case where the landowner has taken steps, such as fencing or posting, to indicate that privacy is exactly what is sought.

IV

We now hold that a lawful possessor may claim privacy in "open fields" under Article 11 of the Vermont Constitution where [circumstances] would lead a reasonable person to conclude that the area is private. On the other hand, Article 11 does not afford protection against searches of lands where steps have not been taken to exclude the public.

Where the indicia, such as fences, barriers or "no trespassing" signs reasonably indicate that strangers are not welcome on the land, the owner or occupant may reasonably expect privacy. The inquiry is objective—whether a reasonable person should know that the occupant has sought to exclude the public. Whether the steps taken are adequate for this purpose will depend on the specific facts of each case.

V

[W]e differ from federal doctrine by placing on the State the burden to prove that a warrantless search of open fields is not prohibited under the principles we announce today. Federal law places the burden on the defendant to establish a reasonable expectation of privacy in the area searched in order to claim rights under the Fourth Amendment. In contrast, we view government searches of a person's land as presumptively implicating Article 11, and consequently the State has the burden of proving that such a search does not violate Article 11.

VI

Given the extensive posting of the land [in the present case], defendant's intent to exclude the public was unequivocal. On these facts, we find that the officers' walk over defendant's logging roads and through his woods violated his right to privacy under Article 11, and the evidence obtained thereby may not be used against him.

The rule announced here does not significantly hamper the police from investigating suspected criminal activity. It does require police to obtain a warrant, based upon probable cause, before they enter land where it is apparent to a reasonable person that the owner or occupant intends to exclude the public.

Reversed.

Peck, J., dissenting. I am not prepared to countenance in silence the extreme and unwarranted judicial activism of which the [majority] opinion is an example. Accordingly, I dissent....

I The "Possessions" Enigma

In my view, the word "possessions" in Article Eleven means "personalty," [i.e., personal property] and the majority is well aware of it.

The honest approach would have been a neutral analysis of Article Eleven and not merely shaping it to fit a desired result. The word "land," as such, does not appear expressly in Article Eleven, nor is it employed in the Fourth Amendment. "Land" has been incorporated into both constitutional provisions by judicial interpretation over a period of time and, in the case of Article Eleven, without relying on the word "possessions." The same is true of the word "effects" in the Fourth Amendment.

As I read these two constitutional provisions, the implicit inclusion of the word "lands" in both Article Eleven and the Fourth Amendment stems from the word "houses." Extending the application of these provisions to so much of the land as surrounds and serves the primary residential purposes of the **house**, that is the curtilage, is a logical and reasonable interpretation. Open fields are simply not within the scope of Article Eleven or the Fourth Amendment.

Open fields, like all lands, [are protected] by the criminal trespass statutes enacted by the Legislature. For all … practical purposes, the *sole* beneficiary of today's decision is the owner of open fields who conducts criminal activity thereon in defiance of the law. In short, the majority has given birth to a right of privacy to commit crime.

The word "possessions" in Article Eleven, like "effects" in the Fourth Amendment, should be interpreted to mean "personalty," and should not be deleted as meaningless.

II Unreasonable Searches

I would remind the majority, as it sheds its tears for the defendant, that the entry [of the police onto the defendant's property] was not arbitrary. It was not an afternoon of sport for the police, on the off-chance they might just happen to stumble on marijuana or some other contraband…. The entry was undertaken in reliance on a "tip"; with every reason to believe the search was legitimate, and it was done in good faith.

Under these circumstances, in *this* case, I think a neutral fairness … should require a conclusion that the police acted reasonably and in good faith.

IV Summary and Conclusions

The refusal of the majority to concern itself with, or to give any consideration to, the most significant of the key words in Article Eleven, "possessions," and indeed to treat all the key words as meaningless, is irresponsible. It permits the majority to abandon restraint, and adopt a purely subjective, wish-fulfillment standard of constitutional interpretation…. The virus which infects so many courts in criminal cases, and leaves them with tunnel vision, seeing only the criminal as having any rights, continues to ravage this Court.

QUESTIONS FOR DISCUSSION

1. What constitutional issue did this appeal raise?
2. What actions by police officers gave rise to this appeal?

3. What decision by the trial court gave rise to this appeal?
4. Why did Kirchoff base his appeal on the Vermont Constitution instead of on the U.S. Constitution?
5. On what basis did Kirchoff argue that the Vermont Constitution contains greater protection for personal privacy in cases like this one than the U.S. Constitution does?
6. Did the Court agree with Kirchoff? Explain.
7. What rule of law did the majority announce in this case? How did that rule differ from the rule that applies to such cases in federal court?
8. What *legal* reasons did the dissent give for its conclusion that the majority had reached an incorrect result?
9. What *public policy* reasons did the dissent give for its conclusion?
10. Do you agree with the majority opinion, or with the dissent? Explain.

Pines v. Perssion
14 Wis. 2d 590, 111 N.W. 2d 409 (1961)

MARTIN, C. J. At the time this action was commenced the plaintiffs were students at the University of Wisconsin in Madison. Defendant was engaged in the business of real estate development and ownership. During the 1958–1959 school year plaintiffs were tenants of the defendant in a student rooming house. In May of 1959 they asked the defendant if he had a house they could rent for the 1959–1960 school year. Defendant told them he was thinking of buying a house on the east side of Madison which they might be interested in renting. This was the house involved in the [disputed lease that caused this lawsuit]. The house had in fact been owned and lived in by the defendant since 1951, but he testified he misstated the facts because he was embarrassed about its condition.

Three of the plaintiffs looked at the house in June, 1959 and found it in a filthy condition. Pines testified the defendant stated he would clean and fix up the house, paint it, provide the necessary furnishings and have the house in suitable condition by the start of the school year in the fall. Defendant testified he told plaintiffs he would not do any work on the house until he received a signed lease and a deposit. Pines denied this.

The parties agreed that the defendant would lease the house to plaintiffs commencing September 1, 1959 at a monthly rental of $175 prorated over the first nine months of the lease term, or $233.33 per month for September through May. Defendant was to have a lease drawn and mail it to the plaintiffs.

Defendant mailed the lease to Pines in Chicago in the latter part of July. Because the plaintiffs were scattered around the country, Pines had some difficulty in securing the necessary signatures. Pines and the defendant kept in touch by letter and telephone concerning the execution of the lease, and Pines came to Madison in August to see the defendant and the house. Pines testified the house was still in terrible condition and defendant again promised him it would be ready for occupancy on September 1st. Defendant testified he said he had to receive the lease and the deposit before he would do any work on the house, but Pines could not remember him making such a statement.

On August 28th, Pines mailed defendant a check for $175 as his share of the deposit and on September 1st he sent the lease and the balance due. Defendant received the signed lease and the deposit about September 3rd.

Plaintiffs began arriving at the house about September 6th. It was still in a filthy condition and there was a lack of student furnishings. Plaintiffs began to clean the house themselves, providing some cleaning materials of their own, and did some painting with paint purchased by defendant. They became discouraged with their progress and contacted an attorney with reference to their status under the lease. The attorney advised them to request the Madison building department to inspect the premises. This was done on September 9th and several building code violations were found. They included inadequate electrical wiring, kitchen sink and toilet in disrepair, furnace in disrepair, handrail on stairs in disrepair, screens on windows and doors lacking. The city inspector gave defendant until September 21st to correct the violations, and in the meantime plaintiffs were permitted to occupy the premises. They vacated the premises on or about September 11th.

The trial court concluded that defendant represented to the plaintiffs that the house would be in a habitable condition by September 1, 1959; it was not in such condition and could not be made so before October 1, 1959; that … plaintiffs were entitled to surrender the premises; that they were not liable for rent for the time subsequent to the surrender date, which was found to be September 30, 1959.

In our opinion, there was an implied warranty of habitability in the lease and that warranty was breached by the [landlord].

There was no express provision in the lease that the house was to be in habitable condition by September 1st.

The general rule [under the common law] is that there are no implied warranties to the effect that at the time a lease term commences the premises are in a tenantable condition or adapted to the purposes for which leased. A tenant is a purchaser of an estate in land, and is subject to the doctrine of *caveat emptor* (buyer beware). His remedy is to inspect the premises before [renting] them or to secure [from the landlord] an express warranty [that they will be habitable]. Thus, a tenant is not entitled to abandon the premises on the ground of uninhabitability.

There is an exception to this rule, some courts holding that there is an implied warranty of habitability and fitness of the premises where the subject of the lease is a furnished house. This is based on an intention inferred from the fact that under the circumstances the [prospective tenant] does not have an adequate opportunity to inspect the premises at the time he accepts the lease.

We have not previously considered this exception to the general rule. Obviously, however, the frame of reference in which the old common law rule operated has changed.

Legislation and administrative rules, such as … building codes and health regulations, all impose certain duties on a property owner with respect to the condition of his premises. Thus, the legislature has made a policy judgment—that it is socially (and politically) desirable to impose these duties on a property owner—which has rendered the old common law rule obsolete. To follow the old rule of no implied warranty of habitability in leases would, in our opinion, be inconsistent with the current legislative policy concerning housing standards. The need and social desirability of adequate housing for people in this era of rapid population increases is too important to be rebuffed by that obnoxious legal cliché, *caveat emptor*. Permitting landlords to rent "tumbledown" houses is at least a contributing cause of such problems as urban blight, juvenile delinquency and high property taxes for conscientious land-owners.

There is no question in this case but that the house was not in a condition reasonably and decently fit for occupation when the lease term commenced. [The landlord] himself admitted it was "filthy," so much so that he lied about owning it in the first instance, and he testified that no cleaning or other work was done in the house before the [tenants] moved in. The filth, of course, was seen by the [tenants] when they inspected the premises prior to signing the lease. They had no way of knowing, however, that the plumbing, heating and wiring systems were defective.

The evidence clearly showed that the implied warranty of habitability was breached. [The tenants' promise] to pay rent and [the landlord's promise] to provide a habitable house were mutually dependant, and thus a breach of the latter by [the landlord] relieved [the tenants] of any liability under the former.

[The tenants] are absolved from any liability for rent under the lease and their only liability is for the reasonable rental value of the premises during the time [that they lived there]. [W]e direct the trial court to find what a reasonable rental for that period would be and enter judgment for the [tenants] in the amount of their deposit plus the amount recoverable for their labor [in cleaning and painting the house minus the rental value of the house during the time that the tenants lived there].

Cause **remanded** [to the trial court] with instructions to enter judgment for the [tenants] consistent with this opinion.

QUESTIONS FOR DISCUSSION

1. What facts gave rise to this appeal?
2. What legal rule did the landlord presumably think should govern this appeal?
3. Did the appellate court follow that rule?
4. What legal rule did the appellate court conclude should govern this case?
5. What circumstances, according to the appellate court, made its choice of governing rule appropriate in this case?
6. How was the Court's rule different from the old common law rule?
7. What public policy reasons did the Court cite for applying its rule in cases like this one?

8. Who owed money to whom as a result of the Court's decision?
9. Do you think that the Court reached the correct result? Explain.
10. Do you think that a different result would have been appropriate if the tenants had rented an *unfurnished* house or apartment? Is *caveat emptor ever* justified?

NOTES

1. Ruggero J. Aldisert, *Winning on Appeal: Better Briefs and Oral Argument* (New York: Clark Boardman Callaghan, 1992), p. 85.
2. The judicial norm that appellate courts cannot consider any issue that counsel did not raise at trial is known as the *sua sponte* **doctrine**. There is a debate among political scientists about whether the U.S. Supreme Court honors this doctrine. Some political scientists argue that the High Court honors it and other political scientists contend that the Court often manipulates cases in order to raise and consider issues that the parties did not argue at trial. See Lee Epstein, Jeffrey A. Segal, and Timothy Johnson, "The Claim of Issue Creation on the U.S. Supreme Court," *American Political Science Review* 90 (December 1996): 845–849; and Kevin T. McGuire and Barbara Palmer, "Issues, Agendas, and Decision Making on the Supreme Court," *American Political Science Review* 90 (December 1996): 853–863.
3. Frank M. Coffin, *On Appeal: Courts, Lawyering, and Judging* (New York: W. W. Norton, 1994), p. 13.
4. Douglas O. Linder, "How Judges Judge: A Study of Disagreement on the United States Court of Appeals for the Eighth Circuit," *Arkansas Law Review* 38 (1985): 479–560.
5. *Id.*
6. *Id.* Political science research has identified factors other than the nature of cases and the philosophies of the justices (e.g., appointive selection procedures, random assignment of opinion-writing tasks, and the existence of an intermediate appellate court) that are associated with increased rates of dissent on state supreme courts. See, for example, Paul Brace and Melinda Gann Hall, "Neo-Institutionalism and Dissent in State Supreme Courts," *Journal of Politics* 52 (1990): 54–70.
7. Coffin, *On Appeal: Courts, Lawyering, and Judging*, p. 214.
8. *Id.*, pp. 258–260.
10. See Robert H. Dorff and Saul Brenner, "Conformity Voting on the United States Supreme Court," Journal of Politics 54 (1992): 762–775.
11. Some states require a losing party in the trial court to file a motion for a new trial (e.g., Tennessee) or a motion to correct errors (e.g., Indiana) in the trial court before filing an appeal. See Richardson Lynn, Appellate Litigation, Second Edition (San Francisco: Austin & Winfield, 1993), pp. 132–133.
12. Richard B. McNamara, *New Hampshire Practice: Criminal Practice and Procedure*, Third Edition, Volume 2 (Charlottesville, Va.: Lexis Law Publishing, 1997), p. 502.
13. *Id.*, p. 2.
14. *Id.*, p. 29.
15. *Id.*, p. 17.
16. Aldisert, *Winning on Appeal: Better Briefs and Oral Argument*, p. 51.
17. *Id.*

18. Lynn, *Appellate Litigation*, Second Edition, p. 185.
19. *Id.*
20. *Id.*, pp. 114–115.
21. See Myron Moskovitz, *Winning an Appeal*, Revised Edition (Charlottesville, Va.: The Michie Company, 1985), p. 112.
22. McNamara, *New Hampshire Practice: Criminal Practice and Procedure*, Third Edition, Volume 2A, p. 17.
23. *Id.*
24. *Id.*, p. 18.
25. *Id.*, pp. 18–19.
26. *Id.*, p. 29.
27. Aldisert, *Winning on Appeal: Better Briefs and Oral Argument*, p. 17.
28. McNamara, *New Hampshire Practice: Criminal Practice and Procedure*, Third Edition, Volume 2A, p. 31.
29. *Id.*, p. 32.
30. *Id.*, p. 6.
31. Aldisert, *Winning on Appeal: Better Briefs and Oral Argument*, p. 107.
32. McNamara, *New Hampshire Practice: Criminal Practice and Procedure*, Third Edition, Volume 2A, p. 32.
33. *Id.*
34. Aldisert, *Winning on Appeal: Better Briefs and Oral Argument*, p. 177.
35. Priscilla Anne Schwab, ed., *Appellate Practice Manual* (Chicago: American Bar Association, 1992), p. 104.
36. Andrew L. Frey and Roy T. Englert, Jr., "How to Write a Good Appellate Brief," *Litigation* 20, no. 2 (Winter 1994): 6–63.
37. Coffin, *On Appeal: Courts, Lawyering, and Judging*, p. 108.
38. *Id.*, p. 197.
39. Joel F. Dubina, "Effective Appellate Advocacy," *Litigation* 20, no. 2 (Winter 1994): 3–71.
40. Aldisert, *Winning on Appeal: Better Briefs and Oral Argument*, p. 20.
41. Lynn, *Appellate Litigation*, Second Edition, p. 216.
42. Schwab, ed., *Appellate Practice Manual*, p. 18.
43. Lynn, *Appellate Litigation*, Second Edition, p. 213.
44. *Id.*
45. Coffin, *On Appeal: Courts, Lawyering, and Judging*, p. 97.
46. 385 U.S. 206.
47. *State v. Seymour*, 140 N.H. 736, 673 A.2d 786, *cert. denied*, 117 S. Ct. 146, 136 L. Ed.2d 93 (1996).
48. *State v. Santana*, 133 N.H. 798, 586 A.2d 77 (1991).
49. See *United States v. Peskin*, 527 F.2d 71 (7th Cir.), *cert. denied*, 429 U.S. 818 (1975); and *United States v. Berrios*, 501 F.2d 1207 (2d Cir. 1974).
50. *State v. Seymour*, 140 N.H. 736, 673 A.2d 786, *cert. denied*, 117 S. Ct. 146, 136 L. Ed.2d 93 (1996).
51. McNamara, *New Hampshire Practice: Criminal Practice and Procedure*, Third Edition, Volume 2A, p. 32.
52. *United States v. Peskin*, 527 F.2d 71 (7th Cir.), *cert. denied*, 429 U.S. 818 (1975); *United States v. Berrios*, 501 F.2d 1207 (2d Cir. 1974).
53. Aldisert, *Winning on Appeal: Better Briefs and Oral Argument*, p. 260; see also Schwab, ed., *Appellate Practice Manual*, p. 135.
54. Aldisert, *Winning on Appeal: Better Briefs and Oral Argument*, pp. 29–30.

55. *Id.*, p. 330.
56. Lynn, *Appellate Litigation*, p. 277.justices select determine the cases in which they will write majority opinions.
57. Aldisert, *Winning on Appeal: Better Briefs and Oral Argument*, p.304.
58. In the New Hampshire Supreme Court, contrary to the U.S. Supreme Court and many state supreme courts, the chief justice (or, alternatively, the most senior justice who is in the majority) does not make opinion-writing assignments. Instead, at conference, the justices randomly select from an urn slips of paper that contain the names of cases argued that day. The slips that the respective justices select determine the cases in which they will write majority opinions.
59. Richard Wiebusch, *New Hampshire Practice: Civil Practice and Procedure*, Second Edition, Volume 5 (Charlottesville, Va.: Lexis Law Publishing, 1998), p. 416.
60. *Id.*, p. 415.
61. See N.H.R.S.A. 225-A:24,   I(a) and (d).
62. Wiebusch, *New Hampshire Practice: Civil Practice and Procedure*, Second Edition, Volume 5, p. 418.
63. *Id.*, p. 419.
64. Schwab, ed., *Appellate Practice Manual*, p. 54.
65. Lynn, *Appellate Litigation*, Second Edition, pp. 178–180; Coffin, *On Appeal: Courts, Lawyering, and Judging*, pp. 98–99.
66. Schwab, ed., *Appellate Practice Manual*, p. 18.
67. Wiebusch, *New Hampshire Practice: Civil Practice and Procedure*, Second Edition, Volume 5, p. 521.
68. *Id.*, pp. 522–523.
69. Moskowitz, *Winning an Appeal*, Revised Edition, p. 112.
70. N.H.R.S.A. 225-A:24, I.
71. 140 N.H. 675, 671 A.2d 548 (1996).
72. Wiebusch, *New Hampshire Practice: Civil Practice and Procedure*, Second Edition, Volume 5, pp. 530–531.
73. *Id.*, pp. 529–530.
74. *Id.*, p. 530.
75. *Id.*, p. 452.
76. Lynn, *Appellate Litigation*, Second Edition, p. 135; Aldisert, *Winning on Appeal: Better Briefs and Oral Argument*, p. 51.
77. Wiebusch, *New Hampshire Practice: Civil Practice and Procedure*, Second Edition, Volume 5, pp. 552–553.
78. *Id.*, p. 527; pp. 558–563.
79. *Id.*, p. 577.
80. Schwab, ed., *Appellate Practice Manual*, p. 18.
81. 140 N.H. 675, 671 A.2d 548.
82. 140 N.H. at 680, 671 A.2d at 551.
83. Wiebusch, *New Hampshire Practice: Civil Practice and Procedure*, Second Edition, Volume 5, pp. 561–562.
84. *Nutbrown v. Mt. Cranmore, Inc.*, 140 N.H. at 680.
85. Wiebusch, *New Hampshire Practice: Civil Practice and Procedure*, Second Edition, Volume 5, p. 563.
86. 156 Vt. 1, 587 A.2d 988 (1991).
87. 14 Wis. 2d 590, 111 N.W. 2d 409 (1961).

Chapter 8

LEGAL AND POLITICAL INFLUENCES ON JUDICIAL DECISION MAKING

INTRODUCTION

A political scientist has observed that judges' decisions are "a function of what they prefer to do, tempered by what they think they ought to do, but constrained by what they perceive is feasible to do."[1] That observation is perceptive for two reasons. First, it recognizes that numerous factors can influence judicial decisions. Second, it rejects both the old myth that only "the law" influences judicial decisions and the newer myth that only judges' public policy preferences influence their decisions (see Chapter 1). Instead, it contemplates that, sometimes, judicial decisions result from *political influences* (e.g., judges' public policy preferences), at other times they result from *legal influences* (e.g., *stare decisis*, statutory language), and at still other times they result from a combination of influences.

This chapter will show how legal and political influences shape judicial decisions. It will also explain how the methods that political scientists use to study the judicial process differ from the methods that lawyers use. Lawyers stress the legal influences, and political scientists emphasize the political influences, but both influences affect judicial decisions, which is why this chapter will examine both.

Lawyers favor the **legal model** of judicial decision making. It assumes that judges' decisions result from the application of legal principles and of techniques of interpreting statutory and constitutional language to the facts of the cases at hand.[2] It also assumes that the most important principle that guides judges is *stare decisis*, which directs them to decide today's cases according to rules established in prior, similar cases (see Chapter 1). The legal model downplays the influence that judges' public policy preferences have over their decisions. Indeed, lawyers are often critical of "result-oriented" (i.e., ideologically motivated) judging; they praise the judge who reaches whatever conclusion the precedents and the relevant statutory or constitutional language lead her to, not the judge who searches for precedents and linguistic interpretations that coincide with his political philosophy.

Many political scientists reject the legal model precisely because it downplays the political influences that they believe shape judicial decisions. They prefer the **attitudinal model** of judicial decision making. The attitudinal model assumes that judges' decisions result from their public policy preferences; in other words, judges decide cases according to their political philosophies.[3] Unlike the legal model, the attitudinal model assumes that most judges are result-oriented, and it expresses no opinion about whether that is good or bad. According to this view, conservative Supreme Court justices vote to restrict the rights of criminal defendants, to limit the rights of individuals relative to government, to end race-based or gender-based affirmative action programs, to restrict federal court jurisdiction, especially in *habeas corpus* cases (see Chapter 2), and to protect states against federal interference. Liberal justices vote for the opposite results.[4]

Nevertheless, some political scientists have concluded that the attitudinal model is incomplete because it does not account for the cases in which judges vote contrary to their policy preferences in the short term in order to achieve long-term goals for themselves or their courts. These political scientists favor the **rational-choice model** of judicial decision making, which assumes that judges sometimes vote contrary to their policy preferences for **strategic** reasons.[5] One such reason would be to preserve public support for their court so that the court can draw on public goodwill when it decides controversial cases. Under those circumstances, compromise is required, and some judges moderate or even disregard their policy preferences in order to reach a decision that maintains the court's institutional strength. The joint opinion by Justices Kennedy, O'Connor, and Souter in *Planned Parenthood v. Casey*, which appears in the Epilogue to this chapter, illustrates strategic voting by judges.

The rational-choice model does not reject the attitudinal model. Instead, it complements the attitudinal model by helping to explain judicial decisions that do not result from judges' public policy preferences. It also recognizes the capacity of the legal model to help us understand judicial decisions.[6] The rational-choice theorists wisely recognize the value of political *and* legal influences on the judicial process. One must appreciate both in order to understand fully how judges decide cases. The rest of this chapter will explain how law and politics shape judicial decisions.

LEGAL INFLUENCES

Legal influences on judicial decision making are divisible into the **procedural** and the **substantive**. The procedural influences cause judges to refuse to hear certain cases, and the substantive influences cause them to decide cases according to legal, not political, criteria. The following two sections explain procedural and substantive legal influences, respectively.

Procedural

C. Herman Pritchett, a political scientist who pioneered the use of the attitudinal model, nevertheless advised his colleagues to remember that judging involves both law and politics. Pritchett observed that:

> [P]olitical scientists who have done so much to put the "political" in "political jurisprudence" need to emphasize that it is still "jurisprudence." It is judging in a political context, but it is still judging; and judging is something different from legislating or administering. Judges make choices, but they are not the "free" choices of Congressmen.... Any accurate analysis of judicial behavior must have as a major purpose a full clarification of the unique limiting conditions under which judicial policy making proceeds.[7]

A major "limiting condition" on judicial power is Article III of the federal Constitution, which defines the scope of federal court authority.[8] The Supreme Court has interpreted Article III to authorize several legal doctrines that enable judges to refuse to hear cases that they believe are not proper lawsuits. These **justiciability doctrines**, which concern the appropriateness of particular cases for judicial resolution, include the **advisory opinion doctrine**, **standing**, **mootness**, **ripeness**, and the **political question doctrine**.

The advisory opinion doctrine prohibits federal courts from issuing "advisory opinions," which determine the legality of a congressional or presidential act that does not involve an actual "case."[9] Typically, there is no case because the action has not occurred yet; it is contemplated, and the potential actor wants advice about its likely legality. The Supreme Court announced the advisory opinion doctrine in 1793, after President Washington sought the Court's advice concerning legal questions that arose out of America's neutrality in the war then in progress between England and France.[10] The Court declined to give the advice sought, concluding that Article III confined judicial power to "cases or controversies," namely, actual disputes between adverse parties in which it is likely that a court decision would produce a meaningful result.[11] That conclusion is still good law. It honors the separation-of-powers principle on which the federal government is built by restricting judicial power to justiciable disputes.

The requirement that one have "standing" to file a lawsuit is closely related to the prohibition on advisory opinions. Both doctrines derive from the "case or controversy" command of Article III, which permits federal courts to consider only actual disputes between adverse parties. In order to have standing, a plaintiff must allege that: (1) he has suffered an injury (to body, property, financial condition, psyche, and/or reputation) or will suffer an injury imminently; (2) the injury is traceable to the defendant's conduct (action or inaction); and (3) a decision in the plaintiff's favor by the court would remedy the injury.[12] Standing, then, is the direct personal stake that one must have in a dispute in order to convince a court to resolve it;[13] one must stand to gain or lose something as a result of the court's decision.[14]

Standing serves three important purposes. It preserves the separation of powers, and it enables courts to conserve their limited resources for "real" cases. It also

ensures that the parties to those cases will be genuine adversaries who will prepare their cases carefully and argue them aggressively. Motivated parties are important because American judges rely on the parties to furnish the information
necessary to decide cases.[15]

In *Raines v. Byrd* (1997),[16] the Supreme Court denied standing to six members of Congress who challenged the constitutionality of the **Line Item Veto Act**,
which gave the President the power to cancel individual budgetary items without
vetoing the larger bill(s) of which the cancelled items were a part.[17] The justices,
by a 7–2 vote, concluded that the plaintiffs lacked standing because President
Clinton had not yet used the power that the act gave him; therefore, the plaintiffs could not claim that they had suffered any immediate, direct, or personal
injury from the act.[18] The Court honored the separation of powers and conserved
its limited resources by refusing to decide a dispute that the majority felt was not
a "case or controversy" within the meaning of Article III. Nevertheless, the power
to determine whether the plaintiffs in *Raines v. Byrd* had standing lay in the Court
itself. The Court subsequently used that power to grant standing to new plaintiffs
in *Clinton v. City of New York* (1998), which raised the same issue that *Raines* had
raised.[19] In *Clinton*, which the plaintiffs filed after President Clinton exercised the
line-item veto to their economic disadvantage the Court concluded that the plaintiffs had met the requirements for standing.[20] Thus, standing is a speed bump, not
a brick wall; it can postpone, but not prevent, judicial policy making. Courts establish the requirements for standing, so a court majority that is determined to address
emerging legal issues will be able to do so sooner or later.

Mootness, like standing, derives from the "case or controversy" requirement
of Article III.[21] Mootness prevents a court from deciding a case in which the plain-
tiff(s) had standing to sue when the case began, but changes in the facts or in the
law, while the case was pending, have deprived the plaintiff(s) of the stake in the
outcome that is necessary to maintain standing throughout the case.[22] In other
words, mootness requires that there be an actual controversy at every stage of a
case, not merely when the plaintiff files the complaint.[23] Therefore, if a criminal
defendant or a civil plaintiff dies while a case is pending, if the parties settle a civil
case out of court, or if the legislature repeals a challenged law, the case becomes
moot, and the court must dismiss it.[24]

Mootness is not always so clear-cut, though; there can be sound arguments
for and against declaring a case moot. A good example is *DeFunis v. Odegaard*
(1974), which was the first challenge to the constitutionality of affirmative action
programs brought in the Supreme Court.[25] The University of Washington Law
School denied admission to DeFunis, a white applicant, although his undergraduate grades and his score on the Law School Admission Test (L.S.A.T.) were
higher than those of some minority applicants who were admitted. He sued, claiming that the law school's affirmative action policy in admissions discriminated
against him on the basis of race.

The trial court found in DeFunis's favor, and ordered the law school to admit
him. The university appealed, and DeFunis lost, but the appeals court permitted
him to remain in school until his case was resolved. He filed a *writ of certiorari* in

the Supreme Court, but by the time the Court heard oral argument, DeFunis had registered for his final term of law school. He was on schedule to graduate, and the law school had indicated that it would permit him to do so regardless of the outcome of the case. The majority concluded that there was no longer a controversy between the parties, and a decision by the Court in favor of the university would not adversely affect DeFunis. Therefore, the case was moot.

The four dissenters argued that the case was still a live controversy because DeFunis's graduation was not assured; he could fail to pay his bill, become ill, or fail his courses, in which case he would have to seek continued admission later, and could still lock horns with the affirmative action policy. Moreover, the issue that DeFunis raised was important and likely to recur, so the Court should resolve it now by deciding this case.

The *DeFunis* case shows why mootness can be a judgment call. It also suggests why courts have created two exceptions to the mootness doctrine. One exception permits a court to hear a case in which the defendant tries to avoid an adverse court decision by suspending the activity of which the plaintiff complains, in hopes that the plaintiff will drop the suit or the court will dismiss it.[26] The other exception permits judicial resolution of an issue that is likely to recur, but would usually be moot unless the court made an exception. Abortion is the classic example of the second exception; births usually occur nine months after conception, but courts rarely resolve cases that quickly. Consequently, absent an exception, abortion cases would always be moot because the plaintiff would have given birth before the court could decide the case.[27]

Ripeness is another derivative of the "case or controversy" requirement. A case must be **ripe** in order for a court to decide it, which means that (1) the parties will suffer a hardship without a decision and (2) the parties can present enough evidence to enable the court to reach a decision.[28] The ripeness doctrine exists to prevent what the Supreme Court has called "premature adjudication."[29] It therefore honors the separation of powers and conserves limited judicial resources.[30]

Ripeness is often at issue when a plaintiff seeks a court order that either prevents the defendant from taking certain action that will harm the plaintiff (**injunction**) or that informs the plaintiff what her legal rights are relative to the defendant's proposed action (**declaratory judgment**).[31] For example, in *Poe v. Ullman*, 367 U.S. 497 (1961), a married couple sought a declaratory judgment against the threatened enforcement of a Connecticut law that prohibited married couples from using contraceptives. The Court dismissed the case for lack of ripeness because Connecticut had not prosecuted anyone for violating the 1879 law and it showed no sign of doing so in the immediate future. The plaintiffs' suit was premature.

The political question doctrine also derives from the "case or controversy" requirement. Like the other justiciability doctrines, it honors the separation of powers, and ensures that federal court decisions will produce meaningful results. Federal courts use it as the basis for refusing to consider subjects that they deem inappropriate for judicial resolution.[32] The courts thus leave those subjects to the elected branches of government.[33] A federal court is likely to rely on the political question doctrine when it feels that: (1) the Constitution clearly assigns a subject to another branch of government; (2) the subject would be unmanageable for a court to resolve; and/or that (3) it would be unable to enforce whatever decision it reached.[34] Those criteria are hardly chiseled in stone, though. The Supreme Court has defined "political questions" differently at different times in its history, which has left scholars confused as to what is and what is not a political question.[35]

Nixon v. United States (1993) provides a recent illustration of the political question doctrine.[36] Walter Nixon, a federal district judge whom the Senate had removed from office after an impeachment trial, challenged the constitutionality of the procedure that the Senate had used, whereby a committee, rather than the full Senate, gathered evidence and heard testimony. The Court concluded that the case presented a political question because the Constitution plainly gave the Senate the power to try impeachments free from judicial review. For the same reason, there was no remedy that the Court could give to the plaintiff that would change his position; it could void his conviction, but probably could not reinstate him as a judge. Thus, the Court affirmed the conclusions of two lower federal courts that Nixon's claim was not justiciable.

Not all of the procedural devices that restrict judicial power, however, derive from Article III of the federal Constitution. State constitutions, and/or judicial interpretations thereof, prohibit most state courts from issuing advisory opinions (see Chapter 2), and state courts observe the same justiciability doctrines that federal courts observe, although not on the basis of Article III. Both state and federal courts routinely refuse to hear cases in which the plaintiff has not exhausted the other legal remedies (administrative hearing, arbitration, etc.) to which he is entitled.[37] Jurisdictional statutes limit the cases that both state and federal courts may hear.[38] The Texas Supreme Court cannot hear criminal appeals because the state legislature has designated the Court of Criminal Appeals as the final arbiter of criminal cases in Texas.[39] A federal district court cannot hear a personal-injury suit unless the plaintiff resides in a different state than the defendant does and the amount in controversy is at least $50,000, because a federal statute so stipulates.

Last but not least, **statutes of limitations** prohibit state and federal courts from hearing criminal or civil cases that commence after the **limitations period** set by statute has expired.[40] For example, a state statute may set the limitations period for personal-injury suits at three years after the date of the injury or, for long-dormant illnesses such as cancer, three years after the date when the plaintiff should have discovered the injury. A court must dismiss criminal charges (except for murder) or a civil complaint filed after the limitations period has expired.

Lawyers perceive procedural restraints to be more significant influences on judicial decisions than political scientists do. Political scientists believe that judges' policy preferences (i.e., the attitudinal model) are the greatest influence on their decisions. Nevertheless, two political scientists who are advocates for the attitudinal model have acknowledged that procedural restraints influence case outcomes. They observed that:

> Entirely apart from the factors we have addressed are questions of standing and jurisdiction. Also relevant are such considerations as ... whether the issue the case poses is sufficiently "ripe" for review or whether it should be allowed to "per-

colate" further in the lower court and among scholars…. Though all but unexplained by political scientists, they obviously affect the [Supreme] Court's decisions concerning review.[41]

An example of the influence of procedural restraints will conclude this discussion. During the 1963 Supreme Court term, Justice Arthur Goldberg sent a memorandum to his colleagues about *Rudolph v. Alabama*, in which the Court would soon decide whether or not to grant *cert*.[42] *Rudolph* was an appeal by a black man whom an Alabama jury had sentenced to death for the rape of a white woman. The defendant asked the Court to reverse his conviction because his confession had not been voluntary; he did not challenge the constitutionality of the death penalty. Nevertheless, Justice Goldberg informed his colleagues that he wanted them to consider: "Whether and under what circumstances, the imposition of the death penalty is proscribed by the Eighth and Fourteenth Amendments to the U.S. Constitution?" His own view was that "the evolving standards of decency that mark the progress of our maturing society now condemn as barbaric and inhumane the deliberate institutionalized taking of human life by the state."[43]

Goldberg's memorandum shocked and dismayed most of his colleagues because it violated the norm of judicial self-restraint that states that courts can consider only those issues that parties properly present to them. To do otherwise would be to act more like legislators than judges. In *Rudolph*, neither party had addressed the constitutionality of the death penalty in its brief.[44] Six members of the Court not only rejected Goldberg's position, but voted to deny *cert*., thereby thwarting Goldberg's plan.[45] Thus, *Rudolph* illustrates Herman Pritchett's observation that "Judges make choices, but they are not the free choices of Congressmen."[46]

Substantive

Legal influences not only cause judges to refuse to hear some cases, but also to decide cases on grounds other than their public policy preferences. The nature of the cases themselves often predetermines their outcomes. Most of the cases that state and federal courts decide are "easy," which means that the facts and the law dictate one correct result. Such cases do not usually activate judges' policy preferences; neither do they produce dissents. They are common in state appellate courts that have mandatory jurisdiction. Typically, the legal issues are narrow, the law is clear, and it favors the appellee.[47] That is why, as a law clerk at the Indiana Court of Appeals, I drafted many an opinion that affirmed a criminal conviction because, contrary to the defendant's claim, the trial court judge had properly informed him that, by plea bargaining, he would waive his right to a jury trial.

The federal courts decide many easy cases too. Indeed, Judge Harry Edwards of the U.S. Court of Appeals for the District of Columbia Circuit estimates that one-half of the approximately 200 cases he hears each year are easy.[48] Statistics compiled for the period from July 1, 1983, through June 30, 1984, support his view. During that period, the "D.C. Circuit," as it is popularly known, decided 1146 cases, usually by means of three-judge panels. More than 94 percent of those decisions were unanimous.[49] The court decided 347 cases that year by means of a full written opinion; the other 799 merited only a brief order. Of the 347 full-opinion cases, 80 percent were unanimous, 7 percent produced at least one concurring opinion, and 13 percent contained a dissent.[50]

Judge Edwards estimates that 5 to 15 percent of cases per year raise "very hard" questions related to matters such as individual rights, the separation of powers, and the proper role of the federal courts in the American system of government. Those are the cases in which "the law" yields no clear answer, and the judges' public policy preferences influence their votes.[51] Those cases are the exception that proves the rule, which is that most cases in most courts neither arouse nor reveal judges' public policy preferences.

Constitutional and statutory language also influence judicial decisions, and can blunt the power of judges' policy preferences, especially when the meaning of the text is clear.[52] Consider, for example, Article II, Section 1, Clause 4 of the federal Constitution, which states: "No person except a natural born Citizen of the United States, at the time of the Adoption of this Constitution, shall be eligible to the Office of the President." That language leaves little room for interpretation. There could, perhaps, be a debate about whether one born overseas to American parents is a "natural born citizen," but it is clear that one born overseas to foreign nationals is ineligible to be President.[53]

The Fourth Amendment's prohibition against "unreasonable" searches and seizures is more open to interpretation, but it has meaning too. Besides, years of judicial interpretation have clarified it. Consequently, no judge, regardless of his policy preferences, is likely to conclude that a warrantless nighttime search of every house on a city block is constitutional.[54]

Statutory language has meaning too. Title XI of the Organized Crime Control Act of 1970 prohibits the willful use of the mails, a telephone, a telegraph, or another instrument of commerce to threaten to kill or injure a person, or damage or destroy property, *by means of fire or an explosive*.[55] In 1997, a federal appeals court reversed in part a conviction based on that statute because the prosecutor had failed to charge in the indictment that the defendant threatened harm to persons or property *by means of fire or an explosive*.[56] Statutory language, not judges' public policy preferences, produced that decision.

Norms of proper judicial behavior, which many judges hold dear, also shape their decisions, often regardless of, or even contrary to, their individual policy preferences. Almost all judges attend law school, where professors often criticize result-oriented judges. After graduation, they typically practice law, which requires them to view issues in legal terms and to use the techniques of legal reasoning that they learned in law school. By the time they become judges, it is likely that their professional socialization has caused them to believe that judges should decide cases on the narrowest possible grounds and that they should honor *stare decisis*.[57] State judges may also honor those norms in order to cultivate the support of the local legal community, especially if they must periodically stand for election. Federal district judges may honor those norms in order to avoid reversal on appeal, and both district and appellate judges may honor them to enhance their chances for promotion to a higher court.

Regardless of their motivations, many judges follow the norm that counsels them to decide cases on the narrowest possible grounds. Justice Ruth Bader Ginsburg, who has served on the Supreme Court since 1993, is a good example. One commentator has described her as having "an affinity for resolving cases on narrow procedural grounds rather than appealing to broad principles of social justice; a preference for small steps over sweeping gestures, and an aversion to bold assertions of judicial power."[58] That was evident in *Agostini v. Felton* (1997), in which the Court considered whether New York City public school teachers could provide remedial education services to disadvantaged students at church-affiliated schools without violating the First Amendment's requirement of separation between church and state.[59] The majority said yes, thereby reversing *Aguilar v. Felton* (1985), its earlier ruling on the same issue.[60] Justice Ginsburg wrote a dissent in which she side-stepped the constitutional question, and argued instead that the majority had misinterpreted Rule 60(b) of the Federal Rules of Civil Procedure, which she believed prevented the Court from revisiting its *Aguilar* decision in *Agostini*.[61]

Finally, many judges adhere to the norm of *stare decisis*. *Stare decisis* is less important to Supreme Court justices than to state court and lower federal court judges because the Supreme Court need not fear reversal by a higher court if it fails to follow precedent. Nevertheless, *stare decisis* is an important norm that influences judicial behavior even at the Supreme Court. Political scientist Lawrence Baum has observed that:

> The Court adheres to precedents far more often than it overturns them, either explicitly or implicitly.... Certainly most justices accept the principle that any departure from the doctrine of *stare decisis* demands special justification. Like the law in general, the rule of adhering to precedent hardly controls the Court's decisions, but it does structure and influence them.[62]

The discussions that Supreme Court justices have during their twice-weekly conferences reflect the influence that *stare decisis* has on their decisions. Their conversations during conferences are sprinkled with references to precedents. For example, during conference discussion about *Atascadero State Hospital v. Scanlon* (1985), Justice O'Connor said that: "*Pennhurst* [*State Hospital v. Halderman* (1984)] decided this case and I'd reverse".[63] Similarly, in conference discussion about *Green v. Mansour* (1985), Justice Harry Blackmun noted that he would "reverse on *Atascadero*," meaning that he would vote to reverse the lower court's decision in *Green* based on the *Atascadero* precedent.[64]

In *Edelman v. Jordan* (1974), several precedents competed for the justices' loyalty, and the decision would vary considerably, depending on which precedent they chose to follow. Justice Potter Stewart said during the conference discussion: "Same jurisdiction issue here as in *Hagans* [*v. Lavine* (1974)] but can't solve it the same way. Can't possibly find *Parden* [*v. Terminal Railway Company* (1964) type waiver here. My problem comes down to *Ex Parte Young*."[65]

Some judges honor *stare decisis* even when it conflicts with their policy preferences. For example, Justice Lewis Powell, who served on the Supreme Court from 1972 until 1988, followed precedents of which he disapproved, until the Court overruled them.[66] He therefore voted to decide cases in accordance with *Mapp v. Ohio* (1961), which made illegally seized evidence inadmissible in criminal trials in every state,[67] and *Miranda v. Arizona* (1966), which required police officers to read suspects their rights when arrested,[68] despite his misgivings about both decisions.[69]

Still, Justice Powell wore *stare decisis* like a seatbelt, not a straitjacket. During conference discussion of a case in 1983, he said of a prior decision, "It's bad law. I would want to limit it to its own facts, without overruling it in so many words."[70] That strategy offered Powell a chance to reconcile his respect for *stare decisis* with his policy preferences; he hoped to preserve the precedent, but to prevent it from governing the later case. To paraphrase Professor Baum, *stare decisis* influenced Justice Powell's strategy without controlling it.

Not all judges value *stare decisis* as much as Justice Powell did. Consider Chief Justice William Rehnquist's majority opinion in *Payne v. Tennessee* (1991),[71] which reversed two late-1980s precedents, and permitted a murder victim's friends and family to discuss, at a sentencing hearing, the effects of the murder on their lives.[72] Rehnquist observed in *Payne* that *stare decisis* is not "an inexorable command," and that it is more important to honor *stare decisis* in cases that involve property rights and contract rights than in cases that feature noneconomic rights.[73]

Indeed, judges are more likely to honor *stare decisis* in cases that concern wills, titles to land, commercial transactions, and contracts.[74] Judges frequently conclude, in such cases, that **reliance interests** outweigh the need for change because parties to wills and contracts expect that the documents they sign today will be valid tomorrow.[75] Judges are also more likely to honor *stare decisis* in cases that involve a long-standing interpretation of a statute because the legislature can change any statute that it thinks courts have misinterpreted.[76] Courts are reluctant to change a statute themselves by means of a reinterpretation.

There is less judicial adherence to *stare decisis* in cases that involve rules that courts themselves have established, such as the rule that interprets ambiguities in insurance policies in favor of the policyholder, and in cases that require interpretation of constitutional language.[77] Courts feel freer to revisit constitutional interpretations than statutory interpretations because constitutions are difficult to change; bad constitutional law is likely to survive unless a court changes it by means of a reinterpretation. That helps to explain the Supreme Court's willingness to overturn two precedents in *Payne v. Tennessee*, which interpreted the Eighth Amendment's prohibition against cruel and unusual punishments.

Cases like *Payne* will figure prominently in the next section of this chapter, which examines the political influences on judicial decision making. Those influences, especially judges' policy preferences, are most apparent in *Payne*-type cases, which feature constitutional interpretation and public policy dilemmas.

POLITICAL INFLUENCES

Political influences on judicial decision making are divisible into the **attitudinal**, the **organizational**, and the **institutional**. The attitudinal influences are judges' individual public policy preferences, the organizational influences are interest-group activities, and the institutional influences are judicial colleagues, higher courts, other branches of government, and public opinion. The following three subsections will explain each influence in turn.

Attitudinal

During the past forty years, political scientists (i.e., judicial behaviorists) have amassed substantial evidence that judges' public policy preferences influence their decisions. Indeed, the judicial behaviorists' fundamental assumption is that judicial decisions are primarily, if not exclusively, the products of judges' policy preferences.[78] That assumption underlies the attitudinal model of judicial decision making. The attitudinal model focuses not on the reasons that judges cite for their conclusions, but on the conclusions themselves. Judicial behaviorists study the votes that judges cast instead of the opinions that they write, on the theory that the votes reveal policy preferences more clearly than the opinions do.

Early on, judicial behaviorists discovered that Supreme Court justices who shared similar policy preferences voted together consistently, forming liberal and conservative **blocs**. Not every justice belonged to a **bloc**, but most did. Blocs first became evident on economic issues; later studies showed that they existed on "political" (i.e., individual rights versus law-and-order) and "social" (e.g., racial equality) issues too.[79] Gradually, the recognition of blocs expanded beyond judicial behaviorists; today, lawyers and journalists routinely speak of the Supreme Court's "liberal" and "conservative" blocs. Figure 8.1 shows the blocs on the contemporary Court, as reflected in votes cast during the 1997–1998 term.

Figure 8.1 shows interagreement between Chief Justice Rehnquist and Justices Scalia, O'Connor, Kennedy, and Thomas in nonunanimous cases during the 1997–1998 term. For example, Chief Justice Rehnquist and Justice Scalia voted together in 63.8 percent of those cases; Chief Justice Rehnquist and Justice Kennedy voted together in 85.1 percent of them. Figure 8.1 also shows interagreement between Justices Stevens, Souter, Ginsburg, and Breyer. For example, Justices Stevens and Souter agreed in 63.8 percent of the nonunanimous cases, and Justices Stevens and Breyer agreed in 72.3 percent. If you were to read a few of the 1997–1998 opinions, you would quickly conclude that the group that includes Chief Justice Rehnquist is the Court's "conservative" bloc, and that the group that includes Justice Stevens is its "liberal" (some would say "moderate") bloc.

Figure 8.2 supports that conclusion. It shows that during the 1997–1998 term, the conservative bloc held firm in six cases that the Court decided by a 5–4 vote. That is why the conservatives dominate the current Court: they have five firm

	Rehnquist	Stevens	O'Connor	Scalia	Kennedy	Souter	Thomas	Ginsburg	Breyer
Rehnquist		31.9*	76.1	63.8	85.1	42.6	70.2	59.6	42.6
		64.4	87.6	85.6	92.2	70.0	84.4	78.9	70.0
Stevens	31.9		34.8	21.3	42.6	63.8	27.7	63.8	72.3
	64.4		66.3	58.9	70.0	81.1	62.2	81.1	85.6
O'Connor	76.1	34.8		69.6	74.0	47.8	71.8	45.7	47.8
	87.6	66.3		84.3	86.6	73.0	85.4	68.5	73.0
Scalia	63.8	21.3	69.6		58.7	37.0	85.1	61.7	32.0
	85.6	58.9	84.3		77.8	66.7	92.2	64.4	64.4
Kennedy	85.1	42.6	74.0	58.7		55.3	63.8	63.0	53.2
	92.2	70.0	86.6	77.8		76.7	81.1	80.0	75.6
Souter	42.6	63.8	47.8	37.0	55.3		36.2	68.1	76.6
	70.0	81.1	73.0	66.7	76.7		66.7	83.3	85.6
Thomas	70.2	27.7	71.8	85.1	63.8	36.2		38.3	29.8
	84.4	62.2	85.4	92.2	81.1	66.7		67.8	63.3
Ginsburg	59.6	63.8	45.7	61.7	63.0	68.1	38.3		74.5
	78.9	81.1	68.5	64.4	80.0	83.3	67.8		86.7
Breyer	42.6	72.3	47.8	32.0	53.3	76.6	29.8	74.5	
	70.0	85.6	73.0	64.4	75.6	85.6	63.3	86.7	

FIGURE 8.1 Justices' Voting Blocs, 1997–1998 Term
*The first number in each cell represents the percentage of agreement in nonunanimous cases. The second number represents the percentage of agreement in all signed opinions (including unanimous decisions).
Source: Kenneth Jost, *The Supreme Court Yearbook, 1997–1998* (Washington, D.C.: CQ Press, 1999), p. 4.

votes, so they win unless one of the five, most often Justice Kennedy, defects, as he did three times in 1997–1998.

Judicial behaviorists can account for more than just voting blocs, though. They can explain *why*, for instance, Democratic judges are more likely than Republican judges to decide cases in favor of labor unions. Judges decide labor–management disputes on the basis of a set of related **attitudes** (freedom, equality, social mobility, limited government) that cluster together to form a **value**, **economic liberalism/conservatism**. Democratic judges tend to be economic liberals who favor "underdogs," including labor unions, consumers, and debtors, while Republican judges tend to be economic conservatives who favor "upperdogs," including management, manufacturers, and creditors. Thus, Democratic judges consistently side with labor, and Republican judges consistently side with management, in labor–management disputes.[80]

That consistency makes it possible to measure the degree to which each member of an appellate court supports economic liberalism/conservatism. Each judge's voting record in disputes between employees and employers, consumers and man-

Justices Constituting the Majority	Number of Decisions
Rehnquist, O'Connor, Scalia, Kennedy, Thomas	6
Stevens, Kennedy, Souter, Ginsburg, Breyer	3
Rehnquist, O'Connor, Kennedy, Thomas, Breyer	2
Rehnquist, Scalia, Kennedy, Thomas, Ginsburg	1
Stevens, O'Connor, Kennedy, Thomas, Breyer	1
Stevens, O'Connor, Souter, Ginsburg, Breyer	1
Stevens, Souter, Thomas, Ginsburg, Breyer	1
	Total 15

FIGURE 8.2 5–4 Decisions, 1997–1998 Term
Source: "Annual Summary of Supreme Court Term," Harvard Law Review 112 (1998), pp. 366–378. Reprinted with permission.

ufacturers, and debtors and creditors will place her at a different point on a **cumulative scale** of support for economic liberalism/conservatism. The more frequently she votes in favor of employees, consumers, and debtors, the more support she demonstrates for economic liberalism.[81] The judge who shows a high degree of support for economic liberalism holds attitudes that predispose her to favor employees, consumers, and debtors, while the judge who shows a low degree of support for economic liberalism holds attitudes that predispose him to favor employers, manufacturers, and creditors.[82] Nevertheless, not even the staunch economic liberal is likely to favor the employee, the consumer, or the debtor in every case. The attitudinal model assumes that, for each judge, there is a point beyond which her liberalism will not go; at that **indifference point**, the economic liberal votes for the employer.[83] Her indifference point may be a labor–management case in which the employees are well-paid airline pilots or professional athletes. The usual stimulus (i.e., support for the underdog employee) is absent, so the response is unusual. When the usual stimulus is present, however, the response will be predictably liberal. The conservative judge will reach his indifference point toward the claims of economic underdogs much sooner than the liberal judge will; for example, the conservative may vote in favor of the underdog only when that person is an elderly victim of consumer fraud.

Figure 8.3 depicts a cumulative scale on the dimension of economic liberalism/conservatism. Each judge will vote in favor of the economic underdog in cases that do not reach his indifference point; that is, cases located to the right of his

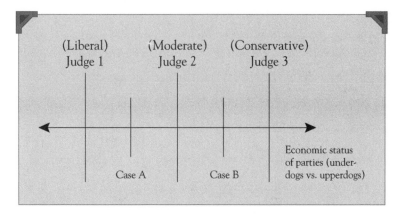

FIGURE 8.3 Cumulative Scale: Economic Liberalism/Conservatism
Source: Adapted from Lee Epstein, ed., *Contemplating Courts* (Washington, D.C.: CQ Press, 1995), p. 231.

indifference point in the diagram. Each judge will vote against the economic underdog in cases that reach her indifference point; that is, cases located to the left of her indifference point in the diagram. Liberal judge 1 will vote in favor of the economic underdog in both case A and case B; moderate judge 2 will vote in favor of the economic underdog in case A, but not in case B; and conservative judge 3 will vote against the economic underdog in case A and in case B.[84] Thus, the attitudinal model enables political scientists to *predict* judicial behavior with a degree of accuracy that lawyers' traditional educated guesses cannot match.

The attitudinal model is particularly accurate when applied to the Supreme Court. That is because its assumption that public policy preferences drive judges' votes is more applicable to the Supreme Court than to any other American court. The justices enjoy lifetime tenure and almost complete discretion to choose the cases that they wish to hear. They therefore have more freedom than most policy makers have to act on their policy preferences because they need not fear losing their jobs as a result of their decisions. The justices need not fear reversal by a higher court either, because there is no higher court; Congress can reverse their interpretation of a statute, but that occurs infrequently. There is no higher office to aspire to, so justices need not mute their views to please the voters or another official.[85] Last but not least, the justices hear almost only difficult cases, many of which force them to choose between deeply held values, such as life and repro-ductive freedom or the American flag and free speech.[86] Thus, the Supreme Court epitomizes the attitudinal model of judicial decision making.

Still, the attitudinal model can only show patterns in the justices' votes that are consistent with certain attitudes; it cannot establish that such attitudes *cause* those votes.[87] That is because it uses those same votes as evidence that the atti-tudes exist. Accordingly, the attitudinal model cannot show that the justices' eco-nomic liberalism or conservatism causes them to vote in favor of employees or employers because it cites the same votes as evidence of economic liberalism or conservatism.[88] To suggest a causal relationship, under such circumstances, would be to indulge in circular reasoning, which is pointless. Thus, two prominent judicial behaviorists have observed that, based on the attitudinal model, one cannot say that attitudes *cause* votes; one can say only that "judges tend to behave *as if* their attitudes and values governed their voting choices."[89]

Organizational

Interest groups, most of which are private, nongovernmental organizations (e.g., National Association of Realtors, National Rifle Association, American Association of Retired Persons), influence judicial decisions indirectly and directly. Their principal means of indirect influence is to support or oppose the selection of particular judicial candidates. In other words, groups try to influence judicial decisions by influencing the selection of the judges who will make those decisions. Their support and their opposition are most visible with respect to Supreme Court nominations, but groups also work for and against candidates for lower federal court judgeships and state court judgeships.

For example, in 1979, the National Rifle Association (N.R.A.) worked to defeat President Carter's nomination of Representative Abner Mikva (D.-IL.) to the U.S. Court of Appeals for the District of Columbia Circuit because Mikva had consistently supported gun-control legislation. The Senate confirmed Mikva, but only by a 58–31 margin, after a bitter battle.[90] In the ten states in which judges run for election as the nominees of political parties, labor unions and business organizations often raise money for and contribute money to judicial campaigns. Fund raising is especially important in judicial elections in large states, such as Texas, where a partisan campaign for a seat on the state supreme court can cost more than $1 million.[91] In those states, there is no question that interest groups influence judicial selection; the real question is whether their influence is improper.

Federal judges are appointed, not elected, so interest groups cannot contribute money to nominees for federal judgeships. Instead, they build support for or opposition to a nominee, both in the Congress and in the country. In 1991, the groups that opposed President Bush's nomination of Judge Clarence Thomas to the Supreme Court devised a four-part plan to defeat the nominee. It included: (1) making sure that Senators who would be likely to oppose Judge Thomas would, in fact, oppose him; (2) convincing undecided senators, especially Republicans who supported abortion rights, and Southern Democrats, to oppose Thomas; (3) mobilizing constituents to send postcards and to make telephone calls to their senators, expressing their opposition to Thomas; and (4) convincing editorial boards of local newspapers around the country to oppose him.[92] The plan failed, as the Senate confirmed Judge Thomas by a 52–48 vote; it nevertheless produced the most votes ever cast in the Senate against a successful Supreme Court nominee.[93]

Interest groups need not always campaign for or against a nominee to influence judicial selection; sometimes, their *potential* opposition is enough to subtly influence a President's choice. For example, in 1990, President George Bush anticipated opposition from conservative groups if he nominated a well-known moderate and opposition from liberal groups if he nominated a well-known conservative. He chose the largely unknown David Souter to avoid arousing strong opposition from either the left or the right.[94] Similarly, President Clinton chose moderates Ruth Bader Ginsburg (1993) and Stephen Breyer (1994) for the Court, apparently to avoid determined opposition from conservative groups.[95]

The other way in which interest groups influence judicial decisions indirectly is to publish their views on emerging legal issues in **law reviews** (or **law journals**), which are student-edited periodicals that most law schools produce. Judges read law review articles, and sometimes cite them in opinions, so lawyers who work for interest groups write to influence the outcomes of future cases. There is a tradition of interest groups using law review articles to influence judicial decisions. Lawyers for the **National Association for the Advancement of Colored People (N.A.A.C.P.)** wrote often in conjunction with their successful challenges to racial segregation in education during the 1940s and 1950s.[96] In the early 1970s, lawyers for women's groups wrote law review articles that paved the way for landmark decisions that ended many forms of discrimination against women.[97] In the 1990s, the N.R.A. encouraged scholars who opposed gun control to write law review articles that supported the N.R.A.'s interpretation of the Second Amendment.[98]

Interest groups influence judicial decisions directly by **sponsoring litigation** and by filing *amicus curiae* **briefs** during litigation. When an interest group sponsors litigation, it pays the attorney's fees and court costs for the party it supports, usually the plaintiff in civil litigation. The party may have his own lawyer, or lawyers who work for the group may represent him.[99] The American Civil Liberties Union (A.C.L.U.) and the N.A.A.C.P.'s **Legal Defense Fund (L.D.F.)** pioneered group sponsorship of litigation. L.D.F.-sponsored litigation during the 1940s and 1950s resulted in Supreme Court decisions that outlawed racial segregation in education, from kindergarten through graduate and professional programs.

In the 1990s, a wide array of groups, from the conservative **American Center for Law and Justice** to the liberal **National Women's Law Center**, sponsored litigation. The National Women's Law Center and **Trial Lawyers for Public Justice** represented female undergraduates who sued their colleges in federal court for denying them the same athletic opportunities that their male classmates received.[100] The American Center for Law and Justice and the **Rutherford Institute** represented student religious groups, anti-abortion advocates, and religious schools in litigation at the Supreme Court.[101] Interest groups were also active in state courts in the 1990s. Group-sponsored lawsuits upheld an anti-gay rights ordinance in Colorado, invalidated an assisted-suicide law in Oregon, and overturned an anti-illegal immigration ballot initiative in California.[102]

Nevertheless, most groups prefer to file *amicus curiae* briefs rather than to sponsor litigation because it is much less expensive to be an *amicus* than it is to sponsor litigation, yet an *amicus* can still present arguments to the court, albeit only in writing.[103] It is not surprising, then, that nearly 200 groups joined in filing more than thirty *amicus curiae* briefs with the Supreme Court in *Planned Parenthood of Southeastern Pennsylvania v. Casey.*[104] Amicus curiae ("friend of the court") briefs are the work of groups that are interested in a case, but are not parties to it. Early in the twentieth century, these briefs were neutral efforts to inform courts about matters with which they were unfamiliar, such as the social and physical consequences of child labor. Today, *amicus curiae* briefs take sides, and present arguments for the party they favor that include data or perspectives that the party's lawyer does not present in writing or orally.

The Supreme Court has more "friends" than any other court. Its Rule 37 permits a nonparty to file a brief in a case, with the consent of the parties or the Court, if the brief "brings to the attention of the Court relevant matter not already brought to its attention by the parties."[105] The Court's high-profile cases attract a flood of *amici*; for example, during the 1995–1996 term, groups filed *amicus curiae* briefs in nearly 90 percent of the cases in which the Court heard oral arguments.[106] The Court has more "friends" now than in the past; in 1980–1981, 71 percent of its orally argued cases attracted *amicus curiae* briefs, while in 1965–1966, the comparable figure was 35 percent.[107]

Interest-group efforts to influence court decisions show how law and politics intersect. Groups try to affect judicial selection because they care about the law, but they affect judicial selection by relying on political skills. Those skills enable them to build coalitions and public support, and to convince voters or legislators to support certain candidates and to reject others. Groups write law review articles and *amicus curiae* briefs, or sponsor litigation, because they care about public policy, but their audience is lawyers and judges, so they rely primarily on legal arguments that contend that the results favored are good law. For example, a group that asks the Supreme Court to outlaw the death penalty cannot win by showing that the death penalty discriminates against racial minorities or causes the executions of innocent people; it can win only by showing that the death penalty is "cruel and unusual" punishment prohibited by the Eighth Amendment to the U.S. Constitution. The latter is a *legal* argument, despite its *political* implications.

Institutional

Institutional influences, including the ways in which courts are structured, the rules by which they operate, and their relationships to the public and to other branches of government, affect their decisions, regardless of the judges' public policy preferences. Institutional influences can cause judges to vote **strategically** instead of **sincerely** (according to their policy preferences). When judges vote strategically, they put their policy preferences aside in order to achieve a majority or to avoid alienating the public or another branch of government.[108]

Colleagues are perhaps the most important institutional influence. Judge Alex Kozinski of the U.S. Court of Appeals for the Ninth Circuit has observed that colleagues constrain each other. District court judges' opinions are subject to review (and reversal) by appellate judges. Appellate judges hear cases in three-member panels, so the author of a majority opinion must convince at least one colleague, preferably two, to join his opinion. "Even then," Judge Kozinski notes, "Litigants petition for rehearing and *en banc* review with annoying regularity. Your shortcuts, errors and oversights are mercilessly paraded before the entire court and, often enough, someone will call for an *en banc* vote."[109] Thus, the desire to avoid reversal can outweigh the desire to advance one's policy preferences, thereby constraining judicial behavior. As a result, according to Judge Patricia Wald of the U.S. Court of Appeals for the District of Columbia Circuit:,

> The elegant prose, the visionary idea, the qualitative leap forward in the law will probably be cancelled by the practical necessity of getting consensus among more cautious colleagues. Final opinions will usually be committee products with all the obstacles to virtuoso performance that entails.[110]

Supreme Court justices do not fear reversal, but the need to build majorities constrains them too. The late Justice Harry Blackmun, who served on the Supreme Court from 1970 until 1994, said of coalition building there:

> One thing that the public often does not appreciate is that much of what we do, up here, is done ... by way of compromise. There are nine of us. And ... many times, the prevailing opinion, it might be five to four, or six to three, or even seven to two sometimes, there are paragraphs or sentences or statements in the prevailing opinion that the primary author would prefer not to have there. But in order to get five votes together we have to get something that those five can agree to. We try to accommodate everyone that we can. But, sometimes, a judgement here is by a vote of five.[111]

The justices compromise in written memos that they exchange during the opinion-writing process. Some memos openly acknowledge that their purpose is compromise. For example, during the 1983–1984 Supreme Court term, then-Associate Justice Rehnquist, in a memo to Chief Justice Burger and Justices Powell and O'Connor, wrote:

> I have been *negotiating* with John Stevens for considerable time in order to produce a fifth vote in my *Bildisco* opinion. I have agreed to make the following changes in the currently circulating draft, and he has agreed to join if I do [emphasis added].[112]

Other memos are less direct, but still offer a vote for the majority in return for changes in the majority opinion. A classic example is a memo from Chief Justice Harlan Stone to Justice Owen Roberts during the Court's consideration of *Cantwell v. Connecticut* (1940).[113] It said:

> I doubt if we are very far apart in the *Cantwell* case, but in order that you might get exactly my views, I have written them out and enclosed them herewith. If you feel that you could agree with me, I think you would find no difficulty in making some changes in your opinion which would make it unnecessary for me to say anything.[114]

It is difficult to reject such an offer when rejection would mean the loss of a majority. That is why Justice Samuel Miller accommodated the wishes of Justice Horace Gray, which Gray expressed in a memo to Miller in 1899. It said:

> After a careful reading of your opinion in *Shotwell v. Moore*, I am very sorry to be compelled to say that the first part of it ...is so contrary to my conviction, that I fear, unless it can be a good deal tempered, I shall have to deliver a separate opin-

ion on the lines of the enclosed memorandum. I am particularly troubled about this, because, if my scruples are not removed, and Justices Field, Bradley, and Lamar adhere to their dissent, your opinion will represent only four judges, half of those who took part in the case.[115]

Compromise occasionally causes justices to change their minds and switch sides during the opinion-writing process. It often causes them to support majority opinions with which they disagree in part. For example, in *Craig v. Boren* (1976), the Court considered the constitutionality of an Oklahoma law that prohibited males from buying beer until age 21, but that allowed females to buy "low" beer (3.2 percent alcohol) at age 18.[116] The Court invalidated the Oklahoma law, and announced that classifications based on sex were unconstitutional unless substantially related to an important governmental purpose. That meant that states had more freedom to classify according to sex than according to race or national origin; classifications based on race or national origin receive **strict scrutiny**, which means they are unconstitutional unless they serve a compelling governmental interest. Nevertheless, classifications based on sex would receive **heightened scrutiny**—that is, a state would have to prove that a law that treated men differently from women served an important public goal.

Heightened scrutiny was a compromise. Justice William Brennan, who wrote the majority opinion, would have preferred to apply strict scrutiny to sex-based classifications. Justice Thurgood Marshall agreed, but two votes were not enough. Therefore, Brennan agreed to accept heightened scrutiny, in return for which he obtained the votes of Justices Powell, Blackmun, Stewart, and Stevens.[117] Thus, Brennan and Marshall muted their policy preferences in order to build a majority and to move the law in the right direction, albeit not as far as they wanted to go. Brennan feared that if he did not compromise, the Court would apply **minimum scrutiny** to sex-based classifications, which would make them presumptively constitutional.[118]

Justice Brennan directed his strategic behavior in *Craig* toward his colleagues. Sometimes, justices must consider not only the views of their colleagues, but also those of the other branches of government and of the public.[119] They must take Congress into account because Congress can deny them salary increases, remove them from office by impeachment and conviction, and reduce their appellate jurisdiction.[120] That can force the Court to put its policy preferences aside and bow to the will of Congress, as it did in *Ex parte McCardle* (1869).[121] William McCardle was a Mississippi newspaper editor whom a military commission arrested in 1867 and held for trial, pursuant to one of Congress's **Reconstruction Acts**, which governed the former Confederate states shortly after the Civil War.[122] The charges against McCardle derived from editorials he had published that criticized the generals who commanded military districts in those states.[123]

McCardle sought a *writ of habeas corpus* (see Chapter 2) in a federal circuit (i.e., appellate) court, and argued that military detentions and trials of civilians were unconstitutional. The court denied his request, and McCardle appealed to the Supreme Court under an 1867 law that authorized appeals from circuit court decisions in cases that involved detentions that allegedly violated the Constitution or a federal statute.[124] The Supreme Court heard oral arguments, and the justices' questions to the lawyers suggested that they would decide in McCardle's favor. That angered congressional leaders, who feared that the Court would use *McCardle* to invalidate the military governments they had established in the former Confederacy.

Congress quickly repealed the 1867 law that was the basis for McCardle's appeal, before the justices could decide the case. The Court then heard new arguments about Congress's authority to withdraw jurisdiction in a case after oral arguments. The justices concluded that the repeal of the 1867 law ended their jurisdiction in *McCardle*; "this court cannot proceed to pronounce judgment in this case, for it has no longer jurisdiction of the appeal," their unanimous opinion said.[125] Thus, the justices deferred to Congress, despite their opposition to military prosecutions of civilians, because they feared permanent damage to the Court's institutional strength if they decided for McCardle and Congress ignored their decision.

The justices must also take the American public into account, because public respect for the law is essential to the Court's continued institutional strength. Justices Kennedy, O'Connor, and Souter took the public into account in *Planned Parenthood of Southeastern Pennsylvania v. Casey*, wherein their joint opinion preserved the constitutional right to an abortion that the Court had announced nineteen years before in *Roe v. Wade*. The three justices believed that honoring a precedent on which Americans had come to rely, even an arguably flawed one, was necessary to preserve the public's faith in the Court and respect for the law.[126] They wrote:

> A decision to overrule *Roe's* essential holding under the existing circumstances would address error, if error there was, at the cost of both profound and unnecessary damage to the Court's legitimacy, and to the Nation's commitment to the rule of law. It is therefore imperative to adhere to the essence of *Roe's* original decision, and we do so today.[127]

McCardle and *Casey* show that even at the Supreme Court, decisions do not always result from the justices' public policy preferences. Both decisions turned on a concern for the Court's institutional integrity, while *stare decisis* was also pivotal in *Casey*. Still, justices' public policy preferences matter; after all, the four dissenters in *Casey* wanted to overturn *Roe* and end the constitutional right to an abortion. Thus, it is necessary to reconcile the multiple influences that can shape judicial decisions. That is the task of the following section.

RECONCILING LEGAL AND POLITICAL PERSPECTIVES

H. W. Perry, Jr., has criticized his fellow political scientists for showing a "lack of appreciation" for the legal influences on judicial decisions, which he contends causes lawyers to disregard political scientists' work on courts.[128] Perry may have been unduly pessimistic about political scientists' visibility among lawyers. For instance, the required reading for a first-year course at Vermont Law School in the fall 1999 term included two books by political scientists.[129] Still, Perry is correct that, even at the Supreme Court, legal factors influence decisions more than political scientists generally acknowledge.

Justices often grant or deny *cert.* in cases regardless of their merits, as when appellate circuits have resolved the same issue differently.[130] The same occurs in cases that do not arouse the justices' policy preferences. In those cases, justices consider whether: (1) the issues are presented clearly and "squarely"; (2) the facts are unambiguous; (3) it is possible to decide the major issue or it is necessary to decide a secondary issue first; and (4) potential problems exist, such as standing or mootness.[131]

When policy preferences are aroused, justices who believe they will win usually vote for *cert.*, and those who fear they will lose usually vote against *cert.*, unless an overriding institutional influence intervenes.[132] For example, the Court felt compelled to grant *cert.* in *United States v. Nixon* (1974), and to decide whether President Nixon could defy an order of a federal district court to relinquish tape recordings that were evidence in criminal trials.[133] Thus, Perry concludes, the *cert.* process is neither wholly legalistic nor entirely political; both legal and political influences affect it, and the latter include institutional concerns in addition to the justices' policy preferences.[134]

Multiple influences also affect outcomes in cases that receive full consideration. Legal influences are prominent when the precedents, statutes, or constitutional provisions that guide the result are sufficiently clear and applicable to the facts at hand to limit the exercise of judicial discretion.[135] Most cases that state courts and lower federal courts decide fit into this category. Therefore, legal influences account for most decisions by most courts.[136] Attitudinal (and sometimes organizational) influences are important when: (1) the evidence is contradictory or equally compelling on both sides; (2) a new area of law is involved, and no precedents exist; or (3) the issues trigger the judges' policy preferences, and judicial lawmaking results.[137]

Attitudinal influences were important in *Davis v. Davis*, which the Tennessee Supreme Court decided in 1992.[138] At issue was whether Tennessee could force a man to become a father. Before divorcing, the Davises had placed in frozen storage seven of Mrs. Davis's eggs, fertilized by Mr. Davis's sperm. After the divorce, Mrs. Davis sought custody of the "frozen embryos" so she could donate them to a childless couple. Mr. Davis argued that donation would force him to become a father against his will; therefore, he sought custody of the embryos in order to discard them. The Court agreed with Mr. Davis, reasoning that because Mrs. Davis could undergo *in-vitro* fertilization again or could adopt a child with her new husband, her interest in donation was less significant than Mr. Davis's interest in avoiding involuntary fatherhood. Thus, the Court awarded custody of the embryos to Mr. Davis. The judges' public policy preference that Tennessee not force Mr. Davis to become a father necessarily determined their conclusion because no statute or prior court decision was available to guide them.

Institutional influences often shape judicial decisions in the most controversial cases. For example, the need for unanimity affected the outcome in *Brown v. Board of Education*, wherein the Supreme Court outlawed racial segregation in public schools.[139] The justices feared that a nonunanimous decision would encourage segregated school districts to resist desegregation more vigorously than a unanimous decision would. They therefore compromised and achieved unanimity. A draft opinion in *Brown* had urged desegregation "at the earliest practicable date," and had not determined whether to limit relief to the plaintiffs or to extend it to all black children who attended segregated schools. The final opinion, in contrast, required desegregation "with all deliberate speed," and limited relief to the *Brown* plaintiffs. It accommodated justices who believed that desegregation would occur sooner if the Court showed some sympathy for the concerns of whites and promised that desegregation would be gradual.[140] The unanimous result was necessary for the Court to convince reluctant school districts that it was serious about desegregation.

Thus, Perry's observation that the Supreme Court's *cert.* process is neither wholly legalistic nor wholly political characterizes judicial decision making in general. It is a complex process that reflects legal and political influences.[141] Moreover, the political influences are not merely attitudinal; they are organizational and institutional too.[142]

CONCLUSION

Neither law nor politics alone can account for judicial decisions; both law and politics affect case outcomes. The legal model is still relevant because law still matters to judges. Law matters most when precedents and statutory or constitutional language make the correct result clear. The correct result is clear in most cases. Politics matters in unprecedented and controversial cases. The attitudinal and rational-choice models have broadened and deepened our understanding of the results in those circumstances.

Thus, both law and political science help us understand courts because courts operate at the crossroads of law and politics. That means that you should appreciate both the legal and the political influences on judicial decisions. *Planned Parenthood of Southeastern Pennsylvania v. Casey*, which follows, reflects both types of influence. As you read, identify the multiple influences at work in the case. Then decide whether the influences that shaped the Kennedy–O'Connor–Souter joint opinion justified the result.

Epilogue: The Law and Politics of Abortion

Planned Parenthood of Southeastern Pennsylvania v. Casey
505 U.S. 833 (1992)

JUSTICE O'CONNOR, JUSTICE KENNEDY, and JUSTICE SOUTER announced the judgment of the Court. [**Editor's Note:**] Justices Stevens and Blackmun joined those portions of the Kennedy–O'Connor–Souter opinion that upheld the essence of *Roe v. Wade* and that invalidated Pennsylvania's spousal notification rule for married women who sought abortions there. Those positions prevailed by a 5–4 vote].

I

Liberty finds no refuge in a jurisprudence of doubt. Yet 19 years after our holding that the Constitution protects a woman's right to terminate her pregnancy in its early stages,... *Roe v. Wade*, 410 U.S. 113 (1973) that definition of liberty is still questioned. [T]he United States [in an *amicus curiae* brief], as it has done in five other cases in the last decade, again asks us to overturn *Roe*....

At issue in these cases are five provisions of the Pennsylvania Abortion Control Act of 1982 as amended in 1988 and 1989.... The Act requires that a woman seeking an abortion give her informed consent prior to the abortion procedure, and specifies that she be provided with certain information at least 24 hours before the abortion is performed. For a minor to obtain an abortion, the Act requires the informed consent of one of her parents, but provides for a judicial bypass option if the minor does not wish to or cannot obtain a parent's consent. Another provision of the Act requires that, unless certain exceptions apply, a married woman seeking an abortion must sign a statement indicating that she has notified her husband of her intended abortion. The Act exempts compliance with these three requirements in the event of a "medical emergency," which is defined in ...the Act. In addition to the above provisions regulating the performance of abortions, the Act imposes certain reporting requirements on facilities that provide abortion services.

After considering the fundamental constitutional questions resolved by *Roe*, principles of institutional integrity, and the rule of *stare decisis*, we are led to conclude this: the essential holding of *Roe v. Wade* should be retained and once again reaffirmed.

It must be stated at the outset and with clarity that *Roe's* essential holding, the holding we affirm, has three parts. First is a recognition of the right of the woman to choose to have an abortion before viability and to obtain it without undue interference from the State. Before viability, the State's interests are not strong enough to support a prohibition of abortion or the imposition of a substantial obstacle to the woman's effective right to elect the procedure. Second is a confirmation of the State's power to restrict abortions after fetal viability, if the law contains exceptions for pregnancies which endanger a woman's life or health. And third is the principle that the State has legitimate interests from the outset of the pregnancy in protecting the health of the woman and the life of the fetus that may become a child. These principles do not contradict one another; and we adhere to each.

II

Our law affords constitutional protection to personal decisions relating to marriage, procreation, contraception, family relationships, child rearing, and education.... These matters, involving the most intimate and personal choices a person may make in a lifetime, choices central to personal dignity and autonomy, are central to the liberty protected by the Fourteenth Amendment. At the heart of liberty is the right to define one's own concept of existence, of meaning, of the universe, and of the mystery of human life. Beliefs about these matters could not define the attributes of personhood were they formed under compulsion of the State.

It should be recognized, moreover, that in some critical respects the abortion decision is of the same character as the decision to use contraception, to which [the Court's prior decisions] afford constitutional protection. We have no doubt as to the correctness of those decisions. They support the reasoning in *Roe* relating to the woman's liberty because they involve personal decisions concerning not only the meaning of procreation but also human responsibility and respect for it....

While we appreciate the weight of the arguments made on behalf of the State in the case before us, arguments which in their ultimate formulation conclude that *Roe* should be overruled, the reservations any of us may have in reaffirming the central holding of *Roe* are outweighed by the explication of individual liberty we have given combined with the force of *stare decisis*. We now turn to that doctrine.

III

A

The obligation to follow precedent begins with necessity, and a contrary necessity marks its outer limit. With Cardozo, we recognize that no judicial system could do society's work if it eyed each issue afresh in every case that raised it. See B. Cardozo, *The Nature of the Judicial Process* (1921). Indeed, the very concept of the rule of law underlying our own Constitution requires such continuity over time that a respect for precedent is, by definition, indispensable....

So in this case we may inquire whether *Roe*'s central rule has been found unworkable; whether the rule's limitation on state power could be removed without serious inequity to those who have relied upon it or significant damage to the stability of the society governed by the rule in question; whether the law's growth in the intervening years has left *Roe*'s central rule a doctrinal anachronism discounted by society; and whether *Roe*'s premises of fact have so far changed in the ensuing two decades as to render its central holding somehow irrelevant or unjustifiable in dealing with the issue it addressed.

1

Although *Roe* has engendered opposition, it has in no sense proven "unworkable," ...representing as it does a simple limitation beyond which a state law is unenforceable....

2

The inquiry into reliance counts the costs of a rule's repudiation as it would fall on those who have relied reasonably on the rule's continued application....

... [F]or two decades of economic and social developments, people have organized intimate relationships and made choices that define their views of themselves and their places in society, in reliance on the availability of abortion in the event that contraception should fail. The ability of women to participate equally in the economic and social life of the Nation has been facilitated by their ability to control their reproductive lives....

3

No evolution of legal principle has left *Roe's* doctrinal footings weaker than they were in 1973. No development of constitutional law since the case was decided has implicitly or explicitly left *Roe* behind as a mere survivor of obsolete constitutional thinking.

4

We have seen how time has overtaken some of *Roe's* factual assumptions: advances in maternal health care allow for abortions safe to the mother later in pregnancy than was true in 1973,... and advances in neonatal care have advanced viability to a point somewhat earlier.... But these facts go only to the scheme of time limits on the realization of competing interests, and the divergences from the factual premises of 1973 have no bearing on the validity of *Roe's* central holding, that viability marks the earliest point at which the State's interest in fetal life is constitutionally adequate to justify a legislative ban on nontherapeutic abortions. The soundness or unsoundness of that constitutional judgment in no sense turns on whether viability occurs at approximately 28 weeks, as was usual at the time of *Roe*, at 23 to 24 weeks, as it sometimes does today, or at some moment even slightly earlier in pregnancy, as it may if fetal respiratory capacity can somehow be enhanced in the future....

5

The sum of the precedential inquiry to this point shows *Roe's* underpinnings unweakened in any way affecting its central holding.... Within the bounds of normal *stare decisis* analysis, then, and subject to the considerations on which it customarily turns, the stronger argument is for affirming *Roe's* central holding, with whatever degree of personal reluctance any of us may have, not for overruling it.

B

[**Editor's Note:** This section contrasts *Roe* with two Supreme Court decisions that the justices subsequently overruled. It explains why the Court was justified in overruling the other cases, but would err if it overruled *Roe*.]

C

... Our analysis would not be complete, however, without explaining why overruling *Roe's* central holding would not only reach an unjustifiable result under principles of *stare decisis*, but would seriously weaken the Court's capacity to exercise the judicial power and to function as the Supreme Court of a Nation dedicated to the rule of law.

... [O]nly the most convincing justification under accepted standards of precedent could suffice to demonstrate that a later decision overruling the first was anything but a surrender to political pressure, and an unjustified repudiation of the principle on which the Court stakes its authority in the first instance. So to overrule under fire in the absence of the most compelling reason to reexamine a watershed decision would subvert the Court's legitimacy beyond any serious question....

... A decision to overrule *Roe's* essential holding under the existing circumstances would address error, if error there was, at the cost of both profound and unnecessary damage to the Court's legitimacy, and to the Nation's commitment to the rule of law. It is therefore imperative to adhere to the essence of *Roe's* original decision, and we do so today.

IV

From what we have said so far it follows that it is a constitutional liberty of the woman to have some freedom to terminate her pregnancy.

We conclude the line should be drawn at viability, so that before that time the woman has a right to choose to terminate her pregnancy. We adhere to this principle for two reasons. First, as we have said, is the doctrine of *stare decisis*....

The second reason is that the concept of viability, as we noted in *Roe*, is the time at which there is a realistic possibility of maintaining and nourishing a life outside the womb, so that the independent existence of the second life can in reason and all fairness be the object of state protection that now overrides the rights of the woman.... The viability line also has, as a practical matter, an element of fairness. In some broad sense it might be said that a woman who fails to act before viability has consented to the State's intervention on behalf of the developing child....

Though the woman has a right to choose to terminate or continue her pregnancy before viability, it does not at all follow that the State is prohibited from taking steps to ensure that this choice is thoughtful and informed. Even in the earliest stages of pregnancy, the State may enact rules and regulations designed to encourage her to know that there are philosophic and social arguments of great weight that can be brought to bear in favor of continuing the pregnancy to full term and that there are procedures and institutions to allow adoption of unwanted children as well as a certain degree of state assistance if the mother chooses to raise the child herself....

A finding of an undue burden is a shorthand for the conclusion that a state regulation has the purpose or effect of placing a substantial obstacle in the path of a woman seeking an abortion of a nonviable fetus. A statute with this purpose is invalid because the means chosen by the State to further the interest in potential life must be calculated to inform the woman's free choice, not hinder it.

... In our considered judgment, an undue burden is an unconstitutional burden...

V

[**Editor's Note:** This section of the opinion upholds the restrictions on abortion contained in the Pennsylvania law except spousal notification, which violated the "undue burden" standard].

Chief Justice Rehnquist, with whom **Justice White, Justice Scalia**, and **Justice Thomas** join, concurring in the judgment in part and dissenting in part.

... We believe that *Roe* was wrongly decided, and that it can and should be overruled consistently with our traditional approach of the plurality in *Webster v. Reproductive Health Services*, 492 U.S. 490 (1989), and uphold the challenged provisions of the Pennsylvania statute in their entirety.

Justice Scalia, with whom the **Chief Justice, Justice White**, and **Justice Thomas** join, concurring in the judgment in part and dissenting in part.

... The states may, if they wish, permit abortion-on-demand, but the Constitution does not *require* them to do so. The permissibility of abortion, and the limitations upon it, are to be resolved like most important questions in our democracy: by citizens trying to persuade one another and then voting....

That is, quite simply, the issue in this case: not whether the power of a woman to abort her unborn child is a "liberty" in the absolute sense; or even whether it is a liberty of great importance to many women. Of course it is both. The issue is whether it is a liberty protected by the Constitution of the United States. I am sure it is not....

QUESTIONS FOR DISCUSSION

1. What statute was at issue in this case, and how did it restrict abortion rights?
2. Why did the Bush Administration file an *amicus curiae* brief in this case?
3. How did the Court's decision differ from the view that the Bush Administration expressed in its *amicus curiae* brief?
4. What was the "central holding" of *Roe v. Wade?*
5. How did *stare decisis* influence the joint opinion in *Casey* by Justices Kennedy, O'Connor, and Souter?
6. Had new social and medical circumstances made *Roe* "unworkable" by 1992?
7. What institutional influences shaped the Kennedy–O'Connor–Souter joint opinion, and in what way(s)?
8. Why did the dissenters insist that "*Roe* was wrongly decided," and that the Court should have overruled it?
9. What mechanism did the dissenters think should resolve the abortion issue?
10. What practical effect(s) would a decision in *Casey* to overrule *Roe* have had on efforts by women to obtain abortions?
11. Did the institutional interests that the joint opinion cited justify the result in *Casey?* Explain.
12. If not, what alternative result should the Court have reached, and why?

NOTES

1. The quote, by James L. Gibson, appears in Lawrence Baum, *The Puzzle of Judicial Behavior* (Ann Arbor, Mich.: University of Michigan Press, 1997), p. 18.
2. Richard A. Brisbin, Jr., "Slaying the Dragon: Segal, Spaeth and the Function of Law in Supreme Court Decision Making," *American Journal of Political Science* 40 (1996): 1004–1017.

3. Baum, *The Puzzle of Judicial Behavior*, p. 18.

4. Erwin Chemerinsky, "The Crowded Center," *American Bar Association Journal* (October 1994): 78–81.

5. Baum, *The Puzzle of Judicial Behavior*, pp. 6–7.

6. See, for example, Lee Epstein and Jack Knight, *The Choices Justices Make* (Washington, D.C.: CQ Press, 1998); Robert A. Carp and Ronald Stidham, *The Federal Courts*, Third Edition (Washington, D.C.: CQ Press, 1998), p. 141; Joseph F. Kobylka, "The Mysterious Case of Establishment Clause Litigation," in Lee Epstein, ed., *Contemplating Courts* (Washington, D.C.: CQ Press, 1995), pp. 93–128; Lee Epstein and Joseph F. Kobylka, *The Supreme Court and Legal Change: Abortion and the Death Penalty* (Chapel Hill, N.C.: University of North Carolina Press, 1992), p. 310.

7. C. Herman Pritchett, "The Development of Judicial Research," in Joel Grossman and Joseph Tanenhaus, eds., *Frontiers of Judicial Research* (New York: Wiley, 1969), p. 42. The same quote also appears in H. W. Perry, Jr., *Deciding to Decide: Agenda Setting in the United States Supreme Court* (Cambridge, Mass.: Harvard University Press, 1991), p. 3.

8. Erwin Chemerinsky, *Federal Jurisdiction*, Third Edition (New York: Aspen Law & Business, 1999), 41.

9. Gerald Gunther and Kathleen M. Sullivan, *Constitutional Law*, Thirteenth Edition (Westbury, N.Y.: The Foundation Press, 1997), p. 28.

10. *Id.*

11. Chemerinsky, *Federal Jurisdiction*, Third Edition, pp. 48–49.

12. *Id.*, p. 59.

13. Gunther and Sullivan, *Constitutional Law*, Thirteenth Edition, p. 27.

14. Bruce E. Altschuler and Celia A. Sgroi, *Understanding Law in a Changing Society* (Englewood Cliffs, N.J.: Prentice-Hall, 1992), p. 115.

15. *Id.*

16. 117 S. Ct. 2312.

17. The Line Item Veto Act began at Volume Two of the United States Code, Section 691. However, the Court declared it unconstitutional in 1998, so it is no longer part of the United States Code.

18. Carp and Stidham, *The Federal Courts*, Third Edition, p. 49.

19. *Clinton v. City of New York*, 118 S. Ct. 2091 (1998).

20. In *Clinton*, the Court proceeded to declare that the Line-Item Veto Act violated the **Presentment Clause**, which is Article I, Section 7, Clause 2 of the Constitution, and which, in the Court's view, requires that the president either approve or reject a bill in its entirety.

21. Chemerinsky, *Federal Jurisdiction*, Third Edition, p. 127.

22. Gunther and Sullivan, *Constitutional Law*, Thirteenth Edition, p. 43.

23. *Id.*, p. 44.

24. Chemerinsky, *Federal Jurisdiction*, Third Edition, p. 126.

25. 416 U.S. 312.

26. Altschuler and Sgroi, *Understanding Law in a Changing Society*, p. 116.

27. *Id.*; See also Carp and Stidham, *The Federal Courts*, Third Edition, pp. 50–51.

28. Chemerinsky, *Federal Jurisdiction*, Third Edition, p. 116.

29. *Pacific Gas & Electric Company v. State Energy Resources Conservation & Development Commission*, 461 U.S. 190 (1983).

30. Chemerinsky, *Federal Jurisdiction*, Third Edition, pp. 116–117.

31. Gunther and Sullivan, *Constitutional Law*, Thirteenth Edition, pp. 44–45.

32. *Id.*, p. 144.

33. *Id.*

34. *Id.*, p. 46.

35. Chemerinsky, *Federal Jurisdiction*, Third Edition, pp. 144–145.

36. 506 U.S. 224.

37. Carp and Stidham, *The Federal Courts*, Third Edition, p. 55.

38. Harry T. Edwards, "Public Misperceptions Concerning the 'Politics' of Judging: Dispelling Some Myths About the D.C. Circuit," *University of Colorado Law Review* 56 (1985): 619–646.

39. Court Statistics Project, *State Court Caseload Statistics, 1996* (Williamsburg, Va.: National Center for State Courts, 1997), p. 52.

40. Altschuler and Sgroi, *Understanding Law in a Changing Society*, p. 117.

41. Jeffrey A. Segal and Harold J. Spaeth, *The Supreme Court and the Attitudinal Model* (New York: Cambridge University Press, 1993), p. 199.

42. *Cert. denied*, 375 U.S. 889 (1963).

43. Epstein and Kobylka, *The Supreme Court and Legal Change*, pp. 42–43.

44. *Id.*, p. 43.

45. *Id.*

46. Perry, *Deciding to Decide: Agenda Setting in the United States Supreme Court*, p. 3.

47. Baum, *The Puzzle of Judicial Behavior*, p. 67.

48. Harry T. Edwards, "Public Misperceptions Concerning the "Politics" of Judging: Dispelling Some Myths About the D.C. Circuit," *University of Colorado Law Review* 56 (1985): 619–646.

49. *Id.*

50. *Id.*

51. *Id.*

52. Alex Kozinski, "What I Ate for Breakfast and Other Mysteries of Judicial Decision Making," in David M. O'Brien, ed., *Judges on Judging: Views from the Bench* (Chatham, N.J.: Chatham House, 1997), pp. 71–76.

53. *Id.*

54. *Id.*

55. The relevant portion of this statute appears at Title 18 of the United States Code, Section 844(e).

56. *United States v. Spruill*, 118 F.3d 221 (4th Cir. 1997).

57. Baum, *The Puzzle of Judicial Behavior*, p. 62.

58. Jeffrey Rosen, "The New Look of Liberalism on the Court," *The New York Times Magazine*, October 5, 1997, p. 58.

59. 117 S. Ct. 1997.

60. 473 U.S. 402.

61. Rosen, "The New Look of Liberalism on the Court," p. 58. Pursuant to *Aguilar*, a federal district court in New York City had issued an injunction that prohibited the City from sending public school teachers into parochial schools to provide remedial services. Twelve years later, the losing parties in *Aguilar*, who were the plaintiffs in *Agostini*, sought to have that injunction cancelled, pursuant to Rule 60(b)(5), which permits relief from decisions that are no longer viable because of a change in the law. They claimed that *Aguilar* was no longer good law because of two subsequent Supreme Court decisions that were contrary to it. On that basis, the Supreme Court revisited the constitutionality of the remedial education program in *Agostini*, and the majority upheld it, thereby overruling *Aguilar*. Justice Ginsburg, in dissent, argued that the plaintiffs' Rule 60(b)(5) motion only permitted the Supreme Court to decide whether

the district court had properly rejected the plaintiffs' request to cancel the injunction; it did not permit the Court to decide whether the remedial education program was constitutional. The latter question, in Ginsburg's view, was a matter for another case.

62. Lawrence Baum, *The Supreme Court*, Fifth Edition (Washington, D.C.: CQ Press, 1995), p. 149, quoted in Epstein and Knight, *The Choices Justices Make*, p. 177.

63. *Id.*

64. *Id.*

65. *Id.*

66. *Id.*, p. 317.

67. 367 U.S. 643.

68. 384 U.S. 436.

69. *Id.*, p. 317.

70. *Id.*

71. 501 U.S. 808.

72. James F. Simon, *The Center Holds: The Power Struggle Inside the Rehnquist Court* (New York: Simon & Schuster, 1995), p. 210.

73. *Id.*, p. 211.

74. Altschuler and Sgroi, *Understanding Law in a Changing Society*, p. 95.

75. *Id.*

76. *Id.*

77. *Id.*, p. 96.

78. Baum, *The Puzzle of Judicial Behavior*, p. 25.

79. *Id.*, p. 174.

80. Segal and Spaeth, *The Supreme Court and the Attitudinal Model*, p. 69.

81. Carp and Stidham, *The Federal Courts*, Third Edition, pp. 174–175.

82. Segal and Spaeth, *The Supreme Court and the Attitudinal Model*, p. 69.

83. Carp and Stidham, *The Federal Courts*, Third Edition, p. 175.

84. Jeffrey A. Segal, Donald R. Songer, and Charles M. Cameron, "Decision Making on the U.S. Courts of Appeals," in Lee Epstein, ed., *Contemplating Courts* (Washington, D.C.: CQ Press, 1995), p. 231.

85. Baum, *The Puzzle of Judicial Behavior*, p. 36.

86. *Id.*, p. 82.

87. *Id.*, p. 38.

88. *Id*, p. 40; see also Sheldon Goldman and Thomas Jahnige, *The Federal Courts as a Political System*, Third Edition (New York: Harper & Row, 1985), p. 137.

89. Goldman and Jahnige, *The Federal Courts as a Political System*, Third Edition, p. 137.

90. Ronald J. Hrebenar, *Interest Group Politics in America*, Third Edition (Armonk, N.Y.: M. E. Sharpe, 1997), p. 222.

91. *Id.*, p. 225.

92. *Id.*, p. 229.

93. Jane Mayer and Jill Abramson, *Strange Justice: The Selling of Clarence Thomas* (New York: Plume/Penguin, 1995), p. 348.

94. Gregory A. Caldeira and John R. Wright, "Lobbying for Justice: The Rise of Organized Conflict in the Politics of Federal Judgeships," in Epstein, ed., *Contemplating Courts*, pp. 44–70.

95. *Id.*, p. 70.

96. Hrebenar, *Interest Group Politics in America*, Third Edition, p. 225.

97. *Id.*

98. *Id.*

99. *Id.*, p. 226.
100. See: *Cohen v. Brown University*, 101 F.3d 155 (1st Cir. 1996); *Favia v. Indiana University of Pennsylvania*, 7 F.3d 332 (3d Cir. 1993); *Roberts v. Colorado State Board of Agriculture*, 998 F.2d 824 (10th Cir. 1993); and *Cook v. Colgate University*, 992 F.2d 17 (2nd Cir. 1993). For a discussion of these cases, see Brian L. Porto, "Completing the Revolution: Title IX as Catalyst for an Alternative Model of College Sports," *Seton Hall Journal of Sport Law* 8 (1998): 352--418.
101. Hrebenar, *Interest Group Politics in America*, Third Edition, p. 234.
102. *Id.*, p. 230.
103. *Id.*, p. 228; see also Alexander Wake, "Friends with Agendas," *American Bar Association Journal* (November 1996): 46–48.
104. Hrebenar, *Interest Group Politics in America*, Third Edition, p. 228.
105. Wake, "Friends with Agendas," pp. 46–48.
106. *Id.*
107. *Id.*
108. Epstein and Knight, *The Choices Justices Make*, p. 13.
109. Kozinski, "What I Ate for Breakfast and Other Mysteries of Judicial Decision Making," pp. 71–76.
110. Patricia M. Wald, "Some Real-Life Observations about Judging," *Indiana Law Review* 26 (1992): 173–186.
111. Phillip J. Cooper, *Battles on the Bench: Conflict Inside the Supreme Court* (Lawrence, Ks.: University Press of Kansas, 1995), pp. 139–140.
112. Epstein and Knight, *The Choices Justices Make*, p. 74.
113. 310 U.S. 296.
114. Walter F. Murphy, *Elements of Judicial Strategy* (Chicago: University of Chicago Press, 1964), p. 59.
115. Charles Fairman, *Mr. Justice Miller and the Supreme Court, 1862–1890* (Cambridge, Mass.: Harvard University Press, 1939), p. 320, quoted in Carp and Stidham, *The Federal Courts*, Third Edition, p. 162.
116. Epstein and Knight, *The Choices Justices Make*, p. 1.
117. *Id.*, p. 9.
118. *Id.*, p. 56.
119. *Id.*, p. 13.
120. *Id.*, pp. 142–143.
121. 74 U.S. (7 Wall.) 506.
122. Bernard Schwartz, *A History of the Supreme Court* (New York: Oxford University Press, 1993), p. 140.
123. *Id.*
124. *Id.*
125. *Id.*, p. 141.
126. Simon, *The Center Holds: The Power Struggle Inside the Rehnquist Court*, p. 157.
127. 505 U.S. 833 (1992).
128. Perry, *Deciding to Decide: Agenda Setting in the United States Supreme Court*, p. 3.
129. They were Lief Carter, *Reason in Law*, Fifth Edition (New York: Addison Wesley Longman, 1998); and Epstein and Knight, *The Choices Justices Make*.
130. *Id.*, p. 270.
131. *Id.*, p. 279
132. *Id.*, p. 280.
133. *Id.*

134. *Id.*, p. 289; see also Epstein and Knight, *The Choices Justices Make*, pp. 87–88.
135. Paul Brace and Melinda Gann Hall, "Integrated Models of Judicial Dissent," *Journal of Politics* 55 (1993): 914–935.
136. Carp and Stidham, *The Federal Courts*, Third Edition, p. 141.
137. *Id.*, p. 148.
138. 842 S.W. 2d 588.
139. 347 U.S. 483.
140. Mark Tushnet and Katya Lezin, "What Really Happened in *Brown v. Board of Education*," *Columbia Law Review* 91 (1991): 1867–1930.
141. Perry, *Deciding to Decide: Agenda Setting in the United States Supreme Court*, p. 289.
142. Brace and Hall, "Integrated Models of Judicial Dissent".

Chapter 9

THE LIMITS OF JUDICIAL
POLICY MAKING

INTRODUCTION

In his classic book, *Democracy in America*, Alexis DeTocqueville wrote that in the United States:

> … few laws can escape the searching analysis of the judicial power for any length of time, for there are few which are not prejudicial to some private interest or other, and none which may not be brought before a court of justice by the choice of parties, or by the necessity of the case.[1]

Those words are even more true at the dawn of the twenty-first century than they were in 1831–1832, when DeTocqueville visited America. Since the end of World War II, the size and power of government in America have increased dramatically; judicial power has grown tremendously as a part of that trend.[2]

The exercise of judicial power frequently results from the exercise of legislative power. When legislatures enact statutes to solve social and economic problems, disputes arise about the meanings of those statutes, and parties bring those disputes to courts for resolution.[3] Thus, the post-World War II "age of statutes" has been an "age of courts" too.[4] For example, in 1972, Congress enacted the **Education Amendments Act; Title IX** of that statute prohibited sex discrimination by colleges that received funds from the federal government.[5] Title IX did not specify, though, whether it prohibited sex discrimination throughout a college or only in those offices and departments that received federal funds. Thus, the reach of the Title IX prohibition became the subject of a lawsuit that the U.S. Supreme Court decided in 1984.[6]

Courts must not only determine the meanings (and the constitutionality) of statutes; they must also decide whether the manner in which administrative agencies (e.g., the U.S. Department of Education, the Wisconsin Department of Natural Resources, etc.) enforce statutes coincides with legislative intent and/or constitutional command.[7] The agencies are themselves often products of the post-World War II expansion of government, which has included an increased federal role in public education and greater state attention to environmental protection. Judicial review of administrative decisions makes courts even more important political institutions today than they were in DeTocqueville's time.

The growth of judicial power has changed the nature of civil lawsuits and the remedies that courts impose to resolve them. Courts still hear disputes about private rights, such as an injured skier's right to compensation from a ski area operator for her injuries (see Chapter 6). Yet they also hear an increasing number of disputes in which plaintiffs allege that public institutions (e.g., prisons, nursing homes, schools) have violated statutory requirements, constitutional rights, and/or administrative regulations. Plaintiffs in such **public law litigation** do not necessarily seek damages, as civil plaintiffs traditionally do, because damages will not make a prison safe, a nursing home clean, or a school district attentive to the needs of disabled children. Instead, they request **structural injunctions**, in which courts order defendant institutions to reform themselves.[8]

In other words, courts no longer just say no to illegal or unconstitutional actions; rather, they tell public institutions what to do and how to do it, sometimes for many years. For example, the same federal district judge who ordered the Kansas City (Mo.) School District to implement a desegregation plan in 1977 continued to supervise the operation of that plan in 1995.[9] In such cases, courts try to change defendants' future behavior instead of merely compensating plaintiffs for defendants' past wrongs.[10] The behavior at issue might be the treatment of inmates by a prison or the treatment of female athletes by a college. The remedy imposed might require the prison to stop censoring inmates' mail and to hire additional medical staff, or it might require the college to reinstate its women's softball team and to establish a women's soccer team within two years. In the Kansas City school desegregation case, the judge imposed an increase in property taxes to fund the desegregation plan,[11] and ordered salary increases for all but three of the Kansas City School District's nearly 5000 employees.[12]

Such remedies have generated an important debate among scholars of the judicial process. Scholars disagree vehemently about whether courts, which are not always accountable to the voters (e.g., federal courts), *should* make such broad policy decisions; they also disagree about whether courts, which are staffed by generalists and have limited access to information, *can* make those decisions competently. Furthermore, they disagree about whether courts' policy decisions produce the social change that the courts intend. This debate is the subject of the next section.

The Debate About Judicial Policy Making

Overview

The debate about judicial policy making pits supporters of **judicial activism** against supporters of **judicial restraint**. The former believe that courts should and can make broad public policy decisions; the latter believe that courts should not make such decisions and doubt that they can do so wisely. This debate also pits supporters of the **dynamic court** model against supporters of the **constrained court** model of judicial policy making.[13] The former believe that courts produce significant social reform; the latter believe that courts rarely, if ever, produce significant social reform.

Judicial Restraint Versus Judicial Activism

Judicial Restraint

Conflicting views about the wisdom of "majority rule" lie at the heart of the debate about judicial activism. Scholars and judges who revere majority rule and who believe that only the elected branches of government should make public policy reject judicial activism and favor restraint. Their colleagues who are skeptical about majority rule and who believe that courts best protect minority rights reject judicial restraint and favor activism, especially if they think that courts can make public policy wisely.[14]

Supporters of judicial restraint fear judicial tyranny. They contend that Americans' rights are most secure when legislators make public policy. That is because the difficulty of building legislative majorities can prevent the passage of unwise laws, and because legislators who pass unwise laws are accountable to the voters on election day. Our rights are threatened when courts make public policy because of the relative ease of building a judicial majority of three votes or five votes for an unwise decision, and because judges who make unwise decisions are not accountable to the voters on election day.[15] Professor Raoul Berger voiced this concern in a 1980 article. He wrote:

> We are dealing with a question of power: who is to govern in our democracy, who is to make policy choices for the nation—a group of unelected and virtually unaccountable Justices or the elected representatives of the people, indeed, the people themselves?[16]

Thus, supporters of judicial restraint would put more power in the hands of legislators and executives, and less power in the hands of judges.[17] One has even recommended that Congress restrict the power of federal courts to order expenditures of public funds, to interfere in the administration of state governments, and to oversee public institutions.[18] Supporters of judicial restraint are as concerned about who makes public policy as they are about what policies are made.[19]

Supporters of judicial restraint are especially critical of judicial activism in constitutional cases. They contend that judges should enforce the Constitution's clear commands. Judges should not use the Constitution's vague general commands as legal authority for imposing their personal policy preferences on the American people. To enforce clear constitutional language is to properly exercise the power of judicial review; to manipulate vague constitutional language is to "legislate" from the bench, which abuses judicial power.[20]

The late Justice Hugo Black, who supported judicial restraint, thought that the Supreme Court majority had legislated from the bench in *Griswold v. Connecticut* (1965), in which the Court held that the Constitution contains a **right of privacy** that entitles married couples to use contraceptive devices, and bars states from prohibiting married couples from using them.[21] Justice Black wrote a dissent in which he noted that there was no constitutional language or reasonable interpretation thereof that supported a right of privacy. The Court had crossed the boundary of proper judicial review by creating and seeking to enforce a right that the Constitution neither specified nor included by implication.[22] "Use of any such broad, unbounded judicial authority," Justice Black wrote, "would make of this Court's members a day-to-day constitutional convention."[23] Simply put, judges should read (and apply) the Constitution, not rewrite it.

Judge J. Clifford Wallace of the U.S. Court of Appeals for the Ninth Circuit shares Justice Black's preference for judicial restraint. He suggests that in constitutional cases judges should: (1) follow the clear language of the Constitution unless doing so would contradict the Founding Fathers' intent; (2) clarify unclear constitutional language consistent with the Founding Fathers' intent if that intent is reasonably certain; (3) clarify unclear constitutional language, when neither of the previous principles applies, by choosing the alternative that least restricts the policy-making discretion of elected officials; and, (4) when none of the previous principles applies, clarify unclear constitutional language according to the best estimate of the Founding Fathers' intent or in the manner most consistent with past practice.[24]

Those principles, in Judge Wallace's view, recognize the inherent value of democracy by leaving policy making to legislative majorities. Therefore, even wrong-headed policy making by legislative majorities is better than judicial policy making because in our constitutional scheme, policy making is the function of legislative, not judicial, majorities.[25] That is why Justice Black voted to uphold the Connecticut statute at issue in *Griswold*. No constitutional language prohibited Connecticut from outlawing the distribution or use of contraceptives, so the law should stand, even it was unwise and largely unenforceable.

Supporters of judicial restraint not only argue that courts *should not* make public policy because they lack accountability to the voters. They also argue that courts *cannot* make wise public policy because they are not equipped to do so. That is, unlike legislatures, courts lack the staffs, the financial resources, and the power to hold comprehensive hearings in which multiple witnesses can examine all aspects of a public policy issue and present a variety of viewpoints.[26] Legislatures are also more aware of society's needs than courts are because legislators are immersed in the political process, while judges are insulated from it.[27]

Perhaps the most important critique of the judicial capacity for policy making is contained in the writings of lawyer and political scientist Donald L. Horowitz.[28] The essence of Horowitz's critique is that courts are not suited to make public policy because they were not designed for that purpose. They were designed instead to resolve individual disputes, and they remain best suited to that purpose.[29]

According to Horowitz, six features of the judicial process leave courts ill suited to making broad policy decisions. First, judges are generalists who decide cases on many different subjects; therefore, they often lack the information necessary to make broad policy decisions and the expertise necessary to interpret the information that they do receive during litigation.[30] There is no judicial equivalent of the senator or representative who has made educational or health-care matters her specialty during her congressional career. Moreover, even if a judge could develop a specialty, chances are that few, if any, cases on that subject would land in his court, because judicial administrators assign cases to individual judges at random. Thus, a judge is likely to be inexperienced in the subject matter of most public law litigation.[31]

Second, the judicial process usually focuses on the parties' respective rights and duties rather than on policy alternatives for resolving social problems and the relative costs of those alternatives. That can result in structural injunctions that require school districts, prisons, and hospitals to rectify violations of constitutional rights regardless of the cost of the remedy. In other words, the nature of the judicial process causes judges who find violations of constitutional rights to order remedies without regard to their costs.[32]

Third, the judicial process proceeds case by case, which means that a single court decision cannot address a subject as comprehensively as a single piece of legislation can. That is why the Supreme Court, despite having decided cases concerning public school prayer since the 1960s, did not decide until 2000 that student-led prayers before high school football games were constitutional. That particular issue did not come to the Court until its 1999–2000 term. Thus, the judicial process is too slow and narrowly focused to make broad public policy decisions.[33]

Fourth, the judicial process functions only in response to the lawsuits that parties bring to court. That means that a particular case may not present a public policy problem in its full or in its usual dimensions. The plaintiff may not be representative of the universe of potential plaintiffs in such cases, and the facts may not reflect the problem at issue in its most serious form. A court decision in that case may therefore be inappropriate to the problem and a poor precedent for future cases on that subject.[34]

For example, in 1983 the Indiana Supreme Court and the Michigan Court of Appeals both held that injured college football players were not entitled to receive workers' compensation benefits because they were not "employees" of their universities within the meaning of their states' workers' compensation laws.[35] The nature of the athletic programs at the defendant colleges influenced those decisions. The two colleges did not field nationally ranked football and basketball teams, their athletic budgets were not among the largest in college sports, and they did not compete against prestigious opponents. Consequently, the plaintiffs could not convince the courts that their athletic scholarships were employment contracts that included workers' compensation rights. The results might have been different had the plaintiffs played for universities where athletic budgets were large, media scrutiny and the pressure to win were intense, and athletes routinely trained for careers in professional sports. The courts might then have concluded that the college–player relationship was akin to an employer–employee relationship, which included workers' compensation rights.[36] In those circumstances, the courts would have seen the full dimensions of the problem that the plaintiffs sought to remedy.

Fifth, judicial fact finding is ill suited to finding **legislative facts**, which are the recurrent patterns of behavior on which public policy should be based. In the prior example, relevant legislative facts would have been the employment-like relationships that exist between some colleges and their athletes and the financial consequences for athletic scholarship recipients of career-ending athletic injuries. Courts rarely receive such information from litigants, and they do not conduct independent research in order to discover it. Instead, courts rely on **adjudicative facts**, which are the particular events that have transpired between the parties to a lawsuit. Interrogatories, depositions, examination, and cross-examination are designed to find adjudicative facts. Adjudicative facts are sufficient to resolve private disputes, but not to make public policy.[37]

Sixth, the judicial process is not designed to review and to correct past mistakes. Unlike legislatures, courts rarely oversee the implementation of their decisions, so they cannot readily detect or remedy unintended consequences. Courts only learn about such consequences if and when parties to prior cases return to court seeking to modify the original decisions. Corrective action may not occur until years after the original decisions, if it occurs at all.[38] Thus, Horowitz concludes that courts should restrict themselves to resolving private disputes, and should refrain from making broad public policy decisions.

Judicial Activism

Supporters of judicial activism reject both justifications for judicial restraint. They argue that courts should make public policy, and that courts can do so effectively. Specifically, courts should use their power not just to decide cases, but to serve the cause of human dignity by expanding equality and personal freedom.[39] For judicial activists, to promote human dignity is to do justice, and justice is the goal of the judicial process. A judge promotes human dignity when, having concluded that prison conditions violate the Eighth Amendment's prohibition of "cruel and unusual punishment," she orders prison authorities to remedy the violations, and retains jurisdiction of the case until they have done so.[40]

Judicial activists contend that courts must exercise such broad powers when elected officials fail to respond to pressing social needs because the likely beneficiaries of change (e.g., prisoners, mental patients, or children in poor school districts) lack the political power necessary to make it happen. When courts review administrative practices, they must do more than just approve or disapprove of those practices, because administrative actions are usually continuous. Courts must identify the steps that an institution needs to take in order to satisfy the constitutional or statutory requirements that gave rise to the current litigation.[41]

Judicial activists also contend that supporters of judicial restraint scrutinize court orders that require improvements in institutional conditions, but ignore failures by legislators and administrators to remedy the appalling conditions that necessitate those orders.[42] Supporters of judicial restraint also fail to recognize that many court orders are **consent decrees** that the parties have negotiated and have agreed to without judicial coercion. Indeed, the administrator of the defendant institution may welcome that result in hopes that it will force legislators to appropriate the funds necessary to upgrade the institution.[43]

Judicial activists cite the saga of school desegregation as evidence of the need for courts to prod reluctant public officials to respect human rights. The Supreme Court ruled in 1954 that racial segregation in public schools was unconstitutional, but Southern school districts made little progress toward desegregation during the 1950s and 1960s.[44] In 1966, only 12.5 percent of black students in the South attended desegregated schools; in 1968, more black students (2.5 million) attended segregated schools in the South than had done so in 1954 (2.2 million).[45]

The school district of New Kent County, Virginia, which contained two schools, reflected the lack of progress in desegregation since 1954. Before 1954, one school had only white students and the other school had only black students. In 1968, even though there was no residential segregation and the district was about evenly divided between whites and blacks, one school was 85 percent white and the other school was 100 percent black. The county had enacted a "freedom of choice" plan that supposedly let parents send their children to the school they preferred. The result was continued segregation because no white parents sent their children to the black school and, faced with intimidation by whites, few black parents dared to send their children to the white school.[46]

In *Green v. New Kent County School Board* (1968), the Supreme Court abandoned the gradualism in desegregation that it had approved in 1954, and ordered the defendant school board to desegregate its public schools immediately.[47] The justices rejected the freedom-of-choice plan as insufficient to achieve desegregation. Impatient with the school board's delays, they ordered it to "come forward with a [desegregation] plan that promises realistically to work, and promises realistically to work *now*."[48] If that was judicial activism, its supporters say, such action was necessary to obtain justice for persons who lacked the political power required to obtain justice for themselves.

Judicial activists question whether legislatures are as democratic as supporters of judicial restraint say they are. The activists do not view the legislative process as being significantly more democratic than the judicial process is.[49] They observe that courts most often invalidate state laws, which may not reflect the views of a majority of Americans. An example would be Pennsylvania's requirement that a married woman who seeks an abortion first obtain her husband's consent, which the Supreme Court invalidated in *Planned Parenthood v. Casey*. Moreover, courts frequently review administrative decisions, and appointed administrators are no more representative of public opinion or accountable to the voters than judges are.[50] The courts in Michigan and Indiana that denied work-ers' compensation to injured college athletes reviewed and affirmed the decisions of appointed administrators in those states. Furthermore, even judges who are not accountable to the voters must write opinions that explain their decisions, and higher courts can reverse decisions that ignore precedent or misstate the law. Leg-islators are electorally accountable, but they need not disclose publicly the rea-sons for their decisions.[51]

Like supporters of judicial restraint, judicial activists devote particular attention to constitutional cases. Unlike supporters of judicial restraint, judicial activists do not insist that adherence to the intentions of the Founding Fathers limit constitu-tional interpretation. One judicial activist, Professor Arthur Selwyn Miller, has writ-ten that to so restrict constitutional interpretation is to establish a "dictatorship over the living by the dead."[52] Similarly, the late Justice William Brennan wrote that when judges interpret the Constitution, they should consider not what the Founding Fathers intended, but instead, what the Constitution means in the present day. Indeed, the value of the Constitution lies not in what it might have meant in an ear-lier era, but rather its capacity to serve current needs and to solve current problems.[53]

Judge Richard Posner of the U.S. Court of Appeals for the Seventh Circuit illus-trates this point in a discussion of the right to counsel contained in the Sixth Amend-ment.[54] The Sixth Amendment states: "In all criminal prosecutions, the accused shall enjoy the right... to have the assistance of counsel for his defense." Read nar-rowly, that language merely means that the government cannot forbid the defendant to hire a lawyer; if the defendant cannot afford a lawyer, he must do without one. Read broadly, though, it not only entitles the well-off defendant to hire a lawyer, it guarantees to the indigent defendant the effective assistance of counsel.[55]

The narrow interpretation is more consistent with the Founding Fathers' intent, which was to abolish the English rule that prohibited a defendant from hir-ing a lawyer unless complex issues arose in his case. In those days, no one contem-plated government hiring a lawyer to represent an indigent defendant; government had meager funds, and criminal trials were short and simple, so it was reasonable to expect that a defendant would defend himself if he could not afford a lawyer. How-ever, the narrow interpretation does not fit today's circumstances; government can now afford to hire lawyers for indigent defendants, and criminal law and procedure are so complex that an unrepresented defendant is at a great disadvantage relative to the government.[56] Thus, courts read the Sixth Amendment's right-to-counsel language broadly in order to serve current needs and solve current problems.

That is proper, according to political scientist Judith Baer, because the Found-ing Fathers did not create a pure democracy; they created instead a republic that places constitutional rights outside majority control and gives the authority to pro-tect those rights to judges, who need not answer to the voters.[57] The late Supreme Court Justice Robert Jackson expressed this idea eloquently when he wrote:

> The very purpose of the Bill of Rights was to withdraw certain subjects from the vicissitudes of political controversy, to place them beyond the reach of majori-ties and officials and to establish them as legal principles to be applied by courts.[58]

Judicial activists believe that courts should apply those principles openly and often in the pursuit of human dignity.

Judicial activists also believe that courts are capable of making public policy, and that supporters of judicial restraint exaggerate courts' activism and their limitations. The activists note that courts do not resolve most civil cases; settlement agreements between the parties do. Courts encourage settlements, which may be as important as policy making, but the parties negotiate for themselves.[59] Therefore, judicial policy making occurs much less frequently than the supporters of judicial restraint allege. Furthermore, the judicial policy making that occurs requires less skill than its critics suggest because it often takes the form of consent decrees that the parties negotiate and then present to the court for approval. In those cases, the court relies on the expertise of the parties to remedy the problem(s) that sparked the litigation.[60]

Professor Abram Chayes argues that courts possess six institutional features that equip them well to make public policy.[61] First, judges are relatively insulated from political pressures because of their job security, but they often have experience with public policy issues because of prior law practice or government service. Therefore, they can usually decide policy issues competently and independently. Second, cases present national problems in a manageable size, which enables courts to tailor remedies to the parties' needs and to modify them later if necessary. Third, courts, unlike legislatures and administrative agencies, always permit representatives of the persons whom the outcome will affect (i.e., lawyers for prisoners and prison administrators, respectively) to participate actively in their decision-making process.

Fourth, the adversarial nature of the judicial process gives parties strong incentives to supply the court with ample information on which to base its decision. Fifth, unlike administrative agencies, courts must respond to the claims of aggrieved parties; they can reject those claims, but they must consider them. Sixth, courts are flexible enough to obtain help from outside the government in finding legislative facts and in evaluating potential remedies. For example, they can appoint **special masters** to assist parties in negotiating consent decrees and **monitors** to inform them whether their orders are working and whether defendants are complying with those orders. That is no worse an arrangement than legislators' reliance on colleagues for advice before voting on unfamiliar or complex legislation. In Chayes's view, then, courts are well suited to make public policy.

Constrained Court Versus Dynamic Court

Constrained Court

The constrained court model maintains that courts usually cannot achieve significant social change because: (1) constitutional rights are limited; (2) courts lack independence from the elected branches of government; and (3) courts are ill equipped to make and to implement public policy.[62] There is not a constitutional right on which to base every claim for social reform. For example, there is not a constitutional right to affordable housing, adequate levels of public assistance, or clean air. That means that courts cannot consider claims of entitlement to such benefits, even if those claims present compelling moral or public policy arguments. Thus, the limited nature of constitutional rights limits courts' capacity to reform society.[63]

Moreover, assuming limitless constitutional rights, courts still lack the independence from the elected branches of government that would enable them to produce significant social reform. Courts depend on legislatures for financial resources and on administrators to implement their decisions; therefore, they are reluctant to anger the other branches of government by making decisions that those branches are likely to oppose and subvert.[64] The political question doctrine (see Chapter 8) reflects that reluctance, which was evident in the Supreme Court's refusal to decide whether America's participation in the Vietnam War was unconstitutional because it occurred without a declaration of war by Congress. Furthermore, even if courts could overcome the two previous constraints, they are not equipped to make or to implement social reforms by themselves. They lack the policy expertise, the monitoring capacity, or the political skills necessary to make reforms work, especially when there is opposition.[65]

Courts can produce significant social reform only when their decisions coincide with social, political, and economic conditions that support such reform. In other words, the "constrained court" requires help in order to make social change. Help occurs when: (1) the other branches of government give defendants incentives to induce their compliance with court decisions; (2) the other branches of government impose costs on defendants to induce their compliance; (3) the economics of the marketplace induce compliance; or (4) court decisions themselves give reform a legitimacy that spurs persons who can implement it (e.g., prison wardens or hospital administrators) to begin doing so.[66] Thus, courts must overcome the constraints of limited constitutional rights, political dependence, and unsuitability for policy making, *and* one of four favorable conditions must exist before courts can *help to produce* significant social reform.[67]

Professor Gerald Rosenberg cites Supreme Court decisions about civil rights and abortion, respectively, as evidence that the constrained court model accurately depicts the impact of judicial policy making. He observes that the impact of *Brown v. Board of Education* (1954) in the South was minimal for more than ten years afterward because the authorities whose job it was to implement desegregation either supported segregation or were unwilling to confront those who did, and the Court could not implement its decision alone. Conditions did not begin to change until a decade later, when President Lyndon Johnson made civil rights a cornerstone of his administration's policy agenda, Congress outlawed racial segregation in all public facilities, and public attitudes outside the South coalesced against racial segregation. Those changes removed the constraints that had limited the impact of *Brown*, and established both incentives for compliance and costs for noncompliance.

Professor Rosenberg also downplays the impact of the Supreme Court's decision in *Roe v. Wade* (1973), which legalized abortion nationwide. He argues that compliance occurred more readily in response to *Roe* than to *Brown* because public opinion favored *Roe*, a movement to liberalize abortion laws existed at the time of *Roe*, members of Congress did not initially oppose *Roe*, and the economics of the marketplace encouraged the establishment of women's health clinics to perform abortions when hospitals refused to do so. Unlike *Brown*, *Roe* did not require implementation by people who opposed it or who were fearful of its consequences, and those who favored it could profit by implementation. In other words, the constraints that could have limited *Roe's* success were weak, and a condition existed that hastened its implementation. Despite favorable circumstances, then, *Roe* accomplished little by itself, but instead, merely contributed to a process of social change.[68]

Thus, Professor Rosenberg concludes that courts almost never produce significant social reform, and that, at best, courts can validate social reforms that other branches of government initiate. Therefore, advocates of social reforms ought to devote fewer resources to litigation and more resources to lobbying legislators and administrators in pursuit of their public policy goals.[69]

Dynamic Court

The dynamic court model rejects the notion that courts are inherently ineffective at social reform. Indeed, it argues that courts can effect social reform when the elected branches of government refuse to do so because judges do not face the voters at frequent intervals. That is especially true of federal judges, who do not face the voters at all; they can uphold minority rights without fear that the majority will vote them out of office. Moreover, according to the dynamic court model, a plaintiff need not have economic and political power in order to win a lawsuit because legal arguments, not financial contributions or angry telephone calls, win lawsuits.[70]

Political scientist Bradley Canon argues that Supreme Court decisions alone have removed religious observances from public schools. Neither legislators nor governors assisted the Court in that effort; indeed, many legislators and governors bitterly opposed ending prayer and Bible readings in public schools.[71] Nevertheless, although religious observances still occur in schools, such as student-led prayers at graduations, they are unusual and, almost invariably, controversial.[72]

Professor Cannon also contends that Supreme Court decisions are solely responsible for the greater availability of sexually oriented books and films today than a generation ago. No President or governor ever urged greater availability for such material. It is not a dubious accomplishment for the Court to have increased the accessibility of sexually oriented books and films. The Court's interpretation of the freedom of speech has ensured readers access to literary classics as well as to more low-brow fare. It has also ensured that adults are not restricted to reading or to viewing materials that are suitable for children. Professor Cannon concedes that Americans' attitudes toward sexually oriented material did not change because of the Court's landmark decision in *Roth v. United States* (1957), which liberalized the standard for constitutionally protected speech.[73] Instead, attitudes changed on their own, but *Roth* facilitated that change by making sexually oriented material more readily available and more socially acceptable than it had ever been before.[74]

Finally, Professor Canon observes that the Supreme Court is more responsible than any other institution of government for the survival of abortion rights in

America during the anti-abortion presidencies of Ronald Reagan and George Bush. That undoubtedly is also a dubious accomplishment in the minds of some, but it nevertheless casts doubt on the validity of the constrained court model. Professor Canon acknowledges that abortion would most likely be legal in some states even if the Court had not legalized it nationwide in *Roe*. The Court, though, did make abortion a nationwide option, and the Court has preserved that option despite determined challenges by Congress and two presidents.[75]

Professor Canon thus concludes that the constrained court model overstates its case, and that courts can and do effect significant social reform in the United States. Professors David Schultz and Stephen Gottlieb echo Canon's view, and argue that courts effect social change by placing on the political agenda issues that elected officials prefer to ignore and by giving elected officials a reason or an excuse to address those issues.

Schultz and Gottlieb concede that courts rarely, if ever, produce social change alone, but they contend that it is unrealistic to expect courts to do that because they are only one institution in a government of shared powers. Instead, courts assist social change, and they even initiate it when the elected branches of government are unwilling to do so.[76] That is sufficient evidence of judicial vitality to validate the dynamic court model. Now that you know the opposing viewpoints in the debate about judicial policy making, it is time to analyze the debate in order to help you develop your own vision of judicial policy making. That is the task of the next section.

AN ASSESSMENT OF JUDICIAL POLICY MAKING

Legitimacy

The Founding Fathers recognized that democracy can enable the majority to tyrannize the minority unless a mechanism exists to protect minority rights. That is why they created a republic instead of a pure democracy; a republic contains nondemocratic elements that prevent tyranny of the minority by the majority. One such nondemocratic element is a federal judiciary comprised of appointed judges who enjoy lifetime tenure in office.[77] Job security helps federal judges to protect a timeless constitutional value such as the freedom of speech from majorities who would limit it when the message or the messenger is unpopular.[78] For example, the Supreme Court invalidated two statutes that prohibited the desecration of an American flag because the First Amendment protects the expression not only of popular ideas, but also of unpopular ideas.[79]

When the Court declared the two flag-burning laws unconstitutional, it fulfilled the role that the Founding Fathers envisioned for it. That role is to ensure that individual freedom, as enshrined in the Constitution, does not fall victim to the momentary passions of temporary majorities. The judicial role is as important as any role that the Congress or the president plays, which reminds us that the judiciary is a co-equal branch of government in the United States. That is why judicial policy making is inevitable. It is impossible to be a co-equal branch of government that preserves core constitutional guarantees without making difficult choices between competing values, such as patriotism and the freedom of speech. When courts choose between competing values, they necessarily make policies that shape individual and institutional behavior, because court decisions are "the law," just as statutes and regulations are.

Thus, it is pointless to argue that courts must merely "interpret the law" and must not make public policy. Courts' constitutional role makes judicial policy making legitimate; unclear statutory and constitutional language, and legislators' tendency to dodge divisive social problems, make it necessary. Courts should not overstep constitutional bounds, though, as judicial tyranny is as bad as tyranny in its other forms. The appropriate inquiry, then, is not whether, but rather how, courts should make public policy.

Wisdom counsels moderation in judicial policy making, as in all other human endeavors. Moderation means, in part, that judges' interpretations of constitutional concepts such as "due process" and "equal protection" should reflect the broad philosophical outlines of the Founding Fathers' design. Otherwise, judges are simply more powerful "legislators" than those the voters elected, which was not the Founding Fathers' wish.[80] Moderation also means, though, that modern judges must not be captives of eighteenth-century thinking, which held African-Americans in perpetual bondage and prevented women from voting or owning property.[81]

Moderation seems incompatible with capital punishment, which stirs strong feelings for and against, but moderation is in order when judging the constitutionality of capital punishment. The Fifth and Fourteenth Amendments state that government shall not deprive a person of "life, liberty, or property, without due process of law," and the Eighth Amendment states that government shall not inflict "cruel and unusual punishments." Moderation here means that government may take a life, because the Constitution plainly contemplates that action, but it also means that scrupulously fair judicial procedures must precede an execution. Capital punishment cannot be the product of whim or prejudice.

Former Justice William Brennan rejected this view, and interpreted the Eighth Amendment to prohibit capital punishment, which he believed was "utterly and irreversibly degrading to the very essence of human dignity."[82] That might be a correct policy judgment, but it is a doubtful constitutional judgment. The Constitution provides for capital punishment, but it does not state that "human dignity" is its governing standard. Thus, moderation counsels judges to uphold the constitutionality of capital punishment, regardless of their policy views; only a constitutional amendment can properly end capital punishment.[83]

Moderation, however, neither ends social progress nor stifles judicial creativity, as the Supreme Court's landmark decision in Gideon v. Wainwright (1963) illustrates.[84] In Gideon, the Court held that states must provide lawyers for criminal defendants in felony cases who cannot afford to hire lawyers to defend themselves. The Court interpreted the Sixth Amendment, which states that "[i]n all criminal prosecutions, the accused shall enjoy the right to have the assistance of counsel for his defense," to encompass not only the historic right to hire a lawyer, but also a new right to obtain a lawyer at government expense if the defendant cannot afford to pay one.

The new interpretation was broader than the Founding Fathers' view, which included only the right to hire a lawyer, but it still honored the constitutional text, which contained room for expansion. The Court concluded that expansion was necessary because criminal trials had become so complex that defendants required the services of lawyers to ensure fair results. That was a moderate conclusion because (1) the Court read the Sixth Amendment (albeit broadly), but did not try to rewrite it, and (2) the result was a fairer system of criminal justice in America.[85] *Gideon* exemplifies what Professor Judith Baer calls "disciplined, principled creativity" in constitutional interpretation.[86]

Moderation is also the measure of wisdom when courts require public institutions to reform themselves. Here, moderation means redressing the plaintiffs' legal injury without exercising legislative power.[87] Put another way, moderation means that courts act as a co-equal, rather than as a superior, branch of government. Courts can meet that standard in public-law cases by: (1) upholding constitutional rights; (2) telling public institutions what they cannot do; and (3) giving them the chance to reform themselves. That strategy enables courts to do what they do best, namely, to identify past violations of constitutional rights, and it enables legislators and administrators to do what they do best, namely, to make laws that address current problems and to enforce them.

The federal district judge who ordered the Kansas City School District to increase local property taxes in order to fund a desegregation plan failed the moderation test by violating the separation-of-powers principle. He exercised the power to tax, which is plainly a legislative power in the American constitutional scheme, as the Supreme Court reminded him on appeal.[88] The Kansas City case notwithstanding, there are numerous instances in which courts have decided public-law litigation within constitutional parameters. For example, Judge Frank Johnson's controversial orders to reform Alabama's schools and prisons (see Chapter 1) respected constitutional parameters.

Early in 1963, parents of black students petitioned Judge Johnson to desegregate the schools in Macon County, Alabama, pursuant to the Supreme Court's decision in *Brown v. Board of Education*. Judge Johnson granted the plaintiffs' petition. He ordered the Macon County School Board to begin desegregation by the start of the fall term and to submit a general desegregation plan by mid-December 1963.[89] When Governor George Wallace and the state board of education tried to prevent desegregation in Macon County and elsewhere in Alabama, Judge Johnson and two other federal judges enjoined the governor and the board from "interfering with court-ordered desegregation anywhere in the State of Alabama."[90]

Still, the three-judge panel declined to order the desegregation of every public school in Alabama "upon the assumption that the Governor, the State Superintendent of Education, and the State Board of Education will comply with the injunction."[91] Only after those officials failed to comply did Judge Johnson and his colleagues issue, on March 22, 1967, a statewide desegregation order that required every school district in Alabama to adopt a desegregation plan for all grades, effective at the start of the 1967–1968 school year.[92]

Judge Johnson and his colleagues thus acted with moderation in the Alabama school desegregation cases. They enforced the *Brown* decision, prohibited the defendants from interfering with desegregation, and gave public school authorities the chance to desegregate their own schools. They did not issue a statewide desegregation order until Alabama's leaders had repeatedly prevented the voluntary integration of public schools.

Acting alone, Judge Johnson also exhibited moderation when inmates alleged in several lawsuits that conditions in the Alabama prison system violated the constitutional prohibition against cruel and unusual punishment. The evidence supported the allegations. An expert witness characterized conditions in Alabama's prisons as "sickening" and "uncivilized"; a federal public health officer said that the prisons in Alabama were "unfit for human habitation."[93] Judge Johnson agreed.

In *Newman v. Alabama* (1972),[94] Judge Johnson ordered prison officials to stop depriving inmates of basic medical care, and he specifically prohibited officials from using unqualified personnel and inmates to deliver medical services or to prescribe, dispense, or administer drugs.[95] In *Diamond v. Thompson* (1973),[96] he stopped arbitrary limitations on inmates' access to religious literature, and held that inmates are entitled to be notified and to receive a hearing before they can be subjected to solitary confinement.[97] In *James v. Wallace* (1976),[98] Judge Johnson held that prison conditions in Alabama violated the constitutional prohibition against "cruel and unusual punishment" because they prevented the achievement of legitimate institutional goals, namely, deterrence, rehabilitation, and security.[99] He compiled a detailed list of "minimal constitutional standards" of inmate confinement that applied to everything from lighting to toothpaste.[100] Finally, he created a human rights committee to monitor compliance with his order.[101]

Judge Johnson demonstrated moderation in the prison cases, even though he ordered prison authorities to meet a detailed set of "minimal constitutional standards." The Constitution prohibits "cruel and unusual punishment," and the conditions in Alabama's prisons were certainly cruel, if not unusual. Judge Johnson did not read a "right of rehabilitation" into the Constitution; he merely required Alabama to meet the basic human needs of the inmates in its custody. Moreover, prison conditions in Alabama were largely the result of legislative inattention, which reflected the majority's contempt for a minority, inmates. That situation warrants judicial policy making. Thus, Judge Johnson's orders were hardly rash or excessive.

Judge Johnson's response to conditions in Alabama's mental hospitals was not so moderate. He held in *Wyatt v. Stickney* (1971) that patients involuntarily committed to mental hospitals have a constitutional right to receive "adequate" treatment, and that Bryce Hospital in Tuscaloosa violated that right by failing to treat its patients.[102] Bryce Hospital deprived the plaintiffs of their liberty without due process of law, in violation of the Fourteenth Amendment. Judge Johnson ordered state mental health officials to prepare a plan for adequate treatment within ninety days, and to implement it within six months.[103]

Judge Johnson later issued an order that required each of Alabama's three public mental-health facilities, including Bryce Hospital, to implement a list of "Minimal Constitutional Standards for Adequate Habilitation of the Mentally Retarded."[104] The list included detailed regulations for patients' treatment, health, comfort, hygiene, and privacy.[105] He appointed a human rights committee for each facility to ensure that the authorities met the constitutional standards.[106]

Judge Johnson abandoned moderation in *Wyatt* when he concluded that Alabama had violated a constitutional "right to treatment." The Constitution mentions no such right. Nor can one infer that right from the text, as one can infer a right to counsel for indigent defendants from the text of the Sixth Amendment. Judge Johnson could properly have ordered Alabama not to commit persons to mental hospitals involuntarily without a hearing, counsel, and an opportunity to confront adversary witnesses, because the Fourteenth Amendment prohibits deprivations of liberty without **due process** (fair procedures). Instead, he ruled that due process includes a right to treatment, despite the Constitution's silence on that subject.

One need not be an advocate of judicial restraint to criticize the decision in *Wyatt*. It epitomizes result-oriented judging. Admittedly, Alabama treated its mental patients inhumanely, and the state legislature ignored them as much as it ignored prison inmates. Still, the Constitution prohibits cruel and unusual punishment, but it does not prohibit inadequate mental-health treatment. That distinction should have produced a different outcome in *Wyatt* than in the prison cases.[107]

Thus, judicial policy making is legitimate when it vindicates constitutional rights *and* respects constitutional principles, the limits of its own power, and the authority and expertise of institutional defendants. That moderate course liberates judges from the eighteenth century without empowering them to shape the twenty-first to their own design.

Capacity

Courts have the capacity for the moderate policy making advocated here. Indeed, several features equip courts well to make policy. First, their detachment from the hustle and bustle of politics offers opportunities for reflection and analysis that legislators rarely enjoy. Appellate judges in particular devote considerable time to researching and writing opinions. That makes a hasty vote for a half-baked idea less likely on the bench than on the floor of the legislature.[108]

Second, courts are accountable for their actions within the legal fraternity and within the larger political system. They are accountable to the legal fraternity because their written opinions are subject to immediate critiques by dissenters and to long-range critiques by lawyers, legal scholars, and higher courts.[109] Reversals and professional criticism can prevent promotions. Courts are accountable to the public because their opinions are public documents that are accessible in print and electronic form.[110] Public anger can result in electoral defeat for state judges and in salary freezes for federal judges. Accountability to the legal fraternity and to the public encourages persuasive and moderate judicial opinions.

Third, in cases that call for institutional reform, courts can select from a menu of potential remedies that encourage defendants to reform themselves. **Process remedies** are the least intrusive category; they include advisory committees, evaluation committees (which Judge Johnson ordered for Alabama's prisons and mental hospitals), citizen participation in institutional governance, educational programs for employees, and dispute-resolution procedures, all of which aim to correct problems without forcing an institution to make specific policy changes.[111] **Performance standards** are more intrusive, but they still allow defendants to decide what means they will use to achieve those standards. Examples include racial attendance figures in schools, the ratio of medical personnel to inmates in prisons, and the qualifications of personal-care attendants at mental hospitals.[112] **Specified remedial actions** are highly intrusive because they impose on defendants remedial goals and the means of achieving them. Judges tend to use these actions, such as the busing of students and the modification of school attendance zones to desegregate schools, or changes in the size and condition of prison cells or hospital rooms, when defendants refuse to reform themselves.[113]

Fourth, courts are better able than their critics believe to monitor the results of their policy making. Courts can require defendants to submit progress reports or to participate in periodic hearings during which defendants must indicate what progress they have made since the previous hearing. Courts can hire special masters to help the parties develop reform plans, and can retain the masters' services during implementation of those plans. Alternatively, courts can appoint monitors to report on defendants' compliance after implementation. Courts can even reward defendants who comply with their orders by relaxing the monitoring process, or by ending it ahead of schedule.[114] Thus, courts not only *should* make policy decisions when circumstances require; courts *can* do so, especially when defendants are willing to reform and when courts give them opportunities and incentives to do so.

Impact

Even if courts should make policy in some circumstances, and can do so, the truest measure of the value of judicial policy making is its impact on American society. According to the dynamic court model, that impact is significant; according to the constrained court model, it is minimal. Both models are overstatements: the impact of judicial policy making is less than the dynamic court model imagines, but more than the constrained court model admits.

The Supreme Court's identification of a particular constitutional right does not necessarily mean that Americans will soon be able to exercise that right. Institutional resistance, opposition from powerful interest groups, prejudice, cultural practices, and indecision can hinder, and even prevent, the exercise of a constitutional right.[115] That is why the public schools in New Kent County, Virginia, were still segregated fourteen years after *Brown v. Board of Education*, and it is why there are states in which it remains extremely difficult to obtain an abortion despite *Roe v. Wade*. Thus, the impact of *Brown* and of *Roe* on American society was probably less than their respective supporters would have liked. That does not mean, though, that the impact of either decision was insignificant.

Court decisions need not produce rapid and dramatic change alone in order to affect American society. Indeed, court decisions rarely initiate broad social change. Rather, they enshrine in law emerging public sentiments, thereby making those sentiments the bases for public policy. That influences public opinion in favor of the emerging sentiments, which gradually become mainstream views.[116] Thus, courts spur social change by giving emerging sentiments a legitimacy they previously lacked. That does not immediately desegregate schools, or make abortion services available, but it signals to society that change is in the wind. Courts also spur social change by forcing public officials to face issues they have long avoided, and by giving them an excuse to make hard policy choices.[117] During the past generation, for example, state supreme courts in more than half of the states have held that reliance on local property-tax revenues to fund public schools violates the right to a free public education contained in their respective state constitutions.[118] Property-rich towns enjoy low tax rates yet generate large amounts of money for their schools, while the reverse is true in property-poor towns. The rulings by the state supreme courts have forced state legislators to confront this historic inequity and to rectify it by finding means of funding public schools other than local property taxes. Those rulings have also given legislators who have long advocated reform in public school finance an unprecedented opportunity, because they must replace the local property tax with an alternative funding mechanism or the public schools will close.

Thus, neither the dynamic court model nor the constrained court model captures the impact of judicial policy making on social change. The dynamic court model overestimates the impact of judicial policy making, and the constrained court model underestimates it. Courts usually do not initiate social change, and they cannot accomplish it alone. That is probably as it should be in a large, diverse country in which the separation of powers is a cornerstone constitutional principle. Still, courts influence social change because they legitimize emerging sentiments, force public officials to address long-standing problems, and justify action when the majority would prefer inaction. That is significant, especially to plaintiffs whom politicians have long ignored.

CONCLUSION

There is limited benefit in a debate about whether courts should make public policy, because they most assuredly do. Indeed, judicial policy making is inevitable, because courts' most important function is to protect constitutional principles against tyranny by the majority. They cannot do so without periodically making policy choices between competing values, such as patriotism and free speech. Thus, courts' constitutional role legitimizes their policy making.

Still, courts are a co-equal, not a superior, branch of government, so their power is limited. They must respect the constitutional text when they uphold constitutional rights; try, as much as possible, to tell public institutions what not to do instead of what to do; and give those institutions opportunities to reform themselves. Their deliberative nature, detachment from politics, and access to numerous remedies and mechanisms for evaluating those remedies equip them well for these tasks.

Courts do not initiate significant social change nor can they achieve it single-handedly, but they can influence it. Courts influence social change by legitimizing emerging views, by forcing public officials to address long-standing problems, and by enabling them to do so without paying a high political price for it. Thus, the impact of court decisions may be less than the dynamic court model envisions, but it is more than the constrained court model suggests.

Rose v. Council for Better Education, Inc., which follows, shows a court forcing legislators to address long-standing problems in the operations of a state's public school system. In *Rose*, the Kentucky Supreme Court held that Kentucky's public schools violated the state constitution's requirement that the legislature establish an "efficient system of common schools throughout the State." The court imposed an "absolute duty" on the legislature to create a new system of public schools in Kentucky. *Rose* is a bold exercise in judicial policy making; after reading it, try to decide whether it is *legitimate* and whether it seems likely to work.

Epilogue: A School System Flunks Out

Rose v. Council for Better Education, Inc.
790 S.W.2d 186 (Ky. 1989)

STEPHENS, Chief Justice.

The issue we decide on this appeal is whether the Kentucky General Assembly has complied with its constitutional mandate to "provide an efficient system of common schools throughout the state."

In a word, the present system of common schools in Kentucky is not an "efficient" one in our view of the clear mandate of Section 183 [of the Kentucky Constitution]. The common school system in Kentucky is constitutionally deficient.

The framers of our constitution intended that each and every child in this state should receive a proper and an adequate education, *to be provided for by the General Assembly.* This opinion dutifully applies the constitutional test of Section 183 to the existing system of common schools. We do no more, nor may we do any less.

I. Procedural History

This declaratory judgment action was filed in the Franklin Circuit Court by multiple plaintiffs, including the Council for Better Education, Inc., a non-profit Kentucky corporation whose membership consists of sixty-six local school districts in the state.

The defendants named in the complaint were the Governor, the Superintendent of Public Instruction, the State Treasurer, the President *Pro Tempore* of the Senate, the Speaker of the House of Representatives, and the State Board of Education and its individual members.

The complaint included allegations that the system of school financing provided for by the General Assembly is inadequate; places too much emphasis on local school board resources; and results in inadequacies, inequities and inequalities throughout the state so as to result in an inefficient system of common school education in violation of Kentucky Constitution, Sections 3 and 183.... Additionally the complaint maintains the entire system is not efficient under the mandate of Section 183.

The case was tried by the court without the intervention of a jury. The trial court entered the first of several orders, findings of fact and judgments on May 31, 1988. Generally, that order found Kentucky's common school finance system to be unconstitutional and discriminatory and held that the General Assembly had not produced an efficient system of common schools throughout the state. On October 14, 1988, a final, appealable judgment was entered.

A notice of appeal was timely filed by the present appellants, John A. Rose, President *Pro Tempore* of the Senate of Kentucky, and Donald J. Blandford, Speaker of the House of Representatives of Kentucky.

II. Analysis of Trial Court's Findings of Fact

The trial judge [concluded] that the separation of powers doctrine would prohibit courts from directing the General Assembly as to how the school system should be financed. But, he reiterated that the General Assembly must provide an efficient system.

In the "judgment," the trial judge retained continuing jurisdiction over the subject matter for the purpose of enforcing the judgment. To that effect, he ordered a progress report be made to him on a day certain.

V. The Evidence

As we proceed to summarize the evidence before us, the legal test we must apply is whether that evidence supports the conclusion of the trial court that the Kentucky system of common schools is not efficient. It is textbook law that before an appellate court may overturn the trial court's finding, such finding must be clearly erroneous. *Yates v. Wilson*, 339 S.W.2d 458 (Ky. 1960).

[T]here are wide variations in financial resources and dispositions thereof which result in unequal educational opportunities throughout Kentucky. The local districts have large variances in taxable property per student. Even a total elimination of all mismanagement and waste in local school districts would not correct the situation as it now exists. A substantial difference in the curricula offered in the poorer districts contrasts with that of the richer districts, particularly in the areas of foreign language, science, mathematics, music and art.

Students in property poor districts receive inadequate and inferior educational opportunities as compared to those offered to those students in the more affluent districts.

The numerous witnesses that testified before the trial court are recognized experts in the field of primary and secondary education. Without exception, they testified that there is great disparity in the poor and the more affluent school districts with regard to classroom teachers' pay; provision of basic educational materials; student-teacher ratio; curriculum; quality of basic management; size, adequacy and condition of school physical plants; and per year expenditure per student. Kentucky's children, simply because of their place of residence, are offered a virtual hodgepodge of educational opportunities. The quality of education in the poorer local school districts is substantially less in most, if not all, of the above categories.

Appellants conceded, the trial court found and we concur that in spite of legislative efforts, the total local and state effort in education in Kentucky's primary and secondary education is inadequate and is lacking in uniformity. It is discriminatory as to the children served in 80% of our local school districts.

The disparity in per pupil expenditure by the local school boards runs in the thousands of dollars per year. Moreover, between the extreme high allocation and the extreme low allocation lies a wide range of annual per pupil expenditures. In theory (and perhaps in actual practice) there could be 177 different per pupil expenditures, thus leading to 177 different educational efforts. The financing effort of local school districts is, figuratively speaking, a jigsaw puzzle.

X. What is an "Efficient" System of Common Schools?

In a few simple, but direct words, the framers of our present Constitution, set forth the will of the people with regard to the importance of providing public education in [Kentucky].

> "*General Assembly to provide for school system*—The General Assembly shall, by appropriate legislation, provide for an efficient system of common schools throughout the State." Ky. Const. Sec. 183.

A brief sojourn into the Constitutional debates will give some idea—a contemporaneous view—of the depth of the delegates' intention when Section 183 was drafted and eventually made its way into the organic law of this state. It will provide a background for our definition of "efficient."

Comments of Delegate Beckner on the report which led to the selection of the language in Section 183 reflect the framers' cognizance of the importance of education, and emphasized that the educational system in Kentucky must be improved. Referring to the education of our children, he admonished the delegates, "do not let us make a mistake in dealing with the most vital question that can come before us." III *Debates Constitutional Convention 1890* [p.] 4459.

Beckner set out four permanent justifications for and characteristics of state provided schools:

1. The education of young people is essential to the prosperity of a free people.
2. The education should be universal and should embrace all children.
3. Public education should be supervised by the State, to assure that students develop patriotism and understand our government.
4. Education should be given to all—rich and poor—so that our people will be homogeneous in their feelings and desires.

This Court, in defining efficiency must, at least in part, be guided by these clearly expressed purposes. The framers of Section 183 emphasized that education is essential to the welfare of the citizens of [Kentucky]. By this animus to Section 183, we recognize that education is a fundamental right in Kentucky.

The system of common schools must be adequately funded to achieve its goals. The system of common schools must be substantially uniform throughout the state. Each child, *every child,*... must be provided with an equal opportunity to have an adequate education. Equality is the key word here. The children of the poor and the children of the rich, the children who live in the poor districts and the children who live in the rich districts must be given the same opportunity and access to an adequate education. This obligation cannot be shifted to local counties and local school districts.

Having declared the system of common schools to be constitutionally deficient, we have directed the General Assembly to recreate and redesign a new system that will comply with the standards we have set out. Such system will guarantee to all children the opportunity for an adequate education, through a *state* system. To allow local citizens and taxpayers to make a supplementary effort in no way reduces or negates the minimum quality of education required in the statewide system.

We do not instruct the General Assembly to enact any specific legislation. We do not direct the members of the General Assembly to raise taxes. It is their decision how best to achieve efficiency. We only decide the nature of the constitutional mandate. We only determine the intent of the framers. Carrying out that intent is the duty of the General Assembly.

The essential, and minimal, characteristics of an "efficient" system of common schools, may be summarized as follows:

1. The establishment, maintenance and funding of common schools in Kentucky is the sole responsibility of the General Assembly.
2. Common schools shall be free to all.
3. Common schools shall be available to all Kentucky children.
4. Common schools shall be substantially uniform throughout the state.
5. Common schools shall provide equal educational opportunities to all Kentucky children, regardless of place of residence or economic circumstances.
6. Common schools shall be monitored by the General Assembly to assure that they are operated with no waste, no duplication, no mismanagement, and with no political influence.
7. The premise for the existence of common schools is that all children in Kentucky have a constitutional right to an adequate education.

8. The General Assembly shall provide funding which is sufficient to provide each child in Kentucky an adequate education.

9. An adequate education is one which has as its goal the development of the [following] seven capacities:

oral and written communication skills;

knowledge of economic, social, and political systems;

an understanding of governmental processes;

self-knowledge and knowledge of one's physical and mental wellness;

appreciation for one's cultural and historical heritage;

sufficient training or preparation for advanced training in either academic or vocational skills to enable each child to choose and pursue life work intelligently;

sufficient skills to compete favorably with counterparts in surrounding states, in academics or in the job market.

XI. Is the Present System "Efficient"?

In spite of the past and present efforts of the General Assembly, Kentucky's present system of common schools falls short of the mark of the constitutional mandate of "efficient." When one juxtaposes the standards of efficiency as derived from our Constitution, the cases decided thereunder, the persuasive authority from our sister states and the opinion of experts, with the virtually unchallenged evidence in the record, no other decision is possible.

Summary/Conclusion

We decline to issue any injunctions, restraining orders, writs of prohibition or writs of mandamus.

Lest there be any doubt, the result of our decision is that Kentucky's *entire system* of common schools is unconstitutional. This decision applies to the entire sweep of the system—all its parts and parcels. This decision applies to the statutes creating, implementing and financing the *system* and to all regulations, etc., pertaining thereto. It covers school construction and maintenance, teacher certification—the whole gamut of the common school system in Kentucky.

Since we have, by this decision, declared the system of common schools in Kentucky to be unconstitutional, Section 183 places an absolute duty on the General Assembly to re-create, re-establish a new system of common schools in the [state].

The General Assembly must provide adequate funding for the system. How they do this is their decision. However, if …taxes on real and personal property are used by the General Assembly as part of the financing of the redesigned state system of common schools, the General Assembly has the obligation to see that *all such property* is assessed at 100% of its fair market value. Moreover, because of the great disparity of local tax efforts in the present system of common schools, the General Assembly must establish a uniform *tax rate* for such property. In this way, all owners of real and personal property throughout the *state* will make a comparable effort in the financing of the state system of common schools.

GANT, Justice, concurring.

The majority accurately acknowledges that this Court has a *constitutional duty* to [hold that the Kentucky General Assembly has not provided for "an efficient system of common schools throughout the State."] However, the Court's *constitutional duty* is not fulfilled merely by declaring that the common school system in Kentucky is constitutionally deficient. This Court must take the additional step of directing the Trial Court to issue appropriate writs to compel correction of this constitutional deficiency.

The majority finds that the General Assembly has failed to perform a major mandatory duty imposed on it by § 183 of the [Kentucky] Constitution, yet it grants appellees no remedy for the grievous wrongs they suffer from this dereliction of duty. To declare the right but withhold a remedy is to shirk the Court's own duty.

This action should be remanded to the Franklin Circuit Court with direction to immediately issue writs of mandamus requiring the Governor to call an Extraordinary Session of the General Assembly; requiring the Governor, the Superintendent of Public Instruction, and members of the State Board of Education to recommend appropriate corrective measures; and requiring the General Assembly to enact legislation necessary to bring the Kentucky school system into compliance with § 183 of the Kentucky Constitution.

VANCE, Justice, dissenting.

I respectfully dissent. I believe the majority opinion is inherently inconsistent in that it says that our system of common schools, to be constitutionally efficient, must provide substantially equal educational opportunity for children throughout [Kentucky], yet it actually permits the continuation of a system which does not provide substantially equal educational opportunity.

I believe this is so because the opinion expressly holds that individual school districts may continue to levy [property] taxes for school purposes to be used solely within the district. Primarily, it is the levy of these [property] taxes by local school districts, which produces greatly disparate revenues in richer counties than in poorer ones, that has caused the great disparity in school funding per child in the various districts throughout [Kentucky].

[T]he continued levy of school taxes for use within individual districts, even if levied at a uniform rate throughout the state and property is assessed at 100 percent of its value, will continue to produce much more revenue in richer counties than in poorer ones. It follows that the continuation of such a tax policy will leave us exactly where we are now, and the school system will not provide substantially equal educational opportunity throughout [Kentucky], but will in fact, result in better educational opportunity for those who reside in the wealthier sections of the state.

LEIBSON, Justice, dissenting.

Respectfully, I dissent.

I agree in principle with the majority's opinion that the General Assembly has failed thus far to, "by appropriate legislation, provide for an efficient system of common schools throughout the State." Ky. Const., § 183. Nevertheless, this case should be reversed and dismissed because it does not present an "actual" or "justiciable" controversy.

Prominent on the surface of any case held to involve a political question is found a textually demonstrable constitutional commitment of the issue to a coordinate political department; or a lack of judicially discoverable and manageable standards for resolving it; or the impossibility of deciding without an initial policy determination of a kind clearly for nonjudicial discretion." *Baker v. Carr*, 369 U.S. 186 (1962).

Viewed objectively, the issues in this case fail to qualify under the standards for justiciability in *Baker v. Carr*, falling instead squarely within its description of a nonjusticiable case: there is (1) in our Kentucky Constitution a "textually demonstrable ... commitment of the issue to a coordinate political department," ... the General Assembly; (2) "a lack of judicially discoverable and manageable standards"; and (3) "the impossibility of deciding without an initial policy determination of a kind clearly for nonjudicial discretion." *Id.*

The case as presented to us neither asks for nor is amenable to specific relief through a decree conclusive in character. The appellees have made it painfully clear that they do *not* want our Court to declare any particular statute or group of statutes unconstitutional, including the system of local school districts, local financing and local administration now in place.

At oral argument appellees' counsel conceded that, in asking that we declare the system unconstitutional but not the statutes, they were presenting us with a "Gordian" knot. But ask they did, thus presenting us with an insolvable, nonjusticiable dilemma. And, we have responded with what could be expected when you open Pandora's box, an Opinion which at the same time declares everything unconstitutional and nothing unconstitutional. This is more than just a vain act or a bad precedent. This result may well create havoc in the educational process. It adds to the General Assembly's burden in seeking to improve our educational system rather than lightening the load.

We were only asked to decide one issue in this lawsuit: whether the General Assembly has responded adequately to its constitutional responsibility. This is a political question, pure and simple. We have undertaken to "enter upon policy determinations for which judicially manageable standards are lacking." Baker v. Carr, 369 U.S. 186 (1962). Without such standards, a case is not justiciable. It is not enough to decide that Kentucky does not have an "efficient system of common schools throughout the State," as Section 183 of the Constitution requires, without specifying what statutes are unconstitutional, and why. Yet, the former is not asked, and the latter is not possible. I repeat, this case is not justiciable.

QUESTIONS FOR DISCUSSION

1. What issue did the Kentucky Supreme Court have to decide in this case?
2. Who were the plaintiffs, and what did their complaint allege?

3. What did Section 183 of the Kentucky Constitution state, and why did the plaintiffs allege that Kentucky's system of public schools violated Section 183?
4. What decision had the trial court reached in this case? Did the Kentucky Supreme Court agree with the trial court's decision?
5. What evidence (i.e., "legislative" facts) did the majority of the Kentucky Supreme Court cite in support of its decision?
6. How did the majority try to learn what the framers of Section 183 intended?
7. What did the majority conclude the framers of Section 183 intended?
8. What did the majority conclude are the characteristics of an "efficient" system of public schools? Whose responsibility was it to make Kentucky's public schools "efficient"?
9. Why did Justice Gant, in his concurrence, claim that the majority had declared a right, but withheld a remedy? What remedy did he favor?
10. Why did Justice Vance, in dissent, argue that the majority's decision would permit the inequities in Kentucky's public schools to remain?
11. Why did Justice Leibson, in dissent, contend that the Kentucky Supreme Court should have reversed the trial court's decision and dismissed this case?
12. Who reached the correct result in this case? Explain.

NOTES

1. Alexis DeTocqueville, *Democracy in America* (Richard D. Heffner, ed.) (New York: Mentor, 1984), p. 75.
2. Stephen C. Halpern, "On the Imperial Judiciary and Comparative Institutional Development and Power in America," in Stephen C. Halpern and Charles M. Lamb, *Supreme Court Activism and Restraint* (Lexington, Mass.: Heath, 1982), pp. 221–247.
3. Lynn Mather, "The Fired Football Coach (Or, How Trial Courts Make Policy)," in Lee Epstein, ed., *Contemplating Courts* (Washington, D.C.: CQ Press, 1995), pp. 170–202.
4. For a discussion of this "age of statutes," see Guido Calabresi, *A Common Law for the Age of Statutes* (Cambridge, Mass.: Harvard University Press, 1982).
5. 20 U.S.C. §§ 1681–1688.
6. *Grove City College v. Bell*, 465 U.S. 555. The *Grove City* decision only settled this dispute temporarily, though. In *Grove City*, the Court interpreted Title IX to prohibit sex discrimination only in college offices and departments that received federal funds. In 1988, Congress reversed the Court's interpretation when it enacted amendments to the Civil Rights Restoration Act of 1987, which extended the reach of Title IX to "all of the operations of a college...." See Brian L. Porto, "Completing the Revolution: Title IX as Catalyst for an Alternative Model of College Sports," *Seton Hall Journal of Sport Law* 8 (1998): 352–418.
7. Abram Chayes, "The Role of the Judge in Public Law Litigation," *Harvard Law Review* 89 (1976): 1281–1316.
8. Phillip J. Cooper, *Hard Judicial Choices: Federal District Judges and State and Local Officials* (New York: Oxford University Press, 1988), p. 20.
9. See *Missouri v. Jenkins*, 515 U.S. 70 (1995).

10. Abram Chayes, "The Role of the Judge in Public Law Litigation;" see also Judith Resnick, "Managerial Judges," *Harvard Law Review* 96 (1982): 374–448.

11. *Missouri v. Jenkins*, 495 U.S. 33 (1990).

12. *Missouri v. Jenkins*, 515 U.S. 70 (1995).

13. Gerald N. Rosenberg, *The Hollow Hope: Can Courts Bring About Social Change?* (Chicago: University of Chicago Press, 1991), pp. 21–24.

14. Christopher Wolfe, *Judicial Activism: Bulwark of Freedom or Precarious Security?* (Pacific Grove, Calif.: Brooks/Cole, 1991), p. 5.

15. *Id.*

16. Raoul Berger, "The Role of the Supreme Court," *University of Arkansas at Little Rock Law Journal* 3 (1980): 1–12.

17. William Lasser, *The Limits of Judicial Power* (Chapel Hill, N.C.: University of North Carolina Press, 1988), p. 227.

18. Gary L. McDowell, *Curbing the Courts: The Constitution and the Limits of Judicial Power* (Baton Rouge, La.: Louisiana State University Press, 1988), p. 203.

19. Lasser, *The Limits of Judicial Power*, p. 231.

20. Wolfe, *Judicial Activism: Bulwark of Freedom or Precarious Security?*, p. 32.

21. 381 U.S. 479.

22. David M. O'Brien, ed., *Judges on Judging: Views from the Bench* (Chatham, N.J.: Chatham House, 1997), p. 136.

23. *Griswold v. Connecticut*, 381 U.S. 479 (1965).

24. J. Clifford Wallace, "The Jurisprudence of Judicial Restraint: A Return to the Moorings," in O'Brien, *Judges on Judging: Views from the Bench*, pp. 163–174.

25. *Id.*

26. Halpern and Lamb, *Supreme Court Activism and Restraint*, p. 12.

27. Wallace, "The Jurisprudence of Judicial Restraint: A Return to the Moorings," pp. 163–174.

28. Donald L. Horowitz, *The Courts and Social Policy* (Washington, D.C.: The Brookings Institution, 1977); "The Courts as Guardians of the Public Interest," *Public Administration Review* 37 (1977): 148–154.

29. Horowitz, *The Courts and Social Policy*, p. 23.

30. *Id.*, p. 31.

31. *Id.*, p. 30.

32. *Id.*, p. 34.

33. *Id.* The Supreme Court's decision concerning prayer at high school football games is *Santa Fe Independent School District v. Doe*, No. 99-62 (June 20, 2000).

34. *Id.*, pp. 38–41.

35. See *Rensing v. Indiana State University*, 444 N.E.2d 1170 (1983); and *Coleman v. Western Michigan University*, 336 N.W.2d 224 (1983).

36. Brian L. Porto, "Legal and Constitutional Challenges to the N.C.A.A.: The Limits of Adjudication in Intercollegiate Athletics," in Arthur T. Johnson and James H. Frey, *Government and Sport: The Public Policy Issues* (Totowa, N.J.: Rowman and Allanheld, 1985), pp. 117–139.

37. Horowitz, *The Courts and Social Policy*, pp. 45–47.

38. Id., pp. 51--54.

39. Wolfe, *Judicial Activism: Bulwark of Freedom or Precarious Security?*, p. 3.

40. *Id.*, p. 5.

41. Halpern, "On the Imperial Judiciary and Comparative Institutional Development and Power in America," pp. 221–247.

42. Stephen L. Wasby, "Arrogation of Power or Accountability: 'Judicial Imperialism' Revisited," *Judicature* 65 (1981): 209–219.

43. *Id.*, p. 213.

44. *Brown v. Board of Education*, 347 U.S. 483 (1954).

45. Lasser, *The Limits of Judicial Power*, p. 197.

46. *Id.*

47. 391 U.S. 430 (1968).

48. *Id.*

49. Wolfe, *Judicial Activism: Bulwark of Freedom or Precarious Security?*, p. 76.

50. *Id.*, p. 77.

51. Wasby, "Arrogation of Power or Accountability: 'Judicial Imperialism' Revisited," pp. 209–219.

52. Arthur Selwyn Miller, *Toward Increased Judicial Activism: The Political Role of the Supreme Court* (Westport, Conn.: Greenwood Press, 1982), p. 249.

53. William J. Brennan, Jr., "The Constitution of the United States: Contemporary Ratification," in O'Brien, ed., *Judges on Judging: Views from the Bench*, pp. 200–210.

54. Richard A. Posner, "What Am I, a Potted Plant? The Case Against Strict Constructionism," in O'Brien, ed., *Judges on Judging: Views from the Bench*, pp. 182–186.

55. *Id.*

56. *Id.*

57. Judith A. Baer, "The Fruitless Search for Original Intent," in Michael W. McCann and Gerald L. Houseman, *Judging the Constitution: Critical Essays on Judicial Lawmaking* (Glenview, Ill.: Scott, Foresman, 1989), p. 65.

58. *West Virginia Board of Education v. Barnette*, 319 U.S. 624 (1944).

59. Ralph Cavanaugh and Austin Sarat, "Thinking About Courts: Toward and Beyond a Jurisprudence of Judicial Competence," *Law and Society Review* 14 (1980): 371–420.

60. *Id.*

61. Chayes, "The Role of the Judge in Public Law Litigation," pp. 1281–1316.

62. Rosenberg, *The Hollow Hope: Can Courts Bring About Social Change?*, p. 10.

63. *Id.*, p. 13.

64. *Id.*, p. 15.

65. *Id.*, p. 21.

66. *Id.*, pp. 33–35.

67. *Id.*, p. 338.

68. Gerald N. Rosenberg, "The Real World of Constitutional Rights: The Supreme Court and the Implementation of the Abortion Decisions," in Epstein, ed., *Contemplating Courts*, pp. 390–419.

69. Rosenberg, *The Hollow Hope: Can Courts Bring About Social Change?*, pp. 338–339.

70. *Id.*, pp. 24–25.

71. *Engel v. Vitale*, 370 U.S. 421 (1962), outlawed prayer in the public schools, and *Abington School District v. Schempp*, 374 U.S. 203 (1963), ended school-sponsored Bible readings.

72. Bradley C. Canon, "The Supreme Court and Policy Reform: The Hollow Hope Revisited," in David A. Schultz, ed., *Leveraging the Law: Using the Courts to Achieve Social Change* (New York: Peter Lang, 1998), pp. 215–249.

73. 354 U.S. 476.

74. Canon, "The Supreme Court and Policy Reform: The Hollow Hope Revisited," pp. 215–249.

75. *Id.*, pp. 240–241.
76. David A. Schultz and Stephen E. Gottlieb, "Legal Functionalism and Social Change: A Reassessment of Rosenberg's *The Hollow Hope*," in Schultz, ed., *Leveraging the Law: Using Courts to Achieve Social Change*, pp. 169–207.
77. Wolfe, *Judicial Activism: Bulwark of Freedom or Precarious Security?*, p. 50.
78. Brennan, "The Constitution of the United States: Contemporary Ratification," pp. 200–210.
79. The Court declared a Texas flag-burning statute unconstitutional in *Texas v. Johnson*, 491 U.S. 397 (1989). It declared a federal flag-burning statute unconstitutional in *United States v. Eichman*, 496 U.S. 310 (1990).
80. Alan M. Dershowitz, "The Sovereignty of Process: The Limits of Original Intention," in National Legal Center for the Public Interest, *Politics and the Constitution: The Nature and Extent of Interpretation* (Washington, D.C.: National Legal Center for the Public Interest and the American Studies Center, 1990), pp. 11–16.
81. *Id.*
82. Brennan, "The Constitution of the United States: Contemporary Ratification," pp. 200–210.
83. See Henry J. Abraham, "Line-Drawing Between Judicial Activism and Restraint: A 'Centrist' Approach and Analysis," in Halpern and Lamb, eds., *Supreme Court Activism and Restraint*, pp. 201–219.
84. 372 U.S. 335.
85. *Id.*
86. Baer, "The Fruitless Search for Original Intent," pp. 49–71.
87. Cooper, *Hard Judicial Choices: Federal District Judges and State and Local Officials*, p. 341.
88. *Missouri v. Jenkins*, 495 U.S. 33 (1990).
89. Tinsley E. Yarbrough, *Judge Frank Johnson and Human Rights in Alabama* (University, Ala.: University of Alabama Press, 1981), p. 91.
90. *Id.*, p. 99. The case was *Lee v. Macon County*, 231 F. Supp. 743 (M.D. Ala. 1964).
91. *Id.*
92. *Id.*, pp. 139–140.
93. *Id.*, pp. 192–193.
94. 349 F. Supp. 278.
95. *Id.*, pp. 186–187.
96. 364 F. Supp. 659.
97. *Id.*, p. 187.
98. 406 F. Supp. 318.
99. Yarbrough, *Judge Frank Johnson and Human Rights in Alabama*, p. 200.
100. *Id.*
101. *Id.*, p. 207.
102. 325 F. Supp. 781.
103. Yarbrough, *Judge Frank Johnson and Human Rights in Alabama*, p. 159.
104. *Id.*, p. 169.
105. *Id.*
106. *Id.*, p. 170.
107. The U.S. Court of Appeals for the Fifth Circuit did not think that Judge Johnson had acted improperly in *Wyatt*. It affirmed his decision in *Wyatt* in 1974. See Yarbrough, *Judge Frank Johnson and Human Rights in Alabama*, p. 174.
108. Wolfe, *Judicial Activism: Bulwark of Freedom or Precarious Security?*, p. 81.
109. *Id.*

110. Wasby, "Arrogation of Power or Accountability: 'Judicial Imperialism' Revisited," pp. 209–219.
111. Cooper, *Hard Judicial Choices: Federal District Judges and State and Local Officials*, p. 20.
112. *Id.*
113. *Id.*
114. Cavanaugh and Sarat, "Thinking About Courts: Toward and Beyond a Jurisprudence of Judicial Competence," 371–420.
115. Gerald N. Rosenberg, "Knowledge and Desire: Thinking About Courts and Social Change," in David A. Schultz, ed., *Leveraging the Law: Using the Courts to Achieve Social Change*, pp. 251–291.
116. Wolfe, *Judicial Activism: Bulwark of Freedom or Precarious Security?*, p. 65.
117. Halpern, "On the Imperial Judiciary and Comparative Institutional Development and Power in America," p. 234; Schultz, ed., *Leveraging the Law: Using the Courts to Achieve Social Change*, p. 200.
118. See, for example, *Claremont School District v. Governor*, 142 N.H. 462, 703 A.2d 1353 (1997); *Brigham v. State*, 166 Vt. 246, 692 A.2d 384 (1997); *Roosevelt Elementary School District No. 66 v. Bishop*, 877 P.2d 806 (Ariz. 1994); *Tennessee Small School Systems v. McWherter*, 851 S.W.2d 139 (Tenn. 1993); and *Edgewood Independent School District v. Kirby*, 777 S.W.2d 391 (Tex. 1989). Another of these cases, *Rose v. Council for Better Education, Inc.*, 790 S.W.2d 186 (Ky. 1989), is featured in the epilogue to this chapter.

Chapter 10

SUMMARY AND CONCLUSION

SUMMARY

The judicial process occurs at the intersection of law and politics; both law and politics influence court decisions. Courts make public policy decisions, notwithstanding their use of legal rules, language, and reasoning, and they enforce those decisions by exercising the coercive power of government.

Law and politics are related, but they are not identical. Their connections include lawyers' participation in politics, the influence of political party affiliations and ideology on judicial selection, the election of judges in many states, and decisions by the U.S. Supreme Court about election law. Still, their differences are as important as their connections. Law is more structured and more narrowly focused than politics; rules of evidence, burdens of proof, and legal language constrain lawyers and judges. Therefore, a court decision can be "good law" because it properly construes statutory or constitutional language, or relevant precedents, but be bad politics because it upholds minority rights that the majority opposes. Judge Frank Johnson's controversial decisions concerning school desegregation and prison conditions, respectively, in Alabama, illustrate this point.

Modern judges are well aware that both law and politics influence their decisions. Indeed, modern judges try to reconcile law and politics so that Americans will respect and obey the law and courts will remain vital institutions within the American political system. For example, in *Planned Parenthood of Southeastern Pennsylvania v. Casey*,[1] the Supreme Court honored *stare decisis* and Americans' longstanding reliance on *Roe v. Wade*, and recognized that the preservation of *Roe* was necessary to the preservation of its own institutional strength.[2] *Casey* shows the importance of both legal and political influences on courts; thus, in order to understand the judicial process, one must understand both law and politics.

Federalism reflects the interaction between law and politics in America. Federalism, which divides political power between a national government and fifty state governments, is a core constitutional principle born of a political compromise between supporters of federal power and supporters of state power at the Constitutional Convention in 1787. It aims to achieve national unity while respecting the states' diverse traditions; the most noteworthy result of that philosophy is a dual system of state and federal trial and appellate courts that is unique in the world. The federal government and each state has a system of trial courts and appellate courts, including a court of last resort.

The dual court system flows from federalism, and important consequences flow from the dual court system. One consequence is that there is considerable diversity among states in the penalties imposed for criminal offenses. The most stark example of that is the death penalty, which Texas imposes regularly, but Vermont opposes. Another consequence is that the Supreme Court must periodically decide whether the federal government or a state has exceeded the powers granted to it in the Constitution. Thus, in cases such as *Martin v. Hunter's Lessee*, the Court shapes the fundamental political relationship between federal power and state power.[3] Put another way, the judicial process molds the political process in those cases.

The judicial process also substitutes for the political process in the United States. We Americans want protection from life's emotional pain and physical hazards, but we do not trust the elected branches of government to protect us. Therefore, we reject the means of self-protection that other postindustrial democracies use, including administrative regulations and national health insurance, and instead hail into court the individuals and institutions that injure us or that fail to prevent our injuries. Ironically, despite our professed distrust of government, we readily seek protection or compensation in courts, which, of course, are part of government.

For that reason, political controversies frequently become lawsuits. Some political controversies even begin as lawsuits that seek to force elected officials to act. The public school funding issue has evolved that way in most states. When major political controversies become lawsuits, courts become important policy makers in the American political system. Lawyers become public figures who can lay the groundwork for future political careers through their involvement in high-profile cases. Under these circumstances, it is no wonder that Professor Mary Ann Glendon has characterized America as *A Nation Under Lawyers*.[4]

Judicial selection and removal further demonstrate the interaction between law and politics. Indeed, there is an unresolved tension in judicial selection between independence (law) and accountability (politics); Americans want judges to decide cases based on the law, but also to reflect mainstream political views. Accountability sometimes trumps independence in state court elections, as occurred in 1986 in California, where voters unseated three state supreme court justices who had consistently voted to reverse death sentences. The greatest cost of accountability is the appearance of impropriety that results when judges who run for reelection accept campaign contributions from lawyers who argue cases in their courtrooms.

Politics also influences the appointment of federal judges. Candidates for federal judgeships usually belong to the same political party as the presidents who nominate them, and they are often politically active prior to being nominated to the bench. The president's staff, the Senate Judiciary Committee, and interest groups screen them for ideological acceptability. Finally, their nominations may reflect not only legal competence and ideological compatibility with the president, but other political influences such as race, gender, religion, or geography. All of the above observations apply especially to Supreme Court nominees.

Even the removal of judges is subject to political influences because the institutions that remove judges from office, namely, legislatures (state and federal judges) and the electorate (state judges only), are inherently political. That was evident in 1996, when voters ousted Justice Penny White of the Tennessee Supreme Court. Her defeat followed an aggressive campaign by the state's Republican Party to defeat her after she voted to grant a new hearing to a convicted murderer.

Justice White's defeat shows that politics is the frequent companion of criminal law because many voters believe that judges favor defendants' rights over victims' rights. There are other reasons, though, for the link between politics and criminal law. Prosecutors and judges are elected officials in many states, so politics influences who will prosecute and who will preside at criminal trials. Prosecutors decide whether or not to prosecute certain crimes, so politics indirectly influences prosecutors' choices of whom and what to prosecute. Legislators write criminal statutes, so politics influences substantive criminal law too.

Still, politics must take a back seat to law in the courtroom, and it usually does. Law must resolve the key issues in a case, such as whether an illegal search occurred or whether the defendant was the victim of selective prosecution. Otherwise, denials of constitutional rights, such as the Supreme Court reversed in *Sheppard v. Maxwell*, would likely occur with tragic frequency.[5]

Politics accompanies civil law, too, especially tort law. Indeed, in recent years, "tort reform" has been the subject of a lively political debate. Business people, defendants' lawyers, and Republican politicians charge that tort litigation has damaged America's competitiveness in the global marketplace. Plaintiffs' lawyers and Democratic politicians counter that litigation is a necessary incentive to manufacturers to produce safe and effective products. The results of the presidential election in 2000 are likely to influence future developments on this issue.

Appellate courts, state and federal, make the most consequential public policy decisions. Those decisions, which are a distinct minority except at the U.S. Supreme Court, force appellate judges to choose between competing visions of how America ought to work. They therefore arouse the judges' public policy preferences, which interact with the law, the case record (including the facts), the judges' desire for collegiality, and the court's institutional norms (e.g., respect for precedent) to produce results. Thus, appellate judges correct lower court errors in the vast majority of their cases, but they also make public policy in their most important cases.

In *State v. Kirchoff*, for example, the Vermont Supreme Court held that a warrantless police search of open fields is unconstitutional when the owner of those fields has taken steps to exclude the public from his property.[6] In *Pines v. Perssion*, the Wisconsin Supreme Court held that there is an implied warranty of habitability in a lease for a furnished house, which entitles tenants to abandon the premises without incurring liability if those premises are unfit for human habitation.[7] *Kirchoff* and *Pines* were important policy decisions; *Kirchoff* gave Vermonters more privacy from police searches than they previously had, and *Pines* gave Wisconsin tenants legal recourse against unscrupulous landlords. Thus, Vermont was more free after *Kirchoff*, and Wisconsin was more just after *Pines*.

Both law and politics influence judicial policy making; therefore, both law and political science help us to understand the judicial process. The legal influences include procedural devices, such as the justiciability doctrines, jurisdictional statutes, and statutes of limitations, all of which enable judges to sidestep cases that they think are inappropriate for judicial resolution. The Supreme Court used one of the justiciability doctrines, namely, the political question doctrine, to avoid deciding whether the Vietnam War was unconstitutional. The legal influences also include substantive considerations, such as the comparatively easy nature of most cases, the clarity of some legislative and constitutional language, and norms of proper judicial behavior, especially fidelity to *stare decisis*. The Supreme Court majority honored *stare decisis* in *Casey* when it preserved the right to obtain an abortion.

The political influences are attitudinal, organizational, and institutional. The attitudinal influences are judges' public policy preferences, the organizational influences are interest-group activities, and the institutional influences are colleagues, higher courts, other branches of government, and public opinion. Policy preferences trumped *stare decisis* in *Payne v. Tennessee*, wherein the Supreme Court reversed two precedents, and permitted victim-impact statements at a sentencing hearing.[8] Elaborate campaigns for and against the Supreme Court candidacies of Robert Bork in 1987 and Clarence Thomas in 1991 revealed that interest groups can influence judicial decisions by influencing judicial selection. Had the Senate confirmed Bork, he would probably have cast the fifth vote in *Casey* to overturn *Roe*. Instead, Justices Kennedy, O'Connor, and Souter demonstrated in *Casey* that institutional influences, such as concern for the Court's public image and future strength, can sometimes cause judges to cast votes that do not necessarily reflect their policy preferences.

Casey, *Roe*, and other judicial policy decisions have spawned a lively debate among scholars about whether: (1) courts *should* make public policy; (2) courts *can* make public policy effectively; and (3) courts can produce significant social change. Supporters of judicial restraint argue that courts should typically refrain from making public policy. Instead, the legislative and executive branches of government should make policy because they are accountable to the voters.

Courts, then, should defer to the will of the majority by interpreting statutory or constitutional language according to the intent of its authors. Supporters of judicial restraint also argue that courts cannot make public policy wisely because they were designed to resolve individual disputes about past events, not to shape future events.

Judicial activists counter that courts should foster human dignity by expanding equality and personal freedom, especially when elected officials fail to do so because the likely beneficiaries of change lack the political power necessary to achieve it. Indeed, the Constitution envisions that courts will play that role because the Bill of Rights places individual rights beyond majority control, and it empowers courts to protect them.

Supporters of the constrained court model contend that it is pointless to debate whether or not courts should make public policy because courts do not produce significant social change. At most, courts assist social changes that would have occurred anyway. Supporters of the dynamic court model respond that judicial independence enables courts to jump-start social change when elected officials are unwilling to do so.

One searches in vain for a reason why courts should not make public policy. Indeed, judicial policy making is inevitable because courts must preserve constitutional principles against tyranny by the majority. In so doing, courts choose between competing values, such as patriotism and the freedom of speech. When courts make such choices, they make public policy. Courts can make public policy wisely when they respect the constitutional text, tell defendants what they cannot do instead of what they must do, and, if they must tell defendants what to do, give the defendants an opportunity to devise plans to reform themselves. Courts will rarely initiate significant social change, nor can they achieve it alone. Still, as *Rose v. Council for Better Education, Inc.* shows, courts can influence social change by legitimizing emerging views, by forcing public officials to address long-standing problems, and by enabling them to do so without paying a high political price.[9] That may not epitomize a "dynamic court," but it is no small accomplishment in a political system built on separated powers and a belief in limited government.

CONCLUSION

Courts are critical decision makers within the American political system, which is why political scientists study them as much as lawyers do, albeit differently. Courts are keepers of the constitutional flame; their decisions remind us what values we hold dear, and enforce those values when legislative majorities would act otherwise. To enforce constitutional values is to give shape and form to the relationships that exist between: (1) the branches of the federal government and the state governments, respectively; (2) the federal government and the states; (3) government (federal or state) and individuals; (4) individuals and institutions;

and (5) individuals in their personal and professional lives. Thus, court decisions often have enormous political consequences.

Consider, for example, the cases that appear in the epilogues to the preceding chapters. *United States v. Eichman* (Chapter 1) invalidated a federal anti-flag-desecration statute because flag desecration is constitutionally protected speech, even when a majority in Congress disagrees. *Rose v. Council for Better Education, Inc.* (Chapter 9) invalidated Kentucky's system of public schools because it was not the "efficient" system that the Kentucky Constitution contemplated, despite the state legislature's efforts to improve it. *Martin v. Hunter's Lessee* (Chapter 2) held that the U.S. Supreme Court could review the decision of a state supreme court because the supremacy clause of the Constitution makes federal power superior to state power in our federal system. *Chisom v. Roemer* (Chapter 4) applied the antidiscrimination provisions of the federal Voting Rights Act to state judicial elections.[10]

Sheppard v. Maxwell (Chapter 5) held that a violation of the Sixth Amendment right to a fair trial occurs when a judge fails to protect a defendant from adverse publicity before or during trial. *State v. Kirchoff* (Chapter 7), which restricted police searches of "open fields" in Vermont, also expanded personal freedom and limited governmental power. So did *Planned Parenthood of Southeastern Pennsylvania v. Casey* (Chapter 8), which, despite approving restrictions on abortion, preserved the constitutional right to obtain an abortion.

Even court decisions in nominally private disputes can have public policy consequences. For example, *Florida Bar v. Went For It, Inc.* (Chapter 3) upheld Florida Bar rules that prohibited lawyers from soliciting personal-injury and wrongful-death clients by mail within thirty days of an accident.[11] Those rules aimed to improve the public image of Florida lawyers. *B.M.W. of North America, Inc. v. Gore* (Chapter 6) reversed an award of $2 million in punitive damages to a car owner whom the manufacturer failed to notify that his car had been repainted prior to sale.[12] Supporters of "tort reform" applauded the reversal, which reinforced their view that Congress ought to impose a nationwide "cap" on the amount of money that juries can award in punitive damages.

Thus, if you study the judicial process carefully, you will unlock the door to a sophisticated understanding of the entire American political system. This book aims to be the key that opens the lock.

NOTES

1. 505 U.S. 833 (1992).
2. 410 U.S. 113 (1973).
3. 14 U.S. (1 Wheat.) 304 (1816).
4. Mary Ann Glendon, *A Nation Under Lawyers: How the Crisis in the Legal Profession is Transforming American Society* (New York: Farrar, Strauss and Giroux, 1994).
5. 384 U.S. 333 (1966).
6. 156 Vt. 1, 587 A.2d 988 (1991).

7. 14 Wis.2d 590, 111 N.W.2d 409 (1961).
8. 501 U.S. 808 (1991).
9. 790 S.W.2d 186 (KY. 1989).
10. 501 U.S. 380 (1991).
11. 115 S.Ct. 2371 (1995).
12. 116 S.Ct. 1589 (1996).

Appendix A
RESEARCHING THE LAW

You can determine the current state of the law on a particular subject by learning how to use a few basic legal research tools. This appendix will identify those tools, and it will explain how to use them. If you would like additional instruction in legal research, see William P. Statsky, *Legal Research and Writing: Some Starting Points*, Fifth Edition (Albany, N.Y.: West Legal Studies, 1999).

The legal research tools to be discussed below were once available only in printed form in libraries. They are still available in printed form in libraries, but they are now also available through electronic legal research services, which operate by a hookup between your computer and another computer, often by means of a telephone line. The best known of these services are **WESTLAW**, a product of West Publishing Company, and **LEXIS**, a product of the Mead Data Company. WESTLAW and LEXIS enable you to find and to read cases, statutes, and other legal materials without traveling to a law library. You must pay to use these services, though, and they can be expensive unless your college library offers them (or one of them) to students free of charge. Consult a reference librarian at your college library to find out if either WESTLAW or LEXIS is available to you.

This appendix will show you how to conduct legal research using printed sources, in case electronic sources are unavailable or prohibitively expensive. You can research the law just as well in its printed form as in its electronic form. The process may be slower using printed materials, but it is considerably cheaper. Besides, not all of the sources that exist in print also exist in electronic form.

Suppose that you want to know the state of the law regarding sex discrimination in college sports. The first step is to consult a series of **finding tools**, which help you to find the cases, statutes, and other legal sources that will, in turn, reveal the state of the law on sex discrimination in college sports. The first finding tool you should consult is a legal encyclopedia, either **American Jurisprudence,** Second Edition (commonly known as **Am. Jur. 2d**) or **Corpus Juris Secundum** (commonly known as **CJS**). Law school libraries have both encyclopedias; city, county, and state law libraries have at least one of them; and your college library may have one of them. Let's assume that you decide to use Am. Jur. 2d. Select the volume that contains the index to the remaining volumes; it will say "Index" on the spine. Look in the index for headings that might lead you to cases about sex discrimination in college sports. The likely possibilities include "Discrimination," "Sex Discrimination," and "Civil Rights." The index shows that volume 15 of Am. Jur. 2d contains the heading "Civil Rights," so you should consult volume 15.

In volume 15, study the table of contents for the heading "Civil Rights." You will see that there is a subheading, "Sex Discrimination in Education," that begins on page 268. Examine that subheading, and you will notice that section 88 under "Sex Discrimination in Education" concerns "Athletics." Turn to section 88, and read the paragraph about sex discrimination in sports. Disregard the part about high school sports, but make careful notes from the discussion on college sports. Section 88 identifies the governing statute in this field, **Title IX**, as **20 U.S.C.A. § 1681 et seq.** That means that you can find Title IX in volume 20 of the *United States Code Annotated*, beginning at section 1681. The United States Code Annotated (or **U.S.C.A.**) is available in all law libraries and in some college libraries. Make a note to yourself to read the text of Title IX when you have finished with Am. Jur. 2d.

You are not finished with Am. Jur. 2d yet, though. Section 88 contains a second important reference, **23 A.L.R. Fed. 664**, which is an article about sex discrimination in college sports. Make a note to find that article later in volume 23 of the *American Law Reports Federal* **(A.L.R. Fed.),** beginning on page 664. You are most likely to find A.L.R. Fed. in a law school library.

One important step remains before you are finished with Am. Jur. 2d. Turn to the paperbound **pocket part** that is inserted in the back cover of volume 15, and look for section 88 under the "Civil Rights" heading. The purpose of consulting the pocket part is to find up-to-date information; pocket parts are always more current than the texts of printed sources. Section 88 in the pocket part will refer you to a case, *Haffer v. Temple University*, which is followed by a citation, 688 F.2d 14 (3d Cir. 1982). You should read *Haffer*, so make a note of it, including the citation. The citation means that you can find *Haffer* in volume 688 of the *Federal Reporter*, Second Series, beginning on page 14, and that the U.S. Court of Appeals for the Third Circuit decided *Haffer* in 1982. The *Federal Reporter*, which contains decisions of the federal appellate courts, is available in law school libraries, in city, county, and state law libraries, and in some college libraries.

Section 88 in the pocket part will also refer you to an article about Title IX, which is located at **6 J. Coll. & Univ. Law 345**. You can find this article in volume 6 of the *Journal of College and University Law*, beginning on page 345. The *Journal of College and University Law* will probably be available at a law school library. Finally, section 88 will refer you to a second article on sex discrimination in college sports, which is located at 129 A.L.R. Fed. 571. The volume number 129 tells you that this article is more recent than the article you discovered earlier, at 23 A.L.R. Fed. 664. You are now finished with Am. Jur. 2d. It yielded a wealth of information, including Title IX, a case, a law review article, and two A.L.R. Fed. articles (known as **annotations**). The article and the annotations will undoubtedly identify more cases on sex discrimination in college sports.

Before you read those materials, though, you should consult another finding tool, known as a **digest**, which will locate additional cases for you. Title IX, a federal statute, governs sex discrimination in college sports, so you should consult *West's Federal Practice Digest*, Fourth Edition. Look in the "Index" volume under "Civil Rights," and you will see that volume 13 discusses civil rights. In volume 13, examine the table of contents under "Civil Rights," and you will find a subheading, "Sex Discrimination," which is located at **key number 128**. Key number 128 contains summaries of cases about sex discrimination; if you skim-read these summaries, you will find two cases that concern sex discrimination in college sports. They are *Favia v. Indiana University of Pennsylvania*, 7 F.3d 332 (3d Cir. 1993) and *Roberts v. Colorado State Board of Agriculture*, 998 F.2d 824 (10th Cir.), *cert. denied*, 510 U.S. 1004 (1993). Make a note to read both cases; you can find *Favia* in volume 7 of the *Federal Reporter*, 3d Series, beginning at page 332, and *Roberts* in volume 998 of the *Federal Reporter*, 2d Series, beginning at page 824.

Next, update this information by selecting the paperbound *Supplement* located next to volume 13 on the library shelf, and by consulting key number 128 under the heading "Civil Rights." The *Supplement* contains several more cases on sex discrimination in college sports, including *Beasley v. Alabama State University*, 3 F. Supp. 2d 1325 (M.D. Ala. 1998); *Pederson v. Louisiana State University*, 912 F. Supp. 892 (M.D. La. 1996); *Cohen v. Brown University*, 101 F.3d 155 (1st. Cir. 1996), *cert. denied*, 117 S. Ct. 1469 (1997); *Gonyo v. Drake University*, 879 F. Supp. 1000 (S.D. Iowa 1995); *Kelley v. Board of Trustees*, 35 F.3d 265 (7th Cir. 1994); *Cook v. Colgate University*, 992 F.2d 17 (2d Cir. 1993); and *Bennett v. West Texas State University*, 799 F.2d 155 (5th Cir. 1986). In order to find these later cases, you must skim the summaries of numerous cases that concern sex discrimination outside of college sports. Take note only of the cases that feature sex discrimination in college sports. When you have found all of those cases, you are finished with *West's Federal Practice Digest*.

By now, you should know how to find federal appellate court decisions contained in the *Federal Reporter*, but you are probably unfamiliar with the *Federal Supplement* (F. Supp.), which contains federal district court decisions, such as *Pederson* and *Gonyo*. *Pederson* is in volume 912 of the *Federal Supplement*, beginning at page 892, and *Gonyo* is in volume 879 of the *Federal Supplement*, beginning at page 1,000. The *Federal Supplement* is available in law school libraries; in city, county, and state law libraries; and in some college libraries.

Proceed to the *American Law Reports, Federal* or **A.L.R. Fed.** The annotations in A.L.R. Fed collect and summarize all of the federal court decisions to date on a particular topic. Recall that Am. Jur. 2d referred you to an annotation located at 23 A.L.R. Fed 664; now it is time to find and to read that annotation. You will discover that 23 A.L.R. Fed 664 is out of date, so be sure to consult 129 A.L.R. Fed. 571, which updates 23 A.L.R. Fed. 664. When you consult 129 A.L.R. Fed. 571, you will find, in the research references that precede the text of the annotation, a list of law review articles on sex discrimination in college sports and a book by Walter T. Campion, Jr., titled *Fundamentals of Sports Law*, which discusses sex discrimination in college sports in section 19.4. Make a note to yourself to read the law review articles [e.g., T. J. Wilde, "Gender Equity in Athletics: Coming of Age in the 90's," 4 *Marquette Sports Law Journal* 217 (Spring 1994)] and section 19.4 of Campion's book. Then check the pocket part of volume 129 under the heading "129 A.L.R. Fed 571–586," where you will find another case, *Boucher v. Syracuse University*, 164 F.3d 113 (2d Cir. 1999).

Before reading the cases that you have discovered, you should make sure that they are still "good law"; that is, that a higher court or a later case has not reversed any one of them. Your cases are exclusively federal cases, so you must consult **Shepard's Federal Citations** to find out whether they are still "good law." *Shepard's Federal Citations* is available in law school libraries; in city, county, and state law libraries; and in some college libraries. Using *Shepard's* to make sure that a case is still "good law" is known as **sheparizing** that case.

Suppose that you want to sheparize *Roberts v. Colorado State Board of Agriculture*, 998 F.2d 824 (10th Cir. 1993). Find the most recent volume of *Shepard's Federal Citations*, which will be paperbound, and read the cover to see if it includes case citations from the *Federal Reporter*, Second Series (F.2d) and from volume 998 because that is where *Roberts* is located. If not, select the hardcover volume that includes 998 F.2d 824. Find the page on which "Vol. 998" appears at the top and **824** appears in bold black type; underneath that citation, you will find a list of citations for later cases that refer to *Roberts*. Check to see if any of the later citations has the letter "o" or the letter "l" next to it. The letter "o" would indicate that *Roberts* is no longer good law because the later case **overruled** it. The letter "l" would indicate that *Roberts* is still good law in certain circumstances, but that its reach is **limited** to those circumstances.

The letters "c," "d," and "f" are also important; be sure to read later cases whose citations have any of those letters next to them. The letter "c" indicates that the later case **criticized** the sheparized case. When you sheparize *Roberts*, you will see that in 912 FS (F. Supp) 913, the majority opinion criticized *Roberts*. The letter "d" indicates that the later case is **distinguishable** from the sheparized case, which justifies a different result in the later case. The letter "f" indicates that the court in the later case **followed** the reasoning of the court in the sheparized case. When you sheparize *Roberts*, you will see that in 905 FS 1495 and 3 FS2d 1335, the respective courts followed the reasoning of *Roberts*. Incidentally, you will also find the letter "j" next to the citation 128 F.3d 1046; that means that in the cited case, a judge referred to *Roberts* in a dissenting opinion.

Skim the later cases that do not have a letter after their citations. Often, these cases are not useful because they cite the sheparized case in a way that is irrelevant to the subject of your research. For example, they might cite the sheparized case for its decision on a procedural matter, such as mootness or ripeness, not for its conclusion on the merits of the dispute. Sheparize all of the cases that you found in Am. Jur. 2d, *West's Federal Practice Digest*, and A.L.R. Fed. concerning sex discrimination in college sports. If those cases are still good law, you can either read them now or set them aside and read Title IX first.

You will find Title IX in volume 20 of the *United States Code Annotated* (U.S.C.A.), beginning at section 1681, as you learned from Am. Jur. 2d. If volume 20 of the U.S.C.A. is unavailable, see whether the **United States Code Service** (U.S.C.S.) or the **United States Code** (U.S.C.) is available. Both the

U.S.C.S. and the U.S.C. contain Title IX in volume 20, beginning at section 1681. If possible, use either the U.S.C.A. or the U.S.C.S. when researching statutes, because they refer you to additional sources of information; the U.S.C. does not.

Read Title IX, which you will soon discover encompasses 20 U.S.C.A. §§ 1681–1688. Also read the **Historical and Statutory Notes** about Title IX that are available in the U.S.C.A. (and the U.S.C.S.). The notes contain three important pieces of information. First, Title IX, which Congress enacted in 1972, is Public Law 92–318. That designation is your key to the *U.S. Code Congressional and Administrative News*, which contains the history of Title IX. You can read that history in the volume of the *U.S. Code Congressional and Administrative News* for 1972 that has the words **Legislative History** printed on its spine. This publication is available in law school libraries; in some city, county, and state law libraries; and in some college libraries. It can illuminate the circumstances in which, and the intent with which, Congress enacted a particular law.

Second, there is a list of **regulations** that the former federal Department of Health, Education and Welfare (now Health and Human Services) developed in order to enforce Title IX. Those regulations are located at **45 C.F.R. Part 86**; that refers to volume 45 of the *Code of Federal Regulations* (C.F.R.), beginning at Part 86. These regulations are also located at 34 C.F.R. Part 106. The C.F.R. is available in law school libraries; in some city, county, and state law libraries; and in some college libraries. Search the index to 45 C.F.R. Part 86 for headings that concern college sports. You will find Part 86.37, titled "Financial Assistance," and Part 86.41, titled "Athletics." Both regulations require colleges to satisfy certain criteria in order to comply with Title IX. Identical regulations are located at 34 C.F.R. Part 106.37 (Financial Assistance) and 34 C.F.R. Part 106.41 (Athletics), respectively. Part 86.37 (like Part 106.37) regulates athletic scholarships, and Part 86.41 (like Part 106.41) indicates how colleges can provide "equal educational opportunity" in sports to their male and female students.

Third, another case and several more law review articles on sex discrimination in college sports are available for your consideration. Make a note to yourself to read the case, *National Collegiate Athletic Association v. Smith*, 119 S. Ct. 924 (1999), which is important because it is a decision of the U.S. Supreme Court. You can find this decision at volume 119 of the *Supreme Court Reporter*, beginning on page 924. The *Supreme Court Reporter* is available in law school libraries; in city, county, and state law libraries; and in some college libraries.

You now have a substantial body of information about sex discrimination in college sports. It is time to end your research when you cease to discover new cases or articles. Presumably, you have read carefully the materials that you have found. If so, you have learned what Title IX and its regulations require colleges to do in order to comply with the law against sex discrimination in college athletics. You have also learned what the federal courts have said that Title IX requires colleges to do in order to comply with that law. Thus, you now know the state of the law

on sex discrimination in college sports, and you can use that knowledge to antic-
ipate the outcomes of future cases on this subject.

A similar process would enable you to research an issue of state law. Suppose
that after reading Chapter 6, you want to research the potential liability of Maine's
ski area operators for injuries that alpine skiers suffer at ski resorts in Maine. Begin
by consulting **West's Maine Digest** or **West's Atlantic Digest** (read only cases
from Maine though), using the volume that includes the heading "Negligence"
because that is the subject of the cases you seek. Read the case summaries until
you find Maine cases that arose from alpine skiing injuries; be sure to consult both
the bound volume of the digest and its pocket part. Make a list of the cases to be
read; you can find them in the **Maine Reports** or in the **Atlantic Reporter**. It may
be difficult to locate the *Maine Reports* outside of Maine, but law school libraries
nationwide have the *Atlantic Reporter*, which contains Maine cases. In Maine, you
can also find the *Maine Reports* in city or county law libraries, in the state law
library, and in some college libraries.

You might also be able to find ski liability cases from Maine, and an annotation that explains their rulings, in **A.L.R. 4th** or **A.L.R. 5th**, which are the state-
law equivalents of A.L.R. Fed. You can update the cases you find by using
Shepard's Maine Citations or **Shepard's Atlantic Citations**, both of which are
available in law school libraries nationwide. *Shepard's Maine Citations* is also likely
to be available in city or county law libraries, in the state law library, and in some
college libraries, in Maine. The cases that you discover will undoubtedly refer you
to Maine's statute(s) on ski area operator liability, which you should read carefully
early in your research. You can find Maine statutes in **Maine Revised Statutes
Annotated** (M.R.S.A.), a multivolume set that is available in law school libraries
nationwide, in city or county law libraries, or the state law library in Maine, and
in some college libraries in Maine. If you fail to find cases that refer you to the ski
liability statute(s), search the index volume to the M.R.S.A. under "skiing,"
"alpine skiing," or "ski area operators," and you will find the relevant statute(s).

If you have access to the Internet, you can find some of the materials identified in this appendix online at no extra charge. You will not find privately published materials, such as Am. Jur. 2d, A.L.R. Fed., Shepard's, the U.S.C.A., the
U.S.C.S., *West's Maine Digest*, or *West's Atlantic Digest* online; they are available
electronically only through WESTLAW or LEXIS, which require a subscription
fee. Still, you will find online federal government publications, such as the *United
States Code* and the *Code of Federal Regulations*. You will also find decisions of the
federal district courts, the federal appellate courts, and the U.S. Supreme Court,
in addition to numerous law review articles.

Use the search engine INFOSEEK, ALTA VISTA, or YAHOO to gain access
to the Web sites **Findlaw** (*www.findlaw.com*) and **Jurist** (*www.jurist.law.pitt.edu*).
Findlaw has links to federal court decisions (search by case name or by docket
number), the *United States Code*, the *Code of Federal Regulations*, and law review
articles. Incidentally, you can also locate the *United States Code* directly at
www.uscode.house.gov/usc.htm. Jurist has links to recent Supreme Court decisions,

law review articles, books about the law, and book reviews. Most states have made their statutes and state supreme court decisions available online, so you can find many state legal materials electronically too. Consult a reference librarian at your college library for help in finding Web sites that house state legal materials.

I hope that this appendix will inspire you to undertake legal research, in order to write a term paper for a course or just to learn more about an issue that interests you. Begin by retracing the steps outlined for researching sex discrimination in college sports because they will show you what the various legal research tools look like. Use those tools often; with practice, your research will uncover more information in less time than you once needed.

That will serve you well if you become a lawyer. A lawyer's time and a client's money are finite; therefore, lawyers must conduct legal research efficiently or be willing to work more hours than they can bill to their clients. Until you become efficient, keep your sense of humor by using the search engine Yahoo to find the Web site titled "Attorney Jokes." Good luck with your research!

Appendix B

DOCUMENTS
OF LITIGATION

CRIMINAL

Printed below are replicas of several documents that figure prominently in criminal litigation. Each document pertains to *State v. Johnson*, the fictional criminal case featured in Chapter 5. Nevertheless, these documents do not always follow the format used in New Hampshire; instead, as befits a textbook aimed at a nationwide audience, they are generic documents that criminal courts in any state might use. Indeed, criminal courts in all fifty states use documents similar to those depicted below. Federal courts use the same categories of document, but their formats differ from the formats used in the states. For a comparison of state and federal formats, see F. Lee Bailey and Kenneth J. Fishman, *Complete Manual of Criminal Forms*, Third Edition (St. Paul, Minn.: West Group, 1997).

Application and Supporting Affidavit for Apartment Search

THE STATE OF NEW HAMPSHIRE

GRANITE COUNTY   GRAYSON DISTRICT COURT

99–14–3GR No.

The State of New Hampshire v. Stanley Johnson

BEFORE The Hon. Margaret Levesque, Grayson District Court, Michael Halloran, the undersigned being duly sworn, deposes and says:

That I have reason to believe that on the premises located at 47 Meadow Lane, Apartment B, Grayson, New Hampshire, there is now being concealed certain contraband, namely, cocaine, as might be on the premises.

And the facts tending to establish the foregoing grounds for issuance of a search warrant are as follows:

On January 29, 1998, Trooper Steve Cummings of the New Hampshire State Police posed as a college student and entered the suspect's apartment in order to effect an undercover drug "buy." Trooper Cummings indicated to the suspect that he wished to purchase cocaine, and the suspect agreed to sell it to him. Trooper Cummings requested a $50. bag, and, in exchange for $50. in cash, the suspect handed Trooper Cummings a plastic bag marked "$50." that contained a white powder. A subsequent field test of the powder revealed that it was cocaine.

WHEREFORE, said affiant has reason to believe that the contraband described in the attached warrant is being concealed on the premises located at 47 Meadow Lane, Apartment B, Grayson, New Hampshire.

Michael Halloran
Detective, Grayson Police Dept.

Search Warrant

THE STATE OF NEW HAMPSHIRE
GRANITE COUNTY   GRAYSON DISTRICT COURT
99–14–3GR No.

The State of New Hampshire v. Stanley Johnson
To the Chief of Police, Grayson, New Hampshire,
or any other authorized police officer:

An affidavit having been made before me by Michael Halloran, that he has reason to believe that on the premises known as 47 Meadow Lane, Apartment B, Grayson, New Hampshire, there is now being concealed certain contraband, namely, cocaine, and such other fruits or instrumentalities as might be on said premises, which are instrumentalities and fruits of the sale of a controlled drug, namely, cocaine, in violation of R.S.A. 318-B:2, I.

I am satisfied that there is probable cause to believe that the contraband so described is concealed on the premises above described and that the foregoing grounds for application for issuance of the search warrant exist.

You are hereby commanded to search forthwith the place named and if contraband be found there to seize it, leaving a copy of this warrant, and prepare a written inventory of the property seized, and return this warrant and bring the contraband before me within ten days of this date, as required by law.

Dated: January 29, 1999

Judge

Indictment

THE STATE OF NEW HAMPSHIRE
GRANITE, SS.   February Term, 1999
SUPERIOR COURT
The State of New Hampshire
v.
Stanley Johnson

At the SUPERIOR COURT, begun and holden at Graniteville, within and for said County of Granite, on the 15th day of February in the year 1999:

The jurors for the State of New Hampshire upon their oath present that Stanley Johnson of Grayson in said County of Granite between November 1, 1998, and January 30, 1999, the exact date being unknown to the Grand Jurors, at Grayson in the County of Granite aforesaid, did knowingly and intentionally distribute and possess with intent to distribute a quantity of cocaine, a controlled drug, in violation of R.S.A. 318-B:2, I.

A TRUE BILL:

_____

County Attorney

_____

Foreman of Grand Jury

Motion to Suppress Evidence

THE STATE OF NEW HAMPSHIRE

GRANITE, SS.   March Term, 1999

SUPERIOR COURT

The State of New Hampshire

v.

Stanley Johnson

NOW COMES the Defendant, Stanley Johnson, by his attorney, Eugene Jefferson, and respectfully moves this Honorable Court to suppress evidence illegally seized from his residence on January 30, 1999.

In support thereof, counsel states the following:

1. On or about January 30, 1999, officers of the Grayson Police Department executed a search warrant for 47 Meadow Lane, Apartment B, Grayson, New Hampshire.

2. It is respectfully submitted that the search warrant obtained for 47 Meadow Lane, Apartment B, Grayson, New Hampshire, was illegal because there was insufficient probable cause for the issuance of the warrant.

3. Specifically, there was insufficient evidence to support a finding of probable cause that contraband, or evidence thereof, would be found in the Defendant's residence.

4. Accordingly, all evidence that was seized pursuant to the unlawful search of Defendant's residence must be suppressed.

5. This Court's attention is respectfully directed to the attached Memorandum of Law and Affidavit of Stanley Johnson.

WHEREFORE, the Defendant respectfully requests this Honorable Court to suppress all evidence obtained from the illegal search of the Defendant's residence on January 30, 1999.

Respectfully submitted,

_____

Attorney for Defendant

[**Editor's Note:** The memorandum of law to which paragraph 5, above, refers, would accompany the motion to suppress. The memorandum would be considerably longer than the motion it supports, and it would present the legal argument for Stan's contention that the search of his apartment was unconstitutional. The memorandum would use supportive cases, and would try to distinguish unsupportive cases from this case, in order to show that Trooper Cummings's warrantless entry into Stan's apartment was illegal because Stan did not consent to it. An affidavit signed by Stan would also accompany the motion to suppress. The affidavit would attest to the truth of the facts stated in the motion.]

CIVIL

Printed below are replicas of two documents that figure prominently in civil litigation. Each document pertains to *Peterson v. Big Pine Mountain Ski Corporation*, the fictional civil case featured in Chapter 6. Nevertheless, these documents do not always follow the format used in New Hampshire. Instead, as befits a textbook aimed at a nationwide audience, they are generic documents that civil courts in any state might use. Indeed, civil courts in all fifty states use documents similar to those depicted below. You can see the full range of documents that pertain to civil litigation in *West's Legal Forms*, Third Edition (St. Paul, Minn.: West Group, 2000), or in *American Jurisprudence Legal Forms*, Second Edition (Rochester, N.Y.: Lawyers Cooperative Publishing Co., 1994). Both publications are available in law school libraries; city, county, and state law libraries usually have one of them.

Complaint

THE STATE OF NEW HAMPSHIRE

PINE, SS.   June Term, 1999

SUPERIOR COURT

Shannon Peterson, Plaintiff

v.

Big Pine Mountain Ski
Corporation, Defendant

COMPLAINT

1. Shannon Peterson is a resident of the Town of Madbury in the County of Strafford and State of New Hampshire.

2. Big Pine Mountain Ski Corporation is a New Hampshire corporation that owns and operates Big Pine Mountain Ski Resort (Big Pine).

3. On December 31, 1998, Ms. Peterson spent the day skiing at Big Pine.

4. On December 31, 1998, Big Pine began its snowmaking earlier than usual in order to prepare for the large crowd it expected on New Year's Day, without warning skiers who were on the affected slopes.

5. On December 31, 1998, Ms. Peterson was distracted while skiing by blowing artificial snow, which obscured an icy patch in her path, whereupon she lost her balance, fell, slid downhill 150 feet, and collided with a steel tower that supported chair-lift cables.

6. On December 31, 1998, Ms. Peterson sustained a severe concussion, a broken collarbone, crushed vertebra, broken ribs, and numerous cuts and abrasions as a result of the fall and collision.

7. Because of her injuries, Ms. Peterson suffers from double vision, lower back pain, and depression.

8. Because of her injuries, Ms. Peterson is unable to participate in intercollegiate athletics, and she faces diminished career opportunities in her chosen field, physical therapy.

9. Ms. Peterson's injuries were a direct and proximate result of the Defendant's negligent operation of its business premises.

WHEREFORE, the Plaintiff demands from the Defendant an amount of compensation for her injuries within the jurisdictional limits of this Court, together with interests, costs, and attorneys' fees.

PLAINTIFF DEMANDS A TRIAL BY JURY.

Dated at Graniteville in the County of Granite and State of New Hampshire on this the 17th day of June, 1999.

> SHANNON PETERSON
> By Her Attorney:_____
> Eugene Jefferson

Answer

[**Editor's Note:** Each numbered paragraph below contains the Defendant's response to the assertions made in the corresponding numbered paragraph of the Plaintiff's complaint. Therefore, you should refer back to the complaint as you read the answer.]

THE STATE OF NEW HAMPSHIRE

PINE, SS.   July Term, 1999

SUPERIOR COURT

Shannon Peterson, Plaintiff

v.

Big Pine Mountain Ski
Corporation, Defendant

ANSWER AND AFFIRMATIVE DEFENSE

1. Admitted.

2. Admitted.

3. Admitted.

4. The Defendant lacks sufficient information to either admit or deny this claim; therefore, it is denied.

5. The Defendant lacks sufficient information to either admit or deny this claim; therefore, it is denied.

6. Admitted.

7. The Defendant lacks sufficient information to either admit or deny this claim; therefore, it is denied.

8. The Defendant lacks sufficient information to either admit or deny this claim; therefore, it is denied.

9. Denied.

AFFIRMATIVE DEFENSE

1. Failure to state a claim on which relief can be granted. [**Editor's Note:** This defense results from Big Pine's contention that New Hampshire law, specifically, R.S.A. 225-A:24, I, considers icy trails and collisions with lift towers and components thereof to be inherent risks of alpine skiing for which ski area operators cannot be held liable.]

WHEREFORE, the Defendant, Big Pine Mountain Ski Corporation, respectfully requests that this Honorable Court dismiss this action and award the Defendant its costs, interest, and attorney's fees and such other relief as may be deemed proper.

Dated at Manchester in the County of Hillsborough and State of New Hampshire this 29th day of July, 1999.

> BIG PINE MOUNTAIN
> SKI CORPORATION
> By Its Attorney: _____
> Payson Parker

INDEX